D1083325

A History
of the Theory
of Investments

Founded in 1807, John Wiley & Sons is the oldest independent publishing company in the United States. With offices in North America, Europe, Australia, and Asia, Wiley is globally committed to developing and marketing print and electronic products and services for our customers' professional and personal knowledge and understanding.

The Wiley Finance series contains books written specifically for finance and investment professionals as well as sophisticated individual investors and their financial advisors. Book topics range from portfolio management to e-commerce, risk management, financial engineering, valuation, and financial instrument analysis, as well as much more.

For a list of available titles, please visit our Web site at www.WileyFinance.com.

A History of the Theory of Investments

My Annotated Bibliography

MARK RUBINSTEIN

John Wiley & Sons, Inc.

Published by John Wiley & Sons, Inc., Hoboken, New Jersey.
Published simultaneously in Canada.

For general information on our other products and services or for technical support, please contact our Customer Care Department within the United States at (800) 762-2974, outside the United States at (317) 572-3993 or fax (317) 572-4002.

Wiley also publishes its books in a variety of electronic formats. Some content that appears in print may not be available in electronic books. For more information about Wiley products, visit our web site at www.wiley.com.

Library of Congress Cataloging-in-Publication Data:

Rubinstein, Mark, 1944–
   A history of the theory of investments : my annotated bibliography /
Mark Rubinstein.
      p.   cm.—(Wiley finance series)
   Includes index.
   ISBN-13 978-0-471-77056-5 (cloth)
   ISBN-10 0-471-77056-6 (cloth)
   1. Investments.   2. Investments—Mathematical models.   3.
Investments—Mathematical models—Abstracts.   I. Title.   II. Series.
HG4515.R82 2006
016.3326'01—dc22

                                                    2005023555

Printed in the United States of America.

10   9   8   7   6   5   4   3   2   1

To celebrate the memory and glory
of the ideas of financial economics

Contents

Preface

Ideas are seldom born clothed, but are gradually dressed in an arduous process of accretion. In arriving at a deep knowledge of the state of the art in many fields, it seems necessary to appreciate how ideas have evolved: How do ideas originate? How do they mature? How does one idea give birth to another? How does the intellectual environment fertilize the growth of ideas? Why was there once confusion about ideas that now seem obvious?

Such an understanding has a special significance in the social sciences. In the humanities, there is little sense of chronological progress. For example, who would argue that in the past three centuries English poetry or drama has been written that surpasses the works of Shakespeare? In the natural sciences, knowledge accumulates by uncovering preexisting and permanent natural processes. Knowledge in the social sciences, however, can affect the social evolution that follows discovery, which through reciprocal causation largely determines the succeeding social theory.

In this spirit, I present a chronological, annotated bibliography of the financial *theory* of investments. It is not, however, a history of the *practice* of investing, and only occasionally refers to the real world outside of theoretical finance. To embed this "history of the theory of investments" in a broader context that includes the development of methodological and theoretical tools used to create this theory, including economics, mathematics, psychology, and the scientific method, I am writing companion volumes— a multiyear project—titled *My Outline of Western Intellectual History*, which also serves to carry this history back to ancient times.

Although this work can be used as a reference, to read it as a history one can read from the beginning to the end. For the most part, papers and books are not grouped by topic since I have tried to see the field as an integrated whole, and to emphasize how one strand of research impacts others that may initially have been thought to be quite separate. For this purpose a chronological ordering—though not slavishly adhered to—seems appropriate since a later idea cannot have influenced an earlier idea, only vice versa.

If I may indulge in the favorite pastime of historians, one can divide the history of financial economics into three periods: (1) the Ancient Period before 1950, (2) the Classical Period from about 1950 to 1980, and

(3) the Modern Period post-1980. Since about 1980, the foundations laid down during the Classical Period have come under increasing strain, and as this is written in 2005, it remains to be seen whether a new paradigm will emerge.

Of necessity, I have selected only a small portion of the full body of financial research that is available. Some papers are significant because they plant a seed, ask what turns out to be the right question, or develop important economic intuitions; others are extraordinarily effective in communicating ideas; yet others are important because they formalize earlier concepts, making all assumptions clear and proving results with mathematical rigor. Although I have tried to strike some balance between these three types of research, I have given more prominence to the first two. Unpublished working papers are included only if they either (1) are very widely cited or (2) appear many years before their ideas were published in papers by other authors. A few literature surveys are mentioned if they are particularly helpful in interpreting the primary sources. Mathematical statements or proofs of important and condensable results are also provided, usually set off by boxes, primarily to compensate for the ambiguity of words. However, the proofs are seldom necessary for an intuitive understanding.

The reader should also understand that this book, such as it is, is very much work in progress. Many important works are not mentioned, not because I don't think they are important, but simply because I just haven't gotten to them yet. So this history, even from my narrow vantage point, is quite partial and incomplete, and is very spotty after about 1980. In particular, though it traces intimations of nonrationalist ideas in both the ancient and classical periods, it contains very little of the newer results accumulating in the modern period that have come under the heading of "behavioral finance." Nonetheless, the publisher encouraged me to publish whatever I have since it was felt that even in such a raw form this work would prove useful. Hopefully, in the fullness of time, an updated version will appear making up this deficit.

The history of the theory of investments is studded with the works of famous economists. Twentieth-century economists such as Frank Knight, Irving Fisher, John Maynard Keynes, Friedrich Hayek, Kenneth Arrow, Paul Samuelson, Milton Friedman, Franco Modigliani, Jack Hirshleifer, James Tobin, Joseph Stiglitz, Robert Lucas, Daniel Kahneman, Amos Tversky, and George Akerlof have all left their imprint. Contributions to finance by significant noneconomists in this century include those by John von Neumann, Leonard Savage, John Nash, and Maurice Kendall. Looking back further, while the contributions of Daniel Bernoulli and Louis Bachelier are well known, much less understood but of comparable importance are works of Fibonacci, Blaise Pascal, Pierre de Fermat, Christiaan Huygens, Abraham de Moivre, and Edmund Halley.

Perhaps this field is like others, but I am nonetheless dismayed to see how little care is taken by many scholars to attribute ideas to their original sources. Academic articles and books, even many of those that purport to be historical surveys, occasionally of necessity but often out of ignorance oversimplify the sequence of contributors to a finally fully developed theory, attributing too much originality to too few scholars. No doubt that has inadvertently occurred in this work as well, but hopefully to a much lesser extent than earlier attempts. Even worse, an important work can lie buried in the forgotten past; occasionally, that work is even superior in some way to the later papers that are typically referenced.

For example, ask yourself who first discovered the following ideas:

Present value.

The Modigliani-Miller theorem.

Pratt-Arrow measures of risk aversion.

Markowitz mean-variance portfolio theory.

The Gordon growth formula.

The capital asset pricing model.

The Black zero-beta model.

The Cox-Ross-Rubinstein binomial option pricing model.

The Lucas exchange model.

The Milgrom-Stokey no trade theorem.

The derivation of expected utility from postulates of individual rationality.

The martingale pricing representation with risk-neutral probabilities.

Dynamic completeness.

The association of random walks with rational markets.

The use of nonstationary variance to describe the stochastic process of security prices.

The hypothesized relationship between upwardly biased stock prices, belief heterogeneity, and short-selling constraints.

The size effect.

The abnormal earnings growth model.

Prospect theory.

In most of these cases, the individuals commonly given bibliographical credit in academic papers were actually anticipated many years, occasionally decades or centuries, earlier. In some cases, there were others with independent and near-simultaneous discoveries who are seldom, if ever, mentioned, offering one of many proofs of Stephen Stigler's law of eponymy that scientific ideas are never named after their original discoverer! This includes Stigler's law itself, which was stated earlier by sociologist and philosopher of science Robert K. Merton. A prominent example in financial economics is the Modigliani-Miller theorem, which received possibly its most elegant exposition at its apparent inception in a single paragraph contained in a now rarely referenced but amazing book by John Burr Williams published in 1938, 20 years before Modigliani-Miller. Had his initial insight been well known and carefully considered, we might have been spared decades of confusion. A clear example of Merton's naming paradox is the "Gordon growth formula." Unfortunately, once this type of error takes hold, it is very difficult to shake loose. Indeed, the error becomes so ingrained that even prominent publicity is unlikely to change old habits.

Also, researchers occasionally do not realize that an important fundamental aspect of a theory was discovered many years earlier. To take a prominent example, although the Black-Scholes option pricing model developed in the early 1970s is surely one of the great discoveries of financial economics, fundamentally it derives its force from the idea that it may be possible to make up for missing securities in the market by the ability to revise a portfolio of the few securities that do exist over time. Kenneth Arrow, 20 years earlier in 1953, was the first to give form to a very similar idea. In turn, shades of the famous correspondence between Blaise Pascal and Pierre de Fermat three centuries earlier can be found in Arrow's idea. A field of science often progresses by drawing analogies from other fields or by borrowing methods, particularly mathematical tools, developed initially for another purpose. One of the delightful by-products of historical research is the connections that one often uncovers between apparently disparate and unrelated work—connections that may not have been consciously at work, but no doubt through undocumented byways must surely have exercised an influence.

One can speculate about how an academic field could so distort its own origins. Its history is largely rewritten, as it were, by the victors. New students too often rely on the version of scholarly history conveyed to them by their mentors, who themselves are too dependent on their mentors, and so forth. Seldom do students refuse to take existing citations at their word and instead dust off older books and journals that are gradually deteriorating on library shelves to check the true etiology of the ideas they are using. Scholars have the all-too-human tendency of biasing their attributions in the direction of those whom they know relatively well or those who have written several papers and spent years developing an idea, to the disadvantage of older and more original works by people who are not in the mainstream, either in their approach to the subject, by geography, or by timing. An excellent example of this is the sole paper on mean-variance portfolio selection by A.D. Roy, whom Harry Markowitz acknowledges deserves to share equal honor with himself as the co-father of portfolio theory.[1] Robert K. Merton has dubbed this the "Matthew effect" (particularly apt since it may serve as an example of itself) after the lines in the Gospel According to Matthew (25:29): "Unto everyone that hath shall be given, and he shall have abundance; but from him that hath not shall be taken away even that which he hath."

Of course, financial economics is not alone in its tendency to oversimplify its origins. For example, consider the calculus, well known to have been invented by Isaac Newton and Gottfried Wilhelm Leibniz. Yet the invention of calculus can be traced back to the classical Greeks, in particular Antiphon, Eudoxus, and Archimedes, who anticipated the concept of limits and of integration in their use of the "method of exhaustion" to determine the area and volume of geometric objects (for example, to estimate the area of a circle, inscribe a regular polygon in the circle; as the number of sides of the polygon goes to infinity, the polygon provides an increasingly more accurate approximation of the area of the circle). Although Galileo Galilei did not write in algebraic formulas, his work on motion implies that velocity is the first derivative of distance with respect to time, and acceleration is the second derivative of distance with respect to time. Pierre de Fermat devised the method of tangents that in substance we use today to determine the maxima and minima of functions. Isaac Barrow used the notion of differential to find the tangent to a curve and described theorems for the differentiation of the product and quotient of two functions, the differentiation of powers of x, the change of variable in a definite integral, and the differentiation of implicit functions.

Unlike large swaths of history in general, much of the forgotten truth about the origins of ideas in financial economics is there for all to see, in older books residing on library shelves or in past journals now often available in electronic form. Much of the history of investments has only been *rewritten* by the victors, and can be *corrected* from primary sources. In this book, I have tried my best to do this. For each paper or book cited, my goal is to clarify its *marginal* contribution to the field.

Like the three witches in Shakespeare's *Macbeth* (and I hope the resemblance ends there), with hindsight, I can "look into the seeds of time, and say which grain will grow and which will not." Taking advantage of this, I will deemphasize research (such as the stable-Paretian hypothesis for stock prices) that, although once thought quite promising, ultimately proved to be a false path.

Nonetheless, I am certain that I also have omitted *many important* discoveries (in part because I just haven't gotten to them) or even attributed ideas to the wrong sources, unaware of even earlier work. Perhaps, on the other hand, I have succumbed to the historian's temptation to bias his interpretation of the written record in light of what subsequently is seen to be important or correct. I hope the reader will forgive me. I have already received some assistance from Morton Davis, and I wish to publicly thank him. I also ask the reader to take the constructive step of letting me know these errors so that future revisions of this history will not repeat them.

MARK RUBINSTEIN

Berkeley, California
January 2006

The Ancient Period
Pre-1950

1202 **Fibonacci** or Leonardo of Pisa (1170–1240), *Liber Abaci* ("The Book of Calculation"); recently translated into English by Laurence E. Sigler in *Fibonacci's Liber Abaci: A Translation into Modern English of Leonardo Pisano's Book of Calculation* (New York: Springer-Verlag, 2002).

1478 **Unknown Author,** *The Treviso Arithmetic*; translated into English by David Eugene Smith, pp. 40–175, in Frank J. Swetz, *Capitalism and Arithmetic: The New Math of the 15th Century Including the Full Text of the Treviso Arithmetic of 1478* (LaSalle, IL: Open Court, 1987).

1761 **Edmond Halley** (November 8, 1656–January 14, 1742), "Of Compound Interest," in Henry Sherwin, *Sherwin's Mathematical Tables* (published posthumously after Halley's death in 1742, London: W. and J. Mount, T. Page and Son, 1761).

FIBONACCI SERIES, PRESENT VALUE, PARTNERSHIPS,
FINITE-LIVED ANNUITIES, CAPITAL BUDGETING

Fibonacci (1202) is well-known as the most influential tract introducing positional numerical notation into Europe. Arabic numerals were first developed in India, perhaps in the mid-first millennium A.D. and were subsequently learned by Arab traders and scholars. In turn, Fibonacci learned about them while traveling through North Africa. He begins Chapter 1 with these words:

These are the nine figures of the Indians: 9, 8, 7, 6, 5, 4, 3, 2, 1. With these nine figures, and with this sign 0 which in Arabic is called zephirum, any number can be written, as will be demonstrated.

After the publication of this tract, computation by Arabic numerals using pen and ink gradually replaced the use of the abacus. The book also develops the famous Fibonacci series, 1, 1, 2, 3, 5, 8, 13 . . . .

Much less appreciated is the role *Liber Abaci* plays in the development of present value calculation, as has been quite recently discovered by William N. Goetzmann in [Goetzmann (2003)] "Fibonacci and the Financial Revolution," Yale ICF Working Paper No. 03-28 (October 23, 2003). Fibonacci illustrates his methods of calculation through several numerical examples. Among these are four types of applications to investments: (1) the fair allocation of profits to members of a partnership ("On Companies," pp. 172–173); (2) the calculation of profits from a sequence of investments, with intermediate withdrawals ("Problems of Travelers," pp. 372–373); (3) the calculation of future value ("A Noteworthy Problem on a Man Exchanging One Hundred Pounds at Some Banking House for Interest," pp. 384–386); and (4) the calculation of present value ("On a Soldier Receiving Three Hundred Bezants for His Fief," p. 392). His solution to (1) is simply to divide profits in proportion to contributed capital—a solution that is now obvious. As an example of (3) in Sigler's translation:

> *A man placed 100 pounds at a certain [banking] house for 4 denari per pound per month interest, and he took back each year a payment of 30 pounds; one must compute in each year the 30 pound reduction of capital and profit on the said 100 pounds. It is sought how many years, months, days and hours he will hold money in the house. (p. 384)*

Fibonacci calculates that the man will have some money with the bank for 6 years, 8 days, and "$(^1/_2)(^3/_9)5$" hours. This makes use of Fibonacci's notation whereby the denominator of each fraction is actually the product of its explicit denominator and all the denominators to the right, and the hours are the sum of these fractions. So the number of hours is $5 + (^3/_9)$hours $+ (^1/_{18})$hours $= 5$ and $^7/_{18}$ hours, in modern notation. Note that as antiquated as Fibonacci's notation has become, it still remains very useful in situations where small units are measured in a different number of parts than larger units. For example, Fibonacci would have written 5 weeks, 3 days, 4 hours, 12 minutes, and 35 seconds as $(^{35}/_{60})(^{12}/_{60})(^4/_{24})(^3/_7)5$.

In problem (4), Fibonacci illustrates the use of present value by ranking the present values of two annuities, differing only in the periodicity of payment, where the interest rate that can be earned on the reinvestment of amounts received is 2 percent per quarter: Both pay 300 bezants per year, with one paying quarterly installments of 75 bezants and the other instead paying the entire 300 bezants at the end of each year.

Due to compounding, present value under a constant interest rate is the result of summing a weighted geometric series. Goetzmann speculates that Fibonacci's interest in finance may have provided the spark for his famous work on infinite series. Unfortunately, we know so little about Fibonacci that this cannot be verified.

After Fibonacci's work, Arabic numerals became widely used in Europe, particularly for commercial purposes. The *Treviso Arithmetic* (1478) published by an unknown author is the earliest known dated and printed book on arithmetic and serves as an early attempt to popularize the Arabic numeral system. The book starts by describing how to use Arabic numerals for enumeration, addition, subtraction, multiplication, and division—the same procedures in use today. By the *Treviso's* time, the numerals had just previously reached their modern forms. For example, the practice of writing 0 as Ø died out after 1275. This may be in part due to the *Treviso* itself, since printing technology may have forced standardization. However, notation for the operations of addition, subtraction, multiplication, and division was not introduced until later, "+" and "−" in print in 1489, "×" in 1631, and "÷" in 1659. While we are on the subject, "√" was introduced in 1525, "=" in 1557, "<" and ">" in 1631, "∫" in 1675 (by Gottfried Wilhelm Leibniz), "$f(x)$" in 1735 (by Leonhard Euler), and "dx/dy" in 1797 by Joseph-Louis Lagrange. Representation of fractions as decimals did not occur until 1585. Using letters for unknowns in equations waited until François Vieta's (1540–1603) formulation in about 1580. John Napier invented logarithms in 1614 and brought decimal notation for factions to Europe in 1617.

These operations are illustrated by a number of problems. Partnerships can be traced as far back as 2,000 B.C. in Babylonia. This form of business organization provided a way to finance investments requiring large amounts of capital over extended periods of time. In Christian Europe, partnerships also provided a way to circumvent usury prohibitions against charging interest. Here is the first partnership problem posed in the *Treviso* (p. 138):

> *Three merchants have invested their money in a partnership, whom to make the problem clearer I will mention by name. The first was called Piero, the second Polo, and the third Zuanne. Piero put in 112 ducats, Polo 200 ducats, and Zuanne 142 ducats. At the end of a certain period they found they had gained 563 ducats. Required is to know how much falls to each man so that no one shall be cheated.*

The recommended solution, following the same principle as already set forth by Fibonacci in his problem "On Companies," is to divide the profits among the investors in proportion to their respective investments. The second partnership problem is much more interesting (p. 138):

> *Two merchants, Sebastiano and Jacomo, have invested their money for gain in a partnership. Sebastiano put in 350 ducats on the first day in January, 1472, and Jacomo 500 ducats, 14 grossi on the first day of July, 1472; and on the first day of January, 1474 they found they had gained 622 ducats. Required is the share of each.*

After converting both investments to a common unit, 8,400 grossi for Sebastiano and 12,014 grossi for Jacomo, the *Treviso* adjusts for the timing of the investments by the number of months of the respective investments:

Sebastiano: $8,400 \times 24 = 201,600$ Jacomo: $12,014 \times 18 = 216,252$

The profits are then divided according to these proportions. The sum $201,600 + 216,252 = 417,852$. Sebastiano receives $622 \times (201,600/417,852) = 300$ ducats and Jacomo $622 \times (216,252/417,852) = 322$ ducats.

The modern analyst would approach this allocation in one of two ways, depending on whether Jacomo's delayed contribution were contracted in advance or whether the terms of his contribution were determined near the time of his contribution. In the former case, he would then need to know the interest rate to work out the fair division of profits, and in the second he would need to know the value of a share in the partnership on July 1, 1472. Although the author of the *Treviso* has posed an interesting problem and probably learned much from Fibonacci, his answer suggests he does not yet understand Fibonacci's more sophisticated present value analysis.

But by the 1500s, Fibonacci's work on present value had become better known, despite usury laws. Consider, for example, a problem from Jean Trenchant [Trenchant (1558)], *L'Arithmétique*, 2nd edition, 1637, Lyons (p. 307): Which has the higher present value, a perpetual annuity of 4 percent per quarter or a fixed-life annuity of 5 percent per quarter for 41 quarters? Trenchant solves the problem by comparing the future value at the end of 41 quarters of a 1 percent annuity per quarter, with the present value in the 41st quarter of a perpetual annuity at 5 percent starting then. Trenchant's book also contains the first known table of present value discount factors.

In the forgotten age before computers, once it was desired to determine the effects of interest rates on contracts, much work was devoted to developing fast means of computation. These include the use of logarithms, precalculated tables, and closed-form algebraic solutions to present value problems. Edmond Halley, cataloger of stars in the Southern Hemisphere from telescopic observation, creator of the first meteorological charts, publisher of early population mortality tables, is, of course, best known as the first to calculate the orbits of comets. Not the least of his achievements includes results in financial economics. Halley (1761) derives (probably not for the first time) the formula for the present value of an annual annuity beginning at the end of year 1 with a final payment at the end of year T: $[X/(r - 1)][1 - (1/r^T)]$, where r is 1 plus the annual discrete interest rate of the annuity and X is the annual cash receipt from the annuity. Another relatively early derivation of this formula can be found in Fisher (1906).

Although valuation by present value, as we have seen, had appeared much earlier, Fisher (1907) may have been the first to propose that *any* capital project should be evaluated in terms of its present value. Using an arbitrage argument, he compared the stream of cash flows from the project to the cash flows from a portfolio of securities constructed to match the project. Despite this, according to Faulhaber-Baumol (1988), neither the *Harvard Business Review* from its founding in 1922 to World War II, nor widely used textbooks in corporate finance as late as 1948, made any reference to present value in capital budgeting. It was not until Joel Dean in his book [Dean (1951)] *Capital Budgeting: Top Management Policy on Plant, Equipment, and Product Development* (New York: Columbia University Press, 1951) that the use of present value was popularized. More recently, according to John R. Graham and Campbell Harvey in [Graham-Harvey (2001)] "The Theory and Practice of Corporate Finance: Evidence from the Field," *Journal of Financial Economics* 60, Nos. 2–3 (May 2001), pp. 187–243, most large firms use some form of present value calculation to guide their capital budgeting decisions.

1494 Luca Pacioli (circa 1445-1517), *Summa de arithmetica, geometria, proportioni et proportionalita* ("Everything about Arithmetic, Geometry and Proportions"); the section on accounting, "Particularis de computis et scripturus," translated into English by A. von Gebstattel, *Luca Pacioli's Exposition of Double-Entry Bookkeeping: Venice 1494* (Venice: Albrizzi Editore, 1994).

PROBLEM OF POINTS, ACCOUNTING, DEBITS VS. CREDITS,
ACCOUNTING IDENTITY, ASSETS, LIABILITIES, AND EQUITIES,
CLEAN-SURPLUS RELATION, BOOK VS. MARKET VALUES,
MATCHING PRINCIPLE, CONSISTENCY PRINCIPLE

Pacioli (1494), acknowledging a debt to Euclid (circa 300 A.D.) and Fibonacci (1202), summarizes the basic principles of arithmetic, algebra, geometry, and trigonometry. More important for our immediate purposes, Pacioli is often credited with posing the "Problem of Points," the problem that eventually ignited the explosive development of modern probability theory in the seventeenth century (naturally there is some evidence that this problem originated even earlier):

> *A and B are playing the fair game of* balla. *They agree to continue until one has won six rounds. The game actually stops when A has won five and B three. How should the stakes be divided?*

Pacioli's (incorrect) solution was simply to divide the stakes in proportion to the number of games won by each player. So if the stakes were 56 pistolas, player A would receive 35 and player B would receive 21.

But Pacioli's book is best known for its influence on accounting. Accounting in ancient times took the form of a mere physical listing of inventories. Later accounting methods translated these items into a common unit of measurement, usually a single currency. This mutated into a list of "charges" and "discharges," essentially a cash statement showing the sources and uses of cash designed so that the lord of an estate could monitor his steward who actually dispensed payments. The origins of the more recent methods of double-entry accounting are a bit obscure. We know that an Italian merchant firm, Gallerani company of Siena, used double-entry accounting as early as 1305 (reported by Christopher W. Nobes, [Nobes (1982)] "The Gallerani Account Book of 1305–1308," *Accounting Review* 57, No. 2 (April 1982), pp. 303–310). Although Pacioli did not invent double-entry accounting methods, because he developed double-entry bookkeeping so thoroughly in this influential work he is often referenced as the original source of these methods and considered "the father of accounting." In the accounting section of his book, "Particularis de computis et scripturas," Pacioli writes that he is describing "the Venetian method which certainly among others is much recommended and which can be used as a guide to all others" (p. 42). He even admonishes would-be accountants not to rest easy at night until their credits and debits are equal. Further discussion of the history of financial accounting conventions (for external accounting purposes) takes us beyond the intended scope of this book. However, since accounting concepts are important for measuring the expected return and risk of corporate securities, I instead discuss the key issues.

First, what is the purpose of external accounting statements? In my opinion, their primary purpose is to provide information to stockholders. One could argue that the statements are also useful for employees in evaluating the return and risk of investing their human capital with the firm, or outside suppliers of goods and services who may want to evaluate the return and risk of dealing with the firm, or debt holders who need to assess the likelihood of default. But I think, particularly since the stockholders are the owners of the firm and, by determining the stock price, indirectly make resource allocation decisions for the firm, that the primary constituency for these statements is the stockholders. While the statements may have other goals, their paramount purpose is to help stockholders decide the market price of the firm's stock. This is consistent with the view taken in financial economics, and largely by the law, that the firm should be run for the benefit of its shareholders. In practice, while the employees, suppliers, and debt holders may have access to other information about the firm, the annual report to shareholders, with its balance sheet and income statement, is their primary source of information, particularly for large public firms.

One way the firm could meet the obligation of providing information to shareholders would be to have videos taken of each employee for his or her entire working year, gather these together, and distribute them to each stockholder. That way the stockholder would have a fairly complete and unbiased record of what happened during the year. But, clearly, this is absurd. At the other extreme, the firm could simply report one number to its stockholders at the end of every year—its own estimate of what the stock price should be. But this, too, is not useful since the firm may not have enough information to make a good estimate of its stock price. As Hayek (1945) argues, the information needed to determine the stock price is typically widely dispersed across the economy, and no small subset of individuals, even all the employees of a firm, is sufficient to determine an informationally efficient price. Even setting this aside, the proper technique of aggregating this information into a price is not clear, and firms cannot be relied upon to know how to do this. A firm may also be tempted to manipulate the resources it receives from investors, or the incentive-based compensation paid to its executives, by an intentional overvaluation of its stock. Finally, as if this were not difficult enough, a desirable further constraint is not to require firms to release information that can affect their incentive to compete against other firms, even if this information aids in valuation. So the challenge of accounting is to find a constrained middle ground, some way to summarize what happened during the year without leaving out anything important, without relying on the firm to be completely truthful, and without damaging the firm's incentive to compete.

The solution that has evolved since Pacioli is to provide two financial statements, the balance sheet and the income statement. The first, like a snapshot, captures the relevant aspects of the firm at a single point in time; and the second, like a movie, shows how the firm moves from a balance sheet at an earlier date to a balance sheet at a later date. The balance sheet represents every transaction as giving rise to a change in an asset, on the one hand, and a corresponding change in liability or equity on the other (occasionally transactions also merely interchange some equities with liabilities, or an asset with another asset). This gives us the famous accounting identity that disciplines double-entry accounting:

$$\text{Assets} = \text{Liabilities} + \text{Equities}$$

Every transaction has these two faces. Traditionally *assets* are subdivided into three main categories: current assets (cash, receivables, inventories, and prepaid expenses); long-term physical assets like plant and equipment; and intangible long-term assets like the capitalized value of research and development expenses and the value of established brand names. *Liabilities* are subdivided into two main categories: short-term (payables, deferred taxes, short-term debt) and long-term (long-term bank loans, publicly traded corporate bonds). *Equities* are subdivided into two categories: contributed capital and the accumulated profits. The income statement subtracts several expense items from revenues to yield profits attributed to the period between two balance sheets. These profits are usually divided by the number of shares outstanding to determine earnings per share (EPS), and the proportion of the earnings paid out as dividends is separately reported to determine dividends per share.

If an investor only wants to take away from this a single number, then he should just look at earnings per share. This is the accountant's estimate of how much the stock price should have changed (with dividends added back) between the dates of the two balance sheets. That is, if S_{t-1} and S_t are the stock prices at dates $t-1$ and t, D_t is the dividends paid per share, and X_t the reported earnings per share between the two dates, then

$$(S_t + D_t) - S_{t-1} = X_t$$

There is a sense in which if the accountants and the stock market have got it right, the stock price would have changed by exactly this amount.

Moreover, using the EPS equation and the so-called clean-surplus relation (assuming no new contributed capital),

$$Y_t = Y_{t-1} + X_t - D_t$$

we can prove that the stock price per share S_t equals the corresponding book value Y_t per share. Starting with the date 0 boundary value at the inception of the firm, $S_0 = Y_0$, where the book value Y_0 is contributed capital, and solving these equations recursively:

$$S_t = Y_t = Y_0 + \Sigma_{k=1}(X_k - D_k)$$

In practice, even if the market is working properly, the market and book values of most firms are not equal. Although we can blame this on the accountants, they are in a tough spot. One problem is created by revenues or expenses that are sometimes delayed until after products have been delivered or accelerated before products are delivered. So simply to record as revenues and expenses all transactions during the year can be misleading. Instead, the *matching principle* of accounting requires that only revenues received from products delivered to customers during a year and only the expenses generated to create those products should be reported on the income statement for that year. Cash received or paid out during the year that is not matched to products delivered during the year is recorded as a temporary balance sheet item and typically recognized on the income statement in the succeeding year when the corresponding products are delivered. This is called "accrual accounting" in contrast to "cash accounting," which does not try to match revenues with expenses. So accountants have this trade-off: They can increase the accuracy of the statements by using cash accounting, or they can provide potentially more useful but potentially less accurate comparisons by using accrual accounting. For external accounting statements, this trade-off today has typically been decided in favor of accrual accounting.

As a simple example, the matching principle is the cause of inventories on the balance sheet. These may reflect the purchase of warehoused supplies or finished goods that have been paid for but have not yet been used in production or delivered to a customer. But even this can create accounting questions. If units of a homogeneous item held in inventory have been purchased at different prices, just which price should be used to expense a unit used in a product that is delivered? One approach is to assume that the first unit purchased is the first one used, or first in first out (FIFO) accounting; an alternative is to assume that the last unit purchased is the first one used, or last in first out (LIFO) accounting.

As an even more difficult issue, suppose a firm buys long-lived equipment used to manufacture its products, which gradually wears out or eventually becomes technologically obsolete. The matching principle requires the firm to determine how much of the equipment is used up to make the products it delivers that year. While the initial cost of purchasing the equipment is a known fact, and the liquidation revenues eventually received perhaps years later from selling the equipment will be a known fact, there is generally no magical way of determining the correct rate of depreciation of the equipment in any given year. There is no transaction to prove what this is. So accountants solve this dilemma in one of their favorite ways. Depending on the type of equipment, they simply require that it be depreciated at a specific rate each year. The simplest technique is straight-line depreciation, whereby, say, 10 percent of the purchase price is considered an expense in each year for 10 years. But because that may not correctly represent the rate of depreciation, they may alternatively allow an accelerated form whereby greater depreciation is taken in earlier years compared to later years. Accountants try to find a middle ground between giving firms the latitude they need to do a better job of matching, against the fear that if too much flexibility is permitted, the firm will use that to misstate (usually overstate) its earnings. It is just this sort of balancing act that makes accounting interesting, and its appropriate conventions far from obvious.

The allocation of research and development expense and marketing and advertising expenses can be particularly difficult to get right. Should these be capitalized and then gradually expensed (amortized) over an extended period, or be immediately expensed? To get this right, one needs to answer a very difficult question: To what extent do these expenses affect the revenues and expenses from products delivered not in the years corresponding to these expenses, but in subsequent years?

This example brings out another accounting principle: Since stockholders will use accounting information to project future revenues and expenses, the financial statements need to make it easy for stockholders to separate revenues and expenses due to ongoing sustainable operations from one-shot occurrences. To do this, profits and losses are usually broken up into two categories: ordinary and extraordinary. Extraordinary profits arise from changes in the value of the firm's assets and liabilities that cannot be expected to recur. It is useful to distinguish among three types of extraordinary profits: (1) profits deriving from random changes outside the firm's control, such as movements in interest rates, which affect the present value of the firm's debt obligations; (2) profits from intentional decisions of the firm, outside the normal operations of the firm, such as the decision to hold cash in yen rather than in dollars; and

(3) profits and losses deriving from *ex post* corrections to previous accounting statements, such as losses from stagnant inventories that, because of gradual changes in product demand, will never be used. Unfortunately, this last category all too often reflects the failure to have properly followed the matching principle in prior years. But, for valuation purposes, it is still better to get the old bad news sooner rather than later.

Another very difficult accounting question to resolve is the choice between simply reporting the results of executed transactions and, in addition, amending these results from time to time to reflect changes in market values. For example, suppose the most significant asset of a pineapple firm is land it bought in Hawaii in 1900 at a cost of $1 million. It would then be reported on the balance sheet as an asset valued at $1 million. Over the next century, because of the remarkable rise of tourism, the land gradually becomes worth $100 million. Suppose that today, compared to the value of the land, the remainder of the firm is worth very little. If the firm continues to carry the land on its balance sheet at $1 million, stockholders today may have no idea that the firm has assets that could be liquidated at a significantly higher value. An obvious solution would be for the firm to have gradually recognized over the century changes in the market value of the land every year as an extraordinary profit or loss. Had it done so, it would now have both an offsetting asset and equity: The land would be valued on the balance sheet at $100 million and additional equity would be $99 million. Unfortunately, market value accounting, as it solves one problem, creates another: Since the land has not yet been sold in a closing transaction, how does the firm know what it is really worth? Although this uncertainty can be reduced in a variety of ways, it cannot often be eliminated. If it cannot be eliminated, the profit and loss created from mark-to-market accounting is of a different reliability compared to situations where ownership has been bracketed by both an opening and a closing transaction. Would not stockholders want to distinguish between unrealized profit from land that has not yet been sold and realized profit from land that has? Moreover, different experts will often disagree about the market value of the land until it is actually sold. Which expert should the stockholders believe? In particular, should they believe experts hired by the firm when the management of the firm may have an incentive to overstate the value of the land?

In their schizoid way, generally accepted accounting principles (GAAP) provide a complex answer to this problem: Some assets and liabilities can be revalued at market and others cannot, roughly according to the uncertainty of their market values. Other assets, such as capital equipment, given intermediate treatment through depreciation rules, are being valued neither at cost nor at market, but rather by fairly rigid rules designed to capture their probable decrease in value.

These are only a few of the valuation issues that cause the earlier equation relating stock price changes to earnings and, as a result, market value to book value per share to become misaligned. Perhaps the most significant cause of these differences can be attributed to structural conditions of industry competition. In many industries, firms are able to establish monopolistic or oligopolistic advantages that are not reflected in their book values. The fact that few firms enter an industry before its demand takes off can provide a significant first mover advantage. Microsoft, which has established the most popular personal computer (PC) operating system, provides a textbook example of how to leverage a singular advantage into dominance in many PC software applications. Unfortunately, nothing in Microsoft's past transactions, even if its physical assets are marked to market, can prepare the reader of its financial statements for its high ratio of market value to book value. The difference between market and book reflects not only the very high operating profit margins on its current products, but its unique position to make very profitable investments in the future, investments that would be denied to other firms that do not have Microsoft's monopolistic advantages. The stock market, of course, does not wait for these profits to appear before embedding them into the stock price; it anticipates them, thereby causing market values and book values to diverge significantly.

Because of this argument, financial economists tend to consider firms with high market-to-book ratios as *growth* firms, and those with low market to book as *value* firms. Investors can even invest in mutual funds, some specializing in growth stocks and others in value stocks. But it is hoped that this discussion makes clear that because there are many reasons why book and market values can become misaligned, the metric of the market-to-book ratio to distinguish between growth and value stocks is far from perfect.

Historically, accounting statements designed to measure performance focus on the level of earnings, a return measure. But, ever since Markowitz (1952/March) and Roy (1952), financial economists have argued that a second aspect of performance is also risk. Although it appears that current accounting conventions are not well designed for this purpose (and perhaps need to be redesigned to make risk measurement easier), modern financial statements can still be quite useful. For example, the time series of ordinary earnings per share provided by these statements can be used to calculate variance measures of earnings, as an independent indication of the risk of investing in the stock. Unfortunately, in practice, many firms exercise whatever latitude revenue and expense matching conventions allow to smooth earnings over time and thereby give the appearance of reduced risk.

The common way to measure risk from financial statements is *ratio analysis*. Traditional examples include the ratio of current assets to current liabilities, a crude stock indicator of default risk. The ratio of earnings before interest and taxes (EBIT) to annual interest payments is a flow measure of default risk. The ratio of long-term assets to short-term assets measures liquidity and valuation risk, since presumably of the two, short-term assets are more liquid and have less uncertainty regarding their value. Although the firm's stock derives risk from many sources, both from within the firm and from without, there are three key sources of risk inside the firm: (1) diversification of sources of revenues, (2) operating risk, and (3) financial risk.

Current financial statements by themselves usually do not disaggregate the sources of revenues by product line or industry to help much with measuring diversification, although supporting footnotes and other sources such as registration statements that accompany new securities issues have some of this information.

Operating risk can be defined as the ratio of fixed to variable costs. The higher this ratio for the firm, the more sensitive will be the profits of the firm to changes in revenues. Although fixed and variable costs are not directly broken apart on the income statement, to some extent the categories that are given can be used to disaggregate costs into these two sources, and a time-series regression analysis of reported expenses against revenues over time can be used to get a rough idea of this disaggregation.

The common indicator of financial risk is the liabilities-to-equities ratio, using book values. The higher this ratio, presumably the more highly leveraged the firm and the more sensitive bottom-line earnings will be to changes in earnings before interest and taxes. However, on one hand, the book value of equities is often a very poor indicator of the market value of equities; and on the other, book value liabilities are commonly much more closely aligned with market values. At the same time, the market values of equities are often readily available from the stock market. Therefore, financial economists often prefer the ratio of the book value of liabilities to the market value of equities to measure financial leverage.

Unfortunately, this measure of financial risk is not free from difficulty. Clearly, as a precondition, transactions must be allocated to liabilities or equities. For the purpose of measuring financial risk, the essence of liabilities derives from promised fixed payments over time, and, provided these are paid, liabilities do not share in the success of the firm. At the other extreme, equities have no promised payments, but after paying off all other claimants on the firm (employees, suppliers, debt holders, government) receive whatever is left over. As the "residual claimants" of the firm, equities derive their value directly from the profitability of the firm. Some securities, like preferred stock, convertible debt, or employee stock options, are hybrid securities, containing elements of debt and elements of stock, and their categorization is problematic.

Consistency is another principle of accounting: The rules for implementing first-order economically equivalent decisions by different firms should be designed so that comparative accounting measures of return and risk should not be affected. The controversy in the United States from 1994 to 2005 over accounting for employee stock options illustrates the issue of consistency. As before, consider otherwise identical firms A and B; A compensates its employees entirely with cash; B compensates its employees entirely with stock options, originally issued at-the-money. To simplify, both firms are assumed to receive the same services from their employees. Naturally, A expenses its cash compensation; what should B do? If, as was the standard practice, B does not treat the stock options as an expense, B will report higher profits, even though from an economic point of view the two firms are doing the same thing; B is really no better than A. So, the principle of consistency demands that B determine the market value of its options when they are granted and expense that value.

An insightful example of the difficulty of attaining consistency is accounting for leased assets. Consider two otherwise equivalent firms; firm A borrows the cost of the purchase of a building, and firm B leases the same building. On the balance sheet of firm A, accountants will typically record the purchase price of the building as an asset with an equal offsetting liability. Reported in this way, the purchase creates an increase in the debt-to-equity and debt-to-assets ratios. On the balance sheet of firm B, if the length of the lease is not over the entire life of the building, the value of the leased asset does not appear on the balance sheet, and its effect appears only on the income statement through the expensed lease payments. Reported in this way, firm B will show no change in its debt-to-equity or debt-to-assets ratios, and so will appear to have less financial risk than firm A. The apparent reason for this different treatment is that the legal substance of these two transactions is quite different. Firm A literally owns the building, while firm B does not. But, from the point of view of financial analysis, this is a distinction of form, not first-order economic substance. If the financial economist knew about the lease, he or she would interpret the lease in this way: It is as if firm B borrowed the building instead of borrowing cash, pays what are called lease payments (with a correction for implied depreciation) instead of interest payments, and is obligated to pay back (that is, return) the building, just as firm A is obligated to pay back the cash loan. To abide by the consistency principle, the firm should report the transactions in such a way that the debt-to-equity ratios of the two firms remain equal. One way to do this would be to record the value of the leased building as an asset offset by an equal liability, reflecting firm B's obligation to "pay back" the "borrowed" building.

Unfortunately, as sensible as this sounds, further reflection shows how difficult the standard of consistent accounting is to realize. Accounting for leases in this way implies that assets are not defined by legal *ownership*; rather they are defined by things the firm *uses* to generate revenues—firm B does not own the building, but it is using it to generate revenues, so it is an asset of the firm in this sense. Now, the goal of consistency really gets us into trouble. Consider this: Both firms also use the streets outside their headquarters so employees can come to and leave work; they also use seats on airlines when their employees travel on business; and so forth. To be consistent, these things are therefore assets and need to be reported on the balance sheet. Ideally, a financial economist would want the firm to do this. Again compare two firms, one that uses its own airplanes and roads owned by the firm financed with debt, and another that uses the externally provided roads and airline seats. Clearly, carried to this extreme, consistency becomes impractical.

We should not overplay the significance of designing good accounting rules. External accounting statements are only one source of information about the firm. Some individuals, called professional security analysts, specialize in a single industry and spend a good portion of their lives evaluating public firms in that industry. As a result, if we get accounting rules wrong, although the cost of learning about firm fundamentals will rise, the market may very well continue to price stocks with reasonable accuracy. For example, many corporate executives apparently believe that since expensing stock options reduces their reported earnings per share, their stock price will also fall after the accounting change. But, since the market has other means of learning about their firm's option plans, what is far more likely is that their stock price will be virtually unaffected by the change.

1654 Blaise Pascal (June 19, 1623–August 19, 1662), "Traité du triangle arithmétique avec quelques autres petits traités sur la même matière"; translated into English as "Treatise on the Arithmetical Triangle," and with **Pierre de Fermat** (August 17, 1601–January 12, 1665), "Correspondence with Fermat on the Theory of Probabilities" (1654), Great Books of the Western World: Pascal (Franklin Center, PA: Franklin Library, 1984), pp. 447–487.

PASCAL'S TRIANGLE, PROBABILITY THEORY,
PROBLEM OF POINTS, BINOMIAL CATEGORIZATION,
EXPECTATION, COUNTING PATHS VS. WORKING BACKWARDS,
PATH DEPENDENCE, PASCAL'S WAGER

Early work on combinatorial problems seems to have begun in India,[1] so that by about 1150, Bhaskara understood the general formula for the number of combinations of n things taken j at a time, $n!/[j!(n - j)!]$. The calculation of coefficients from the binomial expansion $(a + b)^n$ as well as arraying these coefficients in the shape of a triangle was known by the Arabian mathematician al-Tusi in 1265, and was known in China in Chu Shi-Chieh's *Ssu Yuan Yü Chien* (1303), the frontispiece of which is reproduced. The equivalence between the combinatorial formula and these coefficients was understood by 1636 by Marin Mersenne (1588–1648).

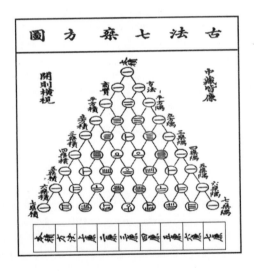

Although clearly the arithmetical triangle was not invented by Pascal (1654), his treatise was the first to bring together all three elements—combinatorics, binomial expansion coefficients, and their triangular array. So thoroughly did Pascal investigate the triangle's properties that ever since it has been commonly referred to as Pascal's triangle. It should be noted that in his discussion of the arithmetical triangle and the Problem of Points, Pascal does not directly use the modern concept of probability, nor even use that term. Instead, he uses combinatoric language, speaking of an event happening so many times out of a total number of possible times. So my discussion that follows is a modernized retelling of Pascal's results.

The triangle starts with 1 in the top row. Each number in a subsequent row is generated by summing the two numbers in the previous row that are just above its location.

$$
\begin{array}{ccccccc}
& & & 1 & & & \\
& & 1 & & 1 & & \\
& & 1 & 2 & 1 & & \\
& 1 & 3 & 3 & 1 & & \\
& 1 & 4 & 6 & 4 & 1 & \\
1 & 5 & 10 & 10 & 5 & 1 &
\end{array}
$$

• • •

Pascal shows that the triangle has a number of surprising properties. For example, numbering the rows starting with 0 for the top row, the nth row contains the coefficients of the binomial expansion $(a + b)^n$. In general, the value of the jth entry (starting numbering from the left from 0) in the nth row is $n!/[j!(n − j)!]$.

Of critical importance for the development of the theory of probability, especially as applied to games of chance (investments?), is the Problem of Points. Recall the basic version of this problem. Two individuals have staked a given amount to be paid to the one who is the first to win n points. A point is awarded in a fair round in which each player has an equal chance of winning. If they decide to stop playing after the first player A has won $x < n$ points and the second player B has won $y < n$ points, what is a fair division of the stakes?

As proposed in Pacioli (1494), suppose the two players have bet 28 pistolas each, $n = 6$ and the points standings are $(x, y) = (5, 3)$, and the game is then called off. Pacioli argues that the fair division is to divide the total stakes in direct proportion to the number of games won by each player. So with 56 pistolas staked, 35 would go to the first player and 21 to the second. Jerome Cardan, better known as Gerolamo Cardano (September 24, 1501–September 21, 1576), in [Cardano (circa 1565)] *Liber de ludo aleae*, first published posthumously in 1663, translated from Latin into English by Sydney Henry Gould as *The Book on Games of Chance* (New York:

Pascal's Triangle

Pascal's triangle exemplifies a recombining binomial tree where the number at each node is the sum of the two numbers lying in the row directly above it. The more general nonrecombining binary tree was originally popularized by Porphyry (circa 234–305), a Neoplatonic philosopher. In his *Introduction to the Categories* (or *Isagoge*), he geometrically represents the relationship of categories from Aristotle's logical work *Categories* as a binary tree, where the set described by each prior category is divided into two mutually exclusive and exhaustive subsets. For example:

$$\text{Substance}$$
$$\text{Corporeal} \qquad \text{Incorporeal}$$
$$\text{Living} \qquad \text{Nonliving}$$
$$\text{Animals} \qquad \text{Plants}$$
$$\text{Rational} \qquad \text{Nonrational}$$

The number of numerical relationships in Pascal's triangle seems endless. Even the Fibonacci sequence lies hidden in the array. Can you find it? Starting from the left side, add the numbers that lie in a diagonal line extending above and to the right, and the sums will make a Fibonacci series. Thus, we have: $1 = 1$, $1 + 1 = 2$, $1 + 2 = 3$, $1 + 3 + 1 = 5$, $1 + 4 + 3 = 8$, and so on.

Holt, Reinhart and Winston, 1961), proposed a more sophisticated solution. He says that the division should depend on the outcome of a new game created from the rounds remaining to be played. So in Pacioli's example, a new game between A and B is imagined where if A can win 1 point before B can win 3 points, then A will win; otherwise B will win. He then asks in this new game what would be the fair stakes contribution of each player. He concludes that B should be willing to stake $1(1 + 1) = 2$ units for every $3(3 + 1) = 12$ units staked by A. So again, if the original stakes were 56 pistolas, he would conclude that A should receive $56(^{12}/_{14}) = 48$ and B should receive $56(^{2}/_{14}) = 8$.

Neither Pacioli's nor Cardano's solution is correct. The problem was finally solved by Pascal-Fermat (1654) in a famous correspondence that gave birth to modern probability theory. They developed the idea of mathematical expectation, and assumed that each player should receive what he would have expected had the game not been stopped.

Fermat's solution simply requires counting the number of ways (or paths) A can win and the number of ways B can win.

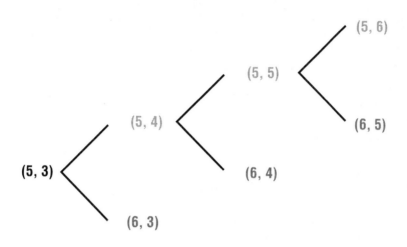

Fermat's Solution

Count paths: 7 vs. 1 ⟶ $^7/_8 \times 56 = 49$

At (5, 3) standings, the possible remaining outcome sequences are (where "a" indicates a point won by the first player and "b" a point won by the second player):

(a a a)   (a b a)   (a b b)   (b b a)

(a a b)   (b a a)   (b a b)   (b b b)

Bolded sequences indicate games won by the first player. Since A wins in 7 out of the 8 possible sequences, A should receive 49 pistolas and B should receive 7 pistolas.

Pascal's alternative but equivalent solution uses the method of backwards recursive dynamic programming.

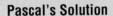

Pascal's Solution

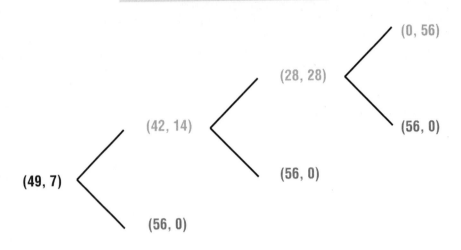

Work backwards

Pascal first asks us to suppose the game is broken off when the standings are (5, 5). Since A and B then both have an equal chance of winning 56 pistolas, they each expect to win 28 pistolas, so the stakes should be divided equally (28, 28). Moving backwards from that, if instead the standings are (5, 4), half the time playing one more round brings the standings to (6, 4) in which case the stakes are divided (56, 0), and half the time the standings end up (5, 5) in which case I have already established the stakes should be divided (28, 28). Therefore, when the standings are (5, 4), A is entitled to $\frac{1}{2}(56) + \frac{1}{2}(28) = 42$, and B is entitled to $\frac{1}{2}(0) + \frac{1}{2}(28) = 14$. Moving back one more round to the current (5, 3) standings, similar reasoning leads to A begin entitled to $\frac{1}{2}(56) + \frac{1}{2}(42) = 49$ pistolas, and B is entitled to $\frac{1}{2}(0) + \frac{1}{2}(14) = 7$ pistolas.[2]

Pascal has also been credited as the originator of decision theory. In [Pascal (1657–1662)] *Pensées*, Great Books of the Western World: Pascal (Franklin Center, PA: Franklin Library, 1984), pp. 173–352, particularly section 3, "Of the Necessity of the Wager," pp. 205–217, Pascal describes his famous "wager," his most unassailable "proof" that you should believe God exists. Consider, he says, two mutually exclusive possibilities. If there is no God, then believing in Him or not believing in Him will be of little matter. However, if there is a God, then believing in Him will bring you the infinite happiness of an eternity in heaven, and not believing in Him will bring you the infinite unhappiness of an eternity in hell. So even if your subjective probability of God existing is arbitrarily small but greater than zero, your expected gain from believing that God exists will be infinite. Of course, we now understand that Pascal's reasoning is seriously flawed since it depends on his particular listing of the possible states of the world. For example, another possibility is that if God exists, believers are sent to hell since no human has enough information to conclude this is true, while doubters, who have the correct view given the information available, go to heaven.

Tempting as it may be, crediting Pascal as the first decision theorist is undeserved. The much earlier Talmud (*Kethuboth* 9q) argues that a man should not be allowed to divorce his wife for adultery before marriage. First, there is the possibility the woman may have lost virginity before marriage through the agency of her new husband; and second, even if this did not happen, the woman may have not been a willing participant. Taken together, there being four possibilities with only one deserving of divorce, the weight of the evidence militates against allowing it. Pascal's wager may also be another instance of Stephen Stigler's law of eponymy since Arnobius of Sicca described a similar choice in his "The Case against the Pagans" (Book 2, Chapter 4), written in about 303 A.D.

As a striking aspect of the birth of modern probability theory, Pascal simultaneously and perhaps unconsciously embraced its duality: the interpretation of probabilities as applying (1) to physical processes like coin flipping and games of chance where probabilities can be indisputably calculated (objective probabilities), which we see in the Problem of Points, or (2) to nonrepeatable events about which there is often considerable disagreement (subjective probabilities), which we see in Pascal's wager. Subsequently, it has been argued, for example, by Savage (1954) in *The Foundations of Statistics*, that the use of subjective probabilities applied to nonrepeatable events necessarily falls out from rational choice among alternatives. But Savage's analysis works only if bets on alternatives are feasible in the sense that the event that determines the outcome of the bets is potentially observable. The outcome of a bet on the existence of life after death is problematic: The winner betting there is no life after death will find it singularly difficult to collect.

In the latter half of the twentieth century, digital computers became critical to the further development of the theory of investments, from empirical tests based on extensive databases to solving mathematical problems with numerical analysis. Very simple calculating machines had long been in use, such as the abacus from 3000 B.C. The slide rule was invented in the years 1630–1632. In 1642–1644, in addition to his many other contributions to science, Pascal, at about age 20, is credited with creating the first digital computer. Numbers are entered by turning dials, and addition and subtraction are accomplished by underlying gears that move as the digits are dialed in, with the total shown in a window above the keys. The 1652 version, signed by Pascal, can be seen in Paris at the Conservatoire National des Arts et Métiers; and for those who prefer London, a copy can be found at the Science Museum in South Kensington.

1657 Christiaan Huygens (April 14, 1629–July 8, 1695), *De ratiociniis in aleae ludo* ("Calculating in Games of Chance"), first published in Latin as an appendix to Frans von Schooten's *Exercitationum mathematicarum libri quinque* (1657) and subsequently in Dutch as *Van rekiningh in spelen van geluck* (1660); reprinted with annotations by **Jakob Bernoulli** in *Ars conjectandi*, Part 1 (1713); English translation available as of March 6, 2004, on the Internet at www.stat.ucla.edu/history/huygens.pdf.

PROBABILITY THEORY, EXPECTATION, ARBITRAGE,
STATE-PRICES, GAMBLER'S RUIN PROBLEM

Already famous for, among other things, the discovery of the rings of Saturn and its largest moon Titan, being the first to notice the markings on the surface of Mars, and his invention of the pendulum clock in 1656, Huygens (1657) in quick succession published the first work on probability—actually a 16-page treatise that includes a treatment of properties of expectation (a word he coined as *expectatio*). Despite the reputation of his treatise and like Pascal (1654) and Pascal-Fermat (1654), Huygens makes no reference to our current notion of probability. Moreover, although Huygens' results can be and have been interpreted in terms of our modern notions of probability and expectation, he had something else in mind. For him, expectation is the amount someone should pay for a gamble. So in one of the curious reversals in intellectual history, a problem in investments provided motivation for the birth of modern probability theory (rather than, as might have been suspected, the other way around)!

Following the commentary of Ian Hacking in [Hacking (1975)] *The Emergence of Probability* (Cambridge: Cambridge University Press, 1975) to provide a basis for Huygens' propositions, consider the following lottery. A promoter offers a lottery to players P1 and P2. He will flip a fair coin and player P1 will try to guess the outcome. If P1 guesses correctly, the payoff will be $X > 0$ to player P1, and 0 to player P2, which I will write $(X, 0)$; if P1 guesses incorrectly, the payoff will be 0 to player P1, and X to player P2, or $(0, X)$. Huygens tacitly assumes that the value of the payoff to any player remains unchanged under a permutation across the states. So in this case the value of payoff $(X, 0)$ should equal the value of the payoff $(0, X)$. He then considers the lottery fair if its price (or stakes) to either player is $P = X/2$ (Assumption 1). This follows from what we now call an arbitrage argument. If instead $P > X/2$, then the promoter makes a sure profit since his total receipts $2P > X$, the prize he must pay out. On the other hand, if instead $P < X/2$, then the two players could collude and make a sure profit at the expense of the promoter.

Huygens now considers a revised lottery in which the winner agrees to pay the loser a consolation prize $0 < K < X$ so that neither player will end up out of pocket; that is, the payoff to each player will be either $X - K$ or K, with equal chance. Huygens assumes this will not change the price P of the lottery (Assumption 2). Huygens also assumes that two lotteries with the same payoffs must have the same price (Assumption 3)—an assumption we would now call "the single-price law."

Huygens starts by proving three propositions:

1. If there are equal chances of obtaining A or B, then the expectation is worth $(A + B)/2$.
2. If there are equal chances of obtaining A, B, or C, then the expectation is $(A + B + C)/3$.
3. If the number of chances of receiving A is n_1 and the number of chances of receiving B is n_2, then the expectation is $(n_1 A + n_2 B)/(n_1 + n_2)$.

Propositions 1 and 2 deal with equiprobable states. Proposition 3, if interpreted as it subsequently was in modern terms, reaches our current notion of expectation where probabilities do not have to be equal; we would identify the ratio $n_1/(n_1 + n_2) \equiv p$, so that the expectation is $pA + (1 - p)B$.

With our several-hundred-year remove, Proposition 1 may seem obvious; but that was not so in 1657.

Proof of Huygens' Proposition 1

Suppose there is a fair lottery I with two players and prize $A + B$ (where $A < B$). It then follows by Assumption 1 that for the lottery to be fair, the price of a ticket to this lottery must be $(A + B)/2$. Suppose also that the winner must pay the loser a consolation prize of A. The payoff from the lottery for one player will then be either $(A + B) - A = B$ if he wins or A, the consolation prize if he loses. Notice that the payoff from this lottery is the same as the payoff for fair lottery II where a player has an equal chance of gaining A or B (by Assumption 2). Since lotteries I and II have the same payoffs, they must have the same price (by Assumption 3). Finally, since the fair price of a ticket to lottery I is $(A + B)/2$, that must also be the fair price for lottery II. Thus, Proposition 1 is proved.

Proposition 2 is proved by extending the side payment idea of Assumption 2 as follows: There are now three players, P1, P2, and P3. Since the gamble is fair, if P1 wins he receives the entire stakes X, but he agrees to pay B to P2 and C to P3. So if P1 wins, P1 nets $A \equiv X - (B + C)$. On the other hand, in return, if P2 wins, he agrees to pay B to P1; and if P3 wins, he agrees to pay C to P1. So P1 has an equal chance of winning A, B, or C. P2 and P3 make arrangements between each other that are similar, so that each player has an equal chance of winning A, B, or C. The following table displays these outcomes:[3]

If the Winner Is:	The Payoff for P1 Is:	The Payoff for P2 Is:	The Payoff for P3 Is:
P1	$X - (B + C) = A$	B	C
P2	B	$X - (A + B) = C$	A
P3	C	A	$X - (A + C) = B$

Proposition 3 uses yet a further extension of Assumption 2. Huygens now proposes a lottery with $n_1 + n_2$ players. Each player stakes X. The lottery is fair since the total payoff is $X \times (n_1 + n_2)$ and each player has an equal chance of winning. The first player makes an agreement with the $n_1 - 1$ players that if he wins he will pay each of them A, and if any one of them wins instead, the winner agrees to pay him A. With the n_2 players, if he wins, he agrees to pay each of them B, and if any one of them wins, the winner agrees to pay him B. From this, by an argument similar to the earlier propositions, he proves Proposition 3.

Surprisingly, the primitive for Huygens is "value," not "probability." Linking this with modern finance, it is as if he were thinking of valuation directly in terms of state-prices (where interest rates can be approximated at zero so $r = 1$) π_a and π_b, where π_a can be identified with $n_1/(n_1 + n_2)$ and π_b with $n_2/(n_1 + n_2)$. So the value of the lottery is $\pi_a(A) + \pi_b(B)$.

In the state-price interpretation, for the same arbitrage reason, the sum of state-prices $\pi_a + \pi_b$ must be 1 and each state-price must be positive. However, the modern theory does not accept Huygens' tacit assumption that value is invariant to permuting the payoffs across equiprobable states. That is, the equal-chance payoffs $(X, 0)$ and $(0, X)$ may not have the same value.

From the modern perspective, state-prices reflect not only probabilities but also levels of risk and risk aversion. We know that Huygens' assertion underlying his Assumption 1 that the gamble with equally likely payoffs X or 0 would be worth $X/2$ would not generally be true if that gamble were traded in a market that did not also include its inverse gamble with payoffs 0 or X in the corresponding states. When both exist in the *same quantity* in the same market (as Huygens seems to assume), since their individual risks can be completely diversified away, they should be priced at their expected payoffs. But if only one were available and not also its inverse, since the risk could not be eliminated by diversification, its price could be more or less than its expected value depending on the correlation of its payoffs with other available investments, the correlation with other factors of importance to the players, and their risk aversion. Or, if the outside wealth of the players was, for reasons other than the gamble, different in the two states, then the prices of the two gambles would generally not be the same. If aggregate wealth were lower in the first state than in the second, even though the gamble is a side bet between two players, the price of the payoff X or 0 would be higher than the price of the payoff 0 or X (of course, the simple arbitrage argument given earlier continues to ensure that whatever their prices, the sum of the two prices must be X).

The winner-take-all University of Iowa presidential election Internet market immediately comes to mind as a real-life example. In the year 2000, participants were able to place a bet at price P_B that would pay $X = \$1$ if George Bush were elected and 0 if not, or place a bet at price P_G that would pay $X = \$1$ if Al Gore were elected and 0 if not. Ignoring the small possibility of a third candidate winning, arbitrage requires that the sum of the prices $P_B + P_G = \$1$. Indeed, this was in fact true to a very close approximation. Should one then, as Huygens argues, interpret P_B as the expected value of a bet that Bush will win and P_G as the expected value of a bet that Gore will win? Not quite. For if it were the case, for example, that participants anticipate better economic times under Bush than under Gore, and if they are risk averse, then the utility of receiving an extra dollar if Gore is elected is higher than the utility of an extra dollar if Bush is elected. Or, it may be that if Bush is elected and he had bet on Bush, a participant may feel so discouraged that he cannot enjoy the extra dollar as much if instead, Gore had been elected and he had bet on Gore. Therefore, the prices of bets on Bush and Gore will be affected not only by subjective probabilities but also by these utilities. In the end, the price P_B of a bet on Bush will be a little lower than the subjective probability of Bush winning, and P_G will be correspondingly higher—in any case, preserving a sum of $1.

Using these three propositions, Huygens then proves 11 others and proposes but does not solve five additional problems suggested by

Fermat. Propositions 4 through 9 relate to the Problem of Points, ana-
lyzed at about the same time by Pascal-Fermat (1654). Propositions 10
to 14 move to new territory. To get a flavor of these, Proposition 10 answers the question: How many times does one need to toss a single fair
die before one can expect to see the first six? Huygens solves the problem recursively. The probability of getting a six in the first toss is X_1 =
1/6 and the probability of not getting a six is 5/6. The probability of getting a six in the first two tosses is the sum of the probability of getting a
six in the second toss 1/6 plus the probability of having instead rolled a
six in the first toss $(5/6)X_1$. Therefore, the probability of rolling a six in
the first two tosses is X_2 = $(1/6)$ + $(5/6)X_1$. The probability of getting a
six in the first three tosses is the sum of the probability of getting a six
in the third toss 1/6 plus the probability of instead having rolled a six in
the first two tosses $(5/6)X_2$. Therefore, the probability of rolling a six in
the first three tosses is X_3 = $(1/6)$ + $(5/6)X_2$. Continuing this line of reasoning, the probability of getting a six by the kth toss is X_k = $(1/6)$ +
$(5/6)X_{k-1}$. From this, it is easy to see that when k = 4 the probability of
having thrown a six crosses over from below $1/2$ to 671/1,296. (Although
Huygens does not solve this sequence of equations analytically, it is easy
to see that X_k = $1 - (5/6)^k$.)

The last proposition, 14, carries this type of recursive solution one
step further to a situation where the potential number of games is unbounded. This proposition answers the question: Suppose two players
take turns tossing two fair dice so that player A wins if he tosses a seven
before player B tosses a six; otherwise player B wins; and B tosses first.
What are the odds that A will win? Clearly, the probability that A will
toss a seven in a single throw is 6/36 and the probability that B will toss
a six in a single throw is 5/36. Huygens solves the problem by setting up
two simultaneous equations. Suppose that the probability that A will
win is p, so that the probability that B will eventually win is $1 - p$. Every
time B throws, since it is as if the game just started, the probability that
A will eventually win is p. But every time A tosses, the probability that A
will eventually win is somewhat higher, say q. Therefore, from Proposition 3, when B tosses, the probability of A eventually winning is also
equal to:

$$\left(\frac{5}{36} \times 0\right) + \left(\frac{31}{36} \times q\right) = p$$

Similarly, when A tosses, the probability of A eventually winning is:

$$\frac{6}{36} + \left(\frac{30}{36}\right)p = q$$

Solving these two simultaneous equations for p and q, we get $p = 31/61$, so the odds that A will win are 31:30.

The last of the five appended problems is the gambler's ruin problem, apparently originally posed by Pascal: Consider a game in which two players start with the same stakes. They play a sequence of rounds. At each round the first player wins with probability p and receives one unit from the stakes of the second player, or the second player wins (with probability $1 - p$) and receives one unit from the stakes of the first player. The game ends as soon as one player has no stakes remaining. What is the probability that this will occur in at most n rounds?

The gambler's ruin problem was to play a critical role in the subsequent development of the mathematics of random walks and Brownian motion. In modern terminology, we have a random walk between absorbing barriers, where one barrier marks the ruin the first player and the other the ruin of the second. As discussed in Hald (2003), p. 352, in his 1713 correspondence with Pierre Rémond De Montmort, Nicholas Bernoulli solves a generalization of this problem when the players start with different stakes and can play any number of rounds. Suppose player A begins with stakes a, and player B begins with stakes b, the probability that A will win any round is p, and the probability that B will win any round is $q = 1 - p$. With this notation, the probability $R(a, b; p)$ that B will be ruined (and perforce A will win all the stakes) is:

$$R(a, b; p) = \frac{p^{a+b} - p^b q^a}{p^{a+b} - q^{a+b}}, \text{ for } a \neq b \text{ and } p \neq \frac{1}{2}$$

$$R(a, a; p) = \frac{p^a}{p^a + q^a}$$

$$R\left(a, b; \frac{1}{2}\right) = \frac{a}{a+b}$$

1662 John Graunt (April 24, 1620–April 18, 1674), *Natural and Political Observations Made Upon the Bills of Mortality* (London: Martyn, 1662); reprinted in B. Benjamin, "John Graunt's 'Observations,'" *Journal of the Institute of Actuaries* 90 (1962), pp. 1–60.

STATISTICS, MORTALITY TABLES, EXPECTED LIFETIME

The field of investments is distinguished by being, after games of chance, the first to feel the benefits of the new probabilistic reasoning. In turn, applications in this area led to further advances in probability theory and literally initiated the related field of statistics. To begin this story, I first need to explain the incipient effort to construct tables of human mortality, and then how these tables were used to determine the present value of life annuities (annuities with payments conditional upon the recipient remaining alive).

The tradition of drawing up a population census dates back at least to republican Rome. The famous Doomsday Book of 1086, put together for the purposes of taxation in England, is a much later example. But it remained for Graunt (1662) to conduct the first published statistical analysis of this type of data, indeed of any type of data, making him the first known statistician. Not only was his analysis the first of its kind, but it is surprisingly sophisticated, largely remaining a model of good statistical procedure to the present day. Of course, he was restricted to displaying data in the form of tables since the representation of time series and cross sections by graphs was not yet the practice.

According to Anders Hald, in [Hald (2003)] *History of Probability and Statistics and Their Applications before 1750* (Hoboken, NJ: John Wiley & Sons, 2003), Graunt's analysis was based on a compendium of vital statistics for the population of London, gathered weekly starting in 1604, with some data as late as 1672 (for subsequent editions). Like a good modern statistician, Graunt first worries about errors by correcting for unreasonable spikes, running consistency checks, and checking for confirmatory evidence. For example, he makes three independent calculations of the number of families in London by looking separately at births, burials, and the number of houses. He then finds useful ways to summarize the data. For example, he aggregates burials over time according to the cause of death (Chapter 2):

Cause of Death	Number of Burials
Plague	16,000
Children's disease	77,000
Aged	16,000

Cause of Death	Number of Burials
"Chronical" diseases	70,000
"Epidemical" diseases	50,000
Total	229,000

He distinguishes between the fixed component of causes of death that are found every year ("chronical") and the variable component of those that change from year to year ("epidemical"). He notes that the fear that many citizens have of dying from particular causes is often quite exaggerated and hopes that his statistics will set them at ease. He also makes other tables that present time-series numbers showing the changes in the cause of death over time. Although Graunt does not yet understand with any precision the effect of sample size on reducing variance, he does know this intuitively since he groups data into subperiods, such as decades, so that trends will be more discernible. Using his data, he is the first to note that the numbers of males and females in the population are consistently nearly equal over time. He formulates and tests the hypothesis that births are lower in years of relatively more deaths.

Most important for the subsequent development of probability theory, Graunt makes the first attempt we know of to create a mortality table. To do this, he has to infer the total population over time from his data and the number of deaths by age. Since he lacks direct information about this, he devises a clever way to guess this information from the data at his disposal. Graunt's resulting mortality table is (Hald 2003, p. 102):

Of the 100 conceived there remains alive at six years end 64.

At sixteen years end	*40*	*At fifty six*	*6*
At twenty six	*25*	*At sixty six*	*3*
At thirty six	*16*	*At seventy six*	*1*
At forty six	*10*	*At eighty*	*0*

It is perhaps worth noting that in the seventeenth century this type of analysis was originally called "political arithmetic," and then subsequently "statistics," originally taken to mean the collection and analysis of facts related to affairs of state (*status* is the Latin word for state).

In 1669, based on Graunt's mortality table, Christiaan Huygens and his brother Ludwig made several statistical innovations (these were finally published in Christiaan Huygens, *Oeuvres Complètes*, Volume 6 of 22, 1895). Ludwig's objective is to use Graunt's table to calculate expected lifetime conditional on current age. To do this, he assumes a uniform distribution of the probability of death in between Graunt's observations.

Hald (2003), p. 107, represents Ludwig's calculations in the following table:

Ludwig Huygens' Mortality Table

Age x	Number of Survivors l_x	Number of Deaths d_x	Midpoint of Age Interval t_x	$t_x d_x$	Accumulation of $t_x d_x$ from Below	Average Age at Death $E(t_x)$	Expected Remaining Lifetime e_x
0	100	36	3	108	1,822	18.22	18.22
6	64	24	11	264	1,714	26.78	20.78
16	40	15	21	315	1,450	36.25	20.25
26	25	9	31	279	1,135	45.40	19.40
36	16	6	41	246	856	53.50	17.50
46	10	4	51	204	610	61.00	15.00
56	6	3	61	183	406	67.67	11.67
66	3	2	71	142	223	74.33	8.33
76	1	1	81	81	81	81.00	5.00
86	0						0.00

The variables x and l_x are taken directly from Graunt's table; d_x is the first difference in l_x; t_x is the midpoint of the beginning and ending of the intervals determined by x. Therefore, assuming a uniform distribution of dying within each interval, t_x equals the expected lifetime for the individuals corresponding to d_x deaths. Ludwig reasons that 1,822 years is the number of years the 100 individuals starting at age 0 will in total live: 36 will live on average 3 years, 24 will live on average 11 years, 15 will live on average 21 years, and so on, so that the sum of all these years is 1,822. Then, each of the 100 individuals at age 0 can expect to live until they are 1,822/100 = 18.22 = $E(t_0)$ years old. By similar logic, each of the 64 individuals at age 6 can expect to live until they are 1,714/64 = 26.78 = $E(t_6)$ years old. Given an individual's age, calculating his or her expected remaining lifetime is then a simple matter of subtracting age x from $E(t_x)$. Interpolating between 17.5 and 15, Ludwig concludes that Christiaan, who at that time was 40, could expect to live 16.5 more years.

Christiaan takes his brother's analysis a few steps further. He represents the first and second columns of the table graphically as an interpolated continuous function, the first appearance of a distribution function. He shows how to calculate the median, as opposed to the expected, remaining life. He also calculates the expected remaining lifetime for the second of two given individuals A and B to die. That is, if T_A, a random variable, is the remaining lifetime for A, and T_B is the remaining lifetime for B, he calculates $E[\max(T_A, T_B)]$. First, for each number of years T_A remaining in the life of A, assuming independence, he calculates $E(T_B | T_B \geq T_A)$. Then he weights each of these conditional expectations by the probability of T_A and sums the products. Here we have one of the earliest uses of the idea of conditional expectations. Identifying $T = \max(T_A, T_B)$, we have the expected remaining lifetime of the survivor $E(T) = E[E(T | T_A)]$, what we now call the law of iterated expectations.

1671 Johan de Witt (September 24, 1625–August 20, 1672), *Value of Life Annuities in Proportion to Redeemable Annuities,* published in Dutch (1671); "Contributions of the History of Insurance and the Theory of Life Contingencies," *Assurance Magazine* 2 (1852), pp. 232–249.

1693 Edmond Halley, "An Estimate of the Degrees of the Mortality of Mankind, Drawn from Curious Tables of the Births and Funerals in the City of Breslaw; with an Attempt to Ascertain the Price of Annuities upon Lives," *Philosophical Transactions of the Royal Society* 17 (1693), pp. 596–610.

1725 Abraham de Moivre (May 26, 1667–November 27, 1754), *A Treatise of Annuities on Lives;* reprinted as an addition to de Moivre's third edition ("Fuller, Clearer, and More Correct than the Former") of *The Doctrine of Chances* (1756); reprinted by the American Mathematical Society (2000), pp. 261–328.

LIFE ANNUITIES, PRESENT VALUE,
MORTALITY TABLES, STATE-PRICES, TONTINES

Today, we think of probability theory as the servant of investments, but this was not always so. In an earlier time, the need to know the present value of cash flows dependent on mortality played a parenting role in developing ideas about probability. A life annuity is a contract that pays the annuitant a given constant amount every year until the death of a given individual, the "nominee" (usually the same as the annuitant), with no repayment of principal. Social Security is today's ubiquitous version of a life annuity. A generalization is a *joint* life annuity, commonly used for married couples or shipmates, which continues only for so long as they both live. A tontine (named after a government funding proposal recommended to the French Cardinal Jules Mazarin in 1653 by Lorenzo Tonti) is similar except that the arrangement continues as long as one member survives. In a typical arrangement, a group of contributors place equal amounts of money in a fund; each then receives an annuity that represents his or her share of a designated total sum that the annuitants divide equally among themselves every year. As the annuitants drop out because of their deaths, those remaining divide the same total, leaving a greater payment to each. After only one annuitant remains, he or she receives the entire annuity payment each year. Once the last annuitant dies, all payments cease and the corpus then reverts to the issuer (e.g., the government). In another version, which provides the theme of Robert Louis Stevenson and Lloyd Osbourne's novella, *The Wrong Box* (1889), the tontine begins with 37 members; no money is paid out until only one remains alive, whereupon he receives the entire initial contribution plus all accumulated income.

According to Roman Falcidian Law passed in 40 B.C., during the Civil War that intervened between the assassination of Julius Caesar in 44 B.C. and the Battle of Actium in 31 B.C. (dates historians now identify with the end of the Roman Republic and the start of the Roman Principate), the legal heir, usually the firstborn surviving male, of an estate was guaranteed to receive at least 25 percent of the value of the estate. Since bequests in classical Rome often took the form of a life annuity to children who were not the firstborn, it was necessary to determine their value. Annuities were quoted in terms of "years' purchase," what we would now call the "payback period." For example, for an annuity of $100 per year, 20 years' purchase implies a current price of $100 × 20 = $2,000. From the third-century Roman jurist Domitius Ulpianus (Ulpian), we have a table of life annuities that apparently recognizes that the value of the annuity should decrease with the age of the annuitant (although there may have been an intentional upward bias to protect the estate of the firstborn). In one of his tables, he quotes that at age 20, a life annuity is valued at 30 years' purchase, while if one were 60, a life annuity is valued at 7 years' purchase. We now know how to calculate a simple upper bound to the years' purchase. Assuming infinite life and a plausible interest rate of 6 percent, the annuity would be worth $1/.06 = $16.67, implying a years' purchase of 16.67. That is the most the annuity could be worth since anything less than an infinite life would produce a smaller value.

The history of life annuities has recently been surveyed in [Poitras (2000)] Geoffrey Poitras, *The Early History of Financial Economics: 1478–1776: From Commercial Arithmetic to Life Annuities and Joint Stocks* (Cheltenham, U.K.: Edward Elgar, 2000). Beginning in the seventeenth century, life annuities were used by governments to raise funds. One reason annuities became quite popular is that they escaped Church usury laws: An annuity was not considered a loan since the buyer received interest only and not return of principal, even though a secondary market in annuities permitted the buyer to cash out early. By that time a more sophisticated notion of years' purchase was used. Suppose that P is the price of an annuity certain lasting until some fixed year in the future, X is the annual annuity payment, and the interest return is r. The years' purchase t satisfies the equation $P = X[\Sigma_{k=1,2,...,t}(1/r^k)]$. In other words, the years' purchase is the time at which the present value of the received annuity equals its price.

Although, as we have seen, the Romans apparently used a crude adjustment for the expected life of the nominee, little attempt was made to make this adjustment with any precision until de Witt (1671). In what may be regarded as the first formal analysis of an option-style derivative, de Witt proposed a way to calculate the value of life annuities that takes account of the age of the nominee. His method was crude by modern standards, but he did make use of one of the first mortality tables. De Witt assumed nominees would die according to the following table. Out of every 768 nominees:

Six will die every six months for the first 50 years.

Four will die every six months for the next 10 years.

Three will die every six months for the next 10 years.

Two will die every six months for the next 7 years.

Assuming a compound interest rate of 4 percent, for each of the 768 times to death, he calculated the present value of the corresponding annuity and then took their arithmetic average to be the price of the annuity. De Witt also mentions that his calculation will be biased low due to what we would now call "adverse selection," since the subset of individuals who purchase annuities will likely contain those who are comparatively healthy and therefore likely to live longer than others of their age.

While this history intentionally focuses on the development of ideas, in contrast to the biographies of the creators of these ideas, I cannot resist mentioning that in 1672, just one year after de Witt published his now-classic work on life annuities, he was publicly hanged by a revolutionary mob in Holland, no doubt because of his prominence as a government minister with special expertise in finance.

Johan van Waveran Hudde (April 23, 1628–April 15, 1704), who had been consulted by de Witt, derived his own annuity values using mortality statistics from 1,495 people who had actually purchased annuities. Halley (1693) made his own calculations. Apart from using different data, Halley's formula led to the same result as de Witt's. But he restructured the solution in a more fundamental way. The present value of an annuity certain terminating at date t is $X[\Sigma_{k=1,2,...,t}(1/r^k)]$. Suppose q_t is the probability the annuitant will *die* in year t. Then, according to de Witt, the present value of a life annuity is:

$$A \equiv X \times \Sigma_t q_t \left[\Sigma_{k=1,2,...,t} \left(\frac{1}{r^k} \right) \right]$$

Alternatively, suppose p_t is the probability the annuitant will be *alive* in year t. Halley first calculated $e_t \equiv p_t/r^t$, and then used these molecular prices to calculate the present value of the life annuity:

$$A = X \times \Sigma_t \left(\frac{p_t}{r^t} \right) = X \times \Sigma_t e_t$$

Proof That Halley's and de Witt's Formulations Are Equivalent

To derive Halley's formulation from de Witt's, first derive the relation between probabilities q_t, that the annuitant *dies* in year t, and p_t, that the annuitant *is alive* in year t. p_t equals the sum of the probabilities of dying at dates $t + 1$, $t + 2$, $t + 3$, ... since if one has not died by date t, one must then die subsequently. So the probability of being alive at date t must equal the probability of dying after date t. Consider a special case where the annuitant must die by date 4. Then:

$$p_1 = q_2 + q_3 + q_4$$
$$p_2 = q_3 + q_4$$
$$p_3 = q_4$$

Solving these equations for q_2 and q_3: $q_2 = p_1 - p_2$, $q_3 = p_2 - p_3$ (and $q_4 = p_3 - p_4$, where by assumption $p_4 = 0$). So generally,

$$q_t = p_{t-1} - p_t$$

This makes intuitive sense since the probability of dying at date t should equal the probability of being alive at date $t - 1$ (and therefore not having died before that) less the lower probability of being alive at date t; the difference between these probabilities can only be explained by having died at date t.

Substituting this into de Witt's formulation:

$$A = X \times \Sigma_t (p_t - p_{t+1}) \left[\Sigma_{k=1,2,\ldots,t} \left(\frac{1}{r^k} \right) \right]$$

Proof That Halley's and de Witt's Formulations Are Equivalent *(Continued)*

Looking at the first few terms:

$$
A = X \times (p_1 - p_2)\left(\frac{1}{r}\right) + (p_2 - p_3)\left(\frac{1}{r} + \frac{1}{r^2}\right) + (p_3 - p_4)\left(\frac{1}{r} + \frac{1}{r^2} + \frac{1}{r^3}\right) + \cdots
$$

$$
= X \times p_1\left(\frac{1}{r}\right) + p_2\left(\frac{1}{r^2}\right) + p_3\left(\frac{1}{r^3}\right) + \cdots = X \times \Sigma_t\left(\frac{p_t}{r^t}\right)
$$

This makes intuitive sense since receiving the annuity at each date is conditional on being alive at that date so that the present value of the expected annuity at any date t equals $p_t(1/r^t)$. The result follows since the present value of a sum equals the sum of the present values.

We can think of the e_t as today's price of your receiving \$1 in year t if and only if you are alive at that time. In today's life insurance parlance, the e_t is called a "pure endowment" price. Actuaries define pure endowment as an amount payable to an insured contingent on surviving for a prespecified length of time; an individual who does not survive receives nothing. Endowment insurance is more inclusive: It pays a stated sum plus accruals either on a prespecified future date or on the date of death if that occurs early. Premiums are typically paid in equal installments during the life of the policy. This type of insurance can therefore be decomposed into pure endowment insurance, which is canceled if death occurs earlier, before the designated period is over, plus term insurance, which pays off only if the insured dies during the period.

The mathematician de Moivre (1725) also worked on the life annuity problem, deriving "closed-form" results for single-life and joint-life annuities, tontines, and reversions. His Problem #1 (pp. 265–266) deals with a *single-life annuity*. To obtain a solution in closed-form, he assumes that the probability of remaining alive decreases with age in an arithmetic progression:

Supposing the probabilities of life to decrease in arithmetic progression, to find the value of annuity upon a life of an age given.

Using Halley's formulation, de Moivre therefore assumes that $p_t = 1 - (t/n)$, where n can be interpreted as some maximum number of years remaining that the individual could survive. For example, consider a man of age 30; if n = 50, the probability he will be alive in one year is $p_1 = 1 - 1/50 = .98$, in two years is $p_2 = 1 - 2/50 = .96$. The probability that he will be alive in 50 years is $p_{50} = 1 - 50/50 = 0$. Under this assumption, the present value of the annuity is:

$$A = X \times \Sigma_t \left(\frac{p_t}{r^t} \right) = X \times \Sigma_t \left(1 - \frac{t}{n} \right) r^{-t}$$

Using the properties of geometric series, de Moivre shows that (where $r^* \equiv r - 1$):

$$A = X \times \left(\frac{1}{r^*} \right) \left(1 - \frac{r}{n} \left[1 - \frac{(1/r)^n}{r^*} \right] \right)$$

De Moivre also provided results for a *joint-life annuity* (Problem #2, pp. 266-268):

The value [of a life annuity] of two single lives being given, to find the value of an annuity granted for the time of their joint continuance.

Suppose that two individuals at ages x and y were to individually buy annuities, which for simplicity each paid off \$1 every year they remain alive. Let the present value of their annuities $A_x \equiv \Sigma_t({}_xp/r^t)$ and $A_y \equiv \Sigma_t({}_yp/r^t)$. Further, suppose the probability of remaining alive is geometrically decreasing with time so that ${}_xp_t = p_x^t$ and ${}_yp_t = p_y^t$. So, for example, for the individual at age x, the probability that he will be alive in one year is p_x, the probability that he will be alive in two years is p_x^2, and so on. De Moivre proves that if the two lives are independent, then the present value of an annuity written on their joint lives (that is, a security that pays off \$1 as long as both are alive) is:

$$A_{xy} \equiv \frac{A_x A_y r}{(A_x + 1)(A_y + 1) - A_x A_y r}$$

To see this, the probability that both individuals will be alive after t years from their present ages is $(p_x p_y)^t$, so that the present value of a joint annuity is $A_{xy} = \Sigma_{k=1,2,\dots,\infty}(p_x p_y/r)^t$. As de Moivre has posed the problem, we need to express this in terms of single-life annuities. The present value of a single-life annuity for the first individual is $A_x = \Sigma_{k=1,2,\dots,\infty}$ $(p_x/r)^t = (p_x/r)/[1 - (p_x/r)] = p_x/(r - p_x)$, and similarly for the second individual $A_y = p_y/(r - p_y)$. Solving each of these single-life formulas for p_x and p_y and substituting these expressions for p_x and p_y in the expression for the joint-life annuity, A_{xy}, brings the result.

De Moivre also considers a *tontine* problem (Problem #4, p. 270):

The values of two single lives being given, to find the value of an annuity from the longest of them, that is, to continue so long as either of them is in being.

which he proves to be $A_x + A_y - A_{xy}$, quite generally without special assumptions regarding the dependence of $_yp_t$ and $_yp_t$ on t.

This follows quite simply from the observation that the probability that at least one of the two individuals remains alive at time t is $1 - (1 - {_xp_t})(1 - {_yp_t})$. Therefore the present value of the tontine is $\Sigma_t[1 - (1 - {_xp_t})(1 - {_yp_t})]/r^t$. Breaking this apart into three separate sums, one for terms $_xp_t$, one for terms $_yp_t$, and one for terms $_xp_t \,{_yp_t}$, yields the result.

De Moivre's Problem #7 (p. 272) deals with a life annuity that results from a *"reversion"*:

Suppose A is in possession of an annuity, and that B after the death of A should have an annuity for his life only; to find the value of the life of B after the life of A.

which he proves to be $A_y - A_{xy}$, again quite generally without special assumptions regarding the dependence of $_xp_t$ and $_yp_t$ on t.

This also follows quite simply from the observation that the probability that A will have died and B will be alive at time t is $(1 - {_xp_t}){_yp_t}$. Therefore the present value of the tontine is $\Sigma_t[(1 - {_xp_t}){_yp_t}]/r^t$. Breaking this apart into two separate sums, one for terms $_yp_t$ and one for terms $_xp_t \,{_yp_t}$, yields the result.

1738 Daniel Bernoulli (February 8, 1700–March 17, 1782), "Specimen Theoriae Novae de Mensura Sortis," in *Commentarii Academiae Scientiarum Imperialis Petropolitannae* (1738); translated from Latin into English by L. Sommer, "Exposition of a New Theory on the Measurement of Risk," *Econometrica* 22, No. 1 (January 1954), pp. 23–36.

1934 Karl Menger (January 13, 1902–October 5, 1985), "Das Unsicherheitsmoment in der Wertlehre," *Zeitschrift für Nationaloekonomie*, Band V, Heft 4 (1934), pp. 459–485, translated from the German into English by Wolfgang Schoellkopf as "The Role of Uncertainty in Economics," in *Essays in Mathematical Economics in Honor of Oskar Morgenstern*, edited by Martin Shubik (Princeton, NJ: Princeton University Press, 1967), pp. 211–231.

RISK AVERSION, ST. PETERSBURG PARADOX,
EXPECTED UTILITY, LOGARITHMIC UTILITY,
DIVERSIFICATION, WEBER-FECHNER LAW OF PSYCHOPHYSICS,
BOUNDED UTILITY FUNCTIONS

In their solution to the Problem of Points, Pascal-Fermat (1654) had assumed that a gamble was worth its expected value. Huygens (1657), as well, as I have noted, developed his entire theory of chance with this presumption. The classic paper of Bernoulli (1738) originates the idea that a gamble is worth less than its expected value because of risk aversion. Bernoulli justified risk aversion by use of the St. Petersburg Paradox. How much would you pay for the opportunity to flip a fair coin until the first time it lands heads? If it first lands heads on the nth toss, you will receive 2^n dollars. The expected value of this gamble equals

$$\left(\frac{1}{2}\right)2 + \left(\frac{1}{2}\right)^2 2^2 + \left(\frac{1}{2}\right)^3 2^3 + \cdots = 1 + 1 + 1 + \cdots = \infty$$

yet you would pay only a finite amount for it, no doubt far less than your total wealth; therefore, the gamble must be worth less than its expected value.

For a solution, Bernoulli proposed that individuals instead maximize expected utility, or as he then phrased it, "moral expectation." In particular, Bernoulli suggested using a utility function $U(W)$ with the property that "the utility resulting from any small increase in wealth will be inversely proportional to the quantity of goods previously possessed [W]"; that is:

$$\frac{dU}{dW} = \frac{b}{W} \text{ for some } b > 0$$

The solution to this is $U(W) = a + b(\log W)$ (where $\log(\bullet)$ represents the natural logarithm), or defined up to an increasing linear transformation, simply $\log W$. In that case, the expected utility of the gamble is:

$$\left(\frac{1}{2}\right)\log 2 + \left(\frac{1}{2}\right)^2 \log 2^2 + \left(\frac{1}{2}\right)^3 \log 2^3 + \cdots = 2(\log 2) = \log 4$$

implying that the individual would pay at most four ducats for the gamble. Bernoulli notes that his cousin, Nicholas Bernoulli (October 10, 1687–November 29, 1759), initially proposed the St. Petersburg Paradox. To Nicholas, the Paradox was quite disturbing since it undermined his sense that expected value was the essence of fairness. Daniel also notes that the mathematician Gabriel Cramer anticipated much of his own solution several years earlier in a letter to his cousin in 1728.

Anticipating Markowitz (1952/March) and Roy (1952), Daniel Bernoulli also argues that risk-averse investors will want to diversify: ". . . it is advisable to divide goods which are exposed to some small danger into several portions rather than to risk them all together." Bernoulli is hardly the first to appreciate the benefits of diversification. For example, according to Talmudic advice, "A man should always keep his wealth in three forms: one third in real estate, another in merchandise, and the remainder in liquid assets." In *The Merchant of Venice*, Act 1, Scene 1, William Shakespeare has Antonio say:

> . . . *I thank my fortune for it,*
> *My ventures are not in one bottom trusted,*
> *Nor to one place; nor is my whole estate*
> *Upon the fortune of this present year.*

Antonio rests easy at the beginning of the play because he is diversified across ships, places, and time, although this turns out to be mistaken security.

An application of Bernoulli's logarithmic utility appears in [Weber (1851)] Ernst Heinrich Weber's (June 24, 1795–January 26, 1878) *Der*

Tastsinn und das Gemeingefühl (1851, "The Sense of Touch and the Common Sensibility"), one of the founding documents of experimental psychology, which defines the threshold of intensity of any stimulus that must be reached before it can be noticed, called the "just noticeable difference." He proposes that this difference divided by the current intensity of the stimulus is a constant (Weber's Law). Gustav Theodor Fechner (April 19, 1801–November 18, 1887), in [Fechner (1860)] *Elemente der Psychophysik* (1860, "Elements of Psychophysics"), adapted this to explain why, although the mind and the body appear separate, they are actually different manifestations of the same reality. He proposed that a change in sensation (as experienced by the mind) is proportional to the constant from Weber's Law.

Menger (1934) points out that concave utility—now commonly termed "diminishing marginal utility"—is not sufficient to solve generalized versions of the St. Petersburg Paradox.[4] For example, suppose the payoff from the gamble were e raised to the power 2^n dollars if heads first appears on the nth toss; then the expected logarithmic utility of the gamble is:

$$\left(\frac{1}{2}\right)\log e^2 + \left(\frac{1}{2}\right)^2 \log e^4 + \left(\frac{1}{2}\right)^3 \log e^8 + \cdots = 1 + 1 + 1 + \cdots = \infty$$

Indeed, Menger shows that as long as the utility function is unbounded, there always exists a St. Petersburg type gamble for which its expected utility will be infinite. As a result, many economists believe that boundedness is a prerequisite for a reasonable utility function, although this continues to be a matter of some controversy.

Menger also discusses another solution to the Paradox that will be picked up much later by behavioral economists, namely that individuals tend to ignore completely outcomes with sufficiently small probability of occurrence—a solution suggested quite early by Georges-Louis Leclerc, Comte de Buffon (September 7, 1707–April 16, 1788), in [Buffon (1777)] "Essai d'arithmétique morale," *Supplément à l'Histoire Naturelle* 4 (1777). Menger notes that individuals tend to underestimate the probabilities of extreme events, small as well as large, and correspondingly overestimate the probabilities of intermediate events.

Menger's observation concerning unboundedness led Kenneth Joseph Arrow, in [Arrow (1965/A)] "Exposition of the Theory of Choice under Uncertainty," Essay 2 in *Essays in the Theory of Risk Bearing* (Chicago: Markham, 1971), pp. 44–89 (part of which was first published in 1965 as

Lecture 1 in *Aspects of the Theory of Risk Bearing*, Yrjo Jahnsson Lectures, Helsinki), reprinted in *Collected Papers of Kenneth J. Arrow: Individual Choice under Certainty and Uncertainty*, Volume III (Cambridge, MA: Harvard University Press, 1984), pp. 5–41, to conclude that not all uncertain outcomes could be admitted under the von Neumann–Morgenstern (1947) axioms since both the completeness and continuity axioms could be violated by St. Petersburg gambles of the Menger type unless the utility function were required to be bounded both below and above. For example, one could easily imagine two such gambles, one clearly preferred to another, but both with infinite expected utility. However, these flights of fancy do not trouble someone like Paul Anthony Samuelson who, in [Samuelson (1977)] "St. Petersburg Paradoxes: Defanged, Dissected, and Historically Described," *Journal of Economic Literature* 15, No. 1 (March 1977), pp. 24–55, consoles himself that such gambles, while interesting thought experiments, "do not seem to be of moment in real life." Nonetheless, the Paradox has played a lengthy and significant role in the history of the economics of uncertainty, causing Samuelson to conclude that it "enjoys an honored corner in the memory bank of the cultured analytic mind."

Samuelson raises perhaps a more troubling objection to unbounded utility that does not rely on the infinities of the St. Petersburg Paradox. Suppose there is a payoff $X, arbitrarily large, that an agent can receive with certainty. If his utility is unbounded above, there will always exist an even larger amount $Y that the agent will prefer even though he has an arbitrarily small probability of obtaining it. Unbounded utility, then, implies a sort of extreme form of nonsatiation. On the other side, in [Arrow (1974)] "The Use of Unbounded Utility Functions in Expected Utility Maximization: Response," *Quarterly Journal of Economics* 88, No. 1 (February 1974), pp. 136–138, reprinted in *Collected Papers of Kenneth J. Arrow: Individual Choice under Certainty and Uncertainty*, Volume III (Cambridge, MA: Harvard University Press, 1984), pp. 209–211, Arrow proves that if the utility function $U(X)$ is monotone increasing and concave with $U(0)$ finite and if $E(X)$ is finite, then $E[U(X)]$ will also be finite. Therefore, if gambles such as the St. Petersburg gamble with infinite expected value are not available, as a practical matter, even utility functions that are unbounded above should not present problems.

1780 **Jeremy Bentham** (February 15, 1748–June 6, 1832), *An Introduction to the Principles of Morals and Legislation* (privately printed); full version published 1789.

1906 Vilfredo Pareto (July 15, 1848–August 20, 1923), *Manual of Political Economy*; translated from Italian into English (New York: Augustus M. Kelly, 1971).

1951 Kenneth Joseph Arrow (August 23, 1921–), "An Extension of the Basic Theorems of Classical Welfare Economics," *Proceedings of the 2nd Berkeley Symposium on Mathematical Statistics and Probability*; edited by J. Neyman (Berkeley: University of California Press, 1951), pp. 507–532; reprinted in *Collected Papers of Kenneth J. Arrow: General Equilibrium*, Volume II (Cambridge, MA: Harvard University Press, 1983), pp. 13–45.

ORDINAL VS. CARDINAL UTILITY, PARETO OPTIMALITY,
OPTIMALITY OF COMPETITIVE EQUILIBRIUM

Bentham (1780) advocates that the goal of human life is to obtain happiness, that happiness can be numerically measured, and that, in their choices, humans make careful hedonic calculations trading off advantages against disadvantages. Bentham writes:

> *Nature has placed mankind under the governance of two sovereign masters, pain and pleasure. It is for them alone to point out what we ought to do as well as to determine what we shall do. On the one hand, the standard of right and wrong, on the other the chain of cause and effects, are fastened to their throne.*

He also believes that wealth is a means to (and hence to some extent a measure of) happiness, but that greater and greater wealth will result in continually diminishing increments to happiness—what is now called "diminishing marginal utility of wealth" (from this he was able to deduce that gambling is "bad" and insurance is "good"). The goal of society is to produce the maximum happiness for all, where the numerical value of the happiness of each of its members is simply equally weighted and summed to produce the total. Combining these ideas results in the prescription of redistribution of wealth from rich to poor, although Bentham realized that the benefits of such a policy had to be balanced against a reduction in productivity incentives. One of the many problems with this prescription is how to decide which people are to be included as "members" of the society (voters only, men only, citizens only, etc.?). Although these views have been significantly modified by modern economists, Bentham is nonetheless rightfully deserving of the title "the father of the utility function."

In contrast, the Greek philosophers believed that each man has a defined place in the broad scheme of the world; some men are born to be slaves, and at the other extreme, others—the philosophers—should be the rulers. Men are naturally superior to women. That one man would work for the happiness of another, or that one man deserved greater happiness than others, was fully compatible with their view of justice.

Pareto (1906) realized that he could dispense with the cardinality of utility (presumed by Bentham) and more weakly simply interpret preferences as an ordering, yet still derive the same results. But more famously, he realized that Alfred Marshall's (July 26, 1842–July 13, 1924) [Marshall (1890)] *Principles of Economics*, Volume 1 (1890), eighth edition retitled *Principles of Economics: An Introductory Volume* (New York: Macmillan, 1920), and others' use of utility to make interpersonal welfare comparisons was too strong, and introduced what has ever since been called "Pareto optimality": a characterization of a candidate equilibrium in which no alternative reallocation of commodities across agents can make some agents better off while making no other agent worse off (where each agent evaluates his own welfare in terms of his own utility). Since it was later shown that a competitive equilibrium is Pareto-optimal, Pareto optimality has become the modern justification for Adam Smith's invisible hand.

Arrow (1951) proves the two optimality theorems for the competitive equilibrium also described in Debreu (1959):

First Optimality Theorem: *If an equilibrium exists and all commodities relevant to preferences and production are priced by the market, then the competitive equilibrium must be Pareto-optimal; that is, any change in the equilibrium allocation of commodities across consumers cannot make some consumers better off while making none worse off.*

Here we have the modern justification for the invisible hand of Smith (1776).

Second Optimality Theorem: *If there are no increasing returns to scale in production and certain other minor conditions are met, then every Pareto-optimal allocation of commodities across consumers is a competitive equilibrium for some initial allocation of endowments.*[5]

The second theorem implies a very useful way to identify whether a proposed allocation is Pareto-optimal. Assuming concave utility for all consumers, an allocation will be Pareto-optimal if and only if it maximizes a positively weighted sum of consumer utilities subject to constraints on the aggregate supply of consumption.

Pareto optimality is one of the modern justifications for a competitive price system (the others have to do with incentives and the communication of information (Hayek 1945)): That is, it leads to an allocation of resources across consumers and firms so that there is no other allocation that can make some consumers better off (relative to it) while making no one worse off. A secondary justification is that the equilibrium of a competitive price system lies within "the core of the economy": the set of allocations that make everyone at least as well off relative to one's endowed allocation (everyone is born into the economy with given endowed resources).

Of course, the set of Pareto-optimal allocations is not unique and the competitive price system simply picks one of them. But Arrow shows that every Pareto-optimal allocation can be attained through a competitive price system by an appropriate reshuffling of endowments (before any exchange or production has occurred) among consumers. So the exact Pareto-optimal allocation the society wants can be reached by first redistributing wealth and then letting the price system do its magic. Since modern economists eschew interpersonal welfare comparisons, it is not the province of economics to say what that initial wealth distribution should be—these are matters for political science. Economics always ducks the really hard questions.

Proofs of these theorems were independently discovered by Gerard Debreu in [Debreu (1951)] "The Coefficient of Resource Utilization," *Econometrica* 19, No. 3 (July 1951), pp. 273–292, and in [Debreu (1954)] "Valuation Equilibrium and Pareto-Optimum," *Proceedings of the National Academy of Sciences* (1954).

1835 Lambert Adolphe Jacques Quetelet (February 22, 1796–February 17, 1874), *Sur l'homme et le développement de ses facultés, ou Essai de physique sociale* (Paris: Bachelier, 1835); translated from French into English as *A Treatise on Man and the Development of His Faculties* (Edinburgh: Chambers, 1942).

AVERAGE OR REPRESENTATIVE MAN, NORMAL DISTRIBUTION,
PROBABILITY IN THE SOCIAL SCIENCES

L'homme moyen, or the "average man," the most famous fictional character in the social sciences, makes his debut in Quetelet (1835). Quetelet constructs his average man from a sample of about 100,000 French conscripts, measuring their average height and weight. He even goes so far as to determine from arrest records the propensity of the average man to commit a crime. The "average man" who became better known as the "representative man," was to play a central role in the development of financial economics more than a century later.

Quetelet's second important contribution was to assume that many natural processes, if properly sorted, conform to a normal curve. As noted to me by my student, Luca Barone, we may also owe to Plato (427 B.C.–347 B.C.), with some liberality of interpretation, the first written description of a unimodal symmetric frequency distribution, along with the belief that most traits are naturally distributed in that manner:

> . . . *for experience would have taught him that the true state of the case, that few are the good and few the evil, and that the great majority are in the interval between them. I mean . . . as you might say of the very large and very small—that nothing is more uncommon than a very large or a very small man; and this applies generally to all extremes, whether of great and small, or swift and slow, or fair and foul, or black and white: and whether the instances you select be men or dogs or anything else, few are the extremes, but many are in the mean in between them. (Great Books of the Western World: Plato, Volume I:* Phaedo, *Franklin Center, PA: Franklin Library, 1979, pp. 385–439, especially p. 415)*

Quetelet added the more specific property of normality,[6] observing that a key requirement for his result is that the sample be sufficiently homogeneous in all ways but the single source of variation under examination. So confident was he of his normal law that when he observed considerably more conscripts in the lowest-height group than he observed in the next higher group, he concluded that the large number in the lowest group, where service was voluntary, was evidence that about 2,000 men had fraudulently avoided conscription.

In 1843, Antoine-Augustin Cournot (August 18, 1801–March 31, 1877) in [Cournot (1843)] *Exposition de la théorie des chances et des probabilities* (Paris: Hachette, 1843) expressed serious reservations about the application of probability theory to the social sciences. This is all the more surprising coming from Cournot, who in 1838 can be credited with introducing mathematical methods into economics. His argument, like his 1838 book, was well ahead of its time. The problem lay in choosing testable hypotheses. He believed that the social sciences offered such a large variety and number of ways of sorting and classifying data that some samples that would seem to support hypotheses could not be relied upon, since by chance some hypotheses would necessarily be spuriously statistically significant. He writes:

> *It is evident that as the number of divisions increases without limit, it is a priori more and more probable that, by chance alone, at least one of the divisions will produce ratios of male to female births for the two classes that are sensibly different.*

In particular, Cournot worried that it would be tempting to choose hypotheses *after* peeking at the data to be used for the test. Today we have a name for this pernicious error: "data mining."

At the other extreme lay the views of Henry Thomas Buckle, who, in *History of Civilization in England*, Volume 1 (London: J.W. Parker, 1857), looked forward to the day when the power of statistics would forge laws of the social sciences and afford a comparable predictability to that acquired by physics through the use of mathematics. The future, of course, was to reveal that the truth lay in between the visions of Cournot and Buckle. But even in the mid-twentieth century, the most famous of science fiction sagas, *The Foundation Trilogy* (1951–1953) by Isaac Asimov (January 2, 1920–April 6, 1992), predicted that a kind of social statistical mechanics applied on a galactic scale would eventually permit statistically significant forecasts of dominant social trends that lay hundreds of years in the future.

1900 Louis Bachelier (March 11, 1870–April 26, 1946), "Théorie de la spéculation," *Annales Scientifiques de l'Ecole Normale Supérieure* 17 (Third Series 1900), pp. 21–86; translated from French into English by A. James Boness, "The Theory of Speculation," in *The Random Character of Stock Market Prices*, edited by Paul H. Cootner; reprinted (London: Risk Publications, 2000), pp. 18–91; also reprinted in the original French as "Théorie de la speculation & théorie mathématique de jeu," Les Grandes Classiques Gauthier Villars (Paris: Éditions Jacques Gabay, 1995), Part 1, pp. 21–86.

BROWNIAN MOTION, OPTION PRICING, RANDOM WALK, NORMAL DISTRIBUTION

Bachelier (1900) in this doctoral thesis shows that probability theory can be used to describe the movement of security prices. His is very likely the first such attempt of which there is record. Bachelier gives the first mathematical description of a continuous-time, continuous-state stochastic process (arithmetic Brownian motion), amazingly with the goal of valuing "options" (French *rentes*, or perpetual government bonds). Although that goal was only partially realized, his paper—a thesis submitted to the Academy of Paris—anticipated Einstein's work on Brownian motion by six years as well as the mathematical basis for the Black-Scholes formula (which is based on geometric Brownian motion) by 73 years.

He precociously anticipated the now-ubiquitous assumption of random walks and normal distributions. He justified randomness by arguing that at the current price there must be as many buyers who believe the price will rise as there are sellers who believe that the price will fall. And since there is no reason to think that either group is wiser than the other, the probability must be about the same that the next price change will be up or down. So he concluded that a trader should expect to make zero profit, and that the market is therefore a "fair game."

The implications of the random walk of prices led Bachelier to discover the now well-known result that volatility expands in proportion to the square root of time,[7] and he derives a differential equation governing the asset price diffusion. He observes that if price changes are serially independent and identically distributed random variables with finite variance observed over reasonably short intervals, then price changes across longer intervals will be approximately normally distributed according to the Pierre-Simon Marquis de Laplace (March 23, 1749—March 5, 1827) central limit theorem from his [Laplace (1814)] *Essai philosophique sur les probabilités* (*A Philosophical Essay on Probabilities*), 1814. Bachelier also derives the first published option pricing formula and then goes on to test it empirically, noting a strong resemblance between his theoretical values and market prices. He ends his thesis by writing:

> *Perhaps a final remark will not be pointless. If, with respect to several questions treated in this study, I have compared the results of observation with those of theory, it was not to verify the formulas established by mathematical methods, but only to show that the market, unwittingly, obeys a law which governs it, the law of probability. (p. 87)*

This Vincent van Gogh of financial economics received only average marks on his thesis. Ironically, we can see now that it is undoubtedly the finest thesis ever written in financial economics. In 1906, he published "Théorie des probabilités continues" (Paris: Gauthier-Villars), in which he defined several types of stochastic processes, including Markov and Ornstein-Uhlenbeck processes, which were subsequently rediscovered; and he described stochastic processes in terms of their drift and diffusion coefficient.

Despite this, he could not find an academic job until several years later; and even then, he had to settle for an obscure teaching post until he retired in 1937, nine years before his death in 1946. Unfortunately forgotten for more than 50 years, Bachelier's thesis was rediscovered by Paul Anthony Samuelson, who said in the transcript of the PBS television program "NOVA 2074: The Trillion Dollar Bet," broadcast February 8, 2000:

> *In the early 1950s I was able to locate by chance this unknown book, rotting in the library of the University of Paris, and when I opened it up it was as if a whole new world was laid out before me. In fact as I was reading it, I arranged to get a translation in English, because I really wanted every precious pearl to be understood.*[8]

1921 Frank Hyneman Knight (November 7, 1885–April 15, 1972), *Risk, Uncertainty and Profit* (Boston: Houghton Mifflin, 1921).

RISK VS. UNCERTAINTY,
SOURCE OF BUSINESS PROFIT, DIVERSIFICATION

Knight (1921) is known primarily for two ideas. The first is his distinction between "risk" and "uncertainty," and the second is his location of the source of "profit" in the returns from exposure of business activities to uncertainty. Knight's analysis is somewhat confusing, tempting the false interpretation of his writing in too modern a light. With that in mind, Knight associates risk with circumstances in which probabilities can be more or less objectively measured, or in which the law of large numbers can be brought into play to eliminate all uncertainty by combining the results of several related endeavors.

> *As we have repeatedly pointed out, an uncertainty which can by any method be reduced to an objective, quantitatively determinant probability, can be reduced to complete certainty by grouping cases. (Chapter 7)*

On the other hand, singular events or events for which science can make no clear predictions are associated with uncertainty. In human affairs, prominent among the latter are judgments of the decision-making skill of other human beings. Knight believed that for uncertain events it is meaningless to speak of them probabilistically—a view that was later to play a significant role in challenges to the usefulness of maximizing expected utility based on subjectively formed probability beliefs, in particular, Ellsberg (1961).

Richard Cantillon (circa 1690–May 14, 1734), in [Cantillon (1755] his 1755 *Essay of the Nature of Commerce* (but written in the 1720s), had realized quite early that the source of profit within a firm was the remuneration that was contingent on the success of the firm after all fixed payment contracts are honored, including interest, wages, and rent. However, in a competitive economy under certainty all profit is competed away so that profits are zero in equilibrium. Knight therefore argued that profits could arise only in an economy where the future was not known with certainty. Perhaps with some license, representing his theory with mathematics (which Knight did not do), I can write:

$$r_j = r + \delta_j + \varepsilon_j$$

where r_j is the realized return to the stockholders of a firm j, r is the riskless return, ε_j is the portion of the realized return of the firm that it can, in principle, eliminate by diversification. Today we would call ε_j the return from "residual risk." That leaves δ_j, the portion of the return that Knight would associate with uncertainty and a measure of Knight's notion of "profit." Knight associates profit then with the random portion of a firm's return that cannot be eliminated by diversification, hedged, or insured. What causes this portion of the return? Knight argues that if probability distributions cannot be objectively measured, their uncertainty cannot be diversified away. And most significantly, the results of human judgments in deciding the course of a firm and in choosing individuals to whom to delegate authority within the firm cannot be measurably predicted with probabilities. So it is "entrepreneurship" that is the ultimate source of profit.

> *The only "risk" which leads to profit is a unique uncertainty resulting from an exercise of ultimate responsibility which in its very nature cannot be insured nor capitalized nor salaried. Profit arises out of the inherent, absolute unpredictability of things, out of the sheer brute fact that the results of human activity cannot be anticipated and then only in so far as even a probability calculation in regard to them is impossible and meaningless. (Chapter 10)*

What is the expected value of δ_j? For Knight, a good guess made by the market would be that $E(\delta_j) < 0$ for what we would now call behavioral reasons: (1) the tendency of entrepreneurs to be overconfident and therefore to overinvest, (2) overpaying because of failure to appreciate the so-called winner's curse, (3) the reluctance to abandon an effort once the commitment has been made, and (4) the satisfaction of working for oneself. But clearly Knight had no real concept of what today we could call "systematic risk," that is, risk borne by the whole society from which an individual cannot escape without sacrificing expected return.

1923 John Maynard Keynes (June 5, 1883–April 21, 1946), "Some Aspects of Commodity Markets," *Manchester Guardian* (1923).

1949 Holbrook Working (1895–October 5, 1985), "The Theory of Price of Storage," *American Economic Review* 39, No. 6 (December 1949), pp. 1254–1262.

SPOT VS. FORWARD PRICES, FORWARD VS. EXPECTED PRICES, NORMAL BACKWARDATION, CONVENIENCE YIELD, HEDGING VS. SPECULATION

One of the earliest issues in financial economics that attracted the attention of economists was the question of the normal relation between today's price for future delivery (the futures or forward price F_0) and the expected future underlying asset price on the delivery date $E(S_t)$. In his newspaper article, Keynes (1923) first formulated his theory of "normal backwardation" in the futures market, arguing that F_0 is typically less than the expected value of S_t. He believed that hedgers who were naturally short would have to pay speculators a risk premium to convince them to accept their risk. Keynes spelled his argument out in more detail in [Keynes (1930)] *A Treatise on Money*, Volume II: *The Applied Theory of Money* (London: Macmillan, 1930), pp. 142–147.

Of course, it was understood quite clearly that for certain types of underlying assets, arbitrage reasoning (and I will update this and add risk aversion) creates a form of normal backwardation. For example, if the underlying asset is a stock market index, assuming no arbitrage and perfect markets, $F_0 = S_0(r/d)^t$, where S_0 is the current underlying asset price, r is the riskless return, d is the payout return on the index, and t is the time to delivery. Typically, since risk aversion implies that $E(S_t) > S_0(r/d)^t$, taken together this implies that $F_0 < E(S_t)$.

The really interesting situation relates to underlying assets that are used for consumption or production purposes (that is, commodities). For these, because the underlying commodity may not be easily shorted (borrowed and sold), arbitrage cannot force $F_0 = S_0(rc)^t$, where c is one plus the rate of storage cost; rather it can only assure that $S_0c^t \leq F_0 \leq S_0(rc)^t$. It is also possible for commodities that $E(S_t) < S_0(rc)^t$. Therefore, the question becomes interesting whether after accounting for the opportunity costs of holding the underlying commodity, its forward price will be less than its expected future spot price: $F_0 < E(S_t)/(rc)^t$. This creates an extra benefit to current owners of the commodity dubbed a "convenience yield" by Nicholas Kaldor in [Kaldor (1939)] "Speculation and Economic Stability," *Review of Economic Studies* 7, No. 1 (October 1939), pp. 1–27.

As stated by John R. Hicks (April 8, 1904–May 20, 1989), in [Hicks (1939)] *Value and Capital: An Inquiry into Some Fundamental Principles of Economic Theory* (Oxford: Clarendon Press, 1939, and revised second edition, 1946), investors will typically have to be induced to buy commodity futures since it is not a position they would naturally prefer:

> *They know that the demands and supplies which can be fixed up in advance for any particular date [by a forward contract] may have little relation to the demands and supplies which will actually be forthcoming at that date; and, in particular, they cannot foretell at all exactly what quantities they will themselves desire to buy or sell at a future period. Consequently, the ordinary business man only enters into a forward contract if by doing so he can "hedge"— that is to ssay, if the forward transaction lessens the riskiness of his position. And this will only happen in those cases where he is somehow otherwise committed to making a sale or a purchase. . . . [T]echnical conditions give the entrepreneur a much freer hand about the acquisition of inputs (which are largely needed to start new processes) than about the completion of outputs (whose process of production . . . may already have begun). Thus, while there is likely to be some desire to hedge planned purchases, it tends to be less insistent than the desire to hedge planned sales. (second edition, p. 137)*

Keynes and Hicks believed that typically businessmen have much more flexibility (today, we might say they have more valuable "real options") in choosing when, if, and from whom to buy inputs needed for production than they have to sell outputs they were often partially or fully committed to produce. So there is, in their language, a "congenital weakness" on the demand side for commodities. Taking up the slack on the buy side of the forward transaction are the speculators who, because they lack a natural reason to be long, require a convenience yield (that is, a lower forward price) to be induced to go long and take that risk.

Since the expected future spot price is not observable, the signature of normal backwardation will be the tendency of the forward price to rise (more than the opportunity costs of holding the commodity would suggest) as the delivery date approaches.

It is commonly thought that today's futures price is largely determined by today's expectation of the future spot price on the delivery date of the future. Further, differences in the futures prices for different delivery dates for otherwise identical futures are often thought to reflect differences in expectations concerning future spot prices corresponding to the two dates. Working (1949/December) argues that this is not generally correct.

He notes that the ratio of the futures prices quoted in the market at time t (say January 2006) for delivery of a commodity at time $t + k$ (say September 2006) to the same commodity at time $t + h$ (say March 2006) where $0 < h < k$ often stays constant even as the spot price of the commodity changes or as changes in expected future harvests occur. Working points out that the key condition for this to hold is that current stocks of the commodity be plentiful relative to expected future stocks and that it be possible to store the commodity to carry it forward. For then, the current price of the commodity can adjust so that an owner of the commodity is indifferent among selling it for consumption at t, $t + h$, or $t + k$, provided only that he is compensated for the cost of storing the commodity should he decide to keep it in inventory. Since storage costs are presumably higher the longer the commodity is stored, the futures price for delivery at increasingly distant dates will be higher than at earlier dates, and the difference will be the cost of storage.

But occasionally the futures prices are inverted so that the nearer-term futures price is higher than the farther-term futures price. This can happen if current stocks may be low relative to current demand and future harvests are expected to be large. In that case, it may not be desirable to carry any of the current stock forward, and all of it should be consumed before the next harvest. This decouples the futures price from the cost of storage and creates "convenience yield."

1930 Irving Fisher (February 27, 1867–April 29, 1947), *The Theory of Interest: As Determined by Impatience to Spend Income and Opportunity to Invest It* (New York: Macmillan, 1930); reprinted (New York: Augustus M. Kelley, 1955).

INTERTEMPORAL CONSUMPTION, PRODUCTION,
AND EXCHANGE, RATE OF INTEREST, FISHER EFFECT,
IMPATIENCE VS. OPPORTUNITY,

FISHER SEPARATION THEOREM, COMPETITIVE MARKETS,
UNANIMITY VS. PARETO OPTIMALITY, REAL OPTIONS,
SPECULATION, CAPITAL BUDGETING

Fisher (1930) is the seminal work for most of the financial theory of investments during the twentieth century. Fisher refines and restates many earlier results that had appeared in his [Fisher (1896)] *Appreciation and Interest*; [Fisher (1906)] *The Nature of Capital and Income* (New York: Macmillan, 1906), reprinted (New York: Augustus M. Kelley, 1965); and [Fisher (1907)] *The Rate of Interest*. As Fisher states, some of his ideas were foreshadowed by John Rae (June 1, 1796–July 12, 1872), to whom Fisher dedicates his 1930 book, in [Rae (1834)] *Statement of Some New Principles on the Subject of Political Economy, Exposing the Fallacies of the System of Free Trade, and Some Other Doctrines Maintained in "The Wealth of Nations"* (Boston: Hilliard Gray & Co., 1834). Fisher develops the first formal equilibrium model of an economy with both intertemporal exchange and production. In so doing, at one swoop, he not only derives present value calculations as a natural economic outcome in calculating wealth, he also justifies the maximization of present value as the goal of production and derives determinants of the interest rates that are used to calculate present value.

He assumes each agent is both the consumer and the producer of a single aggregate consumption good under certainty. This single-good simplification allows him to abstract from the unnecessary complications of the multicommodity Walrasian paradigm, and has ever since been at the heart of theoretical research in finance. At each date, exchange is effected by means of a short-term default-free bond maturing at the end of the period. In this context, among its many contributions to economic thought are (1) an analysis of the determinants of the real rate of interest and the equilibrium intertemporal path of aggregate consumption, (2) the "Fisher effect" relating the nominal interest rate to the real interest rate and the rate of inflation, and (3) the Fisher Separation Theorem justifying the delegation of production decisions to firms that maximize present value, without any direct dependence on shareholder preferences, and justifying the separation of firm financing and production decisions. Most subsequent work in the financial theory of investments can be viewed as further elaboration, particularly to considerations of uncertainty and to more complex financial instruments for the allocation of consumption across time and across states of the world.

Fisher reconciles the two previous explanations of the rate of interest, one based on productivity ("opportunity") and the other based on consumer psychology, or time preference—"impatience," a term coined by

Fisher (1907) in *The Rate of Interest*—showing that they are jointly needed for a comprehensive theory: "So the rate of interest is the mouthpiece at once of impatience to spend income without delay and of opportunity to increase income by delay" (p. 495).

Fisher describes his economy in three ways: in words, with graphs, and with equations. It is interesting that, even at this time in the development of economic thought, Fisher finds it necessary to justify the usefulness of algebraic formulations, pointing out that by this method one could be sure that the number of unknowns and number of independent equations are the same. In addition, he writes:

> *The contention often met with that the mathematical formulation of economic problems gives a picture of theoretical exactitude untrue to actual life is absolutely correct. But, to my mind, this is not an objection but a very definite advantage, for it brings out the principles in such sharp relief that it enables us to put our finger definitely on the points where the picture is untrue to real life. (p. 315)*[9]

Fisher develops a simple example with just two time periods and three consumers for the case where only consumer time preference determines interest rates. Let:

r be the equilibrium riskless return.

$\underline{C}_0^i, \underline{C}_1^i$ be the endowed consumption of consumer i at dates 0 and 1.

x_0^i, x_1^i be the amount of borrowing or lending of consumer i at dates 0 and 1 that each consumer can choose subject to his or her budget constraint: $x_0^i + x_1^i/r = 0$.

$C_0^i \equiv \underline{C}_0^i + x_0^i$, $C_1^i \equiv \underline{C}_1^i + x_1^i$ be the optimal amounts of consumption that consumer i chooses at dates 0 and 1.

He then assumes that a consumer's rate of time preference will depend on the chosen consumption stream: $f_i = F_i(C_0^i, C_1^i)$ is the rate of time preference of consumer i.

In the appendix to his Chapter 12, Fisher relates the rate of time preference to the utility of consumption, $U_i(C_0^i, C_1^i)$ such that: $f_i = [U_i'(C_0^i)/U_i'(C_1^i)] - 1$.

He argues that in equilibrium the rate of time preference of each consumer must equal the riskless return, so that:

$$f_1 = f_2 = f_3 = r$$

For the market to clear, he requires that net borrowing and lending at each date across all consumers be 0: $x_0^1 + x_0^2 + x_0^3 = 0$ and $x_1^1 + x_1^2 + x_1^3 = 0$. The seven unknowns, $C_0^1, C_0^2, C_0^3, C_1^1, C_1^2, C_1^3$, and r are matched by seven independent equations.

Fisher's Economy

A modernized representative agent proof would go something like this. Let:

$U(C_0)$, $U(C_1)$ be the utility of consumption at dates 0 and 1.

ρ be the rate of patience.

Ω_0 be the initial endowment of the consumption good.

X_0 be the amount of Ω_0 used up in production so that $C_0 = \Omega_0 - X_0$.

$f(X_0)$ be the output from production of date 1 consumption so that $C_1 = f(X_0)$.

W_0 be the current wealth of the consumer so that $W_0 = C_0 + C_1/r$.

Assume that $U'(C) > 0$ (nonsatiation), $U''(C) < 0$ (diminishing marginal utility), $0 < \rho < 1$ (tendency to prefer current over future consumption), $f'(X_0) > 0$ (more input yields more output), and $f''(X_0) < 0$ (diminishing returns to scale).

The *production* problem for the consumer is:

$$\max_{C_0, C_1} U(C_0) + \rho U(C_1) \text{ subject to } C_0 = \Omega_0 - X_0 \text{ and } C_1 = f(X_0)$$

Substituting in the constraints, differentiating the utility function, and setting the derivative equal to zero to characterize the maximum, it follows that:

$$\frac{U'(C_0)}{\rho U'(C_1)} = f'(X_0)$$

The *exchange* problem for the consumer is:

$$\max_{C_0, C_1} U(C_0) + \rho U(C_1) \text{ subject to } W_0 = C_0 + \frac{C_1}{r}$$

(Continued)

Fisher's Economy *(Continued)*

Again, substituting in the constraint, differentiating the utility function, and setting the derivative equal to zero, it follows that:

$$\frac{U'(C_0)}{\rho U'(C_1)} = r$$

Gathering these two results together:

$$\frac{U'(C_0)}{\rho U'(C_1)} = r = f'(X_0) \tag{1}$$

Thus, we have Fisher's two-sided determinants of the interest rate: The equilibrium riskless return equals what we would call today the marginal rate of substitution (what Fisher called "the rate of time preference"), and it equals the marginal productivity of capital.

For a more concrete example, suppose $U(C_t) = \log C_t$ and $f(X_0) = \alpha X_0^\beta$ with $0 < \beta < 1$ and $\alpha > 0$. These satisfy the required derivative conditions on utility and the production function. α can be interpreted as a pure measure of productivity since the greater α, the more output from any given input. Substituting into equation (1):

$$\rho^{-1}\left(\frac{C_1}{C_0}\right) = r = \alpha\beta X_0^{\beta-1}$$

Solving this for the unknowns C_0 and r:

$$C_0 = (1+\rho\beta)^{-1}\Omega_0 \quad \text{and} \quad r = \alpha\beta\left[\left(\frac{\rho\beta}{1+\rho\beta}\right)\Omega_0\right]^{\beta-1}$$

Differentiating the solution for the riskless return:

$$\frac{dr}{d\alpha} = \beta\left[\left(\frac{\rho\beta}{1+\rho\beta}\right)\Omega_0\right]^{\beta-1} > 0 \text{ (productivity)}$$

$$\frac{dr}{d\rho} = \alpha(\beta-1)\Omega_0^{\beta-1}\rho^{-2}\left(\frac{\rho\beta}{1+\rho\beta}\right)^{\beta} < 0 \text{ (time preference)}$$

So we see a pure isolation of the effects of Fisher's impatience (ρ) and opportunity (α) on the interest rate.

Fisher also claims that separate rates of interest for different time periods are a natural outcome of economic forces, and not something that can be arbitraged away in a perfect market.

> *The other corollary is that such a formulation reveals the necessity of positing a theoretically separate rate of interest for each separate period of time, or to put the same thing in more practical terms, to recognize the divergence between the rate for short terms and long terms. This divergence is not merely due to an imperfect market and therefore subject to annihilation, as Böhm-Bawerk, for instance, seemed to think. They are definitely and normally distinct due to the endless variety in the conformations of income streams. No amount of mere price arbitrage could erase these differences. (p. 313)*[10]

More generally, Fisher argues that the rate of interest is determined by: (1) the relative distribution of endowed resources across time, (2) time preferences of consumer/investors, (3) production opportunities that provide a way of transforming aggregate current endowments into aggregate future consumption, (4) the general size of endowed resources, (5) risk aversion and the time structure of risk, and (6) the anticipated rate of inflation. With a noticeably behavioral orientation, Fisher attributed factor (2) to lack of foresight, lack of self-control, habit formation, expected lifetime, and a bequest motive. He shows how all six factors will affect the decisions made by economic agents and how these decisions will aggregate up to determine the equilibrium rate of interest.

Fisher then considers a number of potential objections to his theory. An objection still popular is that tying the determinants of interest to aspects of intertemporal consumption choice may be elegant, but narrow. In fact, interest is largely determined by the "supply and demand for loanable funds." Fisher replies that this supply and demand is the intermediate effect of the fundamental underlying needs of producers to maximize present value and of consumers to optimally balance their consumption over their lifetimes. But he also admits that there may be myriad institutional influences on interest rates that he has not considered, but that these factors will be secondary.

Fisher worded his separation result as follows:

> *But we see that, in such a fluid world of options as we are here assuming, the capitalist reaches the final income through the cooperation of two kinds of choice of incomes which, under our assumptions, may be considered and treated as entirely separate.*

> To repeat, these two kinds of choice are: first, the choice from among many possible income streams of that particular income stream with the highest present value, and secondly, the choice among different possible modifications of this income stream by borrowing and lending or buying and selling. The first is a selection from among income streams of differing market values, and the second, a selection from among income streams of the same market value. (p. 141)[11]

This "separation" must be carefully interpreted to mean that the second choice is not independent of the first choice. In order to know what second choice to make, the implications of the first choice must be known. However, the first choice can be made before making the second. Fisher also made it quite clear that his separation result depends on a competitive market where capitalists are "unconscious" of any impact they might have on interest rates, and he made it clear that his result requires the equivalency of borrowing and lending rates (perfect markets).

This suggests that, provided firms act as competitive present value maximizers, firms can make the same production decisions their shareholders would make on their own without knowledge of their time preferences or their endowments. If true, this dramatically simplifies the problem of resource allocation in a competitive economy.

Despite this, Mark Rubinstein, in [Rubinstein (1978)] "Competition and Approximation," *Bell Journal of Economics* 9, No. 1 (Spring 1978), pp. 280–286, argues that the widely believed Fisher Separation Theorem

---

Proof of Fisher's Separation Theorem

To derive the separation theorem, continuing with our earlier example, suppose the production decision were delegated to a competitive present value–maximizing firm. Such a firm would then choose X_0 to:

$$\max_{X_0} - X_0 + \frac{f(X_0)}{r}$$

where it disregards any influence it may have over r (that is, it chooses X_0 as if $dX_0/dr = 0$). Differentiating the present value and setting the derivative equal to zero, it follows that: $r = f'(X_0)$, precisely the decision that representative consumers would have made on their own.

(in perfect and competitive financial markets, firms that choose investments that maximize present value make choices unanimously preferred by
all their stockholders) is essentially incorrect, particularly in a market of
well-diversified investors, because it is not robust to the assumption of
competition.

Perfect competition is sometimes defined to require that no firm by its
actions can have any influence whatsoever on prices. Joan Violet Robinson
(October 31, 1903–August 5, 1983), in [Robinson (1934)] "What Is Perfect Competition?," *Quarterly Journal of Economics* 49, No. 1 (November
1934), pp. 104–120, takes issue with the practical implausibility of this requirement for commodities with rising marginal costs of production (necessary if more than one firm is to survive in a market where all firms sell
the same commodity at the same price), for then the number of firms must
literally be infinite. With a finite number of firms, when one firm increases
its output, the corresponding decrease in the optimal output of other firms
will partially but not completely offset the increase, leaving prices somewhat changed. She concludes:

> *Let us agree to call competition perfect if the price cut associated
> with a unit increase of output by one firm is less than a certain def-
> inite amount. Then for any given slope in the marginal cost curves,
> there is a certain number of firms which will make competition
> perfect. This number will be smaller the smaller the slope of the
> marginal cost curves, and greater the greater the slope of the mar-
> ginal cost curves. (p. 119)*[12]

If competition is defined according to Robinson's classic paper, then
unanimity generally (or, as an empirical matter, probably typically) will not
occur. This can be demonstrated even in a single-period economy under
certainty. The basic idea is that with a large number of small firms, while
the production decision of any one firm has a very small effect on the interest rate (effect 1), well-diversified investors allocate only a very small portion of their wealth to each firm. Therefore, each firm also has only a very
small influence on their wealth (effect 2). Thus, in voting for the firm's production decision, each investor must make the trade-off between two small
effects. Since some investors (lenders) will want a higher interest rate and
others (borrowers) a lower rate, they will disagree. Matters are not saved
by increasing the number of firms, since, as the paper shows, each of the
two effects diminishes at the same rate.

Although the competitive present value decision is not generally
unanimously supported by all investors (unless they are identical),
nonetheless it remains Pareto-optimal. The paper argues that the great

virtue of present value maximization is that it is the only way a firm can make Pareto-optimal investment decisions irrespective of the identities of its shareholders. Despite the publication of this paper more than 20 years ago, introductory texts in finance continue ultimately to justify maximization of present value on the false basis of unanimity. One prominent text continues to list unanimity as the first of seven great ideas of financial economics.

Fisher may also have been the first economist to emphasize the role of what are now called "real options" in increasing the flexibility of production opportunities, which now play a key role in modern treatments of present value for corporate investments:

> *This brings us to another large and important class of options; namely the options of effecting renewals and repairs, and the options of effecting them in any one of many different degrees. . . . But the owner has many other options than that of thus maintaining a constant stock of goods. He may choose to enlarge his business as fast as he makes money from it. . . . A third option is gradually to go out of business. . . . Another case of optional income streams is found in the choice between different methods of production, especially between different degrees of so-called capitalist production. . . . The alternatives constantly presented to most business men are between policies which may be distinguished as temporary and permanent. The temporary policy involves use of easily constructed instruments which soon wear out, and the permanent policy involves the construction at great cost of instruments of great durability. . . . In all cases, the "best" results are secured when the particular series of renewals, repairs, or betterments is chosen which renders the present value of the prospective income stream the maximum. (pp. 194–199)*[13]

Fisher also discusses dynamic properties of interest rate changes, whereby, for example, increasing interest rates leads to a change in the utilization of production opportunities that in turn tends to stabilize interest rates, creating the mean reversion we typically observe.

While Fisher provides a qualitative discussion of the first-order effects of uncertainty, he expresses considerable pessimism about prospects for formal generalization of his theory:

> *To attempt to formulate mathematically in any useful, complete manner the laws determining the rate of interest under the sway of chance would be like attempting to express completely the laws*

which determine the path of a projectile when affected by random gusts of wind. Such formulas would need to be either too general or too empirical to be of much value. (p. 316)[14]

So Fisher left it for others to explain a wide variety of economic phenomena such as insurance, the use of both debt and equity, the demand for liquidity, the use of diversified portfolios, and the extreme diversity of types of securities with differing returns, all of which largely rely on uncertainty for their existence.

In his earlier book, *The Nature of Capital and Income*, Fisher (1906) expressed his views about the rationality of markets and the role of speculation:

The evils of speculation are particularly acute when, as generally happens with the investing public, the forecasts are not made independently. A chief cause of crises, panics, runs on banks, etc., is that risks are not independently reckoned, but are a mere matter of imitation. . . . Where, on the other hand, speculation is based on independent knowledge, its utility is enormous. It operates both to reduce risk by utilizing the special knowledge of speculators, and also to shift risk from those who lack this knowledge to those who possess it. . . . Risk is one of the direst economic evils, and all of the devices which aid in overcoming it—whether increased guarantees, safeguards, foresight, insurance or legitimate speculation—represent a great boon to humanity. (pp. 296–300)

Jack Hirshleifer in [Hirshleifer (1958)] "On the Theory of Optimal Investment Decision," *Journal of Political Economy* 66, No. 4 (August 1958), pp. 329–352, integrates the theory of capital budgeting by firms into Fisher's model of simultaneous consumption and investment choice, setting a strong economic foundation and resolving a number of controversies concerning the use of present value and the internal rate of return as investment criteria. In addition, he considers the impact of certain market imperfections such as differences between borrowing and lending rates and capital rationing, as well as mutually exclusive investments.

1931 Harold Hotelling (September 29, 1895–December 26, 1973), "The Economics of Exhaustible Resources," *Journal of Political Economy* 39, No. 2 (April 1931), pp. 137–175.

EXHAUSTIBLE RESOURCES, HOTELLING'S RULE,
EXTRACTION AS AN OPTION, GOLD

Assuming (as we would say today) no arbitrage, perfect and competitive markets, and certainty, Hotelling (1931) derives the result that the price of an exhaustible resource (e.g., precious metal, copper, oil, etc.) must grow over time at the riskless rate of interest. This is often called "Hotelling's Rule." So if P_0 is its price per unit today, then after elapsed years $t > 0$ with per annum riskless interest return r, its price will be $P_t = P_0 r^t$. He reasons thus. In competitive equilibrium, the resource must be extracted at a rate such that at the margin there will be no gain from shifting extraction between any two periods. For that to be true, the present value of owning the resource must be the same whether one chooses to extract and sell the resource today or at any date $t > 0$. But if that is true, then the undiscounted price must be growing at the riskless rate of interest; that is, if $P_0 = PV_0(P_t)$, then $P_t = P_0 r^t$. With extraction costs, the rule must be revised to say that the price net of extraction costs grows at the rate $r - 1$. Hotelling then argued that the prevalent fear that an exhaustible resource will be exhausted too quickly is typically misplaced. As long as the resource's industry is competitive, it will be extracted at the socially optimal rate, requiring no government intervention.

Hotelling left it for others to generalize his rule to uncertainty. It is useful to distinguish between two types of uncertainty: (1) uncertainty of supply, arising from either extraction costs, the contents of the mine, or the rate of exploration, and (2) uncertainty in demand (that is, in the future value of using the resource). Financial economists have taken a particular interest in the latter. For example, consider an oil well with known contents and known extraction costs; at what rate should the oil be extracted? Octavio A. Tourinho in [Tourinho (1979)] "The Option Value of Reserves of Natural Resources," unpublished working paper (September 1979), University of California at Berkeley, was the first to analyze this problem as an option. He compares the decision to extract the resource to the decision to exercise a perpetual payout-protected American call option on the price of oil with a known and fixed strike price (i.e., the cost of extraction). Paradoxically, just as one would never optimally exercise such a call option early (Samuelson-Merton 1969), so, too, it would seem one would never extract the resource. Tourinho's solution was to suppose that the extraction cost was growing at a sufficient rate over time to make extraction optimal. However, if extraction costs are constant over time, then Tourinho leaves the paradox unresolved. Clearly, the economy should not choose never to consume oil, for example, even if extraction costs were known and fixed. While subsequent analysis has largely resolved this paradox for exhaustible resources used for consumption, the paradox still remains for a resource such as gold, which is overwhelmingly held for investment and not consumption purposes, even in situations where there is no fear of national expropriation of a privately held mine.

Michael John Brennan, in [Brennan (1990)] "Latent Assets," *Journal of Finance* 45, No. 3 (July 1990), pp. 709–730, Presidential Address to the American Finance Association, considers this paradox: Why should anyone mine gold when gold is held almost exclusively for investment purposes, the cost of extraction increases more slowly than the rate of interest, and the mine cannot be expropriated? The opportunity to mine gold is therefore similar to a perpetual American call that it would never pay to exercise early. Brennan observes that firms mine gold nonetheless. He argues that to have their stock price properly valued, they need to mine gold to prove to investors that they have the quantity of gold reserves that they claim. Unfortunately, this strikes me as a very unconvincing solution to the paradox; but like the Sherlock Holmes maxim, when one has considered and rejected the probable, whatever remains, however improbable, must be the truth.

1933 Alfred Cowles 3rd (September 15, 1891–December 28, 1984), "Can Stock Market Forecasters Forecast?," *Econometrica* 1, No. 3 (July 1933), pp. 309–324.

INVESTMENT PERFORMANCE, EFFICIENT MARKETS

Cowles (1933) may be the first published statistical test of the ability of experts to "beat the market." Cowles examines 7,500 recommendations of 16 financial services on individual stocks over the period 1928–1932. He gives the following characterization of this sample:

> *The forecasters include well-known organizations in the different fields represented, many of which are large and well financed, employing economists and statisticians of unquestioned ability. . . . Some of the forecasters seem to have taken a page from the book of the Delphic Oracle, expressing their prophecies in terms susceptible of more than one construction. (p. 309)*[15]

The average recommendation led to market performance worse than the market average by 1.4 percent per annum. After comparing the distribution of returns of the actual forecasters to the distribution of returns of portfolios constructed from randomly selected investments, he also concluded that there was no significant statistical evidence that the best performing forecaster outperformed the market by skill. He also examined the investments of 20 leading fire insurance companies and forecasts of 24 financial publications with similar results, except that here the least successful investors seem to have done even worse than what would have been expected by chance.

J.G. Cragg and Burton G. Malkiel in [Cragg-Malkiel (1968)] "The Consensus and Accuracy of Some Predictions of the Growth of Corporate Earnings," *Journal of Finance* 23, No. 1 (March 1968), pp. 67–84, provide a more recent study of the Cowles type. In particular, they examine the accuracy of consensus forecasts by security analysts of future corporate earnings. To their surprise they find for their sample that these forecasts are little better than forecasts obtained by simple extrapolations of past earnings growth.

1934 Benjamin Graham (May 8, 1894–September 21, 1976) and **David L. Dodd**, *Security Analysis: Principles and Technique* (New York: McGraw-Hill, 1934); revised several times, including Benjamin Graham, David L. Dodd, and Sidney Cottle (New York: McGraw-Hill, fourth edition, 1962).

1949 Benjamin Graham, *The Intelligent Investor*, fourth revised edition (New York: HarperCollins, 1973), first published in 1949.

SECURITY ANALYSIS, FUNDAMENTAL ANALYSIS,
CAPITAL STRUCTURE, GROWTH VS. VALUE, REBALANCING,
DOLLAR-COST AVERAGING, EFFICIENT MARKETS,
MATHEMATICAL FINANCE,
EXTREMES OF INVESTMENT PERFORMANCE

In perhaps the most famous book written on the stock market, Graham-Dodd (1934) advocate the fundamental approach to determining investment value and develop techniques to analyze balance sheets and income statements. From the hindsight of later developments, their primary failings were (1) not to consider the full role of diversification, (2) not to embed the role of risk in determining value in an equilibrium context, and (3) not to give sufficient consideration to the forces that tend to make markets informationally efficient.

Graham and Dodd's handling of the issue of the relevancy of corporate capital structure is instructive. They compare three firms with the same cash flows per annum from operations ($1,000,000), but different capital structures:

Firm	Earnings to Stock	Value of Stock	Value of Bonds	Total Firm Value
A	$1,000,000	$10,000,000	—	$10,000,000
B	750,000	7,500,000	5,000,000	12,500,000
C	500,000	5,000,000	10,000,000	15,000,000

The bonds are all assumed to pay 5 percent and the stocks are all assumed to capitalize earnings in a ratio of 10:1, so for firm B, earnings to stock = 1,000,000 − (.05 × 5,000,000) = 750,000; for firm C, earnings to stock = 1,000,000 − (.05 × 10,000,000) = 500,000; with 10:1 capitalization, for firm B, the value of stock = 750,000 × 10 = 7,500,000; for firm C, value of stock = 500,000 × 10 = 5,000,000 (pp. 461–463, original edition, 1934).

They immediately point out that this situation is at first blush unexpected since three firms with the same cash flows have different total values. It also suggests that firm value can be influenced by voluntary changes in capital structure. This leads them to pose the question: "Can the value of an enterprise be altered through arbitrary variations in capital structure?" Upon closer scrutiny, Graham and Dodd point out that the stock of firm A can be interpreted as really a combination of the bonds and stock of company B. So the stock of firm A should *in theory* be worth 5,000,000 + 10 × (1,000,000 − .05 × 5,000,000) = 12,500,000. This is very close to the analysis of Modigliani-Miller (1958) and Modigliani-Miller (1969). Unfortunately, Graham and Dodd, now on the verge of discovering one of the most important ideas in the history of investments, in the very next sentence turn away from this promising direction with these words:

> But this $12,500,000 value for Company A stock would not ordinarily be realized in practice. The obvious reason is that the common-stock buyer will rarely recognize the existence of a "bond component" in a common-stock issue; and in any event, not wanting such a bond component, he is unwilling to pay extra for it. This fact leads to an important principle, both for the security buyer and for corporate management, viz.:

The optimum capitalization structure for any enterprise includes senior securities to the extent that they may safely be issued
and bought for investment. *(p. 463)*

Graham (1949) forcefully expounds his investment philosophy in the
popular investment classic, *The Intelligent Investor*. Graham, known as
"the father of value investing," advises investing based on a careful analysis of business fundamentals, paying close attention to price-earnings (P/E)
ratios, dividend yield, and other tools of security analysis, and only investing in stocks with market values not far above the value of their tangible
assets. While some growth stocks turn out *ex post* to have high returns,
Graham believes that buyers of these stocks are too subject to unpre-
dictable and extreme price fluctuations to make investment advisable. His
general rule is to divide investible wealth between high-grade bonds and a
portfolio of 10 to 30 stocks, maintaining at least 25 percent in each category, and rebalancing relatively frequently to preset target proportions. He
also advocates dollar-cost averaging, wherein one invests the same dollar
amount in common stocks at fixed periodic intervals, rather than lump-
sum investing. He justifies this strategy by arguing that "In this way, he
buys more shares when the market is low than when it is high, and he is
likely to end up with a satisfactory overall price for his holdings" (p. 10).
Although Graham's conclusion is correct, the implication he draws from it
is not. Paradoxically, just because the average price per share of stock is reduced does not mean the investor is better off.

Unfortunately, some of Graham's prescriptions are little more than
platitudinous common sense. For example, he writes: "To enjoy a reasonable chance for continued better than average results, the investor must follow policies which are (1) inherently sound and promising, and (2) not
popular in Wall Street" (p. 13) and "The more the investor depends on his
portfolio and the income therefrom, the more necessary it is for him to
guard against the unexpected and the disconcerting in this part of his life.
It is axiomatic that the conservative investor should seek to minimize his
risks" (p. 25).

Graham believes that an astute investor can find ample opportunities
to make excess profits:

*It has been an old and sound principle that those who cannot af-
ford to take risks should be content with a relatively low return on
their invested funds. From this there has developed the general notion that the rate of return which the investor should aim for is
more or less proportionate to the degree of risk he is ready to run.
Our view is different. The rate of return sought should be depen-*

dent, rather, on the amount of intelligent effort the investor is willing and able to bring to bear on his task. (p. 40)[16]

This is the diametrically opposite view of those who have come to advocate "efficient markets" wherein no amount of "intelligent effort" can be cost-effective, so that the reward/risk trade-off dominates all other considerations.

And what does Graham think of sophisticated mathematical approaches to investing in stock to detect these inefficiencies? Here is the answer he gave in May 1958 in [Graham (1958)] an address entitled "The New Speculation in Common Stocks" given at the annual convention of the National Federation of Financial Analysts Societies (reproduced in the appendix to *The Intelligent Investor* on pp. 315–325):

> *In forty years of Wall Street experience and study I have never seen dependable calculations made about common-stock values, or related investment policies, that went beyond simple arithmetic or the most elementary algebra. Whenever calculus is brought in, on higher algebra, you could take it as a warning signal that the operator was trying to substitute theory for experience, and usually also to give speculation the deceptive guise of investment. (p. 321)*[17]

Those who would criticize Graham's investment philosophy must contend with his spectacular investment record, purported to have returned about 17 percent per annum from 1929 to 1956. Even worse, one must now deal with the unabashed support and investment results of Graham's most famous disciple, Warren E. Buffett, the most famous and successful stock investor of the twentieth century. In [Buffett (1984)] "The Superinvestors of Graham-and-Doddsville," an edited transcript of a 1984 talk given at Columbia University commemorating the 50th anniversary of the publication of *Security Analysis*, printed as an appendix to *The Intelligent Investor*, pp. 291–313, Buffett readily acknowledges that with enough investors, just random chance will cause some investors to realize extraordinary returns. But he argues that if you could identify many of these investors in advance of their success, and if you found, for instance, that a disproportionate number came from Omaha, yet they made independent investments, you might conclude that there was something about Omaha that creates skillful investing. In his own admittedly casual empirical test, Buffett summarizes the results of nine extremely successful investors with two things in common: (1) they were all identified by Buffett in advance as probable successful investors, and (2) they all by and large follow the tenets of Benjamin Graham. As he writes:

> *Our Graham & Dodd investors, needless to say, do not discuss beta, the capital asset pricing model, or covariance in returns among securities. These are not subjects of any interest to them. In fact, most of them would have difficulty defining these terms. The investors simply focus on two variables: price and value. (p. 294)*[18]

Although these investors followed the same general principles, there was little duplication in the securities they selected, so their portfolios on the surface appear to be relatively independent; in addition, casual observation suggests low risk. Buffett summarizes his attitude toward "efficient markets":

> *I am convinced there is much inefficiency in the market. These Graham-and-Doddsville investors have successfully exploited gaps between price and value. When the price of a stock can be influenced by a "herd" on Wall Street with prices set at the margin*[19] *by the most emotional person, or the greediest person, or the most depressed person, it is hard to argue that the market always prices rationally. In fact, market prices are frequently nonsensical. (p. 299)*[20]

Of course, the highest compound annual rate of return in Buffett's sample is Buffett's own partnership, which from 1957 to 1969 experienced a rate of return of 29.5 percent (23.8 percent to the limited partners), while the average investor who held the Dow Jones Industrial Average (DJIA) would have earned 7.4 percent! More astonishing is the record of Buffett's holding company, Berkshire Hathaway, from its inception in 1965 to 2001, which experienced a compound annual rate of return in book value per share of 22.6 percent compared to 11.0 percent inclusive of dividends for the S&P 500 index. Over these 37 years, in only 4 did Berkshire Hathaway underperform the Index. In particular, from 1980 through 1998, the firm outperformed the index in every single year. Let's face it: It is hard to argue with success.

Or is it? There is a sense in which Buffett "cheats." Buffett is not always passive, like most institutional investors. To the contrary, he often acquires a sufficiently large stake in a few corporations that he is able to influence their internal investment decisions and cost-control policies. Few would argue that the market for physical capital is efficient. In many cases, nothing short of bankruptcy[21] prevents corporate managers from making inefficient productive investments. In contrast, in an efficient stock market, excluding trading costs, there can be no *ex ante* poor investors since all prices are fair.

Another famous investor is Peter Lynch, who managed Fidelity's Magellan (mutual) Fund over the 13 years from 1977 through 1989. Over this period, Magellan outperformed the S&P 500 index in 11 out of 13 years and had an average annualized compound return of 28 percent, considerably exceeding the 17.5 percent annual return of the S&P 500 index over the same period. Perhaps even more astounding, in the first seven years before the fund was burdened with very large size, Magellan beat the S&P 500 by more than 15 percent in *every single year*. Alan J. Marcus in [Marcus (1990)] "The Magellan Fund and Market Efficiency," *Journal of Portfolio Management* 17, No. 1 (Fall 1990), pp. 85–88, asks whether Magellan's performance was due to luck or skill. Suppose in any year the probability of a single fund outperforming the market by chance is $1/2$. Then the probability that a single fund *identified at the outset* could, by chance, outperform the market in at least 11 out of 13 years equals $[13!/(11! \times 2!) + 13!/(12! \times 1!) + 13!/(13! \times 0!)](1/2^{13}) \approx .01$. However, as Marcus points out, Magellan was not identified as a winner in advance, but only after the fact. In that case, the appropriate question is: What is the probability that the best-performing fund out of the universe of competing funds would end up, by chance, outperforming the market in at least 11 out of 13 years? Simulation shows that with 500 competing funds over the 13-year period, the probability that, by chance, the best-performing fund would outperform the market in at least 11 years is 99.8 percent. So measured in these terms, we would hardly be impressed to find that Magellan had done so well.

However, suppose instead we ask: What is the probability that the best-performing fund out of 500 over the 13 years would end up, by chance, having an annualized compound return of at least 28 percent while the market's return was 17.5 percent? The answer to this question depends on the probability distribution of returns of the funds had they selected portfolios by chance. To get a rough answer, Marcus supposes that this distribution is normal with a standard deviation of return of 10 percent over a single year (and an annualized mean of 17.5 percent). Over a 13-year period, the standard deviation of the annualized compound return would then be $10\%/\sqrt{13} = 2.77\%$. A rough estimate from Marcus' paper suggests that the probability that Magellan's performance could have happened by chance is about 17 percent. But this figure does not correct for the fact that the true universe may be even larger than Marcus considers since the time period over which fund performance was measured was selected after the fact. Contrary to Marcus' conclusion, one suspects that if we were to enlarge the universe to consider other 13-year periods, we should not be surprised that in the entire history of U.S. mutual funds, the best-performing mutual fund would have done as well as Magellan.

1936 John Maynard Keynes (June 5, 1883–April 21, 1946), *The General Theory of Employment, Interest and Money* (New York: Macmillan, 1936); reprinted (Norwalk, CT: Easton Press, 1995).

MARKET RATIONALITY, MARKET PSYCHOLOGY,
MARKETS VS. BEAUTY CONTESTS VS. CASINOS,
RISK VS. UNCERTAINTY, LIQUIDITY PREFERENCE

For many economists, even as late as 1936 when Keynes wrote his *General Theory* (no doubt the most influential book written in economics in the twentieth century), the stock market was seen essentially as a casino where economic logic did not apply. Keynes (1936) clearly subscribed to this view:

> *Day-to-day fluctuations in the profits of existing investments, which are obviously of ephemeral and non-significant character, tend to have an altogether excessive, and an even absurd, influence on the market. It is said, for example, that the shares of American companies which manufacture ice tend to sell at a higher price in summer when their profits are seasonally high than in winter when no one wants ice. A conventional valuation which is established as the outcome of the mass psychology of a large number of ignorant individuals is liable to change violently as the result of sudden fluctuation of opinion due to factors which do not really make much difference to the prospective yield; since there will be no strong roots of conviction to hold it steady. In abnormal times in particular, when the hypothesis of an indefinite continuance of the existing state of affairs is less plausible than usual even though there are no express grounds to anticipate a definite change, the market will be subject to waves of optimistic and pessimistic sentiment, which are unreasoning and yet in a sense legitimate where no solid basis exists for a reasonable calculation.*
>
> *But there is one feature in particular which deserves our attention. It might have been supposed that competition between expert professionals, possessing judgment and knowledge beyond that of the average private investor, would correct the vagaries of*

the ignorant individual left to himself. It happens, however, that the energies and skill of the professional investor and speculator are mainly occupied otherwise. For most of these persons are, in fact, largely concerned, not with making superior long-term forecasts of the probable yield of an investment over its whole life, but with foreseeing changes in the conventional basis of valuation a short time ahead of the general public. They are concerned, not with what an investment is really worth to a man who buys it "for keeps," but with what the market will value it at, under the influence of mass psychology, three months or a year hence. (Chapter 7, pp. 153–155)[22]

Then he makes his famous comparison between the stock market and a beauty competition:

[P]rofessional investment may be likened to those newspaper competitions in which the competitors have to pick out the six prettiest faces from a hundred photographs, the prize being awarded to the competitor whose choice most nearly corresponds to the average preferences of the competitors as a whole; so that each competitor has to pick, not those faces which he himself finds the prettiest, but those which he thinks likeliest to catch the fancy of the other competitors, all of whom are looking at the problem from the same point of view. It is not a case of choosing those which, to the best of one's judgment, are really the prettiest, nor even those which the average opinion genuinely thinks the prettiest. We have reached a third degree where we devote our intelligences to anticipating what average opinion expects the average opinion to be. And there are some, I believe, who practice the fourth, fifth, and higher degrees. (Chapter 7, p. 156)

With the prevalence of views such as these, it is easy to understand why it took so long for the study of the stock market to be taken seriously.

In the clarification of his book, in [Keynes (1937)] "The General Theory of Employment," *Quarterly Journal of Economics* 51, No. 2 (February 1937), pp. 209–223, Keynes famously supports Knight (1921) in his distinction between risk and uncertainty:

The calculus of probability, tho mention of it was kept in the background, was supposed to be capable of reducing uncertainty to the same calculable status as that of certainty itself; just as in the Benthamite calculus of pains and pleasures or of advantage and disadvantage. . . . Actually, however, we have, as a rule, only the vaguest idea of any but the most direct consequences of our acts.

By "uncertain" knowledge, let me explain. I do not mean merely to distinguish between what is known for certain and what is only probable. The game of roulette is not subject, in this case, to uncertainty. . . . The sense in which I am using the terms is that in which the prospect of a European war is uncertain, or the price of copper and rate of interest twenty years hence. . . . About these matters there is no scientific basis on which to form any calculable probability whatever. We simply do not know. Nevertheless, the necessity for action and for decision compels us as practical men to do our best to overlook this awkward fact and to behave exactly as we should if we had behind us a good Benthamite calculation of a series of prospective advantages and disadvantages, each multiplied by its appropriate probability, waiting to be summed.

How do we manage in such circumstances to behave in a manner which saves our faces as rational, economic men? We have devised for the purpose a variety of techniques. . . .

1. *We assume the present is a much more serviceable guide to the future than a candid examination of past experience would show it to have been hitherto. In other words we largely ignore the prospect of future changes about the actual character of which we know nothing.*
2. *We assume the existing state of opinion as expressed in prices and the character of existing output is based on correct summing up of future prospects so that we can accept it as such unless and until something new and relevant comes into the picture.*
3. *Knowing that our individual judgment is worthless, we endeavor to fall back on the judgment of the rest of the world which is perhaps better informed. That is, we endeavor to conform to the behavior of the majority or the average.*

. . . All these pretty, polite techniques, made for a well-paneled Board Room and a nicely regulated market, are liable to collapse. At all times the vague panic fears and equally vague and unreasoned hopes are not really lulled, but lie a little way below the surface. (pp. 213–215)[23]

Keynes then uses this argument to justify another determinant of the rate of interest, "liquidity preference," that had not been on the list in

Fisher (1930). He argues that some individuals tend to hoard money, even though it is barren, yielding no explicit return, to protect themselves through its extreme liquidity against the indefinable future. So, in order to be held, interest-bearing securities need to compensate the marginal individual for not holding money. Hence, they have higher rates of interest than they would otherwise have in the absence of liquidity preference.

1938 John Burr Williams (1899–1989), *The Theory of Investment Value* (Cambridge, MA: Harvard University Press, 1938); reprinted (Burlington, VT: Fraser Publishing, 1997).

PRESENT VALUE, DIVIDEND DISCOUNT MODEL,
PERPETUAL DIVIDEND GROWTH FORMULA, ARBITRAGE,
DISCOUNTING EARNINGS VS. DIVIDENDS, VALUE ADDITIVITY,
ITERATED PRESENT VALUE, CAPITAL STRUCTURE,
LAW OF THE CONSERVATION OF INVESTMENT VALUE,
LAW OF LARGE NUMBERS, MARGINAL INVESTOR

The author of an insufficiently appreciated classic, Williams (1938) was one of the first economists to interpret stock prices as determined by "intrinsic value" (that is, discounted dividends). Harry M. Markowitz writes in his Nobel Prize autobiography: "The basic concepts of portfolio theory came to me one afternoon in the library while reading John Burr Williams' *The Theory of Investment Value*" (in [Markowitz (1991)] "Foundations of Portfolio Theory," *Les Prix Nobel* 1990, Nobel Foundation, 1991, p. 292).

While, as we have seen, Williams did not originate the idea of present value, he nonetheless develops many implications of the idea that the value of a stock under conditions of certainty is the present value of all its future dividends. His general present value formula is:

$$P_0 = \frac{\Sigma_{t=1,\dots,\infty} D_t}{r(t)^t}$$

where D_t is the dividend paid at date t, $r(t)$ is the current (date $t = 0$) annualized riskless discount return for dollars received at date t, and P_0 is the current (date $t = 0$) value of the stock. A nice way to build up to this is to start with the recursive relation $P_t = (D_{t+1} + P_{t+1})/r(t + 1)$. Successive substitutions for P_t through date T lead to $P_0 = [\Sigma_{t=1,\dots,T} D_t/r(t)^t] + P_T/r(T)^T$. The result then follows for $T = \infty$.

The modern view would be that this formula follows from no arbitrage. Consider the present value now of receiving a single cash flow of D_t at date t. The present value $PV_0(D_t)$ is defined as the amount of money you would need to set aside today to ensure that you would have D_t at date t. This could be done by investing $D_t/r(t)^t$ today in default-free zero-coupon bonds maturing at date t and holding this position until date t. Note that this investment would grow by date t to $(D_t/r^t)r^t = D_t$. Therefore, $D_t/r(t)^t$ must be the present value of D_t. It must also be what you would need to pay in a market to receive D_t at date t for there to be no arbitrage opportunities between that investment and the zero-coupon bonds. More generally, the date 0 present value $PV_0(D_1, D_2, \ldots, D_t, \ldots)$ is the amount of money you would need to invest today in default-free zero-coupon bonds such that you are sure to have exactly D_1 at date 1, D_2 at date 2, $\ldots$, D_t at date t, $\ldots$, which would clearly be:

$$PV_0(D_1, D_2, \ldots, D_t, \ldots) = \frac{\Sigma_t D_t}{r(t)^t}$$

Williams argues against discounting earnings instead of dividends and quotes the advice an old farmer gave his son (p. 58):

> *A cow for her milk,*
> *A hen for her eggs,*
> *And a stock, by heck,*
> *For her dividends.*

His book contains the derivation of the simple formula for the present value of a perpetually and constantly growing stream of income, $P_0 = D_1/(r - g)$, where r is the constant annualized riskless discount rate and g is the constant annualized growth rate in dividends.

Proof of the Perpetual Dividend Growth Formula

Here is a proof. Define $a \equiv D_1/r$ and $x \equiv g/r$. Then, $P_0 = a(1 + x + x^2 + \cdots)$. Multiplying both sides by x, we have $P_0 x = a(x + x^2 + x^3 + \cdots)$. Subtracting this from the previous expression for P_0, $P_0(1 - x) = a$. Substituting back for a and x, $P_0[1 - (g/r)] = D_1/r$. Therefore, $P_0 = D_1/(r - g)$.

Williams actually writes this formula in the form $P_0 = D_0 x/(1 - x)$ where $x \equiv g/r$—p. 88, equation (17a)—and notes that finite stock prices require $g < r$. This is commonly and mistakenly called the "Gordon growth formula" after its restatement in [Gordon-Shapiro (1956)] Myron J. Gordon and Eli Shapiro, "Capital Equipment Analysis: The Required Rate of Profit," *Management Science* 3, No. 1 (October 1956), pp. 102–110.[24]

Gordon and Shapiro popularized the formula by rewriting it as $k = (D_1/P_0) + g$, where k equals r under certainty, but under uncertainty could loosely be interpreted as the expected return to stock. Breaking apart this expected return into two components, the dividend yield and growth, translated Williams' formula into a language that popularized it among investment professionals. For example, in the early 1960s, although the dividend yield of U.S. Steel was higher than IBM's, IBM could have a higher k and P/E ratio because its prospects for growth were so spectacular.

Here are two useful corollaries in present value calculations:

COROLLARY 1. *Law of Value Additivity:* The present value of a sum of cash flows equals the sum of their present value:

$$PV_0(D_1, D_2, D_3, \ldots, D_t, D_{t+1}, D_{t+2}, \ldots, D_T)$$
$$= PV_0(D_1, D_2, \ldots, D_t) + PV_0(D_{t+1}, D_{t+2}, \ldots, D_T)$$

COROLLARY 2. *Law of Iterated Present Value:* The date 0 present value of a series of cash flows beginning at date $t + 1$ equals the present value at date 0 of the present value of the cash flows at date t:

$$PV_0(D_{t+1}, D_{t+2}, \ldots, D_T) = PV_0[PV_t(D_{t+1}, D_{t+2}, \ldots, D_T)]$$

Derivation and Application of the Present Value Formula for a Finite-Lived Annuity

With these corollaries, one can easily derive a simple formula for a finite-lived constantly growing stream of cash flows; that is, where $D_2 = D_1 g$, $D_3 = D_1 g^2$, $D_4 = D_1 g^3$, $\ldots$, $D_T = D_1 g^{T-1}$. In that case, I can interpret this present value as the difference between the present values of two perpetually growing dividend streams, where the second begins at date D_{T+1}:

By corollary 1: $PV_0(D_1, D_2, \ldots, D_T) = PV_0(D_1, D_2, \ldots) - PV_0(D_{T+1}, D_{T+2}, \ldots)$

(Continued)

Derivation and Application of the Present Value Formula for a Finite-Lived Annuity *(Continued)*

By corollary 2:

$$PV_0(D_1, D_2, \ldots, D_T) = PV_0(D_1, D_2, \ldots)$$
$$- PV_0[PV_T(D_{T+1}, D_{T+2}, \ldots)]$$
$$= PV_0(D_1, D_1g, D_1g^2, \ldots)$$
$$- \left(\frac{g}{r}\right)^T [PV_T(D_1, D_1g, D_1g^2, \ldots)]$$
$$= \frac{D_1}{r-g} - \left(\frac{g}{r}\right)^T \left(\frac{D_1}{r-g}\right) = \frac{D_1}{r-g}\left[1 - \left(\frac{g}{r}\right)^T\right]$$

A nice application of these results is to determine the present value of a series of cash flows growing at g_1 from dates 1 to $t + 1$, and then growing at g_2 from dates $t + 1$ to date T:

$$PV_0(D_1, D_2, \ldots, D_t, D_{t+1}, D_{t+2}, \ldots, D_T)$$
$$= PV_0(D_1, D_2, \ldots, D_t) + PV_0(D_{t+1}, D_{t+2}, \ldots, D_T)$$
$$= PV_0(D_1, D_2, \ldots, D_t) + PV_0[PV_t(D_{t+1}, D_{t+2}, \ldots, D_T)]$$
$$= PV_0(D_1, D_1g_1, \ldots, D_1g_1^{t-1}) + PV_0[PV_t(D_1g_1^t, D_1g_1^tg_2, \ldots, D_1g_1^tg_2^{T-t-1})]$$
$$= PV_0(D_1, D_1g_1, \ldots, D_1g_1^{t-1})$$
$$+ \left(\frac{g_1}{r}\right)^t [PV_t(D_1, D_1g_2, \ldots, D_1g_2^{T-t-1})]$$
$$= \left(\frac{D_1}{r-g_1}\right)\left[1 - \left(\frac{g_1}{r}\right)^t\right] + \left(\frac{g_1}{r}\right)^t\left(\frac{D_1}{r-g_2}\right)\left[1 - \left(\frac{g_2}{r}\right)^{T-t}\right]$$

Following in the footsteps of de Moivre (1725) and Halley (1761), Williams also develops a very extensive analysis of a variety of generalizations, for example for a constant growth rate over n years, followed by dividends that exponentially level off toward a limiting amount that is twice the dividend in the nth year (p. 94, equation [27a]):

$$P_0 = \frac{D_1}{r^n}\left\{\left[\frac{g^n - r^n}{g - r}\right] + \left[\frac{2gr - r - 1}{(r-1)(gr-1)}\right]\right\}$$

His book also contains what is probably the first exposition of the Modigliani-Miller (1958) proposition on the irrelevancy of capital structure, which Williams poetically calls the "Law of the Conservation of Investment Value." Williams writes with borrowed nineteenth-century elegance:

If the investment value of an enterprise as a whole is by definition the present worth of all its future distributions to security holders, whether on interest or dividend account, then this value in no wise depends on what the company's capitalization is. Clearly, if a single individual or a single institutional investor owned all of the bonds, stocks and warrants issued by the corporation, it would not matter to this investor what the company's capitalization was (except for details concerning the income tax). Any earnings collected as interest could not be collected as dividends. To such an individual it would be perfectly obvious that total interest- and dividend-paying power was in no wise dependent on the kind of securities issued to the company's owner. Furthermore no change in the investment value of the enterprise as a whole would result from a change in its capitalization. Bonds could be retired with stock issues, or two classes of junior securities could be combined into one, without changing the investment value of the company as a whole. Such constancy of investment value is analogous to the indestructibility of matter or energy: it leads us to speak of the Law of the Conservation of Investment Value, just as physicists speak of the Law of the Conservation of Matter, or the Law of the Conservation of Energy. (pp. 72–73)[25]

Although this exposition does not use the magical word *arbitrage*, in his next paragraph on the subject Williams says that his Law will not hold exactly in practice (he had not yet absorbed later notions of informationally efficient markets). But, he says, that simply leaves open "opportunities for profit by promoters and investment bankers." From his analysis of United Corporation, it is clear that he sees "promoters" profiting by taking advantage of naive techniques used by investors to value the separate securities in the recapitalization; had the investors but understood the Law of the Conservation of Investment Value, they would have defeated the promoters' efforts.

Williams had very little to say about the effects of risk on valuation (pp. 67–70) because he believed that all risk could be diversified away:

The customary way to find the value of a risky security has been to add a "premium for risk" to the pure rate of interest, and then use the sum as the interest rate for discounting future receipts. . . . Strictly speaking, however, there is no risk in buying the bond in question if its price is right. Given adequate diversification, gains on such purchases will offset losses, and a return at the pure interest rate will be obtained. Thus the net risk turns out to be nil. (pp. 67–69)[26]

As precocious as Williams was, he got this wrong, which makes subsequent discoveries all the more impressive. Knight (1921) also makes a similar error based on the law of large numbers developed by Jakob Bernoulli (1713).

Despite this, because in 1938 Williams had not yet read Markowitz (1952/March) or Roy (1952), he did not appreciate the portfolio point of view. In his discussion of how stock is allocated among different investors, he emphasizes that investors will have different beliefs about the value of that stock, but he believes investors with the highest valuations will end up owning all of the stock. He ignores the good sense of holding some stocks to take advantage of risk reduction through diversification, even if they are not your first choice and may even seem somewhat overpriced. As a result, he argues that the only investor who determines the price of a stock is the *marginal* or last investor who is the most relatively pessimistic among all the optimistic investors who own the stock. With the later perspective of Markowitz and Roy, in the absence of short sales (implicitly assumed by Williams), the modern view is to see each investor who owns the stock as a candidate to purchase even more should its price fall, so that the price of the stock is not simply determined by the preferences and beliefs of the marginal investor, but rather the preferences and beliefs of the *average* investor who holds the stock.

1938 **Frederick R. Macaulay,** *Some Theoretical Problems Suggested by the Movements of Interest Rates, Bond Yields and Stock Prices in the U.S. since 1856*, National Bureau of Economic Research (New York: Columbia University Press, 1938); reprinted (London: Risk Publications, 2000).

DURATION, FOUR PROPERTIES OF DURATION,
PARALLEL SHIFT IN INTEREST RATES, ARBITRAGE

What is the average time to the receipt of cash flow from a bond, usually called the "duration" of the bond? For a zero-coupon bond, this is clearly its time to maturity. For a coupon bond, it must be less than its time to maturity. Let X_t be the cash flow from a bond at date t, and $r(t)$ be the annualized return of a zero-coupon bond maturing at date t. Then $B = \Sigma_t X_t / r(t)^t$ is the present value of the bond. Macaulay (1938) (see in particular pp. 43–53) proposes that its duration D be defined as:

$$D = \Sigma_t \left[\frac{X_t / r(t)^t}{B} \right] \times t$$

where the sum is taken from 1 to T (the date of the last cash flow from the bond). Thus, Macaulay duration is the time to receipt of the average dollar

---

Proof of the Additivity Property of Duration

To see this, consider two bonds 1 and 2:

$$D_1 = \Sigma_t \left[\frac{X_t^1 / r(t)^t}{B_1} \right] \times t$$

$$D_2 = \Sigma_t \left[\frac{X_t^2 / r(t)^t}{B_2} \right] \times t$$

Form a portfolio of the two bonds so that the total value of this portfolio is $B \equiv B_1 + B_2$. Consider the following weighted average of the durations of the two bonds: $(B_1/B)D_1 + (B_2/B)D_2$. Writing this after substituting the definition of duration:

$$\left(\frac{B_1}{B} \right) D_1 + \left(\frac{B_2}{B} \right) D_2 = \left(\frac{B_1}{B} \right) \left\{ \Sigma_t \left[\frac{X_t^1 / r(t)^t}{B_1} \right] \times t \right\}$$

$$+ \left(\frac{B_2}{B} \right) \left\{ \Sigma_t \left[\frac{X_t^2 / r(t)^t}{B_2} \right] \times t \right\}$$

$$= \left\{ \Sigma_t \left[\frac{(X_t^1 + X_t^2) / r(t)^t}{B} \right] \times t \right\}$$

$$\equiv D \text{ (the duration of the portfolio)}$$

of present value from the bond. This has several nice properties. First, the duration of the zero-coupon bond equals its time to maturity. Second, the duration of a portfolio of bonds equals a weighted average of the durations of its constituent bonds, where the weights are the relative values of the bonds.

Third, if forward rates remain unchanged and an unrevised portfolio of bonds experiences no cash flows between dates t and $t + 1$, then if the duration of the portfolio is D measured at date t, the duration will be $D - 1$ at date $t + 1$.

Although Macaulay clearly realized that the prices of bonds with longer durations would be more sensitive to interest rates than shorter-duration bonds, it remained for Hicks (1939) and Paul Anthony Samuelson, in [Samuelson (1945)] "The Effect of Interest Rate Increases on the Bank-

---

Proof of Time Reduction Property of Duration

Proof of third property: changes in duration over time. Consider a three-period coupon bond with:

$$X_1 = 0,\ X_2 > 0,\ X_3 > 0$$

Duration at date 0 is:

$$D_0 = 2\left\{\left[\frac{X_2}{f(1)f(2)}\right] \div \left(\left[\frac{X_2}{f(1)f(2)}\right] + \left[\frac{X_3}{f(1)f(2)f(3)}\right]\right)\right\}$$

$$+ 3\left\{\left[\frac{X_3}{f(1)f(2)f(3)}\right] \div \left(\left[\frac{X_2}{f(1)f(2)}\right] + \left[\frac{X_3}{f(1)f(2)f(3)}\right]\right)\right\}$$

Duration at date 1, assuming unchanged forward returns, is:

$$D_1 = 1\left\{\left[\frac{X_2}{f(2)}\right] \div \left(\left[\frac{X_2}{f(2)}\right] + \left[\frac{X_3}{f(2)f(3)}\right]\right)\right\}$$

$$+ 2\left\{\left[\frac{X_3}{f(2)f(3)}\right] \div \left(\left[\frac{X_2}{f(2)}\right] + \left[\frac{X_3}{f(2)f(3)}\right]\right)\right\}$$

$$= D_0 - 1$$

ing System," *American Economic Review* 35, No. 1 (March 1945), pp. 16-27, to point out that the same calculation of duration measures the elasticity of the bond price with respect to the interest rate. Suppose $r(t) = y$ for all t, then it is easy to see that $dB/B = -(D/y)dy$. This implies that the values of bonds with similar durations have similar sensitivities to changes in interest rates; and the greater the duration, the more sensitive the present value of the bond is to changes in interest rates.

Proof of the Risk Quantification Property of Duration

To see this, $B = \Sigma_t X_t y^{-t}$, so that $dB/dy = -\Sigma_t t X_t y^{-t-1}$. Therefore, $dB = -y^{-1}(\Sigma_t t X_t y^{-t})dy$. Then, $dB/B = -y^{-1}[\Sigma_t t(X_t y^{-t})/B]dy$. Then, by the definition of duration, $dB/B = -(D/y)dy$.

Later it was realized that this interpretation of duration, as the sensitivity of bond prices to a *parallel shift* in interest rates, has a technical problem. For example, in a simple situation suppose the term structure of spot returns (and hence forward returns) is flat at r per annum (irrespective of maturity). Now suppose the entire term structure shifts to a new level, say return s (irrespective of maturity) greater or less than r, so that the term structure of spot returns continues to be flat but at a different level $s \neq r$. If this happens, bond prices would change, and the duration of a bond, as we have seen, predicts the price change. Unfortunately, one can show that the assumption that the term structure can only shift in parallel violates the fundamental assumption of financial economics: no arbitrage.

Proof of the Contradiction between Parallel Yield Shifts and No Arbitrage

To see this, I want to borrow from an analysis in [Davis (2001)] Morton D. Davis, *The Math of Money* (New York: Springer-Verlag, 2001), pp. 66–67. Assume as usual no arbitrage and perfect markets. Consider the following portfolio of bonds (each is a zero-coupon bond with a principal payment of $1 at maturity) purchased when the term structure is r:

  (a) Agree now (date 0) to buy one bond at the end of one year (date 1) that matures two years after (date 3); this is called a "forward rate agreement."

(Continued)

Proof of the Contradiction between
Parallel Yield Shifts and No Arbitrage *(Continued)*

(b) Agree now (date 0) to sell $(2/r)$ bonds at the end of one year (date 1) that mature one year after (date 2); this is another forward rate agreement.

Note that under these agreements, no money changes hands at date 0; rather the purchase and sale of the bonds and any payment or receipt of cash for this occurs at date 1.

Now, suppose after having formed this portfolio of forward rate agreements at date 0, the term structure of spot returns then shifts to s after date 0 but before date 1 and remains at this level on date 1. On this date (date 1), liquidate the portfolio.

At date 1, the gain or loss on forward rate agreement (a) is:

$$-\frac{1}{r^2}+\frac{1}{s^2}$$

and at date 1, the gain or loss on forward rate agreement (b) is:

$$\frac{2}{r}\left(\frac{1}{r}-\frac{1}{s}\right)$$

Adding these together, the total liquidation value of the portfolio at date 1 is:

$$-\frac{1}{r^2}+\frac{1}{s^2}+\frac{2}{r}\left(\frac{1}{r}-\frac{1}{s}\right)=\frac{1}{r^2}-2\left(\frac{1}{rs}\right)+\frac{1}{s^2}=\left(\frac{1}{r}-\frac{1}{s}\right)^2$$

Now this must necessarily be greater than 0 (and not equal to 0) since $r \neq s$. Indeed, whatever happens, whether $s > r$ or $s < r$, the liquidation cash flow to the investor will be positive regardless of whether the term structure shifts up or down. But since the portfolio of the two forward rate agreements costs nothing at date 0 but is worth a positive amount for certain at date 1, there is an arbitrage opportunity. This contradicts our original assumption of no arbitrage; hence the situation described is not consistent. To conclude, the assumption that the only way the term structure can shift is in parallel is inconsistent with the most basic principle of financial economics: namely, no arbitrage.

Macaulay was pessimistic about extending his analysis to deal with embedded options. He put it this way:

Convertible bonds and bonds carrying special privileges of any kind, such as "circulation" privileges, present similar difficulties. The promise to make future money payments is only one of elements determining their prices and yields. They are mongrels and it is next to impossible to measure the degree of their contamination. (pp. 70–71)

A historical review of the development of the concept of duration can be found in [Weil (1973)] Roman L. Weil, "Macaulay's Duration: An Appreciation," *Journal of Business* 46, No. 4 (October 1973), pp. 589–592.

Duration is now one of three standard methods to measure the risk of securities. Duration measures the sensitivity of bond prices to changes in interest rates, beta measures the sensitivity of the excess return (over the riskless return) of a stock to the excess return of a stock market index, and delta measures the sensitivity of the value of an option to dollar changes in its underlying asset price. All three measures are linear so that the duration of a *portfolio* of bonds, the beta of a *portfolio* of stocks, and the delta of a *portfolio* of options on the same underlying asset are weighted sums of the corresponding risk measures of their portfolio's constituent securities.

1945 Friedrich August von Hayek (May 8, 1899–March 23, 1992), "The Use of Knowledge in Society," *American Economic Review* 35, No. 4 (September 1945), pp. 519–530.

AGGREGATION OF INFORMATION, PRICE SYSTEM,
EFFICIENT MARKETS, SOCIALISM VS. CAPITALISM

This relatively short and elegantly written paper is surely one of the gems in the crown of economics. Just as Abraham Lincoln's Gettysburg Address (1863) pointed the United States in a new direction, so, too, Hayek (1945) can be viewed as a call for economics to take the crucial next step. The standard competitive equilibrium model, which shows how the price system results in a Pareto-optimal outcome, is in Hayek's words "no more than a useful preliminary to our study of the main problem" (p. 530), for it takes as given the beliefs (and implicitly the information) of each agent and imposes no cost on the operation of the price system. Because there is no treatment of the costs and methods of forming these beliefs or of implementing the price system itself, the economic solution could just as well, in principle, be reached by a benevolent central planner in possession of the same information. While the competitive model proves that the price system can in principle solve the problem of economic order, it does not show that it is the *best* way to solve it.

Hayek then describes qualitatively the key (but not the only) reason why the price system is the preferred method of solution. He argues that the role of the price system is to efficiently aggregate widely dispersed bits of information into a single sufficient statistic, the price, that summarizes for economic agents all they need to know (in addition to the particular knowledge of their own circumstances) about the dispersed information to make the correct decisions for themselves—the essence of the rationalist view of markets. He writes:

> *The peculiar character of the problem of rational economic order is determined precisely by the fact that the knowledge of the circumstances of which we must make use never exists in concentrate or integrated form, but solely as disbursed bits of incomplete and frequently contradictory knowledge which all the separate individuals possess. The economic problem of society is thus . . . a problem of the utilization of knowledge not given to anyone in its totality. (pp. 519–520)*
>
> *The most significant fact about the [price] system is the economy of knowledge with which it operates, or how little the individual participants need to know in order to be able to take the right action. In abbreviated form, by a kind of symbol [the price], only the most essential information is passed on, and passed on only to those concerned. (pp. 526–527)*[27]

He also brilliantly restates the description of Smith (1776)[28] of the key problem that is solved by a competitive price system:

> *I am convinced that if it were the results of deliberate human design, and if the people guided by the price changes understood that their decisions have significance far beyond their immediate aim, this mechanism [the price system] would have been acclaimed as one of the greatest triumphs of the human mind. . . . The problem is precisely how to extend the control of any one mind; and, therefore, how to dispense with the need of conscious control and how to provide inducements which will make the individuals do the desirable things without anyone having to tell them what to do. (p. 527)*[29]

The motivation behind much of Hayek's work was his role in the debate over the social alternatives of capitalism versus socialism. He steadfastly argued that the key issue in this debate was the creation and communication of relevant economic information, and that for a variety of reasons, capitalism was much better suited to that task. He was therefore concerned about the causes of economic failure under capitalism, most prominently experienced as depression. For Hayek, the roundabout nature of production, that it takes time, and that the more sophisticated the economy, the more time production typically takes, is the key economic fact responsible for depression. Production requires a partially irreversible commitment of resources for some time before the resulting output can be consumed. The longer the time for this commitment, and the more prices fail to function as correct signals for production planning, the more likely cumulative errors of over- or underinvestment will lead to economic collapse. For example, if the prices of some commodities needed for production are temporarily artificially low, producers will be tempted to commit to greater production than is profitable, and may suddenly be forced in the future to cut back, while they accumulate inventories and reduce employment.

Hayek distinguishes between two types of economic knowledge: (1) general scientific or theoretical knowledge and (2) specific knowledge of the individual circumstances of time and place. Advocates of socialism implicitly require that economic planners have access to both types, while advocates of rational expectations, such as Lucas (1972) and Grossman (1976), concentrate both types of knowledge with market participants. Both are mistaken. For example, the flaw in rational expectations is that in order for market participants to extract from prices all the information they need to make the correct decisions, they would need to have knowledge of type (2), which includes the aggregated preferences and endowments of all other participants and how these fit together to determine their demands.

Hayek won the 1974 Nobel Prize in Economic Science "for [his] pioneering work in the theory of money and economic fluctuations and for [his] penetrating analysis of the interdependence of economic, social and institutional phenomena."

1947 John von Neumann (December 3, 1903–February 8, 1957) and **Oskar Morgenstern** (January 24, 1902–July 26, 1977), *Theory of Games and Economic Behavior*, second edition (Princeton, NJ: Princeton University Press, 1947) (first edition without appendix, 1944).

1951 Frederick Mosteller (December 24, 1916–) and **Philip Nogee**, "An Experimental Measurement of Utility," *Journal of Political Economy* 59, No. 5 (October 1951), pp. 371–404.

1953 Maurice Allais (May 31, 1911–), "Le comportement de l'homme rationnel devant le risqué: critique des postulats et axioms de l'école Américaine," with English summary, *Econometrica* 21, No. 4 (October 1953), pp. 503–546; reprinted and translated as "The Foundations of a Positive Theory of Choice Involving Risk and a Criticism of Postulates and Axioms of the American School," in *Expected Utility Hypothesis and the Allais Paradox*, edited by Maurice Allais and O. Hagen (Norwell, MA: D. Reidel Publishing, 1979).

1954 Leonard J. Savage (November 20, 1917–November 1, 1971), *The Foundations of Statistics* (New York: John Wiley & Sons, 1954); second revised edition (New York: Dover 1972).

EXPECTED UTILITY, INDEPENDENCE AXIOM,
SUBJECTIVE VS. OBJECTIVE PROBABILITY, ALLAIS PARADOX,
EXPERIMENTAL MEASUREMENT OF UTILITY

Despite the earlier work of Daniel Bernoulli (1738), there was little attempt to analyze the effects of uncertainty on economic decisions for the next 200 years. A notable exception was Knight (1921), who argues that profits and the very existence of the market system are due to the distinction between risk and uncertainty. Although Bernoulli's assumption of diminishing marginal utility had been picked up by Marshall (1890) and other economists, his second great idea of expected utility left a number of economists uncomfortable with the conclusion that fair gambles should be avoided; this suggested that risk taking was irrational and therefore something that would have to be considered outside the normal confines of economics.

John von Neumann and Oskar Morgenstern's *Theory of Games and Economic Behavior* decisively changed this view. To develop their new "game theory," they needed utility-type payoffs with mixed strategy probabilities. So in the second edition of the book, von Neumann-Morgenstern (1947), an appendix (pp. 617–632) provides an axiomatic analysis justifying the idea that rational individuals should make choices by maximizing their expected utility. Unknown to von Neumann-Morgenstern, an earlier and probably first proof, but based on somewhat different rationality axioms, appeared in [Ramsey (1926)] Frank Plumpton Ramsey's (February

22, 1903–January 19, 1930) "Truth and Probability" (1926), published posthumously after his tragic death from an operation for jaundice in 1930 at the age of 26, in the *Foundations of Mathematics and Other Logical Essays* (Harcourt Brace, 1931), reprinted (Totowa, NJ: Littlefield, Adams, 1965), pp. 156–198. In 1937, Bruno de Finetti (June 13, 1906–July 20, 1985), in [de Finetti (1937)] "La Prevision: ses lois logiques ses sources subjectives," *Annales de l'Institut Henri Poincaré* 7 (1937), pp. 1–68, translated and published as "Foresight: Its Logical Laws, Its Subjective Sources," in *Studies in Subjective Probability*, edited by Henry E. Kyburg Jr., and Howard E. Smokler (New York: Robert E. Krieger Publishing, second edition, 1980), unaware of Ramsey, also shows how to deduce subjective probabilities from choices.

A convenient version of the axioms follows. Suppose Ω represents the set of all possible gambles over all possible outcomes, say x_1, x_2, and x_3 and p, q, $r \in \Omega$. Suppose by p we mean a gamble leading to outcomes x_1, x_2, and x_3 with respective probabilities p_1, p_2, and p_3. And suppose q represents a gamble leading to the same outcomes with respective probabilities q_1, q_2, and q_3; and r represents a gamble leading to the same outcomes with respective probabilities r_1, r_2, and r_3. The relation $\geq$ ("is preferred or indifferent to") is a binary relation over gambles. So I write $p \geq q$ meaning gamble p is preferred or indifferent to q. I also write $p = q$ if and only if $p \geq q$ and $q \geq p$; and I write $p > q$ if and only if $p \geq q$ and not $p = q$.

AXIOM 1. *Completeness:* For all p, $q \in \Omega$, either $p \geq q$ or $p \leq q$.

AXIOM 2. *Transitivity:* For all p, q, $r \in \Omega$, if $p \geq q$ and $q \geq r$, then $p \geq r$.

AXIOM 3. *Continuity:* For all p, q, $r \in \Omega$, if $p > q$ and $q > r$, then there exists an α, $\beta \in (0, 1)$ such that $\alpha p + (1 - \alpha)r > q$ and $q > \beta p + (1 - \beta)r$.

AXIOM 4. *Independence:* For all p, q, $r \in \Omega$ and for any $\alpha \in (0, 1)$, $p > q$ if and only if $\alpha p + (1 - \alpha)r > \alpha q + (1 - \alpha)r$.

The expected utility representation theorem says: Axiom 1–4 if and only if there exists a function U defined on the outcomes x_1, x_2, and x_3 such that for every p, $q \in \Omega$:

$$p \geq q \text{ if and only if } \Sigma_j p_j U(x_j) \geq \Sigma_j q_j U(x_j)$$

(where to the right $\geq$ means equal to or greater than)

U is called a utility function. It is easy to see that U is not a unique function, but rather is defined up to an increasing linear transformation; that is, for any real numbers a and $b > 0$, U is a utility function if and only if $V = a + bU$ is also a utility function (in other words, U and V preserve the same ordering of all possible gambles). It follows that simply assuming choices are made by maximizing expected utility is a shorthand for assuming choices are consistent with the von Neumann–Morgenstern axioms—a convenience that many economists have adopted.

The von Neumann–Morgenstern axioms did not explicitly use the "independence axiom," but their axioms were independently reformulated using this axiom by Jacob Marschak in [Marschak (1950)] "Rational Behavior, Uncertain Prospects and Measurable Utility," *Econometrica* 18, No. 2 (April 1950), pp. 111–141, and Paul Anthony Samuelson in [Samuelson (1966)] "Utility, Preference and Probability," an abstract of a paper presented orally May 1952, reprinted in *The Collected Scientific Papers of Paul A. Samuelson*, Volume 1 (Cambridge, MA: MIT Press, 1966), pp. 127-136. Edmond Malinvaud, in [Malinvaud (1952)] "Note on von Neumann–Morgenstern's Strong Independence Axiom," *Econometrica* 20, No. 4 (October 1952), p. 679, then showed that the independence axiom is actually implied by the original von Neumann–Morgenstern axioms. This axiom implies that the utility of the outcome in each state is independent of the outcomes in all other states. Starting with, say, a function $F(C_1, C_2, \ldots C_s, \ldots, C_S)$ describing a preference ordering over consumption in states $s = 1, 2, \ldots, S$, it is easy to understand intuitively that the independence axiom allows this to be written as $\Sigma_s p_s U(C_s)$.

The independence axiom is probably the weakest link in the von Neumann–Morgenstern theory and has led to many ingenious arguments that it can be inconsistent with reasonable behavior. For example, suppose x_1 is a trip to London and x_2 is a trip to Paris, and suppose $p = (1, 0)$ is a sure trip to London, and $q = (0, 1)$ is a sure trip to Paris. Assume $p > q$. Now suppose I introduce a third outcome x_3: viewing a movie about London. Considering this, say your choice is now between $p = (.8, 0, .2)$ and $q = (0, .8, .2)$. The independence axiom requires that as before $p > q$. That is, since the common opportunity to view a movie about London is added to both choices, your preference ordering should remain unchanged. But isn't it possible that if you take p and end up with only a movie about London you will feel so badly about missing an actual trip to London that you will wish you had chosen q instead and then never would have had to bear this disappointment? This kind of reversal is ruled out by the independence axiom.

The most famous early challenge to the independence axiom was invented in Allais (1953). Suppose the outcomes $x_1 = \$0$, $x_2 = \$100$, and $x_3 =$

$500. Consider a pair of gambles, $p^1 = (0, 1, 0)$ and $p^2 = (.01, .89, .10)$. Empirically, for most people $p^1 > p^2$. Now consider a second pair of gambles, $q^1 = (.89, .11, 0)$ and $q^2 = (.90, 0, .10)$. Empirically, the same people for whom $p^1 > p^2$, also $q^2 > q^1$. Yet, it turns out these choices violate the independence axiom. To see this, if $p^1 > p^2$, then by the expected utility representation theorem there exists a function U such that

$$U(\$100) > .01U(\$0) + .89U(\$100) + .10U(\$500)$$

Adding $.89U(\$0)$ to both sides and subtracting $.89U(\$100)$ from both sides:

$$.89U(\$0) + .11U(\$100) > .90U(\$0) + .10U(\$500)$$

which, of course, implies that $q^1 > q^2$.

Von Neumann and Morgenstern took it for granted that agents make choices as if they employ probabilities. Savage (1954) provides an axiomatic analysis justifying the view that all uncertainties may be reduced to subjective probabilities. He shows that if an individual follows certain logical behavioral postulates that he identifies with rational behavior, the individual will behave as if he makes decisions based on maximizing his expected utility where the expectation is taken with respect to his subjective probabilities. Savage's work can also be viewed as an extension of von Neumann–Morgenstern to incorporate subjective probabilities.

About 30 years earlier, Ramsey (1926) had initiated the axiomatic justification of subjective probabilities. He began by rejecting the path of defining probabilities in terms of the intensity of internal human psychological states. Instead, he argued that it would be more useful to deduce the implicit use of subjective probabilities from the actions of individuals, assumed to make choices based on certain postulates that one might associate with rationality. To take a very simple example, suppose there are two equally pleasant stores, equally distant from your home, that both sell your favorite brand of ice cream. However, sometimes one or the other store is temporarily out of stock. I might deduce from your consistent choice of one of the stores that you believe that store is more likely to have the ice cream.

This inference from actions to probabilities proves particularly pragmatic for a theory of human economic choice: It is unnecessary to interrogate individuals about how they think; one need only observe what alternative acts they would choose. Moreover, by observing their choices, it is possible to separate out their preferences from their beliefs, a distinction that was to prove critical to almost all work in "asset pricing" during the remainder of the twentieth century. Ramsey writes:

> *I mean the theory that we act in the way we think most likely to realize the objects of our desires, so that a person's actions are completely determined by his desires and opinions. . . . It is a simple theory and one that many psychologists would obviously like to preserve by introducing unconscious opinions in order to bring it more in harmony with the facts. How far such fictions can achieve the required results I do not attempt to judge: I only claim for what follows an approximate truth, or truth in relation to this artificial system of psychology, which like Newtonian mechanics can, I think, still be profitably used even though it is known to be false. (p. 173)*

Unfortunately, even if an observed agent is perfectly rational, the program of inferring probabilities and preferences from observed choices contains many hidden shoals that can ground the unwary. For example, having observed an individual bet on a racehorse does not necessarily imply that, given the track odds, he believes the horse will win; the bettor may simply like the name of the horse. For an agent to reveal his preferences and probabilities from his choices, the full implications for the agent of each choice must be specified and the menu of all possible choices must be known.

Mosteller-Nogee (1951) describe what was to be the first in a long line of experiments testing the expected utility theory of von Neumann–Morgenstern (1947) and by extension Savage (1954). They confront several college undergraduates and National Guardsmen with a long series of gambles to see if, for each subject, there exists a single utility function consistent with all his choices. Of course, given the complexity of the task, no subject was perfectly consistent. However, Mosteller and Nogee conclude that, with the exception of a few subjects, their responses were sufficiently consistent (1) that it is "feasible to measure utility experimentally, (2) that the notion that people behave in such a way as to maximize expected utility is not unreasonable, [and] (3) that on the basis of empirical curves it is possible to estimate future behavior in comparable but more complicated risk-taking situations."

In 1988, Allais won the Nobel Prize in Economic Science "for his pioneering contributions to the theory of markets and efficient utilization of resources."

1948 **Milton Friedman** (July 31, 1912–) and **Leonard J. Savage,** "The Utility Analysis of Choices Involving Risk," *Journal of Political Economy* 56, No. 4 (August 1948), pp. 279–304.

1952 **Harry M. Markowitz** (August 24, 1927–), "The Utility of Wealth," *Journal of Political Economy* 60, No. 2 (April 1952), pp. 151–158.

1979 **Daniel Kahneman** (1934–) and **Amos Tversky** (March 16, 1937– June 2, 1996), "Prospect Theory: An Analysis of Decision under Risk," *Econometrica* 47, No. 2 (March 1979), pp. 263–291.

RISK AVERSION AND GAMBLING, LOTTERIES,
REFERENCE-DEPENDENT UTILITY,
PROSPECT THEORY, DYNAMIC STRATEGIES

With the work of von Neumann–Morgenstern (1947), which provided a rational justification for maximizing expected utility, the conclusions of Daniel Bernoulli (1738) concerning risk aversion could now be taken seriously. Friedman-Savage (1948) was the first to do so (although their work was partially anticipated by L. Törnqvist in [Törnqvist (1945)] "On the Economic Theory of Lottery Gambles," *Skandinavisk Aktuarietidskrift* 28, Nos. 3–4 (1945), pp. 298–304). Their paper contains the first diagrams of utility as a function of income with the geometric result that an individual will avoid fair binomial gambles if a chord drawn between the two outcomes of the gamble lies below the utility function.

Such a risk-averse agent will never accept a fair or an unfair gamble. Yet curiously it is commonplace for the same individual to be risk averse for the most part and even purchase insurance, yet also quite happily buy lottery tickets. Earlier economists were unable to explain this because they had given up on maximizing expected utility rather than jettison the hypothesis of diminishing marginal utility. Friedman and Savage now reversed this priority of hypotheses and thereby reconciled gambling with rational behavior.

Friedman and Savage begin by postulating a singly inflected utility function with a concave (to the origin) segment over low levels of income followed by a convex segment over high levels of income. Supposing that an individual finds his current wealth in the domain of the concave segment, he will simultaneously buy insurance against small and large losses, avoid all fair gambles with small potential gains, but also accept unfair gambles with potentially large gains. That is, he will willingly buy gambles that have a large probability of a small loss but a small probability of a large gain (long shots). To explain as well why lotteries tend to have many winning prizes of moderate size rather than a single extremely large prize, Friedman and Savage postulate that the convex segment be followed by a second upper concave segment.

Markowitz (1952/April) points out that the simultaneous preference for insurance and long-shot gambles is not confined to individuals with low wealth (whose wealth falls in the domain of the lower concave segment) but rather to individuals with wealth at all levels. So, rather than interpret the Friedman and Savage utility function as static, he prefers to assume that as an individual's wealth changes, the utility function will, perhaps with some short delay, move horizontally, tending to keep the individual's current wealth, low or high, at the origin. This may be the first occurrence of a formally expressed habit formation or reference-dependent behavioral argument in financial economics, anticipating by 17 years the "prospect theory" of Kahneman-Tversky (1979).[30] Markowitz's full theory supposes that an individual's utility function is monotonically increasing and bounded above and below—to avoid the generalized St. Petersburg Paradox (Menger 1934)—and has three inflection points, with the middle inflection point at the origin (the individual's customary wealth level). The first inflection point to the left of the origin separates a convex segment (the farthest left) and a concave segment ending at the origin, and the third inflection point to the right of the origin also separates a convex segment beginning at the origin and a concave segment (the farthest right). Similar to Kahneman-Tversky (1979), Markowitz also assumes that the concave segment just to left of the origin is steeper (that is, more concave) than the convex segment to the right of the origin. This implies that the individual will tend to ignore symmetric gambles but be quite interested in gambles that are highly skewed to the right (long shots or lotteries).

Markowitz argues that behavior that seems to indicate a willingness to accept symmetric gambles is often part of a strategy in which the individual is making a sequence of bets and plans to increase the size of future bets if the person has been winning, and decrease the size of future bets if he has been losing. Taken together, this compound gamble is skewed to the right around the individual's customary wealth, and therefore is just the sort of overall gamble that Markowitz's theory predicts will be attractive. This is the earliest example of a description I can find of a dynamic strategy that produces nonsymmetric outcomes (in this case, similar to a call), anticipating by 20 years the Black-Scholes (1973) equivalence between dynamic strategies and options.

For many years, the Friedman-Savage and Markowitz departures from strictly concave utility were largely discounted. Apparently risk-preferring behavior was explained by the inherent "joy of gambling" that appeals to some individuals. A common proof is that individuals seldom stake a large fraction of their wealth on a fair or an unfair gamble. Instead, they bet only small amounts, perhaps repetitively. However, more recently, the prospect theory of Kahneman-Tversky (1979) has revived interest in utility functions that have a convex region.

In 2002, Daniel Kahneman was awarded the Nobel Prize in Economic Science "for having integrated insights from psychological research into economic science, especially concerning human judgment and decision-making under uncertainty."

1949 Holbrook Working, "The Investigation of Economic Expectations," *American Economic Review* 39, No. 3 (May 1949), pp. 150–166.

RANDOM WALK, MARTINGALES, EFFICIENT MARKETS

Kendall (1953) writes:

> *It may be that the motion [of stock prices] is genuinely random and that what looks like a purposive movement over a long period is merely a kind of economic Brownian motion. But economists—and I cannot help sympathizing with them—will doubtless resist any such conclusion very strongly. (p. 18)*[31]

The fear that the phenomenon one is examining is just random, having neither rhyme nor reason, is the primal fear of the scientist. However, Working (1949/May) observes, perhaps for the first time—apart from Bachelier (1900)—that this is precisely what a good economist would expect from price changes. The profit-seeking behavior of investors will tend to eliminate any predictable movement in prices, leaving a random walk as the only equilibrium outcome:

> *[I]f the futures prices are subject only to necessary inaccuracy (that irreducible minimum of inaccuracy which must result from response of prices to unpredictable changes in supply and in consumption demand schedules), the price changes will be completely unpredictable. The proposition is readily proved from a consideration of the alternative condition in which price changes are predictable. If it is possible under any given combination of circumstances to predict future price changes and have*

the predictions fulfilled, it follows that the market expectations must have been defective; ideal market expectations would have taken full account of the information which permitted successful prediction of the price change. . . . Apparent imperfection of professional forecasting, therefore, may be evidence of perfection of the market. The failures of stock market forecasters, to which we referred earlier, reflect credit on the market. . . . The fundamental statistical basis for discriminating between necessary and objectionable inaccuracy is that necessary inaccuracy produces price changes among which all serial correlations tend to be zero, whereas objectionable inaccuracy tends to produce price changes which have certain serial correlations that differ significantly from zero. (pp. 159, 160, 163)[32]

Although subsequent work has shown this explanation to be over-simplified and incorrect, it has nonetheless become part of the fabric of everyday thinking about markets and is no doubt, in practice, a very useful and close approximation to the truth (particularly over the short run).

So Working provides perhaps the first formulation of the random walk interpretation of what later became known as "efficient markets" (Fama 1965; 1970/May). In [Working (1958)] "A Theory of Anticipatory Prices," *American Economic Review* 48, No. 2 (May 1958), pp. 188–199, Working carries this one logical step further and observes that as a consequence, the current price is the best guess about the future price—what later became known as the "martingale" interpretation of efficient markets (Samuelson 1965).

Another paper often cited for an observation similar to Working's economic interpretation of random walks is [Roberts (1959)] Harry V. Roberts, "Stock Market 'Patterns' and Financial Analysis: Methodological Suggestions," *Journal of Finance* 14, No. 1 (March 1959), pp. 1–10; reprinted in *The Random Character of Stock Market Prices*, edited by Paul H. Cootner (London: Risk Publications, 2000), pp. 7–17. By 1961, the random walk hypothesis was clearly ingrained into the fabric of investment theory. For example, Alexander (1961) could write:

If, however, there are really trends in earnings, so that an increase in earnings this year implies a higher probability of an increase next year than do stable or declining earnings, the stock price right now should reflect these prospects by a higher price and a higher price-to-earnings ratio. . . . If one were to start out with the assumption that a stock or commodity speculation is a "fair game" with equal expectation of gain or loss or, more accurately, with an expectation of zero gain, one would be well on the way to picturing the behavior of speculative prices as a random walk. (pp. 238, 239)

The Classical Period
1950–1980

1951 **John C. Clendenin**, "Quality versus Price as Factors Influencing Common Stock Price Fluctuations," *Journal of Finance* 6, No. 4 (December 1951), pp. 398–405.

VOLATILITY

Clendenin (1951) may be the first to investigate some of the determinants of stock price volatility. In particular, Clendenin confirms one of the predictions of market rationality: Other things being equal, the volatility of the return of a high-priced stock and the volatility of the return of an otherwise similar low-priced stock should be the same. This finding was later confirmed with a more careful analysis by A. James Heins and Stephen L. Allison in [Heins-Allison (1966)] "Some Factors Affecting Stock Price Volatility," *Journal of Finance* 39, No. 1 (January 1966), pp. 19–23. This hypothesis is not to be confused with the suggestion of Black (1976) that the volatility of the return of a given stock typically varies inversely with its stock price. The former is a cross-sectional hypothesis and this latter is a time-series hypothesis.

1952 **Harry M. Markowitz**, "Portfolio Selection," *Journal of Finance* 7, No. 1 (March 1952), pp. 77–91.

1952 **Andrew D. Roy**, "Safety First and the Holding of Assets," *Econometrica* 20, No. 3 (July 1952), pp. 431–449.

1959 **Harry M. Markowitz**, *Portfolio Selection: Efficient Diversification of Investments*, Cowles Foundation Monograph #16 (New York: John Wiley & Sons, 1959); reprinted in a second edition with Markowitz's hindsight comments on several chapters and with an additional bibliography supplied by Mark Rubinstein (Malden, MA: Blackwell, 1991).

DIVERSIFICATION, PORTFOLIO SELECTION,
MEAN-VARIANCE ANALYSIS, COVARIANCE, RISK AVERSION,

LAW OF LARGE NUMBERS, EFFICIENT SET,
CRITICAL LINE ALGORITHM, LONG-TERM INVESTMENT,
SEMIVARIANCE, MARKET MODEL

The assumption that an investor maximizes the expected return of his portfolio implies that he will place all his eggs in one basket, the single security with the highest expected return, and "watch it"—the advice once given by the industrialist and philanthropist Andrew Carnegie.[1] But this leaves unexplained the pervasiveness of diversification. Markowitz (1952/March) is the first mathematical formalization in English of the idea of diversification of investments, the financial version of "the whole is greater than the sum of its parts": Through diversification, risk can be reduced without changing expected portfolio return. Markowitz postulates that an investor should maximize expected portfolio return (μ_p) while minimizing portfolio variance of return (σ_p^2). Variance may have first been suggested as a measure of economic risk by Fisher (1906), reprinted in 1965, pp. 406–410. Jacob Marschak in [Marschak (1938)] "Money and the Theory of Assets," *Econometrica* 6, No. 4 (October 1938), pp. 311–325 (see in particular p. 320), suggested using the means and the covariance matrix of consumption of commodities as a first-order approximation in measuring utility. Markowitz instead looked directly at the single variable of portfolio return and showed how one could, in practice, calculate the mean-variance efficient set: for each possible level of portfolio expected return, the portfolio with the lowest variance of return.

Probably the most important aspect of Markowitz's work was to show that it is not a security's own risk, perhaps as measured by security variance, that is important to an investor, but rather the contribution the security makes to the variance of the entire *portfolio*—and this was primarily a question of its covariance with all the other securities in the portfolio. This follows from the relation between the variance of the return of a portfolio (σ_p^2) and the variance of return of its constituent securities (σ_j^2 for $j = 1, 2, \ldots, m$):

$$\sigma_P^2 = \Sigma_j x_j^2 \sigma_j^2 + \Sigma_j \Sigma_{k \neq j} x_j x_k \rho_{jk} \sigma_j \sigma_k$$

where the x_j are the portfolio proportions (that is, the fraction of the total value of the portfolio held in security j so that $\Sigma_j x_j = 1$) and ρ_{jk} is the correlation of the returns of securities j and k. Therefore, $\rho_{jk} \sigma_j \sigma_k$ is the covariance of their returns. This seems to be the first occurrence of this equation in a published paper on financial economics written in English.

So the decision to hold a security should not be made simply by comparing its expected return and variance to others', but rather the decision to hold any security would depend on what other securities the investor wanted to hold. Securities cannot be properly evaluated in isolation, but only as a group. This perspective was clearly missing from Williams (1938), from Buffett (1984), and from Graham-Dodd (1934); and even in as late as the revised version of *Security Analysis* in 1962, it received scant comment. Markowitz's approach is now commonplace among institutional portfolio managers.

One might ask why Markowitz's insight had been so long in coming. As noted, Williams (1938) argued that risk could be diversified away and was therefore of modest consequence. In [Hicks (1931)] "The Theory of Uncertainty and Profit," *Economica* 0, No. 32 (May 1931), pp. 170–189, John R. Hicks comes tantalizingly close. Hicks argues that diminishing marginal utility suggests that investors will demand extra expected return for bearing risk. But Hicks argues that some risk can be reduced by its transfer to other parties who are more willing to bear risk via insurance or hedging. He also suggests that a key motivation behind firms with many stockholders is to allow the firm to expand while spreading its risk to many investors. And then Hicks falls into the law of large numbers trap, arguing that diversification both across a large number of investments and over time will make the remaining overall risk minimal—a double error:

> *Finally, it must be asked—what light is thrown by the foregoing on the general question of the influence of risk on the distribution of the National Dividend. . . . Most of the groups of persons whose resources with which we are concerned in the theory of distribution seem to be large enough for nearly all risks they bear to cancel out in a moderate period of time. (p. 187)*[2]

But Hicks qualifies this by writing:

> *[T]he affairs of a group, large enough and homogeneous enough to be a convenient object of economic discussion, may fail to be independent. . . . The most obvious are changes in the general level of prices. (p. 188)*

However, Hicks clearly believes this dependence is a second-order problem and does not pursue its implications. He repeats this reliance on the law of large numbers a second time in [Hicks (1935)] "A Suggestion for Simplifying the Theory of Money," *Economica*, New Series 2, No. 5 (February 1935), pp. 1–19 (in particular p. 9).

Contrast this with Markowitz, who states simply:

This presumption that the law of large numbers applies to a port-folio of securities cannot be accepted. The returns from securities are too inter-correlated. Diversification cannot eliminate all variance. (p. 79)[3]

And this key observation encouraged him to take the next steps that others before him had not seen as necessary.

Markowitz argues that investors dislike variance of portfolio return since they are averse to risk. Hicks, in [Hicks (1962)] "Liquidity," *Economic Journal* 72, No. 288 (December 1962), pp. 787–802, his Presidential Address to the Royal Economic Society, instead makes the case that investors dislike variance because it increases the probability that forced selling of securities with significant liquidation costs will be required to meet liquidity needs (that is, consumption), an argument essentially similar to Keynes (1937).

Roy (1952) independently sets down the same equation relating portfolio variance of return to the variances of return of the constituent securities. He develops a similar mean-variance efficient set. Whereas Markowitz left it up to the investor to choose where within the efficient set he would invest, Roy advised choosing the single portfolio in the mean-standard deviation efficient set that maximizes $(\mu_p - d)/\sigma_p$, where d is a "disaster level" return the investor places a high priority not falling below—a ratio similar in spirit to the now popular Sharpe ratio (Sharpe 1966). It is easy to see that if the portfolio return is normally distributed, then his criterion is equivalent to minimizing the probability that the realized portfolio return will end up below d. Roy is thus the first researcher writing in English to emphasize the preference asymmetry between upside and downside outcomes. Many years later, comparing Roy's paper to his own, Markowitz charitably writes in [Markowitz (1999)] "The Early History of Portfolio Theory: 1600–1960," *Financial Analysts Journal* 55, No. 4 (July/August 1999), pp. 5–16:

On the basis of Markowitz (1952/March), I am often called the father of modern portfolio theory (MPT), but Roy (1952) can claim an equal share of this honor. (p. 5)

Markowitz was ultimately interested in providing investors with a workable methodology that would actually be used to make real investment decisions. Therefore, in [Markowitz (1956)] Harry M. Markowitz, "The Optimization of a Quadratic Function Subject to Linear Constraints," *Naval Research Logistics Quarterly* 3 (1956), pp. 111–133, he works out in detail his numerical critical line algorithm for deriving the efficient set, applying mathematical programming results developed by Harold W. Kuhn (July 29, 1925–) and Albert William Tucker (November 28, 1905–January 25, 1995), in [Kuhn-Tucker (1951)] "Nonlinear Programming," *Proceedings of the 2nd Berkeley Symposium on Mathematical Statistics and Probability*, edited by J. Neyman (Berkeley: University of California Press, 1951), pp. 481–492, and George B. Dantzig (1914–May 13, 2005), A. Orden, and P. Wolfe, in [Dantzig-Orden-Wolfe (1956)] "The Generalized Simplex Method for Minimizing a Linear Form under Linear Inequality Restrictions," *Pacific Journal of Mathematics 5*, No. 2 (June 1955).

Markowitz (1959) contains an extended and detailed development of the mean-variance portfolio choice model of Markowitz (1952/March), purposely designed for access by readers with modest quantitative background. In very simple terms, Markowitz develops the mathematics of diversification. He also strives to find a way to reconcile his mean-variance criterion with the maximization of the expected utility of wealth after many reinvestment periods.

The book also foreshadows several avenues of future research. (1) Markowitz advises using the strategy of maximizing the expected logarithmic utility of return each period for investors with a long-term horizon, and he develops a useful quadratic approximation to this strategy that allows the investor to choose portfolios based on mean and variance. (2) Markowitz actually recommends semivariance as a replacement for variance as a measure of risk on the grounds that it is realistically superior, and investigates its properties and optimal portfolio computing procedures:

> *Analysis based on semi-variance tends to produce better portfolios than those based on variance. Variance considers extremely high and extremely low returns equally desirable. An analysis based on variance seeks to eliminate both extremes. An analysis based on semi-variance, on the other hand, concentrates on reducing losses. (p. 194, 1st edition)*

(3) He outlines the diagonal or market model in an extended footnote, which later, at Markowitz's suggestion, Sharpe (1963) will develop more fully. (4) Insisting that investors choose their portfolios to maximize expected utility according to the Savage (1954) axioms, he compares several alternative measures of risk: standard deviation, semivariance, expected value of loss, expected absolute deviation, probability of loss, and maximum loss. (5) Markowitz lays out how to solve the multiperiod expected utility of consumption problem by using the backwards recursive technique of dynamic programming.

In 1970 when Markowitz assessed the chief subsequent discoveries that his 1959 book had not encompassed, he concluded as he wrote in historical perspective (1999):

> *As compared to later analyses, the chapter 13 consumption-investment game was in discrete time rather than in continuous time (as in Merton (1969/September)), did not reflect the discovery of myopic utility functions (as did Mossin (1968) and Samuelson (1969)), and did not consider the behavior of a market populated by consumer/investors playing this game [as in Sharpe (1964)]. (p. 9)*[4]

Thanks to his work in the 1950s on portfolio selection, in 1990 Markowitz was awarded the Nobel Prize in Economic Science.

1953   Kenneth Joseph Arrow, "Le rôle de valeurs boursières pour la répartition le meilleure des risques," in *Econométrie, Colloques Internationaux du Centre National de la Recherche Scientifique* 11 (1953), pp. 41–47; translated into English as "The Role of Securities in the Optimal Allocation of Risk Bearing," *Review of Economic Studies* 31, No. 2 (April 1964), pp. 91–96; reprinted with new commentary as Essay 4 in *Essays in the Theory of Risk Bearing* (Chicago: Markham, 1971), pp. 121–133; reprinted in *Collected Papers of Kenneth J. Arrow: General Equilibrium*, Volume II (Cambridge, MA: Harvard University Press, 1983), pp. 46–47.

1965/c   Kenneth Joseph Arrow, "Insurance, Risk and Resource Allocation," Essay 5 in *Essays in the Theory of Risk Bearing* (Chicago: Markham, 1971), pp. 134–143 (first published in 1965 as Lecture 3 in *Aspects of the Theory of Risk Bearing*, pp. 45–56, Yrjo Jahnsson Lectures, Helsinki); reprinted in *Collected Papers of Kenneth J. Arrow: The Economics of Information*, Volume IV (Cambridge, MA: Harvard University Press, 1984), pp. 77–86.

1968   Roy Radner (June 29, 1927–), "Competitive Equilibrium under Uncertainty," *Econometrica* 36, No. 1 (January 1968), pp. 31–58.

1970   Jacques H. Drèze (1929–), "Market Allocation under Uncertainty," *European Economic Review* 2, No. 1 (Winter 1970), pp. 133–165.

STATE-SECURITIES, COMPLETE MARKETS, STATE-PRICES,
MARKET-EQUIVALENCE THEOREM, DYNAMIC COMPLETENESS,
PORTFOLIO REVISION, MORAL HAZARD,

RISK-NEUTRAL VS. SUBJECTIVE PROBABILITY,
SEQUENTIAL MARKETS,
EXISTENCE AND OPTIMALITY OF COMPETITIVE EQUILIBRIUM

Arrow (1953) may be the most important paper ever written for financial economics. The concept of a competitive equilibrium under uncertainty and the derivation of its optimality seem to have appeared for the first time in this paper. Arrow shows how the certainty economy described in the first six chapters of Debreu (1959) can easily be generalized to deal with uncertainty provided consumers are (weakly) risk averse. To do so, he invents the idea of a state-security (sometimes called a "state-contingent claim," "pure security" or "Arrow-Debreu security"): a security that pays off one unit of the numeraire in one and only one future state. He then assumes that at the beginning of the economy a "complete market" of state-securities exists, that is, one state-security for every possible state. It is fairly easy to see that Debreu's conclusions concerning the existence and optimality of competitive equilibrium remain unchanged (with the additional assumption of risk aversion).

In two papers in the mid-1960s, Jack Hirshleifer in [Hirshleifer (1965)] "Investment Decision under Uncertainty: Choice Theoretic Approaches," *Quarterly Journal of Economics* 79, No. 4 (November 1965), pp. 509–536, and [Hirshleifer (1966)] "Investment Decision under Uncertainty: Applications of the State-Preference Approach," *Quarterly Journal of Economics* 80, No. 2 (May 1966), pp. 252–277, developed a number of applications using state-prices and state-securities, including an analysis of risk aversion, the debt-versus-equity decisions of firms, and the discount rate for public investments. He contrasts what he calls the "state-preference approach" to the mean-variance approach of Markowitz (1959), Sharpe (1964), and others. In each case, he seeks to show that formulating economic issues in terms of state-prices and state-securities often leads to an analysis that is simultaneously more simplified and more general, while reaching similar conclusions.

A key implication of Arrow's results might be called the "market-equivalence theorem": Consider an economy with just as many different securities as states, commonly called a complete market. The equilibrium portfolio choices of each investor and the equilibrium security prices will be the same in that economy as in an otherwise identical economy, but where the original securities are replaced with a full set of state-securities. Once we have the solution in terms of state-prices and state-securities, we can then combine the state-securities into portfolios that have the same payoffs as the original securities and express the solution in terms of choices and prices of the original securities. We can also quite easily then value the original securities in terms of state-prices.

Illustration of Completing the Market

To illustrate this, consider a three-state economy facing a future of either recession, normality, or prosperity. The payoff from an asset corresponding to each of these states is:

$$\text{Asset payoff} = [1\ 2\ 3]$$

By holding a units, an investor can create the more general payoff [a $2a$ $3a$]. Adding riskless cash as a second security, the payoff is the same in every state:

$$\text{Cash payoff} = [1\ 1\ 1]$$

By holding as well c units of cash, an investor can now create the payoff [$a + c$, $2a + c$, $3a + c$]. The investor can purchase the payoff [0 1 2] since [1 2 3] – [1 1 1] = [0 1 2].

Note, however, that with just the asset and cash, the investor cannot purchase the payoff [1 0 0] since there are no values of a and c such that $a[1\ 2\ 3] + c[1\ 1\ 1] = [1\ 0\ 0]$.

Consider a third security:

$$\text{Derivative payoff} = [1\ 1\ 0]$$

By holding as well d units of the derivative, an investor can create the payoff [$a + c + d$, $2a + c + d$, $3a + c$]. Observe more significantly that the investor can now create state-securities (a "basis vector"):

$$[1\ 0\ 0] = -[1\ 2\ 3] + 3[1\ 1\ 1] - [1\ 1\ 0]$$
$$[0\ 1\ 0] = [1\ 2\ 3] - 3[1\ 1\ 1] + 2[1\ 1\ 0]$$
$$[0\ 0\ 1] = 0[1\ 2\ 3] + [1\ 1\ 1] - [1\ 1\ 0]$$

Therefore, having constructed these, fully arbitrary payoffs are now possible using the state-securities (implying a complete market) since

$$[x\ y\ z] = x[1\ 0\ 0] + y[0\ 1\ 0] + z[0\ 0\ 1]$$

As subsequent research has shown—for example, Rubinstein (1974)—it is frequently much easier to derive results using the equivalent economy with state securities in place of the original economy. In effect, the first-order conditions of the economy with state securities invert the matrix of the first-order conditions of the original economy.

Solving the Inverse Problem: Inferring State Prices from Security Prices

We can state the value of traded securities in terms of the value of a portfolio of state-securities. As an example, consider again a three-state economy where π_1, π_2, π_3 are the current state-prices attached to each state, an asset with payoff [1 2 3] has current price S_0, cash with payoff [1 1 1] has price $1/r$, and a derivative with payoff [1 1 0] has current price C_0. Then:

$$S_0 = [1]\pi_1 + [2]\pi_2 + [3]\pi_3$$

$$\frac{1}{r} = [1]\pi_1 + [1]\pi_2 + [1]\pi_3$$

$$C_0 = [1]\pi_1 + [1]\pi_2 + [0]\pi_3$$

The solution is:

$$\pi_1 = \frac{3}{r} - (S_0 + C_0)$$

$$\pi_2 = -\frac{3}{r} + (S_0 + 2C_0)$$

$$\pi_3 = \frac{1}{r} - C_0$$

Solving for the state-prices in terms of the prices of the traded securities is called the "inverse problem." The example illustrates that if the market is complete, the inverse problem can be solved.

As nice as this simplification is, Arrow was troubled by his assumption of a complete market. In practice, the number of possible states is quite large, so the number of required securities would be vast. Somewhat overshadowed by the idea of state-securities, Arrow (1953) also contains Arrow's principal solution to this difficulty: the first published occurrence of the idea that an initially incomplete market can be effectively completed by opportunities for portfolio revision over time—the key idea behind many subsequent models of intertemporal equilibrium as well as modern option pricing theory. For further commentary, see my discussion under Black-Scholes (1973).

Arrow (1965/C) provides a wide-ranging discussion of risk-bearing. Many social arrangements, including most obviously insurance, futures, and stock markets, exist primarily to shift risk from those who are less willing or able to those who are more willing or able to bear it. Moreover, by social pooling of risk though diversification, certain risks can almost magically disappear. Arrow writes, "Under such a system [complete markets], productive activity and risk-bearing can be divorced, each being carried out by the one or ones best qualified." Today this process is called "financial engineering," a term that may have been invented by Mark Garman.

Although a complete market is generally required for an unconstrained Pareto-optimal allocation of resources, in reality markets are far from complete. In this paper, Arrow considers reasons why markets are incomplete and explains several mechanisms that are created in response to make the best of a difficult situation. He singles out "moral hazard"—originally introduced in [Arrow (1963/December)], "Uncertainty and the Welfare Economics of Medical Care," *American Economic Review* 53, No. 5 (December 1963), pp. 941–973, reprinted as Essay 8 in *Essays in the Theory of Risk Bearing* (Chicago: Markham, 1971), pp. 177–222—as possibly the most important factor preventing complete markets. Moral hazard occurs when the existence of a contract itself changes the incentives of the parties involved. For example, fire insurance might reduce the care an owner would take to prevent an accidental fire. As long as the fire insurance company can monitor the insured only at a cost, this will be a problem. A second-best institutional response is coinsurance; this compromise moves the market more toward completeness, but does not go all the way. Other examples of coinsurance include bankruptcy and limited liability laws.

Drèze (1970) is an important but rarely mentioned commentary on Arrow (1953). He shows that the prices of state-securities can be regarded as products of subjective probabilities and risk aversion adjustments and that the present value of an asset can be viewed as its (discounted) expected value where the state-prices equal the subjective probabilities that would adhere in an economy with risk-neutral preferences. These probabilities have become known as "risk-neutral probabilities." Quoting from the abstract,

It is shown that prices for contingent claims to a numeraire commodity have all the formal properties of a probability measure on

the states, but still reflect the relative scarcities under alternative states as well as the probabilities of these states.

Drèze also revisits Arrow's solution for an incomplete market: sequential markets over time. He points out that, although that would seem to conserve the number of markets, it is still generally necessary for agents to know in advance the state-prices established in future markets in order to make their current decisions, even for states that do not end up occurring. So Arrow's solution does not really reduce the information consumers need to make their current decisions compared with a complete market. The same criticism can be made of the Black-Scholes (1973) option pricing model, which assumes that the volatility of the underlying asset can be predicted in advance, since this is tantamount to knowing in advance state-prices established in future markets.

Equivalence of Initially Complete and Sequentially Complete Markets

Consider an economy with three dates, 0, 1, and 2. At date 1, one of E possible states ("events") $e = 1, 2, \ldots, E$ occurs. Then, conditional on what event occurs at date 1, at date 2 one of S possible states $s = 1, 2, \ldots, S$ occurs. For simplicity (and often without loss of generality), I assume state-securities exist. An investor starts out with wealth W_0 which she then invests in available securities. With initially complete markets, at date 0, the investor chooses state-securities that pay off at date 2 contingent on the full state description at that date, which includes the prior event that occurred at date 1 and the following state at date 2, which are denoted by se. The date 0 price, the subjective probability of the sequence e then s, and the number of each security an investor chooses at date 0, paying off at date 2, contingent on the sequence e then s, are denoted respectively by π_{se}, p_{se}, and W_{se}. The investor's risk aversion for wealth at date 2 is captured by the utility function $U(W_{se})$. In this economy $E \times S$ securities are required.

The investor's problem with *initially complete markets* is:

At date 0: $\displaystyle\max_{\{W_{se}\}} \Sigma_e \Sigma_s p_{se} U(W_{se})$ subject to $W_0 = \Sigma_e \Sigma_s \pi_{se} W_{se}$

(Continued)

Equivalence of Initially Complete and Sequentially Complete Markets *(Continued)*

Under an alternative organization of the market, event securities for each event e occurring at date 1 are available at date 0, and then at date 1 depending on the occurred event e, a new market opens up with state-securities newly available for each state s that can then occur at date 2. In this economy, $E + S$ securities are required. The date 0 price, the subjective probability of event e, and the number of each security an investor chooses at date 0, paying off at date 1, contingent on e, are denoted respectively by π_e, p_e, and W_e. The date 1 price, the subjective probability of state s given that event e has occurred, and the number of each security an investor chooses at date 1, paying off at date 2, contingent on s, given the event e has occurred, are denoted respectively by $\pi_{s|e}$, $p_{s|e}$, and $W_{s|e}$. $U_e(W_e)$ associates utility at date 1 with wealth W_e available to invest over the next period. This utility is derived, as specified next, for each event e, from having first solved for the optimal choices for wealth $W_{s|e}$ received at date 2 that can be earned given the constraint of being able to invest W_e only at date 1. $U_e(W_e)$ is called an indirect or derived utility function.

The investor's problem with *dynamically complete markets* (working backwards) is:

At date 1, given event e:

$$U_e(W_e) \equiv \max_{\{W_{s|e}\}} \Sigma_s p_{s|e} U(W_{s|e}) \quad \text{subject to} \quad W_e = \Sigma_s \pi_{s|e} W_{s|e}$$

Then at date 0:

$$\max_{\{W_e\}} \Sigma_e p_e U_e(W_e) \quad \text{subject to} \quad W_0 = \Sigma_e \pi_e W_e$$

To prove equivalence, using the prior two equations, the dynamic problem is equivalent to:

$$\max_{\{W_{s|e}\}} \Sigma_e p_e [\Sigma_s p_{s|e} U_e(W_{s|e})] \quad \text{subject to} \quad W_0 = \Sigma_e \pi_e (\Sigma_s \pi_{s|e} W_{s|e})$$

If pricing and beliefs are consistent, then $p_{se} = p_e p_{s|e}$ and $\pi_{se} = \pi_e \pi_{s|e}$, so that:

$$\max_{\{W_{s|e}\}} \Sigma_e \Sigma_s p_{se} U(W_{s|e}) \quad \text{subject to} \quad W_0 = \Sigma_e \Sigma_s \pi_{se} W_{s|e}$$

Equivalence of Initially Complete and Sequentially Complete Markets *(Continued)*

Then

$$W_{se} = W_{s|e}$$

Observe that the equivalence requires that at date 0, the investor knows the state-prices that would be established at date 1, $\pi_{s|e}$ for all events e, even for the events that do not end up occurring (as Drèze was first to mention).

To illustrate the distinction between state prices, subjective probabilities, and risk-neutral probabilities, consider the possible payoffs from a one-year homeowner earthquake insurance policy (see box below).

Payoffs from a Homeowner Earthquake Insurance Policy

Richter Scale	Damage	Payoff	Subjective Probability	Risk-Aversion Adjustment	Risk-Neutral Probability	State Price
s		X_s	p_s	Y_s	$q_s \equiv p_s Y_s$	$\pi_s \equiv q_s / r$
0.0–4.9	None	$ 0	.850	.9939	.845	.805
5.0–5.4	Slight	750	.100	.9976	.100	.095
5.5–5.9	Medium	10,000	.030	1.0472	.031	.030
6.0–6.9	Severe	25,000	.015	1.1430	.017	.016
7.0–8.9	Large	50,000	.005	1.3787	.007	.007
Sum			1.000		1.000	

The five *states s* are the levels of earthquake damage that could occur during the year.

The *payoffs* X_s are the dollar damages in each state to be recovered by insurance at the end of the year.

The *subjective probabilities* p_s are personal degrees of belief associated with each state.

The variables, Y_s, are *risk adjustment factors*, smaller than 1 for relatively rich states and larger than 1 for relatively poor states.

q_s is also a probability constructed from the subjective probabilities p_s but modified by the risk adjustment factor Y_s; because q_s is so adjusted, it is called a *risk-neutral probability*.

A *state price* π_s is the price that would be paid at the beginning of the year to receive $1 at the end of the year if state s occurs, and $0 if state s does not occur.

The *riskless return* over the (year) is r, so that $r - 1$ is the interest rate.

For simplicity it is assumed that the Richter scale earthquake rating is perfectly determinative of the damage, and that even if the earthquake occurs during the year, the insurance payment (X_s) is not received until the end of the year. The table shows five mutually exclusive and exhaustive events, each generically termed a future *state* (s)—a full description of the relevant aspects of the world. To each state, investors assign a *subjective* probability (p_s) expressing their personal degree of belief the state will occur. Of course, to be probabilities they must all be nonnegative real numbers and sum to one.

One might naively think that the (present) value of the insurance policy would be its expected payoff discounted back to the present by the one-year riskless return r (that is, the riskless interest rate is $r - 1$): $(\Sigma_s p_s X_s)/r$. So if $r = 1.05$, the value of the insurance policy would be:

$$\frac{.850(0) + .100(750) + .030(10,000) + .015(25,000) + .005(50,000)}{1.05} = \$952.38$$

As any student of finance knows, this valuation approach fails to consider risk aversion. A very popular hypothesis contends that individuals receive greater utility from an extra dollar when they are poor (say, high Richter scale states) and less utility from an extra dollar when they are comparatively rich (low Richter scale states). One way to consider this effect is to assign positive risk-aversion adjustment factors Y_s to each state, with the factors being somewhat less than one in rich states and somewhat greater than one in comparatively poor states. This adjustment will place less weight on dollars received in rich states and more weight on dollars received in poor states. I can achieve this by constructing probabilities $q_s \equiv p_s Y_s$ (where the risk adjustment factors have been carefully standardized so that when multiplied by their corresponding subjective probabilities to form q_s, their sum, $\Sigma_s q_s = 1$). So calibrated, the numbers q_s qualify as probabilities since they are all nonnegative and sum to one over all the states. The formula for the value of the policy in terms of these probabilities is: $(\Sigma_s q_s X_s)/r$. Using these probabilities, I would calculate the value of the policy to be:

$$\frac{.845(0) + .100(750) + .031(10,000) + .017(25,000) + .007(50,000)}{1.05}$$

$$= \$1,104.76$$

Notice that the effects of risk aversion have been swallowed up by the probabilities q_s. Using these probabilities to calculate expectations, I have then simply discounted the expected payoff by the riskless return (with no further adjustment for risk aversion) to determine the value of the policy. Hence, the probabilities q_s are called "risk-neutral probabilities." It must be stressed that although they are probabilities, it is not generally true that they will be the same as the subjective probabilities (which express pure degrees of belief untainted by considerations of risk aversion).

"State prices" is a closely allied concept. If I divide each of the risk-neutral probabilities q_s by r and define $\pi_s \equiv q_s/r$, the formula for the value of the policy becomes: $\Sigma_s \pi_s X_s$. Under this formulation, I would equivalently calculate the value of the policy as:

$$.805(0) + .095(750) + .030(10,000) + .016(25,000) + .007(50,000) = \$1,104.76$$

Writing the formula this way, it is natural to interpret the π_s as prices, one each for the receipt of \$1 in its associated state. Hence, the π_s are called state-prices. Correspondingly, a security that has a payoff of \$1 in one state s and \$0 in every other state is called a state-security. Notice that $\Sigma_s \pi_s = 1/r$. This has a natural economic interpretation: The value of a portfolio that pays \$1 in each and every state is the value of receiving \$1 for certain, or $1/r$. Thus, although the state-prices π_s are nonnegative, they are *not* probabilities because they do not sum to one (unless, of course, $r = 1$).

I can summarize this succinctly as follows: In calculating present values, using subjective probabilities p_s considers only beliefs, using risk-neutral probabilities q_s considers the joint effects of both beliefs and risk aversion, and using state-prices π_s simultaneously takes account of beliefs, risk aversion, and time. Academics love different reformulations of present value results. The flavor currently in favor is based on the stochastic discount factor, $Z_s \equiv \pi_s/p_s$. Using this, I have $\Sigma_s p_s X_s Z_s$; using expectation notation, this is usually more simply written as $E(XZ)$.

The idea of risk-neutral probabilities probably made its first appearance in Drèze's much earlier presentation of this paper in September 1965 at the First World Congress of the Econometric Society, or perhaps in even earlier work of Arrow. The concept was apparently independently discovered by Paul Anthony Samuelson and Robert C. Merton in [Samuelson-Merton (1969)] "A Complete Model of Warrant Pricing That Maximizes Utility," *Industrial Management Review* 10 (Winter 1969), pp. 17–46, reprinted in *The Collected Scientific Papers of Paul A. Samuelson*, Volume 3 (Cambridge, MA: MIT Press, 1972), pp. 818–847, and reprinted in Robert C. Merton, *Continuous-Time Finance*, Chapter 7 (Malden, MA: Blackwell, 1990), pp. 215–254. Their name for this concept was "util-prob."

Another early formulation explicitly writing down state-prices as products of subjective probabilities and a risk-aversion adjustment can be found in Myers (1968), in particular p. 12, equation (6), one of the very few papers in the academic literature to reference an early version of Drèze (1970).

Much has been made of the formalization of Drèze's results by J. Michael Harrison and David M. Kreps, in [Harrison-Kreps (1979)] "Martingales and Arbitrage in Multi-Period Securities Markets," *Journal of Economic Theory* 20, No. 3 (June 1979), pp. 381–408. They make it clear that all that is needed is no arbitrage and permit a continuous number of states. But the economic content of their result is almost evident from Drèze, and certainly with the subsequent results of, say, Beja (1971), Rubinstein (1976/Autumn), or Ross (1977), they make only a marginal contribution to the underlying economic intuition: They rule out doubling strategies, which, over any finite time interval in continuous time, can produce arbitrage profits.

Radner (1968) sees how far the economy described by Arrow (1953) and Debreu (1959) can be stretched. He first shows that the main results related to the existence and optimality of equilibrium continue to go through even if agents have different information about the world, in the sense that different agents can distinguish only between different subsets of states, resulting in a type of incomplete market. However, it still continues to be the case that enough markets can exist at the beginning of the history of the economy so as to make the opening of subsequent markets unnecessary. But this framework begins to unravel when agents have computational limitations. These mean that agents must wait for further information about the world over time before they can determine their full lifetime strategy. Similar problems result if agents receive information over time about the behavior of other agents. Both of these give rise to a demand for liquidity in the form of investments held in a numeraire and in the form of future spot markets—both of which are conspicuously absent from an Arrow-Debreu economy. Radner concludes that:

> *The distinction between (1) uncertainty and information about the environment, and (2) uncertainty and information about others' behavior or the outcome of as yet unperformed computations appears to be fundamental.*

In [Radner (1972)] "Existence of Equilibrium of Plans, Prices and Price Expectations in a Sequence of Markets," *Econometrica* 40, No. 2 (March 1972), pp. 289–303, Radner investigates the potential for a sequence of markets to make up for an incomplete market at any date in the history of an economy. This was first suggested by Arrow (1953). This raises the problem first emphasized by Drèze (1970) that agents need to know in advance the state-prices established in future markets. Radner deals with this explicitly. He defines "common expectations" to mean that all agents associate the same future prices to the same future events (of course, he continues to allow heterogeneous probabilities concerning these events), and he assumes the plans of agents are "consistent" since, at every date the market for exchange is open, the planned supply equals the planned demand for each commodity. He then shows that a competitive equilibrium exists, which he calls an equilibrium of plans, prices, and price expectations.

Arrow won the 1972 Nobel Prize in Economic Science "for his pioneering contributions to general economic equilibrium and welfare theory."

1953   Maurice G. Kendall (September 6, 1907–March 29, 1983), "The Analysis of Economic Time-Series, Part I: Prices," *Journal of the Royal Statistical Society* (Series A, General) 116, No. 1 (1953), pp. 11–25; reprinted in *The Random Character of Stock Market Prices*, edited by Paul H. Cootner (London: Risk Publications, 2000), pp. 99–122.

RANDOM WALK, NORMAL DISTRIBUTION, EFFICIENT MARKETS

Kendall (1953) is one of the first to discover from an empirical analysis that stock prices (actually indexes of stocks in the same industry, trusts, and commodity prices) tend to follow a random walk. He writes:

> *The series looks like a "wandering" one, almost as if once a week the Demon of Chance drew a random number from a symmetrical population of fixed dispersion and added it to the current price to determine the next week's price. And this, we recall, is not the behavior in some small backwater market. The data derive from the Chicago wheat market over a period of fifty years during which at least two attempts were made to corner wheat, and one might have expected the wildest irregularities in the figures. (p. 13)[5]*

He stresses that knowledge of past price changes seems to be of no help in forecasting future changes. Kendall may be the first to note empirically that although individual industry stock indexes have *serially* uncorrelated returns and although one cannot be used in advance to predict another, different industry indexes at the same time have significantly *cross-sectionally* correlated return—the key feature considered in Markowitz (1952/March). Kendall is also one of the first to observe that price changes in common stocks are approximately normally distributed, but with too many observations near the mean and too many in the extreme tails.

Almost 20 years earlier, Holbrook Working also noticed that commodity prices moved randomly in [Working (1934)] "A Random-Difference Series for Use in the Analysis of Time Series," *Journal of the American Statistical Association* 29, No. 185 (March 1934), pp. 11–24. Working suggested that changes in security prices result from the accumulation of many independent influences, some positive and some negative. Before that, Eugen Slutzky in [Slutzky (1927)] "The Summation of Random Causes as the Source of Cyclic Processes" in *Problems of Economic Conditions* 3 (edited by the Conjuncture Institute, Moscow, 1927), translated from Russian into English in *Econometrica* 5, No. 2 (April 1937), pp. 105–146, demonstrated that a series generated by summing random numbers resembled an economic time series complete with cycles.

1953/A   Milton Friedman, "The Methodology of Positive Economics," in *Essays in Positive Economics* (Chicago: Chicago University Press, 1953), pp. 3–43.

ASSUMPTIONS VS. CONCLUSIONS,
DARWINIAN SURVIVAL, ARBITRAGE

Can a theory be refuted by proving that its assumptions are incorrect? Not so, argues Friedman (1953/A). The *only* test of the validity of a theory is the degree of correspondence of its predictions with reality. Indeed, since the best theories tend to have the most parsimonious and simple assumptions, these assumptions are almost always untrue. For example, economists often assume perfect and competitive markets—demonstrably untrue—or that agents are fully rational and capable of lightning-fast exact and complex calculations. Yet these simple and false assumptions are able to explain and predict a wide variety of different phenomena. More accurately stated, economists often assume that agents behave *as if* they are fully rational and perfect calculating machines, not that they actually have these abilities. The relevant question is not whether these assumptions are true, but whether a more parsimonious set of assumptions can explain the same phenomena, or whether alternative assumptions, perhaps equally parsimonious, can explain the same phenomena and then some.

Friedman also offers a famous and very controversial justification for the standard economic assumption of agent rationality based on the Darwinian theory of survival:

Let the apparent immediate determinant of business behavior be anything at all—habitual reaction, random chance or whatnot.

> *Whenever this determinant happens to lead to behavior consistent with rational and informed maximization of returns, the business will prosper and acquire resources with which to expand; whenever it does not the business will tend to lose resources. . . . Given natural selection, acceptance of the hypothesis [of maximization of returns] can be largely based on the assumption that it summarizes the conditions for survival. (p. 22)*

Unfortunately, as others have now shown, it is quite easy to invent Darwinian environments where the irrational survive.

In his companion essay, [Friedman (1953/B)] "The Case for Flexible Exchange Rates," in *Essays in Positive Economics* (Chicago: Chicago University Press, 1953), pp. 157–203, in particular p. 184, he is perhaps the first to develop the arbitrage reasoning that underpins much of logic behind the notion of efficient markets (Fama 1970/May). Using the example of currencies in different countries, he argues that if a security becomes mispriced relative to its fundamentals, arbitrageurs will buy or sell it while hedging their risk with a properly priced close substitute. This will tend to eliminate the mispricing. Moreover, the irrational investors who created the mispricing will suffer losses, which in the long run will diminish their wealth and make them a much less potent force in the market in the future.[6]

Friedman won the 1976 Nobel Prize in Economic Science "for his achievements in the fields of consumption analysis, monetary history, and theory and for his demonstration of the complexity of stabilization policy."

1958 James Tobin (March 5, 1918–March 11, 2002), "Liquidity Preference as Behavior Towards Risk," *Review of Economic Studies* 25, No. 2 (February 1958), pp. 65–86.

RISKLESS SECURITY, MEAN-VARIANCE PREFERENCES,
TOBIN SEPARATION THEOREM, QUADRATIC UTILITY,
MULTIVARIATE NORMALITY

Extending the Markowitz (1952/March) and Roy (1952) model of portfolio choice, Tobin (1958) adds a riskless security and shows that the investor's choice of the proportional composition of his subportfolio of risky securities is independent of his degree of risk aversion (and wealth). Geometrically, consider a graph with portfolio mean return along the y-axis and portfolio variance of return along the x-axis. All mean-variance efficient portfolios lie along a straight line through the riskless return and tangent to the hyperbolic curve of Markowitz's efficient set. This is known as the Tobin Separation Theorem, or more simply as portfolio separation. This means that an investor can break down his optimal portfolio choice problem into two sequential steps: First, given the joint distribution of the returns of risky securities and the riskless return, he chooses his optimal subportfolio of risky securities irrespective of his risk aversion and wealth; second, given the return of this portfolio and the riskless return, his risk aversion, and his wealth, he divides his investable wealth between this sub-portfolio and the riskless security. Tobin also shows that for mean-variance portfolio choice to be consistent with expected utility maximization, either the utility function needs to be quadratic or the returns of all possible portfolios must be jointly normally distributed.

Proof That Quadratic Utility or Multivariate Normality Implies Mean-Variance Preferences

Here is a proof that quadratic utility $-(A - W_1)^2$ (where A is a constant and W_1 is end-of-period wealth) implies choice in terms only of mean and variance:

$$U(W_1) = -(A - W_1)^2 = -(A^2 - 2AW_1 + W_1^2) = -A^2 + 2AW_1 - W_1^2$$

Therefore,

$$
\begin{aligned}
E[U(W_1)] &= -A^2 + 2AE(W_1) - E(W_1^2) \\
&= -A^2 + 2AE(W_1) - [\mathrm{Var}(W_1) + [E(W_1)]^2] \\
&= -A^2 + 2AE(W_1) - [E(W_1)]^2 - \mathrm{Var}(W_1) \\
&= f[E(W_1), \mathrm{Var}(W_1)]
\end{aligned}
$$

Note also that $dE[U(W_1)]/dE(W_1) = 2A - 2E(W_1) = 2[A - E(W1)]$, so $dE[U(W_1)]/dE(W_1) > 0$ if and only if $E(W_1) < A$. Also note that $dE[U(W_1)]/d\mathrm{Var}(W_1) = -1 < 0$ (unconditionally).

Here is a proof that joint normality leads to mean-variance preferences. Let W_0 be the beginning-of-period wealth. Say the end-of-period (random) returns of the available securities are $r_1, r_2, \ldots, r_j, \ldots$ and an investor chooses his portfolio proportions $x_1, x_2, \ldots, x_j, \ldots$ such that $\sum_j x_j = 1$ so that the (random) return on his portfolio $r_P \equiv \sum_j x_j r_j$. His

Proof That Quadratic Utility or Multivariate Normality Implies Mean-Variance Preferences *(Continued)*

problem is to maximize his expected utility of end-of-period wealth by choice of the x_j, that is,

$$\max_{\{x_j\}} E[U(W_1)]$$

where $W_1 = W_0 r_P$ and $r_P \equiv \Sigma_j x_j r_j$ and $\Sigma_j x_j = 1$.

It is a property of jointly normally distributed random variables that any linear combination of the variables is itself normally distributed. Therefore, if the returns of *all* securities are jointly normal, then $r_P \equiv \Sigma_j x_j r_j$ will also be normally distributed. Thus, given jointly normal returns, *any* portfolio an investor can form must also have a normal distribution. Moreover, since a normal distribution is completely described by its mean μ_P and variance σ_P^2, I can write $r_P = \mu_P + \sigma_P x$ where x is a standard normal random variable. Thus, there exists a function f such that:

$$E[U(W_1)] = E\{[U[W_0(\mu_P + \sigma_P x)]]\} = f(\mu_P, \sigma_P)$$

where I regard W_0 as a nonrandom parameter of f.

It remains to show that $U'(W_1) > 0$ and $U''(W_1) < 0$ implies that $f'(\mu_P) > 0$ and $f'(\sigma_P^2) < 0$. Let $n(x)$ be the standard normal density function so that $n(x) > 0$. Then

$$f(\mu_P, \sigma_P) = \int U[W_0(\mu_P + \sigma_P x)]n(x)dx \text{ so that } f'(\mu_P) = \int U'(W_1)n(x)dx$$

It follows from this that because $U'(W_1) > 0$ and $f'(\mu_P) > 0$. Also:

$$f'(\sigma_P^2) = \left(\frac{1}{2}\sigma_P\right)\int U'(W_1)xn(x)dx$$

Again because $U'(W_1) > 0$ and $U''(W_1) < 0$ and $xn(x)$ is symmetric around 0, then $f'(\sigma_P^2) < 0.$[7]

Tobin won the 1981 Nobel Prize in Economic Science "for his analysis of financial markets and their relations to expenditure decisions, employment, production and prices."

1958   Franco Modigliani (June 18, 1918–September 25, 2003) and **Merton Howard Miller** (May 16, 1923–June 3, 2000), "The Cost of Capital, Corporation Finance and the Theory of Investment," *American Economic Review* 48, No. 3 (June 1958), pp. 261–297.

1969   Franco Modigliani and **Merton Howard Miller**, "Reply to Heins and Sprenkle," *American Economic Review* 59, No. 4, Part 1 (September 1969), pp. 592–595.

LAW OF THE CONSERVATION OF INVESTMENT VALUE,
CAPITAL STRUCTURE, MODIGLIANI-MILLER THEOREM,
DOMINANCE VS. ARBITRAGE, SHORT SALES,
WEIGHTED AVERAGE COST OF CAPITAL, VALUE ADDITIVITY,
VALUE VS. STOCK PRICE IRRELEVANCY

Modigliani-Miller (1958) extends to uncertainty the idea in Fisher (1930) that the financing and production decisions of a firm can be separated. It is also the first formal treatment of the Williams (1938) Law of the Conservation of Investment Value, showing that in a perfect market, the value of a firm is independent of its capital structure (Modigliani-Miller's Proposition I). Although this result was clearly anticipated by Williams, Modigliani and Miller argue that Williams does not really prove his Law because he has not made it clear how an arbitrage opportunity would arise if his Law were to fail. To quote Modigliani-Miller's complete comment with regard to Williams:

> *A number of writers have stated close equivalents of our Proposition I although by appealing to intuition rather than by attempting a proof and only to insist immediately that the results are not applicable to the actual capital markets. . .*
>
> *. . . See, for example, J.B. Williams [21, esp. pp. 72–73]; David Durand [3]; and W.A. Morton [14]. None of these writers describe in any detail*

the mechanism which is supposed to keep the average cost of capital constant under changes in capital structure. They seem, however, to be visualizing the equilibrating mechanism in terms of switches by investors between stocks and bonds as the yields get out of line with their "riskiness." This is an argument quite different from the pure arbitrage mechanism underlying our proof, and the difference is crucial. (p. 271)[8]

While this criticism, it seems to me, is questionable with respect to Williams, it does seem on the mark with respect to Walter A. Morton, who writes in [Morton (1954)] "The Structure of the Capital Market and the Price of Money," *American Economic Review* 44, No. 2 (May 1954), pp. 440–454:

The essential difference between the obligations of the same company lies in the priority of claim to earnings and assets. If only one security is issued, it bears all the risk whether it be called a bond, preferred stock, or common stock, and would have the same value provided that the security could share in all the earnings. (I ignore at this point the difference that might be made by the fact that interest payments are tax deductible as a cost before computing federal income taxes whereas preferred and common stock dividends are not.) Similarly, if one individual owned all of the various types of securities issued, his risk would be the same. Legal differences in the event of insolvency or reorganization and tax policy will modify this result. If all the securities were sold in "packages" of bonds, preferred and common, the risk to each owner would be the same as if it were all common stock. It follows accordingly that the over-all cost of money would be unaffected by capital structure if individuals could not differentiate risks. (p. 442)[9]

Morton then goes on to argue that once investors can specialize their portfolios in one type of the firm's securities, so that one investor owns only its bonds, say, and another its stock, then clientele effects (some value safety, and others value the higher return that inures to higher risk) can cause the sum of the values the investors place on their positions to exceed the value had they not been able to specialize.

To show this would not happen in a perfect market, with a lengthy argument Modigliani and Miller prove Williams' Law using a number of assumptions that their own later work and the work of several others show to be unnecessary. For example, Modigliani-Miller assume the debt of the firm is riskless and that, to use their terminology, two firms must exist that are in the same "risk class." This means that, as in the proof that follows, the random variables X_U and X_L are equal in all states of the world.

Modigliani-Miller (1969) strip their proof to its essentials and come full circle, it seems to me, to Williams' original insight. They assume there are two otherwise identical firms (that is, with the same total future cash flows from assets), one levered and one not. They then show that if the sum of the current values of the stock and bonds of the levered firm were not equal to the current value of the stock of the unlevered firm, there would be a *weak arbitrage* opportunity (Proposition I). By "weak" I mean that, among two investments, any investor would prefer one over the other. In that sense, one investment would dominate the other. Unlike arbitrage, this weaker notion of dominance does not require that one be sold short against the other to create arbitrage profits. As Modigliani and Miller construct their new proof, they seem to be using the weaker notion of dominance to circumvent the need to allow short sales.

DOMINANCE Proof of the Law of the Conservation of Investment Value

$X \equiv X_U = X_L$ (future operating income of unlevered and levered firms—same "risk class" assumption)

$V_U \equiv S_U$ (unlevered firm relation between current total firm value and its current equity value)

$V_L \equiv D_L + S_L$ (levered firm relation between current total firm value and the current values of its riskless debt and equity)

r (return on default-free bonds)

Suppose first that $V_U > V_L$. Consider the payoffs of the following two portfolios:

	Current Cost	Future Payoff
Buy α% shares of U	$\alpha S_u \equiv \alpha V_U$	αX
Buy α% bonds of L	αD_L	$\alpha r D_L$
Buy α% shares of L	αS_L	$\alpha(X - r D_L)$
Total	$\alpha D_L + \alpha S_L = \alpha V_L$	$\alpha[(r D_L) + (X - r D_L)] = \alpha X$

DOMINANCE Proof of the Law of the Conservation of Investment Value *(Continued)*

The two portfolios have the same payoff, αX. Therefore, if $V_U > V_L$, then no investors would want to hold the stock of the unlevered firm since they could achieve exactly the same cash flows more cheaply by instead buying the portfolio of the bonds and stock of the levered firm. Therefore, an investment in the levered firm dominates an investment in the unlevered firm.

Suppose, alternatively, that $V_L > V_U$. Consider the payoffs of the following two portfolios:

	Current Cost	Future Payoff
Buy $\alpha\%$ shares of L	$\alpha S_L \equiv \alpha\,(V_L - D_L)$	$\alpha\,(X - rD_L)$
Buy $\alpha\%$ shares of U	$\alpha S_U \equiv \alpha V_U$	αX
Borrow αD_L (on personal account)	$-\alpha D_L$	$-\alpha rD_L$
Total	$\alpha(V_U - D_L)$	$\alpha(X - rD_L)$

The two portfolios have the same payoff, $\alpha(X - rD_L)$. Therefore, if $V_L > V_U$, then no investors would want to hold the stock of the levered firm since they could achieve exactly the same cash flows more cheaply by instead buying the portfolio of the bonds and stock of the unlevered firm. Therefore, an investment in the unlevered firm "dominates" an investment in the levered firm.

Taking these together, if no portfolio dominates, then $V_L = V_U$.[10]

Observe two aspects of this proof. First, it requires default-free borrowing by the firm and that the investor must be able to borrow on the same terms (r) as the firm. Hence this method of proof is sometimes called a "homemade leverage argument." Second, it is not really an arbitrage proof as we would mean it today. In fact, it is very much in the spirit of Williams (1938), who seems also to be making a dominance argument.

In both their 1958 and their streamlined 1969 "dominance" proofs, Modigliani and Miller require default-free debt. For example, in order to capture the limited liability of stock, $\alpha(X - rD_L) \geq 0$ so that $X \geq rD_L$, which implies that there must always be sufficient operating income to meet debt payments. On the other hand, it is equally immediately clear from Williams' proof that risky debt (provided there are no bankruptcy costs) does not alter his Law.

A more modern arbitrage proof requires that short selling with full use of the proceeds be allowed (because the positions taken have to be capable of being reversed). Unlike the Modigliani-Miller dominance proof, this proof does not require homemade leverage (only that the investor be able to buy and sell the firms' securities) and also permits firm bond default.

ARBITRAGE Proof of the Law of the Conservation of Investment Value

Using the same notation, compare the costs and payoffs of the following two portfolios:

	Current Cost	Future Payoff
Buy $\alpha\%$ shares of U	$\alpha S_U \equiv \alpha V_U$	αX
Buy $\alpha\%$ bonds of L	αD_L	$\alpha \min(X, rD_L)$
Buy $\alpha\%$ shares of L	αS_L	$\alpha \max(0, X - rD_L)$
Total	$\alpha D_L + \alpha S_L = \alpha V_L$	$\alpha[\min(X, rD_L)$ $+ \max(0, X - rD_L)] = \alpha X$

The two portfolios have the same payoff, αX. Therefore, with no arbitrage, their current costs must be the same so that $\alpha V_U = \alpha V_L$, implying that $V_U = V_L$.

Modigliani-Miller's Proposition II says that the expected return on equity $E(r_S)$ equals the expected return on the portfolio of debt and equity $E(r_V)$ plus the difference between $E(r_V)$ and the return on debt r times the debt-to-equity ratio D/S: $E(r_S) = E(r_V) + [E(r_V) - r](D/S)$. Today, this seems obvious since this is equivalent to saying that the expected return of a portfolio with two securities equals a weighted average of the expected returns of the securities in the portfolio, where the weights are the value-weighted proportions: $E(r_V) = (D/V)r + (S/V)E(r_S)$ where $V = D + S$. $E(r_V)$ is Modigliani-Miller's "weighted average cost of capital," which of course will be invariant to capital structure since by assumption the numerator of r_V is independent of capital structure and by proof (Proposition I) its denominator is as well.

What both Modigliani-Miller initially and Williams failed to notice, and only became clear later in [Stiglitz (1969)] Joseph E. Stiglitz, "A Re-Examination of the Modigliani-Miller Theorem," *American Economic Review* 59, No. 5 (December 1969), pp. 784–793, with an even clearer argument in his sequel paper [Stiglitz (1974)] "On the Irrelevance of Corporate Capital Structure," *American Economic Review* 64, No. 6 (December 1974), pp. 851–866, is that if risky debt is created as the capital structure is shifted more toward debt, in an incomplete market, a fundamentally new security can be created or an old security destroyed (one that cannot be replicated by a portfolio of preexisting securities in the economy) and this may alter state-prices, which will in turn change the discount rates used to determine the present value of the sum of the cash flows to debt and equity. It is thus possible in the Modigliani-Miller proof that with changes in capital structure, although $V_U = V_L$ continues to hold, both could be higher or lower than they were before the change.

However, in many cases, the securities created by changing capital structure are not new since the patterns of their returns across states can be replicated by forming a portfolio of preexisting securities. In other cases, although firms may be able to creatively innovate new securities, investors do not desire these patterns; so these actions should have no effect on their total value. For example, in the mean-variance capital asset pricing model, since all investors divide their investable wealth between cash and the market portfolio, investors do not desire other patterns of returns across states. Or consider an economy, as outlined by Hakansson (1978) with a full set of state-securities on the market portfolio macro-states and homogeneous beliefs about the residual return of the securities of individual firms conditional on the macro-state. In that case, all investors are perfectly happy restricting themselves to a portfolio containing only macro-state securities; so capital structure changes that create new patterns of residual returns for firms are of no interest to investors. Finally, consider the economy described by Ross (1976/December) in which the returns of all securities are approximately spanned by a small set of priced factors and where the cross-sectionally uncorrelated residual return of any security is small relative to the size of the market and hence can be approximately diversified away. As long as changes in capital structure do not create new priced factors or create large residual return, to a good approximation, capital structure changes will not affect value.

In practice, this influence on discount rates, if any, will typically be negligible, but it is a refinement to the proof that could in rare circumstances prove significant. It may very well provide the motivation for some of the highly innovative recapitalizations we see in practice. Charitably interpreted, this seems similar to Morton's argument.

A second, more modern way to look at the Law is to see it as a special case of present value additivity: The present value of the sum of two potentially uncertain income streams equals the sum of their separate present values. Reading Williams' proof one can hardly fail to notice that, as applied to a firm's capitalization, this is exactly what he is saying.

State-Price Proof of the Law of the Conservation of Investment Value

This proof goes like this. Say a firm has two financial claims (possibly stock and bonds) against its assets, A and B with future random payoffs A_s and B_s, across the exhaustive set of states $s = 1, 2, \ldots, n$, and the contractual arrangements of these claims are such that in every state of the world s, the sum of the payoffs to both of these claims exactly exhausts the operating income X_s of the firm in that state. That is, $X_s = A_s + B_s$ for all states s. Let π_s be the economy-wide state-price for state s. Then, the value of the firm:

$$V = \Sigma_s \pi_s A_s + \Sigma_s \pi_s B_s = \Sigma_s \pi_s (A_s + B_s) = \Sigma_s \pi_s X_s$$

Now suppose the firm changes its capital structure in such a way that leaves its operating income unchanged state by state. In other words (assuming for simplicity that a third claim is not thereby created), in state s, Δ_s is now added to the payoff of asset A and correspondingly, to leave X_s unchanged, Δ_s is subtracted from the payoff of asset B. Also assume, as Stiglitz suggests, that the change in capital structure does not create a new desired pattern of payoffs across states (or destroy an old desired pattern across states). In that case, since agents in the economy continue to face the

State-Price Proof of the Law of the Conservation of Investment Value *(Continued)*

same opportunity sets for desired investments, the state-prices π_s will remain unchanged. Then the new value of the firm will be:

$$\Sigma_s \pi_s(A_s + \Delta_s) + \Sigma_s \pi_s(B_s - \Delta_s) = \Sigma_s \pi_s(A_s + B_s) = \Sigma_s \pi_s X_s = V$$

It is clearly unchanged from its previous value. Note that since the payoffs of the two claims are quite arbitrary, one could be risky debt and the other (limited liability) stock.[11]

A similar proof, under the assumption of "complete markets" (the economy has as many different securities as states of the world), so that the state-prices π_s exist and are unique, first appeared in Hirshleifer (1966). As Hirshleifer points out, "the single-price law of markets" implies that a dollar received in the same state but from the payoffs of different securities must have the same state-price to convert it into its present value (an assumption embodied in the preceding proof). Later Rubinstein (1976/Autumn) argues and Ross (1977) clearly proves that, even in the absence of complete markets, although state-prices will not generally be unique, state-prices will nonetheless exist if and only if there is no arbitrage. This latter result is sometimes referred to as "the first fundamental theorem of financial economics." So the existence and application of the same state-price to a dollar payoff received from different securities in the same state merely requires the absence of arbitrage opportunities.

Another confusion in the literature, and I think in the original Modigliani-Miller paper itself, is the difference between the irrelevancy of capital structure for (1) firm value and for (2) the stock price (per share). Modigliani-Miller assert at the outset that they want to prove the latter, but end up proving only the former. Clearly, from the standpoint of stockholder-centered corporate financial theory, it is the latter proposition that is paramount. It is easy to see how even if (1) is true, (2) need not be. Consider a firm with one risky debt issue, and the firm issues new debt senior to the original debt, using the proceeds to repurchase stock. This will increase the risk of the original (now junior) debt holders and transfer value to the stockholders. Fortunately, the jump from (1) to (2) is, with academic hindsight, easy to see: Given (1), as long as with each recapitalization the original debt holders can intelligently renegotiate their debt contracts, then (2) will hold as well.

Proof of Capital Structure Irrelevancy for Stock Prices

To see this, start with an unlevered firm (with n outstanding shares):

$$V_U = nS_U$$

Now suppose the firm alters is capital structure by buying back m shares and replacing them dollar for dollar with debt:

$$V_L = (n - m)S_L + D_L = (n - m)S_L + mS_L = nS_L$$

where, in general, the stock of the levered firm may sell at a different price per share S_L.

However, since $V_L = nS_L$, $V_U = nS_U$, and $V_L = V_U$, then $S_L = S_U$.

It should be kept in mind that the connection of capital structure irrelevancy to present value additivity (which itself must hold if there is no arbitrage in perfect markets) is made with the benefit of hindsight. Academics, perhaps as late as 1970, remained unclear about the exact assumptions needed for Williams' Law to hold, and there was considerable confusion, particularly in the earlier literature. The field figuratively cut its teeth on Modigliani-Miller's Proposition I in a rite of passage from childhood to adulthood.

So what finally are the assumptions needed for Williams' Law or the Modigliani-Miller Proposition I to hold?

1. No arbitrage (that is, "all equal-sized bites of the pie have the same taste").
2. Operating income (from assets) is not affected by capital structure (that is, "the total pie is fixed").
3. The proportion of operating income that is jointly allocated to stocks and bonds is not affected by the firm's capital structure (that is, roughly, "only stockholders and bondholders eat the pie").
4. The present value function (the economy-wide state-prices) is not affected by capital structure (that is, "the taste per bite of the pie is fixed").

Assumption 1 ensures the existence, but not necessarily the uniqueness, of state-prices. Assumption 2 rules out (1) bankruptcy costs, (2) differential transactions costs in issuing or trading stocks and bonds, (3) managerial incentives to alter operating income that are changed by capital structure such as occurs with employee stock options or capital structure effects on managerial salaries and perks, (4) stockholder incentives to accept high-risk, negative net present value projects that shift value from bondholders to stockholders, and (5) conveyance of information about the operating income of the firm to the market by signaling via capital structure. Assumption 3 rules out differential taxes for income from stock and bonds. And assumption 4 disallows the possibility of creating or destroying desired patterns of returns not otherwise existing in the market by changing capital structure.

The second related proposition that capital structure does not affect the stock price requires an additional assumption:

5. There are no pure transfers between bondholders and stockholders, or between new and old shareholders.

This assumption rules out:

- Pure asset substitution, that is, *ex post* risk-changing projects that can shift value between bondholders and stockholders even though they leave the total market value of the firm unchanged.
- Use of contractual arrangements between bondholders and stockholders that permit *ex post* transfers between them such as in the earlier junior debt example.
- Violations of "strong-form market efficiency" that permit stockholders or managers to use inside information to issue bonds or stock in response to the failure of the market to reflect that information in their relative prices (for example, issue stock when it is overpriced and bonds when the stock is underpriced).

Indeed, it has become commonplace to view the Modigliani-Miller Theorem not as a realistic proof that capital structure is irrelevant, but rather as a way of obtaining the list of reasons that make it relevant. Since the publication of the original Modigliani-Miller paper in 1958, each of these reasons has given rise to its own virtual cottage industry of academic research. Tracing these developments takes us beyond the intended scope of this book since, traditionally, that belongs to the subject of corporate finance as opposed to investments.

Not only did Modigliani-Miller not invent the Modigliani-Miller Theorem, Modigliani-Miller did not even invent arbitrage reasoning or proof, as it is sometimes claimed. As if it were needed, I mention just a few examples.

From the ninth century, we have descriptions of what we would now call a "Dutch book," where a middleman places opposite bets with two different individuals, but secretly at different odds so that he is sure of a profit. According to Edward J. Swan in [Swan (2000)] *Building the Global Market: A 4000 Year History of Derivatives* (New York: Kluwer Law International, 2000), evidence from cuneiform tablets inscribed in ancient Mesopotamia indicates that forward transactions have existed at least since 1750 B.C. A forward transaction (agree today to make an exchange tomorrow) is such an obvious idea often motivated by necessity that this is hardly surprising. What is more, by the sixteenth century, secondary markets in forward contracts had developed across much of Europe with forwards on stock trading on the Amsterdam Exchange. Commodity traders for perhaps many centuries and academics from at least early in the twentieth century clearly understood the role of arbitrage in determining the relation between spot and forward prices, as well as triangular currency arbitrage. The Dutch market for calls and puts (or "opsies" as they were then called), colorfully described in de la Vega (1688), surely included put-call parity arbitrage trading in practice. Fisher (1907) used an arbitrage argument to justify why the present value of cash flows from a capital project must be the same as the present value of the cash flows from a portfolio of securities constructed to match the project. In another context, Hotelling (1931) explains that the price of an exhaustible resource should grow at the rate of interest to prevent profitable shifting of extraction between two periods. We have also seen that Friedman (1953/B) employs notions of arbitrage.

With this in mind, we can now see that Modigliani-Miller's real and enduring contribution was to point others in the direction of arbitrage reasoning as the most fundamental tool to derive results in financial economics. Both Modigliani in 1985 and Miller in 1990 won Nobel Prizes in Economic Science, Modigliani "for his pioneering analyses of saving and financial markets" and Miller primarily for his role in their 1958 paper.

1959 Gerard Debreu (July 4, 1921–December 31, 2004), *Theory of Value: An Axiomatic Analysis of Economic Equilibrium*, Cowles Foundation Monograph #17 (New York: John Wiley & Sons, 1959).

EXISTENCE AND OPTIMALITY OF COMPETITIVE EQUILIBRIUM

Debreu (1959) provides a formal and very general mathematical treatment of the existence and optimality of competitive equilibrium, forming the basis for the standard finance model. Debreu establishes competitive equilibrium theory using the more general mathematical tools from topology rather than calculus. *All* the mathematics necessary for the monograph is stated (although not proven) in the first chapter.

The economy has three sets of variables: (1) decision variables that are chosen by agents, (2) environmental variables that are not under the control of any agent, and (3) other variables that are completely determined by the interaction of variables of types (1) and (2) (e.g., prices). The state of the environment is a complete history of all the environmental variables from the beginning to the end of the economy. An event is a set of states. The most important are dated events that are subsets of all the states describing the history of the economy up to a given date. Commodities are distinguished by their physical characteristics, location, dates of availability or use, and the event at which they become available or used. There are two groups of agents: consumers and producers. Each producer chooses a production plan that specifies his input and output of commodities at each dated event. Each producer is characterized by a production function that describes its ability to transform sets of commodities into other sets of commodities, and is assumed to choose the plan permitted by its production function with the highest present value. Each consumer chooses a consumption plan that specifies his consumption of each commodity at each dated event. Each consumer is characterized by the feasible set of consumption plans available to him, his preferences among these plans (utility function), and his endowed commodities and shares of each producer's profits. Each consumer is assumed to choose commodities that maximize his preferences over his feasible consumption plans. Finally, there is a market for exchange of the commodities to which all consumers and producers have access that is available only at the beginning of economy but permits the exchange of any commodity (e.g., for any future dated event). Payment for each commodity is made only at the beginning date, and all consumers and producers are assumed to act as price takers. There are thus two ways for commodities to be transformed: exchange, which preserves the aggregate amount of each commodity, and production, which can increase the aggregate availability of commodities typically at the sacrifice of a reduction in the aggregate availability of other commodities. Prices are then determined by the equilibrium condition that, for each commodity, the aggregate amount demanded via exchange equals the aggregate amount supplied via exchange (that is, aggregate planned consumption equals aggregate endowed consumption plus planned production). Making the weakest possible assumptions restricting the nature of consumer preferences and producer production functions, Debreu then demonstrates the existence and optimality of the resulting equilibrium. The most problematic of his assumptions is convexity of consumer preference and firm production sets.

Among other earlier papers, this monograph draws on John von Neumann in [von Neumann (1938)] "A Model of General Economic Equilibrium," in Karl Menger, editor, *Ergebnisse eines mathematischen Seminars* (Vienna, 1938), translated from German into English in *Review of Economic Studies* 13, No. 1 (1945–1946), pp. 1–9, where von Neumann was the first to use Kakutani's fixed point theorem to prove the existence of equilibrium, and on Kenneth Joseph Arrow and Gerard Debreu in [Arrow-Debreu (1954)] "Existence of an Equilibrium in a Competitive Economy," *Econometrica* 22, No. 3 (July 1954), pp. 265–290, reprinted in *Collected Papers of Kenneth J. Arrow: General Equilibrium*, Volume II (Cambridge, MA: Harvard University Press, 1983), pp. 58–91, and Arrow (1953). Debreu won the 1983 Nobel Prize in Economic Science "for having incorporated new analytical methods into economic theory and for his rigorous reformulation of the theory of general equilibrium."

1959   M.F.M. Osborne, "Brownian Motion in the Stock Market," *Operations Research* 7, No. 2 (March–April 1959), pp. 145–173; reprinted in *The Random Character of Stock Market Prices*, edited by Paul H. Cootner (London: Risk Publications, 2000), pp. 123–157.

BROWNIAN MOTION, RANDOM WALK,
WEBER-FECHNER LAW OF PSYCHOPHYSICS,
LOGNORMAL DISTRIBUTION

Francis Galton (February 16, 1822–January 17, 1911), in [Galton (1879)] "The Geometric Mean in Vital and Social Statistics," *Proceedings of the Royal Society of London* 29 (1879), pp. 365–367, suggests that many phenomena are the result of independent *multiplicative* effects and that the central limit theorem should then imply that the logarithms of the observations would be normal. This led to the development of the lognormal distribution by D. McAlister in [McAlister (1879)] "The Law of the Geometric Mean," *Proceedings of the Royal Society of London* 29 (1879), pp. 367–376.

Apparently written without knowledge of Bachelier (1900), Osborne (1959) proposes that stock prices follow a random walk. However, unlike Bachelier, Osborne proposes lognormal (as opposed to normal) distributions for security returns, resulting from geometric rather and arithmetic Brownian motion. In the context of modeling stock prices, multiplicatively lognormal returns have several advantages over Bachelier's hypothesis: (1) prices cannot become negative; (2) for any $a > 0$, equal returns more than ae^{μ} and less than e^{μ}/a are equally likely, where μ is the expected natural logarithm of the return; (3) products of returns are lognormal if the individual returns are jointly lognormal (multiplicative stability); and (4) even if the individual returns are not lognormal, a multiplicative version of the central limit theorem holds with a limiting lognormal distribution. However, a key drawback of Osborne's hypothesis is that the probability is zero that the price of a security will fall to zero (no bankruptcy is possible). Also, for *security* returns measured over discrete intervals, *portfolio* returns will not be lognormal (additive instability).

Osborne also proposes that the cause of lognormality derives from the Weber (1851) and Fechner (1860) hypothesis of psychophysics: Equal ratios of physical stimulus correspond to equal intervals of subjective sensation. This is none other than the Daniel Bernoulli (1738) assumption of logarithmic utility. The simple argument is this: Suppose investors have logarithmic utility functions; then the utility of return R will be equal in magnitude to the utility of return $1/R$; that is, $\log R = -\log (1/R)$. Only if each of these outcomes is equally likely will the investors be indifferent to the gamble since then $\frac{1}{2} \log (R) + \frac{1}{2} \log (1/R) = 0$. But in that case, the random variable R behaves like a lognormal variable. This observation anticipates much later work suggesting that lognormal distributions are the outcome of an equilibrium in which investors have logarithmic utility functions.

Observing, as had Regnault (1863) and Bachelier (1900) before him, that in a random walk the variance of the return over a time interval increases proportionally with the length of the interval, Osborne is the first to test for a random walk by measuring the dependence of the variance on the time interval. Osborne also seems to be the first person to publish empirical tests of the random walk model using price series of individual stocks (others had used indexes).

1960 Holbrook Working, "Note on the Correlation of First Differences of Averages in a Random Chain," *Econometrica* 28, No. 4 (October 1960), pp. 916–918; reprinted in *The Random Character of Stock Market Prices*, edited by Paul H. Cootner (London: Risk Publications, 2000), pp. 158–161.

INDIVIDUAL OBSERVATIONS VS. AVERAGES,
SPURIOUS CORRELATION,
INDEX CONSTRUCTION AND STALE PRICES

Many economic time series, rather than a sequence of snapshot observations, are actually reported as averages of data sampled at multiple points. Working (1960) points out that even if the individual observations follow a random walk, the series of averages will be spuriously positively serially correlated. Suppose the sequential observations are $X_0, X_1, X_3, \ldots,$ $X_j, \ldots, X_n$, where $X_j = X_{j-1} + \varepsilon_j$, $E(\varepsilon_j) = 0$, $\mathrm{Var}(\varepsilon_j) = 1$ (without any loss of generality), and $\mathrm{Cor}(\varepsilon_j, \varepsilon_{j+k}) = 0$ for $k \neq 0$. Now, suppose the series is placed in groups of m sequential observations, $(X_1, X_2, \ldots, X_m), (X_{m+1}, X_{m+2}, \ldots, X_{2m}), \ldots$. Note that the variance of $X_{j+m} - X_j = m$. Let the averages $Y_1 \equiv (X_1 + X_2 + \ldots + X_m)/m$, $Y_2 \equiv (X_{m+1} + X_{m+2} + \ldots + X_{2m})/m, \ldots, Y_j, \ldots$. First, Working shows that the variance of $Y_{i+1} - Y_i$ equals $(2m^2 + 1)/3m$. Even for m relatively small, the variance is close to its limiting value as $m \to \infty$ of $^2/_3 m$.

Illustration of Working's Result on Spurious Serial Correlation

For example, suppose $m = 3$ and $n = 6$; then $Y_2 - Y_1 = [(X_3 + \varepsilon_4) + (X_3 + \varepsilon_4 + \varepsilon_5) + (X_3 + \varepsilon_4 + \varepsilon_5 + \varepsilon_6)]/3 - [(X_3 - \varepsilon_3 - \varepsilon_2) + (X_3 - \varepsilon_3) + X_3]/3 = (\varepsilon_2 + 2\varepsilon_3 + 3\varepsilon_4 + 2\varepsilon_5 + \varepsilon_6)/3$. Since the ε are uncorrelated and since the $\mathrm{Var}(\varepsilon) = 1$, then $\mathrm{Var}(Y_2 - Y_1) = (1^2 + 2^2 + 3^2 + 2^2 + 1^2)/3^2 = 19/9 < 3$.

Second, Working shows that the correlation of $Y_{i+1} - Y_i$ with $Y_i - Y_{i-1}$ equals $^1/_2(m^2 - 1)/[(2m^2 + 1)]$. Even for m relatively small, the correlation is close to its limiting value as $m \to \infty$ of $+^1/_4$.

To see this intuitively, suppose a time series has moved up in the first period. If I average the observed prices during this period, this average will likely be less than the closing level for the period. But when I observe the average price in the next period, since the constituent price changes are assumed independent, the second-period average is likely to be higher than the first-period average (since the new prices start out as changes from the previous closing level). Continuing to reason out other possible price changes over the two periods in this way, it is easy to see that using averages will generate spurious positive correlation.

An *ex post* application of Working's result applies to Alfred Cowles 3rd's article, [Cowles (1937)] "Some A Posteriori Probabilities in Stock Market Action," *Econometrica* 5, No. 3 (July 1937), pp. 280–294, in which Cowles reports the results of what may be the first published "runs tests" of stock index price changes. These tests check to see if there are more trends (price changes of the same sign following each other) or more reversals (price changes of opposite sign following each other) than should happen under the null hypothesis of a random walk. Cowles had reported that trends outnumbered reversals, and this was statistically significant at a very high level (although perhaps not economically significant enough to lead to a profitable trading strategy after considering trading costs). In his subsequent 1960 article, [Cowles (1960)] "A Revision of Previous Conclusions Regarding Stock Price Behavior," *Econometrica* 28, No. 4 (October 1960), pp. 909–915, published in the very same issue of the journal as Working's paper, Cowles retracts some of his earlier results, having discovered that some of his index numbers had been computed from the average of high and low prices. Although these are not strictly the arithmetic averages of prices Working examined, the same intuition leading to spurious serial correlation should apply.

In addition, Cowles notes that his earlier study could suffer from another related problem. In most cases, he was using closing index levels, but these index levels actually consisted of (possibly weighted) arithmetic averages of the closing prices of individual stocks. If the individual stocks registered their last trades at different times during the day, the index will be an average of relatively new and relatively stale prices. In practice, since the individual stocks in the index tend to have positively correlated price changes with other stocks in the index, the staleness means that if the index has trended up for the day, it will actually register with a smaller price change over the day than would have occurred had all the stocks traded at their (probably) higher levels at the end of the day. Again, because of the independence assumption, the next day changes in the index will really start from this unreported higher level, inducing, as in the averaging case for a single stock, positive serial correlation in day-to-day index changes.

Alexander (1961) also points out a similar error made by Kendall (1953), who examined 22 price series—19 British industrial stock indexes, 2 cash wheat price series, and spot cotton in New York. With one exception, Kendall found all the series behaved like random walks. The one exception was the cotton series, which caused Kendall to conclude that generalization from several confirming data sets can be dangerous (the fact that the only cows one has seen are white does not imply that black cows do not exist). However, as Alexander writes: "Alas, Kendall drew the wrong moral. The appropriate one is that if you find a single exception, look for an error" (p. 241). It turns out that all the other series were single prices observed at a specified time each week or month, while the cotton series was an average of the weekly closing prices over each month.

1960   **Ronald H. Coase** (December 29, 1910–), "The Problem of Social Cost," *Journal of Law and Economics* 3 (October 1960), pp. 1–44; reprinted in R.H. Coase, *The Firm, the Market and the Law* (Chicago: University of Chicago Press, 1988), pp. 95–156.

COASE THEOREM, PROPERTY RIGHTS,
MODIGLIANI-MILLER THEOREM

Does the allocation of property rights affect production? For example, suppose I have a factory upstream from you that spews out pollutants into the water that poison its use so that your downstream factory must pay additional costs to truck in water to operate. Is the production of our two factories affected by the allocation of property rights that might require that I am liable for the damages I cause your business? A corollary question relates to the role of law: To achieve optimal productive outcomes for the economy, do we need laws that make me liable? Coase (1960) is clear that laws need to specify how the property rights to the stream are distributed; his remaining question is whether it matters just how these rights are distributed between us.

Coase argues that the answer is generally no. To see this à la Williams (1938) suppose a single individual owns both factories and maximizes profits (presumed to lead to socially optimal productive outcomes). If the damage to the profits of the downstream factory caused by the pollution exceeds the increase in profits to the upstream factory from polluting, he will not pollute. Consider instead what would happen between us, assuming we are profit maximizers but I am not legally liable for the pollution. If I continue to pollute, our total profits will be lower than if I were to stop. Therefore, as a profit maximizer, you will come to me and offer to pay me to cease pollution. While the size of that side payment will be a matter of negotiation, it will nonetheless be a zero-sum contribution to profits—my gain will be your loss. Nonetheless, it will be mutually optimal if I accept a sufficient side payment that causes me as a profit maximizer to cease polluting. In that way, there will be more profit to be distributed, depending on the negotiation, between us. More generally, it should now be easy to see that the location of property rights should have no effect on the summed profit (and therefore the individual production) from the two factories.

The Coase Theorem, as this is now called, is quite similar to the Modigliani-Miller Theorem (Modigliani-Miller 1958). Both show that a decision, one with regard to legal structure and the other financial structure, is irrelevant to the allocation of real assets. Both argue that the irrelevancy becomes clear if the full range of opportunities is appreciated—in one case, the opportunity for the two individuals to make zero-sum side payments, and in the other case, the opportunity for an investor to obtain homemade leverage by borrowing or lending outside the firm to offset the firm's own financial leverage. Both theorems also require similar circumstances. The Modigliani-Miller Theorem relies on trading costs that do not favor one financial arrangement over another, and the Coase Theorem presumes that the negotiating cost of arranging the side payment is not affected by the allocation of liability. Also, the Modigliani-Miller Theorem presumes that changing capital structure does not affect state-prices, while the Coase Theorem presumes that the change in the output prices and other costs of the factory are not affected by the different decisions we could make due to the dependency of our personal wealth on the allocation of property rights. I think the main lesson of both the Coase Theorem and the Modigliani-Miller Theorem is to consider the full range of choices that are available to economic agents.

In 1991, Coase was awarded the Nobel Prize in Economic Science "for his discovery and clarification of the significance of transactions costs and property rights for the traditional structure and functioning of the economy."

1961 and **1964** **Sidney S. Alexander**, "Price Movements in Speculative Markets: Trends or Random Walks," *Industrial Management Review* 2 (May 1961), pp. 7–26, and "Price Movements in Speculative Markets: Trends or Random Walks, No. 2," *Industrial Management Review* 5, No. 1 (Spring 1964), pp. 25–46, reprinted in *The Random Character of Stock Market Prices*, edited by Paul H. Cootner (London: Risk Publications, 2000), pp. 237–259, 419–457.

RANDOM WALK, FILTER RULES, EFFICIENT MARKETS

A relatively early paper by Alexander (1961) may have been the first to systematically examine mechanical technical trading strategies (and, as a result, test for nonlinear dependence in price series). In particular, Alexander tests the efficacy of the "filter trading rule": After an X percent rise in price, buy and stay long until the price falls X percent from a subsequent high; then sell short and stay short until the next X percent reversal occurs from a subsequent low; ignore price changes less than X percent. Alexander finds that, applied to buying U.S. stock market indexes using daily closing levels from 1897 to 1959, the filter strategy appears profitable before trading costs and annual profits increase systematically as the filter is reduced. However, as frequently happens in this type of research, subsequent scrutiny and analysis reveals hidden biases and reverses previous conclusions, as in Cowles (1960). Benoit Mandelbrot, in [Mandelbrot (1963)] "The Variation of Certain Speculative Prices," *Journal of Business* 36, No. 4 (October 1963), pp. 394–419, reprinted in *The Random Character of Stock Market Prices*, edited by Paul H. Cootner (London: Risk Publications, 2000), pp. 369–412, points out that Alexander biased his results by assuming that an investor could buy (or sell) at exactly X percent higher (or lower) than the new low (or new high), when in fact because of discretely quoted prices and jumps, he would typically only be able to buy (or sell) at somewhat higher (or lower) prices. Adjusting for this bias in his sequel paper, Alexander (1964) finally concludes on a sorrowful note: "The bold profits of Paper 1 must be replaced with rather puny ones. The question still remains whether even these profits could possibly be the result of a random walk. But I must admit the fun has gone out of it somehow" (p. 423).

Eugene F. Fama and Marshall E. Blume, in [Fama-Blume (1966)] "Filter Rules and Stock-Market Trading," *Journal of Business* 39, No. 1, Part 1 (January 1966), pp. 226–241, point out a second bias resulting from failure to consider dividends. Unlike Alexander, who examines indexes for which dividend adjustment is quite difficult, Fama and Blume look at individual stocks and show that since the profits from short sales (part of Alexander's filter strategy) are reduced by dividends, filter rule profits are reduced, when compared to buy-and-hold 100 percent long investing. In addition, the spurious correlation of indexes noted first by Cowles (1960) may also appear in an index filter test but not in a test based on individual stocks. They also show that for all of the 30 Dow Jones Industrial Average (DJIA) stocks during their sample period, even slight trading costs tend to eliminate profits. However, if these costs are ignored, the smallest filters on the order of 0.5 percent, 1.0 percent, and 1.5 percent do show profits (of course, the smaller the filter, the greater the turnover and trading costs). Wrapping up this line of research, Fama and Blume write:

> *In conclusion, there appears to be both positive and negative dependence in price changes. The order of magnitude of the dependence is so small, however, that our results add further evidence that for practical purposes the random-walk model is an adequate description of price behavior. (p. 240)*

1961 John F. Muth (1930–), "Rational Expectations and the Theory of Price Movements," *Econometrica* 29, No. 3 (July 1961), pp. 315–335.

1972 Robert E. Lucas Jr. (September 15, 1937–), "Expectations and the Neutrality of Money," *Journal of Economic Theory* 4, No. 2 (April 1972), pp. 103–124.

RATIONAL EXPECTATIONS, AGGREGATION OF INFORMATION

Muth (1961) is the first to formalize the idea of rational expectations. Muth adopts a new equilibrium concept that adds this to the usual requirements: The expected future price that agents use in determining their own current demands (and a price that their own current aggregate demands affect) is in fact the correct expectation of that price. Muth calls such an expected price the "rational expectations equilibrium price." In particular, suppose that at date 0 each firm must commit itself in advance to produce output q to be sold at date 1 for price p set in the market at date 1, and suppose that each firm seeks to maximize its own expected profits. p is assumed to be a function D of aggregate output Q, and ε is a random variable summarizing all other stochastic factors affecting demand so that $p = D(Q, \varepsilon)$. The optimal q will clearly be some function H of $E(p)$, so that $q = H[E(p)]$. If there are N identical firms, then the aggregate output will be $Q = NH[E(p)]$. Putting this together, $p = D\{NH[(E(p)], \varepsilon\}$. Therefore, $E(p) = E(D\{NH[E(p)], \varepsilon\})$. This is the additional equilibrium condition Muth adds. That is, at date 0 each firm in determining its output q uses its own estimate $E(p)$ of the future selling price such that the price at date 1 that results from all firms then supplying the aggregate output Q, itself, has the same expectation $E(p)$.

Lucas (1972) carries Muth (1961) a valuable step further, delving more deeply into the process of the formation of rational expectations by supposing that agents infer from current prices (p) specific information about the environment (X) that helps them determine their demands, which in turn helps to determine current prices. Before he observes the current price p, no agent knows everything he would like to know about X. Agents then can use current prices, and their assumed knowledge of the pricing function $p(X)$, to learn more about the current realization of X. In essence, they solve $p = p(X)$ implicitly for X. This is perhaps the first example of a formal model in which information that is used to determine prices is extracted by agents from those prices.

J.R. Green in [Green (1973)] "Information, Efficiency and Equilibrium," Discussion Paper #284 (March 1973), Harvard Institute of Economic Research, Harvard University, uses the same concept of equilibrium but in the context of a model with informed and uninformed agents where the uninformed agents use current prices and their knowledge of the pricing function to extract the information only initially given to the informed agents.

Although Muth is surely the first to formalize the idea of rational expectations, he was not the first to state it. Working (1958) was able to anticipate Muth as well as Lucas, and later Grossman (1976):

Traders accustomed to act primarily on the basis of new information recognized as deserving to have a price effect may view an adverse price movement as a warning that the price is responding to other information which they do not have. Such a trader, having bought on the basis of that information, may therefore sell promptly if the price movement goes contrary to his expectations. (p. 196)[12]

Lucas won the 1995 Nobel Prize in Economic Science "for having developed and applied the hypothesis of rational expectations, and thereby having transformed macroeconomic analysis and deepened our understanding of economic policy."

1961 Merton Howard Miller and **Franco Modigliani**, "Dividend Policy, Growth, and the Valuation of Shares," *Journal of Business* 34, No. 4 (October 1961), pp. 411–433.

DIVIDEND POLICY, EARNINGS GROWTH AND SHARE PRICES,
DISCOUNTING EARNINGS VS. DIVIDENDS,
INVESTMENT OPPORTUNITIES APPROACH

It was once popularly believed that since the stock price equals the present value of all future dividends (Williams 1938), firms that voluntarily shift a higher portion of their earnings to dividends might be able to increase their stock price. In a sequel paper to Modigliani-Miller (1958), Miller-Modigliani (1961) show this is not true. Paradoxically, in perfect markets, a firm's dividend policy will not have any effect on its current stock price. The rough intuition is simple: Ceteris paribus, to the extent a firm pays out greater dividends, it will have less earnings to reinvest. In turn, this will reduce future earnings, which will eventually reduce future dividends. One can have more dividends now or more dividends later, but not both; moreover, shareholders are indifferent to this trade-off. Another way to see this is to ask what should happen to the stock price, ceteris paribus, immediately after a dividend is paid. The dividend can be viewed as a partial liquidation (a dividend of 100 percent of the firm would be a complete liquidation after which the stock would be worth zero). On the one hand, shareholders are better off since they receive the dividend; on the other, they are worse off because the firm now has less to invest by the amount of the dividend; so the stock price falls by the amount of the dividend. Taking these together, the shareholder is no better off as a result of the dividend.

Miller and Modigliani's formal proof of dividend irrelevancy can more easily be grasped using a Williams (1938) style argument than using the argument they supplied. To keep matters very simple, assume certainty and perfect markets, and consider an all-equity firm. To focus directly on the marginal effects of dividend policy, hold the investment policy of the firm fixed. In that case, if a firm decides to increase its dividends, in order to undertake the same investments it will need to issue additional shares. Now consider the position of a single investor who not only owns all the current stock of the firm but also purchases all the new shares as they are issued over time. To such an investor, the present value of his investment in the firm will be:

$$P_0 = \frac{\Sigma_t (D_t - N_t)}{r(t)^t}$$

where the sum is taken from 1 to ∞, D_t is the total dividend paid at date t, N_t is the amount of additional equity capital raised at date t, $r(t)$ is the current (date $t = 0$) annualized riskless discount return for dollars received at date t, and P_0 is the current (date $t = 0$) total value of the equity. To keep the investment policy fixed, if the firm now increases its dividend at any date t to $D_t' = D_t + \Delta D_t$, it must also increase the additional equity raised at date t to $N_t' = N_t + \Delta N_t$. Clearly, as long as $\Delta D_t = \Delta N_t$, then P_0 will be unchanged. So I conclude that dividend policy will have no influence on the firm's stock price since its effects can be undone by issuing new or repurchasing old equity. Seen in these terms, Miller and Modigliani's dividend irrelevancy theorem is transparent.

These arguments seem to hold the investment policy of the firm fixed. But that is not really required. Again, as in the case of the Modigliani-Miller (1958), dividend policy irrelevancy can be interpreted as an immediate and simple consequence of present value additivity. From this perspective, it is easy to see that if a firm reduces its dividend in one period and reinvests the extra retained earnings *in a zero net present value project* that provides increased future dividends, then (provided state-prices are not affected) the present value of the firm's dividends, and hence its current stock price, will remain unchanged. Myron J. Gordon, in [Gordon (1963)] "Optimal Investment and Financing Policy," *Journal of Finance* 18, No. 2 (May 1963), pp. 264–272, makes just this argument under certainty, but mistakenly claims that it will not hold under uncertainty. This mistake was corrected first by Michael J. Brennan in [Brennan (1971)] "A Note on Dividend Irrelevance and the Gordon Valuation Model," *Journal of Finance* 26, No. 5 (December 1971), pp. 1115–1121. A two-line parsimonious proof appears in [Rubinstein (1976/September)] Mark Rubinstein, "The Irrelevancy of Dividend Policy in an Arrow-Debreu Economy," *Journal of Finance* 31, No. 4 (September 1976), pp. 1229–1230.

Since many firms have never paid dividends and it is not clear when they will start, dividend discount models are difficult to apply in practice. Academic accountants, in particular, have tried to find some other equivalent way to value stocks without being forced to specify dividends. One might be tempted simply to discount future earnings. However, David Bodenhorn in [Bodenhorn (1959)] "On the Problem of Capital Budgeting," *Journal of Finance* 14, No. 4 (December 1959), pp. 473–492 (see particularly p. 489), is one of the first to argue that simply discounting earnings is double counting. He writes:

> *The dispute between net income and dividends should be settled in favor of dividends. Consider a firm with a net income of $100 the first year, of which it retains $50 and pays $50 in dividends, so that net income in subsequent years is $105. The net income theory says that the value of this stock is the present value of $100 this year plus $105 next year and in perpetuity. This, however, constitutes double counting of the $50 of retained earnings and the resulting $5 a year addition to the income stream. The correct present value of the firm is the value of $100 this year less the $50 which is retained, so that there is only $50 this year, and plus the $105 which will be earned in each subsequent year. Thus the value of the stock is the present value of the net income stream minus the present value of retained earnings. But net income less retained earnings is dividends, so that we are really discounting the dividend stream. (p. 489)[13]*

In their paper, Miller and Modigliani make one of the first careful attempts to reformulate the dividend discount model equivalently in terms of related variables like cash flows, earnings, and growth opportunities—variables that may be more easily directly estimated than dividends from accounting information. For example, according to the investment opportunities approach, $P_0 = (X_0/r^*) + \Sigma_t I_t[(\rho_t - r^*)/r^*]/r^t$, where the summation is taken from 1 to ∞, X_0 is earnings at date 0, I_t is investment at date t, ρ_t is the annualized rate of return on the investment undertaken at date t, and $r^* \equiv r - 1$. This treats net income from the current assets of the firm X_0 as a perpetuity (hence discounted by r^*) and separate from the net income from future investment opportunities. The gross income from investment at date t is $\rho_t I_t$, and the cost of financing this investment is $r^* I_t$, which are themselves perpetuities (hence discounted by r^*) but starting at date t (hence discounted further by r^t).

The sources of value can be given further detail since X_0/r^* can be broken into two parts: the current firm book value Y_0 and the present value of the abnormal future cash flows on this book value investment, $Y_0(\rho_0 - r^*)/r^*$. So putting this all together, I have a tripartite division of value:

$$P_0 = Y_0 + \frac{Y_0(\rho_0 - r^*)}{r^*} + \frac{\Sigma_t I_t[(p_t - r^*)/r^*]}{r^t}$$

In words, the market price per share of a firm equals the sum of its current book value (that is, the date 0 terminal value of retained cash flows from all its previous investments), the present value of the future abnormal earnings from its existing investments (assumed for simplicity to be a perpetuity), and the present value of abnormal earnings from its future investment opportunities (each assumed for simplicity to be a perpetuity).

Derivation of the Investment Opportunities Formulation of Present Value

Here is a derivation of the investment opportunities formulation from the dividend discount model (Williams 1938). Assume the discount rate is constant so that $r \equiv r(t)$. Define $Y_0 \equiv X_0/r^*$. From our prior discussion, $D_t = X_t - I_t$, $X_0 = \rho_0 Y_0$ and $X_{t+1} = X_t + \rho_t I_t$ for $t \geq 1$. Therefore,

$$D_1 = X_1 - I_1 = \rho_0 Y_0 - I_1$$
$$D_2 = X_2 - I_2 = X_1 + \rho_1 I_1 - I_2 = \rho_0 Y_0 + \rho_1 I_1 - I_2$$
$$D_3 = X_3 - I_3 = X_2 + \rho_2 I_2 - I_3 = \rho_0 Y_0 + \rho_1 I_1 + \rho_2 I_2 - I_3$$
$$\cdots$$

Substituting into the dividend discount model:

$$P_0 = \frac{\Sigma_t D_t}{r^t} = \frac{\rho_0 Y_0 - I_0}{r} + \frac{\rho_0 Y_0 + \rho_1 I_1 - I_2}{r^2} + \frac{\rho_0 Y_0 + \rho_1 I_1 + \rho_2 I_2 - I_3}{r^3} + \cdots$$

$$P_0 = \rho_0 Y_0 \left(\frac{1}{r} + \frac{1}{r^2} + \frac{1}{r^3} + \cdots \right) + \rho_1 I_1 \left(\frac{1}{r^2} + \frac{1}{r^3} + \cdots \right) - \frac{I_1}{r} + \cdots$$

$$P_0 = \frac{\rho_0 Y_0}{r^*} + \left(\frac{\rho_1 I_1}{rr^*} - \frac{I_1}{r} \right) + \cdots = Y_0 + \left(\frac{\rho_0 - r^*}{r^*} \right) Y_0 + \left(\frac{\rho_1 - r^*}{r^*} \right) \left(\frac{I_1}{r} \right) + \cdots$$

This approach may have first appeared in simplified form in [Walter (1956)] James E. Walter, "Dividend Policies and Common Stock Prices," *Journal of Finance* 11, No. 1 (March 1956), pp. 29–41 (see particularly p. 32). The more general version appears in Bodenhorn (see particularly p. 490). Alternatively, according to the stream of earnings approach, $P_0 = \Sigma_t[X_t - \Sigma_\tau r^* I_\tau]/r^t$, where the first summation is taken from 1 to ∞, the second summation is taken from 1 to t, and X_t is earnings at date t.

1961   Daniel Ellsberg, "Risk, Ambiguity, and the Savage Axioms," *Quarterly Journal of Economics* 75, No. 4 (November 1961), pp. 643–669.

RISK VS. UNCERTAINTY, ELLSBERG PARADOX,
INDEPENDENCE AXIOM, SUBJECTIVE PROBABILITY

Yes, this is the same Daniel Ellsberg of Pentagon Papers fame. Whether all uncertainty is measurable by probabilities has long been a controversy in economics. The chief advocate of the idea that not all uncertainty can be quantified is Knight (1921), and the chief advocates of the opposite view are de Finetti (1937) and Savage (1954). To show that the issue still has life, Ellsberg (1961) describes a choice of gambles that cleverly sorts this out. Consider two opaque urns, the first known to contain 50 black balls and 50 red balls, and the second containing 100 black or red balls of unknown proportions. You will get a significant prize if you can draw out a red ball in one draw. From which urn do you prefer to draw the ball? In a second chance, you will get a significant prize if you draw out a black ball in one draw. From which urn do you prefer to draw? In each case, if you prefer to draw from the same urn, it is easy to see that you cannot be using the Savage axioms (and are probably influenced by the lack of knowledge about the composition of the second urn). To see this, suppose in both cases you choose to draw from the first urn. If you follow the Savage axioms, in the first chance, one would infer you believe you are more likely to draw a red ball from the first urn; similarly, in the second chance, one would infer you believe you are more likely to draw a black ball from the first urn. Since both statements cannot simultaneously be true, you cannot be using the Savage axioms.

From his experience with the gamble, Ellsberg claims that most individuals prefer to draw in both cases from the first urn. Even after it is explained to them how that preference violates the Savage axioms, many continue to persist in their choice. Diehards like myself, of course, are stubbornly indifferent between drawing from either urn.

To close in on the Savage axiom that is most likely to blame for the failure of the predictions of Savage's theory, Ellsberg proposes a second related gamble. Consider a single opaque urn known to contain 30 red balls and 60 balls that are either yellow or black, in unknown proportion. A single ball is to be drawn at random from the urn. You can make one of two bets with the following payoffs (A) depending on the ball drawn:

	Red	Black	Yellow	
(A1)	$100	$ 0	$0	("Bet on red")
(A2)	$ 0	$100	$0	("Bet on black")

Consider now another choice between two bets under the same circumstances but where the payoffs (B) are:

	Red	Black	Yellow	
(B1)	$100	$ 0	$100	("Bet on red and yellow")
(B2)	$ 0	$100	$100	("Bet on black and yellow")

Savage's axiom, the sure-thing principle, his version of the Marschak (1950) and Samuelson (1966) independence axiom in a von Neumann–Morgenstern (1947) context, says your choice between the gambles in A should not be affected by altering the common yellow outcome in B. Therefore, if you prefer (A1) to (A2), you should also prefer (B1) to (B2).

In Ellsberg's experience, most people prefer (A1) to (A2), since (A1) is merely "risky" while (A2) is "uncertain"; but most also prefer (B2) to (B1), since (B2) is merely "risky" while (B1) is "uncertain."

Illustration of the Sure-Thing Principle

To see this, I can arbitrarily assign utility 1 to $100 and utility 0 to $0, and let p_1, p_2, and p_3 be the subjective probabilities you assign to red, black, and yellow, respectively. Therefore, the corresponding expected utilities of the gambles are:

$$(A1) = p_1, (A2) = p_2, (A3) = p_1 + p_3, (A4) = p_2 + p_3$$

Clearly, if (A1) is preferred to (A2), then I can infer that $p_1 > p_2$. Then, since $p_1 + p_3 > p_2 + p_3$, it must also be true that (B1) is preferred to (B2).

1961   Leo Breiman (January 27, 1928–), "Optimal Gambling Systems for Favorable Games," *Proceedings of the 4th Berkeley Symposium on Mathematical Statistics and Probability* 1 (Berkeley: University of California Press, 1961), pp. 65–78.

LONG-RUN INVESTMENT, LOGARITHMIC UTILITY, REBALANCING, DARWINIAN SURVIVAL

Markowitz (1952/March) concentrates on advisable behavior for an investor with a single-period horizon. Breiman (1961) asks what a "long-run" investor should do who can repeatedly make the same bet, reinvesting his profits as he goes along. Would his optimal betting strategy be any different than if he were faced with only a single bet? Breiman begins:

> *Assume that we are hardened and unscrupulous types with an infinitely wealthy friend. We induce him to match any bet we wish to make on the event that a coin biased in our favor will turn up heads. That is, at every toss we have a probability p > $^1/_2$ of doubling our bet. If we are clever, as well as unscrupulous, we soon begin to worry about how much of our available fortune to bet at every toss. Betting everything we have on heads on every toss will lead to almost certain bankruptcy. On the other hand, if we bet a small, but fixed, fraction of our available fortune at every toss, then the law of large numbers informs us that our fortune converges almost surely to plus infinity. What to do?*[14]

Breiman's answer (for positive expected rate of return gambles even with otherwise arbitrary probability distributions) is to choose a fraction of our fortune at each toss that maximizes the expected logarithmic utility of our fortune after the toss. He advises this because the log strategy possesses a number of attractive features: (1) compared to any different strategy, the log strategy leads almost surely to more wealth in the long run; (2) the log strategy never risks ruin; and (3) the log strategy asymptotically minimizes the expected time to reach a prespecified target level of wealth. Indeed, these features appear so attractive that some have suggested that the log is the best long-run strategy for *any* (nonsatiated and risk-averse) expected utility of wealth maximizer. However, Mossin (1968) shows this conjecture is not true.

Somewhat earlier Henry Allen Latané in [Latané (1959)] "Criteria for Choice Among Risky Ventures," *Journal of Political Economy* 67, No. 2 (April 1959), pp. 144–155, was one of the first to advocate maximizing expected logarithmic utility because of its favorable capital growth properties. His work, initially presented in 1956, was contemporaneous and independent of similar results by J.L. Kelly Jr. in [Kelly (1956)] "A New Interpretation of Information Rate," *Bell System Technical Journal* 35, No. 4 (July 1956), pp. 917–926.

Mark Rubinstein, in [Rubinstein (1991)] "Continuously Rebalanced Investment Strategies," *Journal of Portfolio Management* 18, No. 1 (Fall 1991), pp. 78–81, derives results similar to those of Breiman, but under the assumption that the return of the gamble is lognormal. This leads to simplified derivations and permits the exact calibration of results given the mean and variance of the gamble and the return of a riskless alternative. The paper focuses on the properties of investment strategies that continually rebalance over time between a riskless and a risky security to some constant proportion ($\alpha \geq 0$) in the risky security. Assume X and Y are values after elapsed time t from following two different rebalancing strategies (based on different values of α). Since the risky security is lognormal, X and Y will also be (bivariate) lognormal under continuous rebalancing. A simple expression is then derived for the probability that the first strategy will outperform the second:

$$\text{prob}(X > Y) = N\left[\frac{(\mu_x - \mu_y)\sqrt{t}}{(\sigma_x^2 - 2\rho\sigma_x\sigma_y + \sigma_y^2)^{1/2}}\right]$$

where $x \equiv \log X$, $y \equiv \log Y$, $\mu_x \equiv E(x)$, $\mu_y \equiv E(Y)$, $\sigma_x^2 \equiv \text{Var}(x)$, $\sigma_y^2 \equiv \text{Var}(y)$, and $\rho \equiv \text{Cor}(x, y)$.

Proof of Expression for prob($X > Y$)

For a proof of this, let $z \equiv x - y$:

$$\text{prob}(X > Y) = \text{prob}(\log X > \log Y) = \text{prob}(x > y)$$
$$= \text{prob}(x - y > 0) = \text{prob}(z > 0)$$

Since X and Y are bivariate lognormal, x and y are bivariate normal. Then z must be itself normal with parameters:

$$\mu_z \equiv \mu_x t - \mu_y t = (\mu_x - \mu_y)t$$

$$\sigma_z^2 \equiv (\sigma_x^2 t - 2\rho\sigma_x\sqrt{t}\sigma_y\sqrt{t} + \sigma_y^2 t) = (\sigma_x^2 - 2\rho\sigma_x\sigma_y + \sigma_y^2)t$$

(Continued)

Proof of Expression for prob(*X* > *Y*) *(Continued)*

Since $\text{prob}(z > 0) = \text{prob}[(z - \mu_z)/\sigma_z > -\mu_z/\sigma_z]$ and $(z - \mu_z)/\sigma_z$ is a standard normal variable,

$$\text{prob}\left(\frac{z - \mu_z}{\sigma_z} > \frac{-\mu_z}{\sigma_z} \right) = 1 - N\left(\frac{-\mu_z}{\sigma_z} \right) = N\left(\frac{\mu_z}{\sigma_z} \right)$$

Putting all this together:

$$\text{prob}(X > Y) = N\left[\frac{(\mu_x - \mu_y)\sqrt{t}}{(\sigma_x^2 - 2\rho\sigma_x\sigma_y + \sigma_y^2)^{1/2}} \right]$$

It is easily shown from this that if X is the result of selecting α to maximize logarithmic utility and Y is the result of any different strategy, $\text{prob}(X > Y) > 1/2$. So over *any time period* t, the logarithmic utility strategy will probably beat any other strategy matched against it. Since $\mu_x = E(\log X)$, if α is chosen to maximize this, for a given different strategy leading to Y, that choice will maximize the difference between $\mu_x - \mu_y$, which will in turn maximize $\text{prob}(X > Y)$ and surely make it greater than $1/2$. Moreover, as $t \to \infty$, this probability goes to 1 since $(\mu_x - \mu_y)\sqrt{t} \to \infty$; so we say that given a long-enough time period, the log utility strategy will almost surely beat any other strategy. Also, the expected time in years to reach any pre-specified target return, a, greater than the riskless return, is minimized by the log strategy and equals $(\log a)/\mu$ where μ is the expected logarithm of the return per annum of the log strategy.

Proof of Formula for Expected Time to Reach a Target Return

Here is a proof. Let $a > 1$ be the target return (for example, $a = 2$ means your target is to double your initial stake). The expected time to reach the target return $E(t)$ is:

$$E(t) = \int t\left(\frac{\log a}{\sigma\sqrt{2\pi t^3}} \right) \exp\left[-\frac{1}{2}\left(\frac{\log a - \mu t}{\sigma\sqrt{t}} \right)^2 \right] dt = \frac{\log a}{\mu}$$

where the integral is taken from $t = 0$ to $t = \infty$. Therefore, the strategy that maximizes μ also ends up minimizing $E(t)$.

But how long will it take to be pretty sure the log strategy will be ahead using the empirical reality of the U.S. stock market? Calibrating the model to U.S. data, it would take 208 years for the log strategy to have at least a 95 percent probability of beating an investment of 100 percent in bonds, and 4,700 years for the log strategy to have a 95 percent probability of beating 100 percent stocks. So while the log utility strategy, as is well known from many other papers as well, has theoretically desirable long-run properties, in practice the long run may be long indeed.

An extreme defense of logarithmic utility appears in [Stein (2002)] Hans-Werner Stein, "Weber's Law and the Biological Evolution of Risk Preferences: The Selective Dominance of the Logarithmic Utility Function," CESifo Working Paper No. 770 (September 2002). Echoing Charles Darwin (February 12, 1809–April 19, 1882) in [Darwin (1872)] *The Origin of Species by Means of Natural Selection*, Great Books of the Western World: Darwin (Franklin Center, PA: Franklin Library, 1978), Stein argues that surrogate preferences are formed as the unconscious natural outcome of the struggle for survival:

> *The true preference of evolution is genetic survival and dominance, but for the purpose of efficiently directing our behavior nature has replaced this preference with a rich body of surrogate or instrumental preferences, all too often without even revealing the trick to us. We like to rest after a long walk because we feel tired, and not in order to help our body restore its chemical and physical balance. We avoid pain because it hurts, not because we consciously want to avoid damage to our muscles, tendons, organs or joints. We like to eat because we feel hungry, not to refill our energy reservoirs, and we drink when we are thirsty, not because we have diagnosed that our blood has become too thick. We like it warm when we feel cold, and the other way around, because that gives us a pleasant feeling, not because we know that the body temperature has to stay at 37° Celsius. And of course, we like to have sex when we have found an attractive partner, because this is how we feel, not because we want to reproduce our genes. In all cases, we use our intelligence to find ways to satisfy our surrogate preferences, which basically aim at maintaining our genetic fitness and ensure reproduction, without really making us know what we are doing. (p. 4)*[15]

Stein assumes that humans have lexicographic preferences in that they place survival above all other concerns. He then equates wealth with survival and number of offspring and concludes that preferences must be such that humans never willingly risk zero wealth. Second, he argues that preferences will evolve according to the property of "selective quality," which favors preferences that, with a probability close to one, lead to higher population in the long run. Third, evolved preferences will also have the property of "selective dominance," which results in population path sizes that become infinitely larger than the size of populations with any other preferences. Stein concludes that while nature may have tried many decision rules for managing wealth, once it stumbled upon the rule of maximizing the expected logarithmic utility of wealth, that rule would have forced out all others since it beats all other rules in terms of selective quality and dominance.

1962   James P. Quirk and **Rubin Saposnik,** "Admissibility and Measurable Utility Functions," *Review of Economic Studies* 29, No. 2 (February 1962), pp. 140–146.

1970   Michael Rothschild (August 2, 1942–) and **Joseph E. Stiglitz** (February 9, 1943–), "Increasing Risk, I: A Definition," *Journal of Economic Theory* 2, No. 3 (September 1970), pp. 225–243.

STOCHASTIC DOMINANCE, INCREASING RISK

The von Neumann–Morgenstern (1947) expected utility theorem is silent concerning whether more wealth is preferred to less. To add this condition to the rationality axioms, the assumption is made that utility is a monotonically increasing function of wealth. This raises the interesting question: If all you know is that a rational investor prefers more wealth to less (and his utility depends only on wealth), when comparing two alternative probability distributions of his future wealth, is it ever possible to say that one distribution must be preferred to the other? For two probability distributions of future wealth, Quirk-Saposnik (1962) seek a necessary and sufficient condition such that one of the distributions is preferred to another if and only if the expected utility of one of the distributions is higher than the expected utility from the other, for all monotonically increasing utility functions of wealth. Their condition is this: Wealth distribution A will have this dominance property compared to wealth distribution B if and only if for every level of wealth X, the cumulative probability of wealth under A is lower (or equal) than the cumulative probability under B (that is, for every level X, the probability that wealth $W_A < X$ is lower than or equal to the probability that $W_B < X$).

Intuitive Illustration of Dominance Property

One way to make this intuitive is to consider two identical probability distributions of future wealth A and B such that for all possible wealth levels $W(s)$, probabilities $p_A(s) = p_B(s)$. Suppose, for convenience, the levels of wealth are organized from lowest to highest so that $W(1) < W(2) < \cdots < W(n)$. Therefore, trivially, the expected utility of A and B are equal: $\Sigma_s p_A(s) W(s) = \Sigma_s p_B(s) W(s)$. Now leave B the same but redistribute the probability of A for just two states $k > j$ so that $p_A(k) > p_B(k)$ and to compensate $p_A(j) < p_B(j)$. Clearly, with this change, $\Sigma_s p_A(s) W(s) > \Sigma_s p_B(s) W(s)$. Note also that for every level of wealth $W(h < j)$ and $W(h \geq k)$, $\Sigma_s p_A(s) = \Sigma_s p_B(s)$, where the sum is taken up to h; but for every level of wealth $W(k > h \geq j) = X$, $\Sigma_s p_A(s) < \Sigma_s p_B(s)$, where the sum is taken up to h.

This condition for dominance is superior to conditions based on moments. For example, consider two future wealth distributions across two equally probable states: $W_A = (2 \ 6)$ and $W_B = (1 \ 3)$. A mean-variance moment condition cannot decide between them since A has a higher variance than B. However, the dominance condition implies that as long as more wealth is preferred to less, A is preferred to B.[16]

Josef Hadar and William R. Russell, in [Hadar-Russell (1969)] "Rules for Ordering Uncertain Prospects," *American Economic Review* 59, No. 1 (March 1969), pp. 25–34, and independently G. Hanoch and Haim Levy, in [Hanoch-Levy (1969)] "The Efficiency Analysis of Choices Involving Risk," *Review of Economic Studies* 36, No. 3 (July 1969), pp. 335–346, christen this property "first-degree stochastic dominance." They go on to derive a stronger related condition, "second-degree stochastic dominance," for probability distributions where the utility function exhibits both risk aversion and greed, that is, monotonic conditions on both the first and second derivatives with respect to wealth.

Rothschild-Stiglitz (1970) provides three very general conditions under which an individual will find one gamble (Y) more risky than another gamble (X): (1) Y is equal to X plus noise, (2) every risk averter prefers X to Y, and (3) other things being equal, Y has more weight in the tails than X. The key result is that these three conditions are equivalent.

1962 Edmund S. Phelps (July 26, 1933–), "The Accumulation of Risky Capital: A Sequential Utility Analysis," *Econometrica* 30, No. 4 (October 1962), pp. 729–743.

INTERTEMPORAL CONSUMPTION AND INVESTMENT,
TIME-ADDITIVE UTILITY, LOGARITHMIC UTILITY,
UNCERTAIN LIFETIME, LIFE INSURANCE

Phelps (1962) is the first to consider the multiperiod consumption problem with uncertainty, and so extends Fisher (1930) to uncertain investment returns. Phelps assumes that a risk averse consumer/investor maximizes his time-additive utility function of consumption $U(C_t)$ with constant time preference ρ over a finite lifetime: $\Sigma_t \rho^t E[U(C_t)]$. In each period he allocates his wealth between consumption and an investment in a single risky security with independent and identically distributed returns over time. He solves the problem for the optimal consumption and portfolio choices using dynamic programming as suggested by Markowitz (1959). He shows that in the special case of logarithmic utility, $U(C_t)$ = log C_t, the optimal consumption at each date depends on wealth, time preference, and remaining lifetime, but it does not depend on the probability distribution of the return of the risky security. An earlier paper by Frank Plumpton Ramsey, in [Ramsey (1928)] "A Mathematical Theory of Saving," *Economic Journal* 38, No. 152 (December 1928), pp. 543–559, considered a similar economy but over an infinite horizon and where the problem was to allocate wealth at each date between consumption and a *riskless* security.

Menahem E. Yaari in [Yaari (1965)] "Uncertain Lifetime, Uncertain Insurance, and the Theory of the Consumer," *Review of Economic Studies* 32, No. 2 (April 1965), pp. 137–150, writes another relatively early paper on consumption under uncertainty. In contrast with Phelps, Yaari assumes that the returns on investments are certain but the consumer's lifetime is uncertain. Yaari assumes the consumer knows the probability that he will die at each date in the future. In his most general case, the consumer is assumed to maximize:

$$\int_0 [\Omega(t)\rho(t)U(C_t) + \pi(t)\beta(t)V(W_t)]dt$$

where $\pi(t)$ is the probability of death at date t, $\Omega(t) = \int_t^T \pi(\tau)d\tau$ (integral taken from t to T) is the probability the consumer will still be alive at date t, $\rho(t)$ is the cumulated time preference at date t, $\beta(t)$ is a time-discount function for bequests, and $V(W_t)$ is the bequest utility function of final wealth W_t at death. The integral is taken from 0 to T, after which the consumer will not be alive.

Yaari considers two types of opportunity sets: the first with only a riskless investment available at each date with completely predictable and known returns over time, and the second with life insurance also available. Under the simplest situation, $\beta(t) = 0$ and $\Omega(t) = 1$ for all t, similar to that considered by Fisher (1930), Yaari shows that

$$\frac{dC(t)}{dt} = -[r(t) + \rho]\left[\frac{U'(C_t)}{U''(C_t)}\right]$$

where $r(t)$ is the instantaneous riskless rate of return at date t and for simplicity in this description I assume here that there is a constant $\rho > 0$ such that $\rho(t) = e^{-\rho t}$. If now I add the complication of an uncertain lifetime so that $\Omega(t) < 1$ for all t (but still no bequest), then the same result holds but with ρ replaced by $\rho - [\pi(t)/\Omega(t)]$, so the rate of time preference is reduced by the conditional probability (actually density) of death at date t given that it is known that the consumer has been alive up to that date. Thus the chance of early death, just as Fisher (1930), pp. 216–217, informally suggested, will increase the preference of earlier over later consumption.

How are these conclusions modified by the availability of life insurance? Yaari assumes this exists in the form of an actuarially fair life annuity—see discussion under de Witt (1671)—that pays him an income equal to his optimal consumption each year until he dies, and nothing thereafter. If it is to be actuarially fair, the instantaneous interest rate the consumer receives from the annuity equals $r(t) + [\pi(t)/\Omega(t)]$. Note that this is greater than the market riskless rate of return because the insurance company can afford to compensate the consumer at a higher rate while he remains alive since its obligation ceases at his death. As a result the consumer will choose to invest only in a life annuity and not choose to invest in the purely riskless investment. But, as Yaari interestingly points out, this creates the opportunity for a sort of Ponzi scheme: Since all debts are forgiven at death, the consumer will be tempted to sell an unlimited amount of life annuities, funding the interest owed with the sale of further life annuities, and thereby eliminate all constraints on his consumption. In real life, the fact that this temptation will become stronger as he becomes older may explain why insurance companies essentially refuse to sell life insurance to individuals after they reach a sufficient age; see Akerlof (1970) for another completely different reason for the failure of the life insurance market.

1963 **William Forsyth Sharpe** (June 16, 1934–), "A Simplified Model for Portfolio Analysis," *Management Science* 9, No. 2 (January 1963), pp. 277–293.

1992   William Forsyth Sharpe, "Asset Allocation: Management Style and Performance Measurement," *Journal of Portfolio Management* 18, No. 1 (Winter 1992), pp. 7–19.

PORTFOLIO SELECTION,
MEAN-VARIANCE ANALYSIS,
MARKET MODEL,
RESIDUAL VS. SYSTEMATIC RISK,
MULTIFACTOR MODELS,
STYLE FACTOR PORTFOLIOS

Sharpe (1963) contains the first detailed development of the diagonal or market model of security returns that reduces the number of inputs required for mean-variance portfolio choice, and was shown later (Treynor-Black 1973) to substantially simplify the calculation of optimal mean-variance portfolios. The model can be interpreted as making the following assumption: The realized excess return of security j is a linear regression against the excess return of a single marketwide factor M (which is the same for all securities):

$$r_j - r = \alpha_j + (r_M - r)\beta_j + \varepsilon_j$$

where α_j and β_j are defined such that $E(\varepsilon_j) = \rho(\varepsilon_j, r_M) = 0$.

Tautological Market Model Construction

So far the model is tautological. To see this, suppose we observe a time series of security returns $r_{j1}, r_{j2}, \ldots, r_{jt}, \ldots$ and corresponding market returns $r_{M1}, r_{M2}, \ldots, r_{Mt}, \ldots$. If all we say is that for every date t, $r_{jt} - r = \alpha_j + (r_{Mt} - r)\beta_j + \varepsilon_{jt}$, as long as I place no restrictions on ε_{jt}, there must exist an α_j and β_j such that the equation holds. If I add the requirement that $E(\varepsilon_j) = 0$, this can be done by choosing α_j so that $E(r_j) - r = \alpha_j + [E(r_M) - r]\beta_j = 0$. Now, if I add the further requirement that $\rho(\varepsilon_j, r_M) = 0$, we can guarantee this by choosing β_j such that $Cov(\varepsilon_j, r_M) = 0$, that is, by requiring that $Cov[r_j - r - \alpha_j - (r_M - r)\beta_j] = 0$. Solving this for β_j, we choose $\beta_j = Cov(r_j, r_M)/Var(r_M)$.

If we assume that the "market factor" is literally the return of the "market portfolio" of all securities, then this implies that the beta of the market portfolio, defined as $\beta_M \equiv \Sigma_j \chi_j \beta_j$, where the χ_j are market value proportions, must itself be 1.

To see this, suppose that χ_j for $j = 1, 2, \ldots, m$ represent the total market value proportions of securities j so that $r_M \equiv \Sigma_j \chi_j r_j$ and $\Sigma_j \chi_j = 1$. Then, $\beta_M \equiv \Sigma_j \chi_j \beta_j$ must equal 1 since by the preceding equation for β_j, $\beta_M = \Sigma_j \chi_j \beta_j = \Sigma_j \chi_j \text{Cov}(r_j, r_M)/\text{Var}(r_M) = \text{Cov}(\Sigma_j \chi_j r_j, r_M)/\text{Var}(r_M) = \text{Cov}(r_M, r_M)/\text{Var}(r_M) = \text{Var}(r_M)/\text{Var}(r_M) = 1$.

Another result of some interest is that even though individual stock alphas can be nonzero ($\alpha_j \neq 0$ for any security j), the market alpha, defined as $\alpha_M \equiv \Sigma_j \chi_j \alpha_j$, must itself be 0.

Proof That the Market Alpha Equals Zero

To see this, restating the market model we have

$$r_j - r = \alpha_j + (r_M - r)\beta_j + \varepsilon_j \text{ for all securities } j$$

Multiplying through by χ_j and summing over all securities:

$$\Sigma_j \chi_j r_j - r\Sigma_j \chi_j = \Sigma_j \chi_j \alpha_j + (r_M - r)\Sigma_j \chi_j \beta_j + \Sigma_j \chi_j \varepsilon_j$$

Since $r_M \equiv \Sigma_j \chi_j r_j$, $\Sigma_j \chi_j = 1$, $\alpha_M \equiv \Sigma_j \chi_j \alpha_j$ and $\beta_M \equiv \Sigma_j \chi_j \beta_j$, then:

$$r_M - r = \alpha_M + (r_M - r)\beta_M + \Sigma_j \chi_j \varepsilon_j$$

Taking expectations of both sides and letting $\mu_M \equiv E(r_M)$:

$$\mu_M - r = \alpha_M + (\mu_M - r)\beta_M + \Sigma_j \chi_j E(\varepsilon_j)$$

Since by construction $E(\varepsilon_j) = 0$ and I have shown that $\beta_M = 1$, $\mu_M - r = \alpha_M + (\mu_M - r)[1]$ and therefore $\alpha_M = 0$.

To this tautological construction, Sharpe adds the assumption that for any two different securities j and k, $\rho(\varepsilon_j, \varepsilon_k) = 0$. This allows a clear separation of systematic or marketwide risk measure β_j from residual or security specific risk $\text{Var}(\varepsilon_j)$. Sharpe writes:

The major characteristic of the diagonal model is the assumption that the returns of various securities are related only through common relationships with some basic underlying factor. ... This model has two virtues: it is one of the simplest that can be con-

*structed without assuming away the interrelationships among se-
curities, and there is considerable evidence that it can capture a
large part of such interrelationships. (p. 281)*[17]

Simplification from the Market Model for Solving the Portfolio Selection Problem

Using the market model assumptions, it is easy to show that:

$$(1)\ \mu_j = r + (\mu_M - r)\beta_j + \alpha_j$$
$$(2)\ \sigma_j^2 = \beta_j^2 \sigma_M^2 + \omega_j^2$$
$$(3)\ \sigma_{jk} = \beta_j \beta_k \sigma_M^2$$

where $\mu_j \equiv E(r_j)$, $\mu_M \equiv E(r_M)$, $\sigma_M^2 \equiv \mathrm{Var}(r_M)$, $\omega_j^2 \equiv \mathrm{Var}(\varepsilon_j)$, $\sigma_{jk} \equiv \mathrm{Cov}(r_j, r_k)$.
Without the market model, the inputs required to solve the mean-variance portfolio selection problem selecting from a riskless security and m risky securities would be m means μ_j, m variances σ_j^2, $\frac{1}{2}m(m-1)$ covariances σ_{jk} and 1 riskless return r for a total of $\frac{1}{2}m(m+3)+1$ estimates. *With* the market model, we would need m alphas α_j, m betas β_j, m residual variances ω_j^2, and r, μ_M and σ_M^2 for a total of $3(m+1)$ estimates. For example, if $m = 100$, without the market model we would need 5,151 estimates; with the market model, only 303 estimates.

This is a *cross-sectional* application of the market model. A second application to a *time series* for the same security is rendered nontautological by assuming that $\rho(\varepsilon_{j,t}, \varepsilon_{j,t+k}) = 0$ where $\varepsilon_{j,t}$ is the residual component observed for security j at date t and $\varepsilon_{j,t+k}$ is the residual component observed for the same security k dates after date t.

It is sometimes useful to assume that the market model and capital asset pricing model (CAPM) of Sharpe (1964), Lintner (1965/February), Mossin (1966), and Treynor (1999) hold at the same time. In that case, it is trivial to see that $\alpha_j = 0$ for all securities.

Eugene F. Fama, in [Fama (1973)] "A Note on the Market Model and the Two-Parameter Model," *Journal of Finance* 28, No. 5 (December 1973), pp. 1181–1185, which corrects his earlier article, [Fama (1968)] "Risk, Return and Equilibrium: Some Clarifying Comments," *Journal of Finance* 23, No. 1 (March 1968), pp. 29–40, finds a logical inconsistency in the market model that survives even if r_M and ε_j are jointly normal, as for example, Treynor-Black (1973) were later to assume.

An Inconsistency in the Market Model If the "Index" Is Identified as the Market Portfolio

If χ_{ij} is the market proportion for security j, so that $\Sigma_j \chi_j = 1$, then it follows from the market model that $\Sigma_j \chi_j r_j - r = (r_M - r)\Sigma_j \chi_j \beta_j + \Sigma_j \chi_j \varepsilon_j$. Since $r_M = \Sigma_j \chi_j r_j$ and it is easy to see from the market model that the market portfolio, itself, has $\Sigma_j \chi_j \beta_j = 1$, then $\Sigma_j \chi_j \varepsilon_j = 0$. But this contradicts the market model assumption that for all securities j and k, $\rho(\varepsilon_j, \varepsilon_k) = 0$, since for any values ε_j for all but the last security k, this condition fully determines ε_k. For example, suppose the market contains just two securities, we would then have $\chi\varepsilon_1 + (1 - \chi)\varepsilon_2 = 0$. Therefore, $\varepsilon_1 = -[(1 - \chi)/\chi]\varepsilon_2$. This implies that $\rho(\varepsilon_1, \varepsilon_2) = -1$, which clearly contradicts the key assumption of the market model that $\rho(\varepsilon_1, \varepsilon_2) = 0$. However, for most practical purposes as Fama notes, this inconsistency can be ignored. In a "large" market, say where $\chi_j \cong 1/m$, then $\mathrm{Var}(\Sigma_j \chi_j \varepsilon_j) = [\Sigma_j \mathrm{Var}(\varepsilon_j)]/m^2$. If $\mathrm{Var}(\varepsilon_j)$ is bounded from above, then as $m \to \infty$, $\mathrm{Var}(\Sigma_j \chi_j \varepsilon_j) \to 0$ so that $\Sigma_j \chi_j \varepsilon_j \cong 0$.

This model has provided the standard way of measuring the inputs into models of optimal portfolio construction. In addition, it provides a key ingredient for later empirical tests of the Sharpe (1964), Lintner (1965/February), Mossin (1966), Treynor (1999) equilibrium model of the determinants of security expected returns. Many of its statistical features have been examined in subsequent papers. For example, John D. Martin and Robert C. Klemkosky in [Martin-Klemkosky (1975)] "Evidence of Heteroscedasticity in the Market Model," *Journal of Business* 48, No. 1 (June 1975), pp. 81–86, separately test whether ε_j is independent of r_M. They propose three alternative statistical tests. The first is to calculate the correlation of $|\varepsilon_j|$ with r_M. The second is the Bartlett test, which, for grouped similar-sized observations of r_M, examines the range of the corresponding observations of ε_j. The third is the Goldfield-Quandt test, which begins by ordering the observed r_{Mt} from lowest to highest. Then omit the middle (say, third) range of observations. Separately regress the observations in the lowest third and highest third, separately measuring the standard deviation of ε_j. If there is no heteroscedasticity, the two standard deviations should be close to each other. For their sample, Martin and Klemkosky conclude that heteroscedasticity for most stocks is not a problem for the market model.

About 30 years later, Sharpe (1992) revisits his market model, but now admits many factors. According to a multifactor model of managed portfolio returns:

$$r_{Pt} = \Sigma_k \beta_{Pk} F_{kt} + \varepsilon_{Pt} \text{ for securities } P = 1, 2, \ldots, J$$
$$\text{and factors } h, k = 1, 2, \ldots, K$$

where r_{Pt} is the realized return of portfolio P at time t with enough factors F_k so that the residual component ε_{Pt} is independent across all the managed portfolios (as well as serially independent over time) in the selected universe. Sharpe defines style analysis to be the application of a multifactor model where:

1. The factor exposures for any managed portfolio are constrained to sum to 1 (that is, $\Sigma_k \beta_{Pk} = 1$).
2. Each factor is perfectly replicated by an identifiable portfolio of securities with no short holdings and can be managed at low trading costs.
3. No two factor portfolios contain the same securities.
4. Typically, the factor exposures are constrained to be nonnegative (that is, $\beta_{Pk} \geq 0$).

The factor exposures are derived from observed security and factor returns using quadratic programming to minimize the variance of the residual return ε_{Pt}. These constraints mean that the realized return of a managed portfolio can be broken apart into a style component that can be replicated by a portfolio of factor portfolios and a selection component ε_{Pt}. The squared correlation of the style components with the managed portfolio return measures the proportion of the variance of the portfolio return explained by style, and one minus this squared correlation is the proportion of the variance of the portfolio return explained by selection.

Sharpe suggests using 12-factor portfolios that replicate (1) Treasury bills, (2) intermediate-term government bonds, (3) long-term government bonds, (4) corporate bonds, (5) mortgage-related securities, (6) large-cap value stocks, (7) large-cap growth stocks, (8) medium-cap stocks, (9) small-cap stocks, (10) non-U.S. bonds, (11) European stocks, and (12) Japanese stocks. As an illustration, Sharpe applies style analysis to the performance of the Fidelity Magellan Fund from 1985 to 1989, using monthly returns. The fund's style is to be exposed to large-cap growth stocks, medium-cap stocks, and small-cap stocks; and its style explains 97.3 percent of the variance of its return. The fund outperformed its style benchmark by a cumulated 25 percent over the five years, both highly statistically and economically significant. However, it must be remembered that Sharpe has not adjusted this performance for selecting Magellan after the fact of its extreme performance from a large universe; see comments concerning Magellan under Graham-Dodd (1934). Indeed, Sharpe reports that 636 mutual funds over the same period (his universe of observed funds) underperformed their benchmark style by 0.89 percent per year on average, inclusive of costs.

1963 Paul Anthony Samuelson (May 15, 1915–), "Risk and Uncertainty: A Fallacy of Large Numbers," *Scientia* (May–April 1963), pp. 1–6; reprinted in *The Collected Scientific Papers of Paul A. Samuelson*, Volume 1 (Cambridge, MA: MIT Press, 1966), pp. 153–158.

TIME-DIVERSIFICATION, RISK AVERSION AND GAMBLING,
LAW OF LARGE NUMBERS, PROBABILISTIC PREFERENCES

Some individuals say that while they are not willing to accept a favorable gamble if it is offered only once, they will accept the gamble if it can be accepted repeatedly. For example, while they may be unwilling to accept a one-shot opportunity to win $100 with a two-thirds probability at the cost of losing a like amount one-third of the time, they may be quite happy to accept a multishot opportunity to face this gamble successively 100 times. Implicitly, they may be applying what they think is a version of the Jakob Bernoulli (1713) law of large numbers, or alternatively they may be using a decision rule based on accepting gambles with a sufficiently large probability of winning. The probability of winning the one-shot gamble is $^2/_3$, while the probability of coming out ahead after accepting the multishot gamble is almost 1:

$$\text{Probability of winning} = \Sigma_{j=0,\ldots,49}\left[\frac{100!}{j!(100-j)!}\right]\times\left(\frac{1}{3}\right)^j\times\left(\frac{2}{3}\right)^{100-j}$$

Using the normal approximation to the binomial, this probability approximately equals:

$$N\left[\frac{100(2/3)-50}{\sqrt{100(1/3)(2/3)}}\right] = N(3.536) = .9998$$

Samuelson (1963) shows that under one assumption that may very well apply, such a choice between the one-shot and multishot gambles is time-inconsistent.

Proof of Samuelson's Result on Time Diversification

The proof is simple. Suppose that at each income or wealth level within a range, you are averse to accepting a gamble; then, Samuelson asserts, no sequence of the same independent gambles offered n times (that leaves you within that range) should be accepted. To see this, consider the last or nth gamble in the sequence. By assumption, irrespective of whether you have accepted the $n - 1$ earlier gambles, you will not accept it. Then the nth $- 1$ gamble becomes the last gamble, which by a similar argument you will also not accept. Therefore, working backwards, you will not even accept the 1st gamble; so you will not accept the sequence.

Intuitively, the law of large numbers is inappropriately applied. It relates to situations where risks are subdivided, not added. To see this, had the multishot gamble been a repeated chance to win $1 two-thirds of the time and lose $1 one-third of the time, this could be rationally accepted even though the one-shot opportunity to win $100 would be rejected (in this case, the single-shot and multishot gambles have the same mean outcome, but the multishot gamble has a much lower variance due to the law of large numbers).

Samuelson also shows that the criterion of selecting among pairs of gambles the gamble with the highest probability of winning fails to satisfy the von Neumann–Morgenstern (1947) transitivity axiom. That is, of the outcomes X, Y, and Z of three gambles, even though $\text{prob}(X > Y) > 1/2$ and $\text{prob}(Y > Z) > 1/2$, it may nonetheless be that $\text{prob}(Z > X) > 1/2$.

Illustration of Intransitivity of Probabilistic Preferences

To see this, consider flipping a slightly biased coin twice where the payoffs of the three gambles are:

Outcome	HH	HT	TH	TT
Probability	.26	.25	.25	.24
X	1	1	−10	−10
Y	0	0	0	0
Z	−1	10	−1	10

$\text{prob}(X > Y) = .51$ and $\text{prob}(Y > Z) = .51$, yet $\text{prob}(Z > X) = .74$

Samuelson won the 1970 Nobel Prize in Economic Science "for the scientific work through which he has developed static and dynamic economic theory and actively contributed to raising the level of analysis in economic science."

1964   Lawrence Fisher and **James H. Lorie,** "Rates of Return on Investments in Common Stocks," *Journal of Business* 37, No. 1 (January 1964), pp. 1–21.

HOLDING-PERIOD RETURN, EQUITY RISK PREMIUM PUZZLE

Theoretical models and empirical procedures are only two of the triangular vertices needed for research. The third vertex is reliable data. That is why the founding of the Center for Research in Securities Prices at the University of Chicago, sponsored by Merrill Lynch, Pierce, Fenner & Smith, Inc., marks a significant moment in the development of modern financial economics. For the first time, a systematic attempt was undertaken to carefully construct complete databases covering the historical record of security prices. Fisher-Lorie (1964) is the first survey of this data to be published. It describes the organization of the data file covering monthly closing prices of all New York Stock Exchange (NYSE) stocks from January 1926 through December 1960. It also presents summary results describing the realized holding period returns inclusive of dividends from a portfolio containing all NYSE stocks over different time periods. Many were surprised at the high returns (relative to interest rates) that were reported—an empirical fact called "the risk premium puzzle" 20 years later. Very quickly this database was used in systematic studies measuring the serial correlation of successive price changes, the effects of dividends on stock prices, and the construction of stock market averages.

A subsequent paper by Fisher and Lorie, [Fisher-Lorie (1968)] "Rates of Return on Investments in Common Stocks: The Year-by-Year Record, 1926–65," *Journal of Business* 41, No. 3 (July 1968), pp. 291–316, extends their earlier paper another five years and provides tables of detailed year-by-year returns. A significant expansion of these reported returns to U.S. Treasury bonds, Treasury bills, and U.S. inflation appears in [Ibbotson-Sinquefield (1976)] Roger G. Ibbotson and Rex A. Sinquefield, "Stocks, Bonds, Bills, and Inflation: Year-by-Year Historical Returns (1926–1974)," *Journal of Business* 49, No. 1 (January 1976), pp. 11–47. Ibbotson Associates now commercially sells an annually updated book titled *Stocks, Bonds, Bills and Inflation: Yearbook.*

1964 John W. Pratt, "Risk Aversion in the Large and in the Small," *Econometrica* 32, Nos. 1/2 (January–April 1964), pp. 122–136.

1965/B Kenneth Joseph Arrow, "The Theory of Risk Aversion," Essay 3 in *Essays in the Theory of Risk Bearing* (Chicago: Markham, 1971), pp. 90–120 (first published without appendix in 1965 as Lecture 2 in *Aspects of the Theory of Risk Bearing*, pp. 28–44, Yrjo Jahnsson Lectures, Helsinki); reprinted in *Collected Papers of Kenneth J. Arrow: Individual Choice under Certainty and Uncertainty*, Volume III (Cambridge, MA: Harvard University Press, 1984), pp. 147–171.

RISK AVERSION, ABSOLUTE RISK AVERSION,
RELATIVE RISK AVERSION, FAVORABLE GAMBLES THEOREM

Pratt (1964) develops the ideas of absolute and relative risk aversion in terms of the risk premium demanded to accept a gamble. If $U(W)$ is the utility of wealth, then $A(W) \equiv - U''(W)/U'(W)$ is absolute risk aversion, and $R(W) \equiv - WU''(W)/U'(W)$ is relative risk aversion.

Unlike the utility function itself, which is unique up to an increasing linear transformation, or $U''(W)$, which is unique up to a positive multiplicative constant, $A(W)$ and $R(W)$ are unique functions; that is, they determine the utility function up to an increasing linear transformation. This makes it possible to use these measures to compare risk aversion across different individuals. Consider two investors, a and b, and a gamble that adds or subtracts a small amount Δ to or from their wealth with equal probabil-

---

A measure of risk aversion is the certainty equivalent π defined as around current wealth such that it leads to the same utility as a 50–50 gamble of $\Delta > 0$:

$$U(W_0 - \pi) \approx \frac{1}{2}U(W_0 + \Delta) + \frac{1}{2}U(W_0 - \Delta)$$

For small risks (Δ near zero), it can be shown that $\pi = \frac{1}{2}\sigma_\Delta^2 A(W_0)$.

ity. To accept this gamble, investor a has to be paid more dollars than investor b if and only if $A_a(W) > A_b(W)$. Consider another gamble, which changes wealth either to $W\Delta$ or to W/Δ for small $\Delta > 1$ with equal probability. To accept this gamble, investor a has to be paid a larger fraction of his wealth than investor b if and only if $R_a(W) > R_b(W)$. According to Pratt, the original formulation of the idea of absolute risk aversion was actually contained in an unpublished note by Robert Schlaifer, in [Schlaifer (1961)] "Utility Functions for Reasonably Cautious Behavior," dated November 13, 1961.[18]

Arrow (1965/B) develops properties of absolute and relative risk aversion independently of Pratt. Arrow considers an investor's allocation of his wealth between a riskless and a risky security. If $A'(W) > (=) [<] 0$, the investor is said to have increasing (constant) [decreasing] absolute risk aversion. Arrow shows that, as his wealth rises, an investor will decrease (keep constant) [increase] his *dollar investment* in the risky security if and only if his utility function has increasing (constant) [decreasing] absolute risk aversion. Similarly, if $R'(W) > (=) [<] 0$, the investor is said to have increasing (constant) [decreasing] relative risk aversion. Arrow shows that, as his wealth rises, an investor will decrease (keep constant) [increase] the *proportion* of his wealth that he allocates to the risky security if and only if his utility function has increasing (constant) [decreasing] relative risk aversion. It is generally thought that, empirically, almost all investors behave as if they have decreasing absolute risk aversion, and the majority behave as if they have decreasing relative risk aversion. A summary of Arrow's results first appeared in [Arrow (1963/February)] "Comment on James Duesenberry: The Portfolio Approach to the Demand for Money and Other Assets," *Review of Economics and Statistics* 45, No. 1, Part 2, Supplement (February 1963), pp. 24–27.

Arrow also derives a second fundamental result: Under very general conditions, a nonsatiated risk averter always commits some positive amount of his wealth (perhaps slight) to a favorable gamble. For simplification, suppose the riskless (cash) rate of return is 0 and an investor with initial wealth W_0 must decide how much to allocate from cash into a risky investment R with expected *rate* of return $E(r_R) > 0$, therefore a favorable gamble. Suppose that $0 \leq A \leq W_0$ is the amount of initial wealth allocated to the risky investment. Then future wealth $W_1 = W_0 + Ar_R$. The investor is assumed to choose A so as to maximize his expected utility of future wealth $E[U(W_1)] = E[U(W_0 + Ar_R)] \equiv J(A)$, where J is a function mapping A onto expected utility. Arrow shows that risk aversion $U''(W_1) < 0$ implies that $A > 0$ if and only if $E(r_R) > 0$ (pp. 98–102).

Proof of Arrow's Result That Rational Risk-Averse Investors Always Invest a (Possibly Small) Positive Amount in a Favorable Gamble

To prove this, observe that:

$$J'(A) = E[U'(W_1)r_R] \text{ and } J''(A) = E[U''(W_1)r_R^2]$$

By risk aversion $U''(W_1) < 0$; therefore, $J''(A) < 0$ for all A. Given that $J(A)$ is therefore everywhere concave to the origin, $J(A)$ can have only one of three possible shapes: (1) it can reach a peak at $J(0)$ and be decreasing as A increases from 0 to W_0; (2) it can reach an interior peak at $J(A)$ for $0 < A < W_0$ so that it decreases on each side of A; or (3) it can reach a peak at $J(W_0)$ and be decreasing as A decreases from W_0 to 0. In the first case, $J'(0) \leq 0$. Then at maximum $A = 0$, $W_1 = W_0$ so $U'(W_1) = U'(W_0)$, a positive constant. So from the preceding equation for $J'(A)$, if follows that $J'(A) = U'(W_0)E(r_R) \leq 0$. So for case (1), $A = 0$ if and only if $E(r_R) \leq 0$ and the contrapositive of this states $A > 0$ if and only if $E(r_R) > 0$. For case (2), $J'(A) = E[U'(W_1)r_R] = 0$. This can be decomposed as:

$$J'(A) = E[U'(W_1)]E(r_R) + \text{Cov}[U'(W_1), r_R] = 0$$

Because of risk aversion, as r_R increases, $U'(W_1)$ decreases, so $\text{Cov}[U'(W_1), r_R] < 0$. Therefore $E[U'(W_1)]E(r_R) > 0$, and since nonsatiation implies $E[U'(W_1)] > 0$, then $E(r_R) > 0$. So for case (2), for an interior value of A to be an optimum, $E(r_R) > 0$. For case (3), at maximum $A = W_0$, $J'(W_0) \geq 0$, so by the preceding equation for $J'(A)$, $J'(A) = E[U'(W_0 + W_0r_R)r_R] \geq 0$ so an argument similar to case (2) follows even more strongly. Thus summarizing all cases, $A > 0$ if and only if $E(r_R) > 0$.

Intuitively, for sufficiently small gambles (small because the investor commits only a very small amount of wealth), the risk per unit of the amount committed to the gamble can be made as small as one would like while the positive expected return per unit committed remains constant, and its salubrious effect will eventually at a small enough commitment outweigh the negative effects of the risk. In other words, for small risks the utility function becomes approximately linear and risk aversion almost disappears for gambles with outcomes constrained to this region.

Since the Sharpe (1964), Lintner (1965/February), Mossin (1966), Treynor (1999) CAPM satisfies the conditions for Arrow's result, it can immediately be concluded that in that model no investor shorts the market portfolio. So short-selling constraints will not affect the conclusions of this model.

1964 William Forsyth Sharpe, "Capital Asset Prices: A Theory of Market Equilibrium under Conditions of Risk," *Journal of Finance* 19, No. 3 (September 1964), pp. 425–442.

1965 John Lintner, "The Valuation of Risk Assets and the Selection of Risky Investments in Stock Portfolios and Capital Budgets," *Review of Economics and Statistics* 47, No. 1 (February 1965), pp. 13–37.

1966 Jan Mossin (1936–1987), "Equilibrium in a Capital Asset Market," *Econometrica* 34, No. 4 (October 1966), pp. 768–783.

1999 Jack L. Treynor, "Toward a Theory of Market Value of Risky Assets," written in 1962 but published only recently in *Asset Pricing and Portfolio Performance*, edited by Robert A. Korajczyk (London: Risk Publications, 1999), pp. 15–22.

CAPITAL ASSET PRICING MODEL (CAPM),
MEAN-VARIANCE ANALYSIS, MARKET PORTFOLIO,
BETA, RISK PREMIUM, SYSTEMATIC RISK,
JOINT NORMALITY COVARIANCE THEOREM,
TOBIN SEPARATION THEOREM, HOMOGENEOUS BELIEFS

Markowitz (1952/March) and Markowitz (1959) were interested in decision rules that can be recommended to rational investors (normative modeling). Sharpe (1964) then asked what would happen if everyone in the economy actually followed Markowitz's advice (prescriptive modeling). This led to the first published derivation of the capital asset pricing model (CAPM) that relates expected security return (μ_j) to the sum of the riskless return r plus the product of marketwide risk aversion ($\theta > 0$) and the covariance of security return with the return of the market portfolio [$Cov(r_j, r_M)$]; that is, $\mu_j = r + \theta Cov(r_j, r_M)$.

Actually, Sharpe wrote the equation somewhat differently. Defining $B_j \equiv$ $\text{Cov}(r_j, r_G)/\sigma_G^2$, he shows that $B_j = -[r/(\mu_G - r)] + [1/(\mu_G - r)]\mu_j$, where G is any mean-variance efficient portfolio, all of which are perfectly correlated with each other; see Sharpe (1964), p. 438, footnote 22. Note that he does not draw the inference that G is perfectly correlated with (and therefore could be) the market portfolio containing all securities in the economy in value-weighted proportions.

Alternatively, the CAPM equation can be interpreted as providing a prescription for discounting an uncertain cash flow received at the end of a single period.

To see this, define $r_j \equiv X_j/P_j$ where P_j is the current price of security j and X_j is its (random) end-of-period value (perhaps price plus dividends). Then the CAPM equation can be written equivalently as:

$$P_j = \frac{E(X_j)}{r + \theta\text{Cov}(r_j, r_M)}$$

Fama (1968), p. 37, equation 18, restates the CAPM in what has become its most popular "beta" form:

$$\mu_j - r = (\mu_M - r)\beta_j \quad \text{where} \quad \beta_j \equiv \frac{\text{Cov}(r_j, r_M)}{\text{Var}(r_M)}$$

This can be rearranged to show that $\beta_j = (\mu_j - r)/(\mu_M - r)$. Like the centigrade scale set to 0 at the freezing point of water and 100 at its boiling point, the beta scale for measuring the risk of securities is set to 1 for the market portfolio M. A security, then, with a beta of 2, for example, is expected to have an excess rate of return (over the riskless rate) that is double the excess rate of return of the market. Of all the legacies of the CAPM to civilization, this may turn out to be the most enduring.

Building on Markowitz (1952/March), Roy (1952), and Tobin (1958), the model assumes all investors choose their optimal portfolio of securities considering only its portfolio mean and portfolio variance of return, that investors are greedy in the sense that they like portfolio expected return, portfolio variance held equal, and risk averse in the sense that they dislike portfolio variance, portfolio expected return held equal. A riskless security is available and security markets are perfect and competitive. Although investors are assumed to have the same beliefs (they agree about the expected returns and covariance of returns with each other for all securities), they are allowed to have different degrees of risk aversion (that is, different trade-offs between portfolio expected return and portfolio variance of return). The paper implies that for pricing purposes, the correct measure of security risk is not its own variance of return but rather its systematic risk: its covariance of return with the return of the market portfolio, a portfolio that contains all securities in the economy, each individually weighted by its proportion of the value of all securities in the market.

Rubinstein's Derivation of the Capital Asset Pricing Model (CAPM)

One way to derive the CAPM equation follows (Rubinstein 1973/October). Each investor $i = 1, 2, \ldots, I$ is assumed to solve the following portfolio selection problem:

$$\max_{\{x_{ij}\}} E[U_i(W_1^i)] \quad \text{subject to} \quad W_1^i = W_0^i \Sigma_j x_{ij} r_j \quad \text{and} \quad \Sigma_j x_{ij} = 1$$

by choosing portfolio proportions x_{ij} for securities $j = 0, 1, \ldots, m$, where by convention I regard security $j = 0$ as riskless and securities $j = 1, \ldots, m$ as different risky securities. Using the technique of Lagrangian multipliers, this can be restated as:

$$\max_{\{x_{ij}\}} E[U_i(W_0^i \Sigma_j x_{ij} r_j)] - \xi_i(\Sigma_j x_{ij} - 1)$$

The first-order conditions (which are guaranteed to describe a maximum since $U'(W_1^i) > 0$, $U''(W_1^i) < 0$) are:

$$W_0^i E[r_j U'(W_1^i)] = \xi_i \text{ (all } i \text{ and } j)$$

(Continued)

Rubinstein's Derivation of the Capital
Asset Pricing Model (CAPM) *(Continued)*

In particular, for the riskless security $(j = 0)$: $W_0^i r E[U'(W_1^i)] = \xi_i$. Therefore,

$$rE[U'(W_1^i)] = E[r_j U'(W_1^i)] = \mu_j E[U'(W_1^i)] + \mathrm{Cov}[r_j, U'(W_1^i)]$$

so that,

$$\mu_j = r + \{-E[U'(W_1^i)]\}^{-1}\mathrm{Cov}[r_j, U'(W_1^i)]$$

From Tobin (1958) one way to justify mean-variance preferences is to assume all securities have returns r_j that are jointly normally distributed. Since weighted sums of jointly normally distributed random variables, in particular W_1^i, are themselves normal, it follows that $(r_j$ and $W_1^i)$ are also jointly normal. The joint normality covariance theorem, as derived by Rubinstein (1973/October) and Stein (1973) states: If x and y are jointly normal, $g(y)$ is any differentiable function of y, and $E|g'(y)| < \infty$, then $\mathrm{Cov}[x, g(y)] = E[g'(y)]\mathrm{Cov}(x, y)$. Using this:

$$\mathrm{Cov}[r_j, U'(W_1^i)] = E[U''(W_1^i)]\mathrm{Cov}(r_j, W_1^i)$$

Substituting into our previous result:

$$\mu_j = r + \theta_i \mathrm{Cov}(r_j, W_1^i) \quad \text{with} \quad \theta_i \equiv -\frac{E[U''(W_1^i)]}{E[U'(W_1^i)]} > 0$$

First, rewrite this as:

$$(\mu_j - r)\theta_i^{-1} = \mathrm{Cov}(r_j, W_1^i)$$

Now, sum or aggregate over all investors:

$$(\mu_j - r)\Sigma_i\theta_i^{-1} = \mathrm{Cov}(r_j, \Sigma_i W_1^i)$$

Aggregation requires that $W_0^M r_M = \Sigma_i W_1^i$ since aggregate holdings must total to the market portfolio. Finally, substituting into the previous result:

$$\mu_j = r + \theta\mathrm{Cov}(r_j, r_M) \text{ with } \theta \equiv W_0^M(\Sigma_i\theta_i^{-1})^{-1} > 0 \text{ (for all securities } j)$$

A key intuition behind the CAPM is the implication of Tobin's (1958) portfolio separation result: With the existence of a riskless security, an investor's choice of the proportional composition of his subportfolio of risky securities is independent of his degree of risk aversion and his wealth. In Sharpe's equilibrium extension, this implies that all investors in the economy (since they all have the same beliefs, all have mean-variance preferences, and differ only with respect to their risk aversion and wealth) end up investing in the *same* subportfolio of risky securities. That is, wealthier and less risk-averse investors might allocate more *dollars* to this subportfolio, but the *proportionate composition* of the portfolio will be the same for all investors. If the supply of securities is to equal the demand for them in equilibrium, this portfolio must then be the market portfolio: If all securities are held by someone, that is the only portfolio they can all hold and be holding the same portfolio. That is why all investors will measure the risk of a security by the covariance of its return with the return of the market portfolio, since that measures the contribution of that security to the variance of the return of the portfolio they all end up holding. The market portfolio is Tobin's tangency portfolio, and is therefore itself mean-variance efficient. This model brings the market portfolio front and center for the first time.

In [Merton (1990)] "Introduction to Portfolio Selection and Capital Market Theory: Static Analysis," in Robert C. Merton, *Continuous-Time Finance*, Chapter 2 (Malden, MA: Blackwell, 1990), pp. 16–56, Merton comments:

> *Because the market portfolio can be constructed without the knowledge of preferences, the distribution of wealth, or the joint probability distribution for outstanding securities, models [such as the CAPM] in which the market portfolio can be shown to be efficient are more likely to produce testable hypotheses. In addition, the efficiency of the market portfolio provides a rigorous microeconomic justification for the use of a "representative man" to derive equilibrium prices in aggregated economic models, i.e. the market portfolio is efficient if and only if there exists a concave utility function such that maximization of its expected value with initial wealth equal to national wealth would lead to the market portfolio as the optimal portfolio. (p. 44)[19]*

At once this is good news and bad news. It is good news because the critical variable for measuring risk (the return of the market portfolio) is now finally identified; it is bad news because application of the model to real-life problems, in principle, means one has to know how the market value of the total of all assets in the world changes over time—a number that is clearly hard to find on the Internet!

More empirical effort may have been put into testing the CAPM equation than any other result in finance. The results are quite mixed and in many ways discouraging. Not that the equation has been shown to be false; rather, problems in measuring the return of the market portfolio (Roll 1977) and in measuring expected returns have, perhaps, made it impossible to show that it is true, even if it were. At bottom, as subsequent generalization of the model shows, the central message of the CAPM is this: Ceteris paribus, the prices of securities should be higher (or lower) to the extent their payoffs are slanted toward states in which aggregate consumption or aggregate wealth is low (or high). Intuitively, this follows from consumer/investor diminishing marginal utility (risk aversion) as it aggregates to affect equilibrium prices. The true pricing equation may not take the exact form of the CAPM, but the enduring belief of many financial economists is that, whatever form it takes, it will at least embody this principle.

The discovery of the capital asset pricing model is one of the more mysterious events in the history of the theory of investments. Although Sharpe is invariably given credit, three other financial economists, Lintner (1965/February), Mossin (1966), and Treynor (1999), are variably given equal credit. So what is the story? Fortunately, financial detective Craig W. French, in [French (2003)] "The Treynor Capital Asset Pricing Model," *Journal of Investment Management* 1, No. 2 (Second Quarter 2003), pp. 60–72, provides a solution to the mystery. Motivated by Markowitz (1952/March) and Tobin (1958), all four economists adopted nearly the same set of assumptions (mean-variance preferences, perfect and competitive markets, existence of a riskless security, and homogeneous expectations) and reached nearly the same two key conclusions: (1) all investors, irrespective of differences in preferences and wealth, divide their wealth between the same two portfolios: cash and the market portfolio, and (2) equivalent versions of the CAPM pricing equation given earlier. One can quibble, as shown, that Sharpe actually did not conclude or emphasize that all investors hold the market portfolio since he permitted some securities to be replicable by others and so allowed for a singular covariance matrix of security returns. However, in the absence of replication, all investors under his assumptions would indeed hold the market portfolio.

It seems likely that Treynor and Sharpe discovered these results independently and at nearly the same time. Adding to the mystery is that Treynor had circulated an earlier paper ("Market Value, Time and Risk," dated August 8, 1961), which contained some of the results of his 1962 paper, and Sharpe's preliminary results (which include the result that in equilibrium all securities will have expected return beta ordered pairs that fall along a straight line with an intercept at the riskless rate) first appeared in his June 1961 doctoral dissertation at UCLA, "Portfolio Analysis Based on a Simplified Model of the Relationships among Securities," which was extended to the final form of his version of the CAPM and presented at a seminar in January 1962. Even earlier, in 1960, Treynor gave a draft of his 1961 paper to Lintner at Harvard, so it is unclear to what extent Lintner's 1965 published paper was influenced by Treynor (however, Lintner neither cites nor mentions Treynor in his paper). Since Mossin references Sharpe, it seems likely that his work was not independent.

Compared to the other formulations by Treynor, Lintner, and Mossin, Sharpe derives his using a geometric argument. Of the three derivations, Mossin's, the last to be written, is easily the most clearly and precisely expressed with mathematics.

Lintner (1965/February), published five months following Sharpe, begins with the Tobin (1958) separation property, which follows from mean-variance preferences. Although he states that mean-variance preferences themselves are consistent with expected utility maximization under quadratic utility or jointly normal security returns, he does not take advantage of this correspondence to derive more specific results. But he clearly states and proves that the separation theorem of Tobin (1958), taken to an equilibrium of investors with the same beliefs, leads to "*the same stock mix will be optimal for every investor*," where the proportions for each stock in this portfolio "can be interpreted as the ratio of the *aggregate market* value of the *i*th stock to the total aggregate market value of all stocks" (p. 25). He also usefully decomposes the CAPM risk adjustment term into the product of (1) what he calls the "market price per dollar of risk," which is the same for all securities, and (2) the stock's risk, different for each security, which is the sum of its own variance of returns plus the sum of the covariances of its return with the returns of all other stocks. Lintner's writing style, unfortunately, makes his results difficult to digest. He habitually uses very long sentences stating precisely all conditions and frequently italicizes words to help the reader pull out the most significant ideas. Despite this, it is often difficult to tell what is important and what isn't. In the case of stock risk, for example, he fails to see that in real life with a large number of available stocks, a stock's own variance will almost always be swamped by the sum of its covariances, and is not significant in determining its risk.

Proof That Own Variance Has Negligible Effects on Value in Large Markets

To see this, consider the market portfolio with proportionate holdings $x_1, x_2, \ldots, x_j, \ldots, x_k, \ldots, x_m$ with returns $r_1, r_2, \ldots, r_j, \ldots, r_k, \ldots, r_m$ where m is the number of securities in the market portfolio so that its return $r_M = \Sigma_j x_j r_j$. Now for a given security k, calculate $\text{Cov}(r_k, r_M) = \text{Cov}(r_k, \Sigma_j x_j r_j) = x_k \text{Var}(r_k) + \Sigma_{j \neq k} x_j \text{Cov}(r_k, r_j)$. To highlight the result, suppose that all $x_j = 1/m$ and all the covariances are equal (to Cov). Then

$$\text{Cov}(r_k, r_M) = \left(\frac{1}{m}\right)\text{Var}(r_k) + \left(\frac{m-1}{m}\right)\text{Cov}$$

Therefore, as m becomes large, the relative influence of $\text{Var}(r_k)$ compared to Cov on $\text{Cov}(r_j, r_M)$ becomes negligible.

Lintner's first sequel paper, [Lintner (1965/December)] "Security Prices, Risk and Maximal Gains from Diversification," *Journal of Finance* 20, No. 4 (December 1965), pp. 587–615, lays out the CAPM model more clearly. He tries to generalize the CAPM to heterogeneous beliefs, but is unable to develop closed-form results. In [Lintner (1970)] "The Market Price of Risk, Size of Market and Investor's Risk Aversion," *Review of Economics and Statistics* 52, No. 1 (February 1970), pp. 87–99, Lintner examines a special case of the CAPM in which all investors have exponential utility of wealth functions, with different exponents (A):

$$U(W_i) \sim -A_i e^{-W_i/A_i}$$

With this, he is able to develop a special case of the result in the prior proof, where $\theta_i = A_i$ and $\theta \equiv W_0^M (\Sigma_i \theta_i^{-1})^{-1}$, the harmonic mean of investor risk aversions, a result similar to Wilson (1968). Using these precise results, Lintner becomes the first to develop the comparative statics of the CAPM. For example, he asks what happens to the market price of risk as, other things being equal, more investors are added to the market. Finally, in [Lintner (1969)] "The Aggregation of Investor's Diverse Judgments and Preferences in Purely Competitive Securities Markets," *Journal of Financial and Quantitative Analysis* 4, No. 4 (December 1969), pp. 347–400, Lintner also derives results under the generalizations of heterogeneous investor assessments of security mean returns and covariances and restrictions limiting short selling. Unfortunately, his closed-form results with these two generalizations are quite complex.

Although Mossin seems unaware of Lintner's papers, concerning Sharpe's, he writes:

> *The paper by Sharpe gives a verbal-diagrammatical discussion of the determination of asset prices in quasi-dynamic terms. His general description of the character of the market is similar to the one presented here, however, and his main conclusions are certainly consistent with ours. But his lack of precision in the specification of equilibrium conditions leaves parts of his arguments somewhat indefinite. The present paper may be seen as an attempt to clarify and make precise some of these points. (p. 769)*[20]

A model of clarity, Mossin begins by setting forth all the simultaneous equations that describe the model. He counts unknowns and finds they equal the number of equations. He assumes investors maximize a utility function with arguments that are the mean and variance of the return of his portfolio. However, like Sharpe, Lintner (1965/February), and Treynor, he does not explicitly investigate the implications of quadratic utility or jointly normal distributions (as in the earlier proof). He concludes that "in equilibrium, prices must be set such that *each individual will hold the same percentage of the total outstanding stock of all risky assets*" (p. 775), implying that all individuals hold what we would now call the "market portfolio" along with an investment in cash.

The CAPM has had enormous repercussions on subsequent academic work in finance. It is now commonly used by professionals as the backbone of approaches to evaluate investments and measure the performance of investment managers. Moreover, it can be given some credit for encouraging the development of index funds in the decades since its discovery. The capital asset pricing model takes its name from Sharpe's paper, and his paper was the principal basis for him being awarded the 1990 Nobel Prize in Economic Science.

1965 Eugene F. Fama (February 14, 1939–), "The Behavior of Stock-Market Prices," *Journal of Business* 38, No. 1 (January 1965), pp. 34–105.

RANDOM WALK, LOGNORMAL DISTRIBUTION,
FAT TAILS, STABLE-PARETIAN HYPOTHESIS, RUNS TESTS,

FILTER RULES, EFFICIENT MARKETS,
WEEKEND VS. TRADING DAY VARIANCE,
MUTUAL FUND PERFORMANCE

Fama (1965) empirically informs much of subsequent theoretical work in asset pricing, particularly work based on the random walk model and normality or lognormality of security returns. As Bachelier (1900), Working (1949/May), Roberts (1959), and Alexander (1961) did before him, Fama argues that a random walk (serial independence of successive price changes) should follow as a natural consequence of market equilibrium, since if it were false, investors would try to take advantage of the dependence to earn excess profits and in so doing eliminate the dependence. Fama fails to realize what became apparent later that since the factors used to discount future cash flows need not be serially independent in equilibrium, neither will the price changes themselves. Nonetheless the association of random walks with rationally set equilibrium prices persists, and is, in practice, a reasonable first-order approximation.

His paper provides evidence pertaining to the probability distribution of the natural logarithms of stock returns. Like Kendall (1953) he finds normality an acceptable first-order approximation, but observes there are too many observations near the mean and in the extreme tails— that is, that the kurtosis is much higher than 3 (for the normal distribution). According to Mandelbrot (1963), the first person that he can discover to observe fat tails for price series was Wesley C. Mitchell in [Mitchell (1915)] "The Making of Index Numbers," introduction to *Index Numbers and Wholesale Prices in the United States and Foreign Countries*, Bulletin No. 173 (U.S. Bureau of Labor Statistics, 1915). Among others, it was also noted by Osborne (1959) and Alexander (1961). Fama considers three empirical models of this discrepancy: stable-Paretian distributions (described in Mandelbrot), mixture of normals, and nonstationarity, and concludes after much discussion that the empirical evidence favors the stable-Paretian hypothesis. Unfortunately, it is fair to say that the stable-Paretian assumption has been abandoned by later research, which now seems to favor nonstationarity as the principal source of fat tails. The earliest fairly convincing papers along these lines are Press (1967) and Rosenberg (1972).

Fama also presents empirical evidence from his examination of individual New York Stock Exchange (NYSE) stocks in favor of random walks: serial correlation tests, runs tests, and Alexander (1961)-style filter tests. The one observation that Fama concludes controverts the random walk hypothesis is the Mandelbrot (1963) observation that large price changes tend to be followed by large price changes but of random sign (so they cannot be easily used to make profits). Fama speculates that this would arise in a market in which new highly significant information hits the market, creating an over- or underreaction that is corrected as the market has more time to reach a more precise consensus. He concludes:

> *There is some evidence that large changes tend to be followed by large price changes of either sign, but the dependence from this source does not seem to be too important. There is no evidence, however, that there is any dependence in the stock-price series that would be regarded as important for investment purposes. That is, the past history of the series cannot be used to increase the investor's expected profits. (p. 87)*[21]

Fama summarizes in a famous sentence that the observed verification of the random walk hypothesis is "consistent with the existence of an 'efficient' market for securities, that is, a market where, given the available information, actual prices at every point in time represent very good estimates of intrinsic values" (p. 90).

Fama is one of the first to note an important empirical contradiction to the random walk hypothesis if time is measured by closing prices and calendar days: Weekend variance of returns (typically Friday close to Monday close), instead of being three times the size of intraweek one-day close-to-close as it would be under that hypothesis (Regnault 1863; Bachelier 1900), is actually only 22 percent times larger. For example, if the annualized standard deviation of intraweek one-day closes is 20 percent, instead of being 35 percent over the weekend, it is only 22 percent.

Fama also provides his own test of mutual fund performance—shortly to be eclipsed by tests that correct returns for risk, as in Treynor (1965) and Sharpe (1966). He reaches similar conclusions to earlier mutual fund studies by Irwin Friend, F.E. Brown, Edward S. Herman, and Douglas Vickers, in [Friend-Brown-Herman-Vickers (1962)] *A Study of Mutual Funds: Investment Policy and Investment Company Performance*, Report of the Committee on Interstate and Foreign Commerce, House Report No. 2274, 87th Congress, Second Session (August 28, 1962) and by Ira Horowitz in [Horowitz (1963)] "The Varying (?) Quality of Investment Trust Management," *Journal of the American Statistical Association* 58, No. 304 (December 1963), pp. 1011–1032. He finds neither any evidence that the average fund outperformed the market nor any evidence of performance persistence, casting doubt on whether any mutual fund in his sample outperformed the market by skill.

1965 William Forsyth Sharpe, "Risk-Aversion in the Stock Market: Some Empirical Evidence," *Journal of Finance* 20, No. 3 (September 1965), pp. 416–422.

CAPITAL ASSET PRICING MODEL (CAPM),
RISKLESS RETURN, BETA

Sharpe (1965) is the first (of what was to become several hundred) published empirical tests of the CAPM. Sharpe examines 34 mutual funds during the period 1954–1963, using annual returns. He assumes that their portfolios are mean-variance efficient. In that case the CAPM predicts that their expected return (μ_j) and standard deviation of return (σ_j) will be linearly related: $\mu_j = a + b\sigma_j$, with $b > 0$ and a interpreted as the riskless return. Since the actual (*ex ante*) μ_j and σ_j are unobservable, he employs the now well-established procedure of using the realized mean and standard deviation of returns as *ex post* estimates. He finds that $a = 1.038$ and $b = .836$ and is highly statistically significant, confirming to a good approximation the predictions of the theory.

However, Richard R. West in [West (1968)] "Mutual Fund Performance and the Theory of Capital Asset Pricing: Some Comments," *Journal of Business* 41, No. 2 (April 1968), pp. 230–234, points out that Sharpe's test of the CAPM may not really test that model at all. Suppose that each of the 34 mutual funds P consisted of an investment of proportion $(1 - x_p)$ in cash with return r and $0 < x_p \leq 1$ in the Dow Jones Industrial Average (DJIA) with return r_M. So the realized return r_P of the fund at any time period is $r_P = (1 - x_p)r + x_p r_M$. In this simple case, the standard deviation of the fund return $\sigma_P = x_p\sigma_M$ and beta of the fund are $\beta_P = x_p\beta_M$. The assumption that any of the 34 funds actually held the DJIA, while clearly false, nonetheless, for practical purposes, is a close approximation to the truth since Sharpe finds that 90 percent of the variance of return of a typical fund is explained by the co-movement of the fund's return with the DJIA.

Now suppose we look at the results from investing in these funds over a period in which the market went up, in particular, $r_M > r$. Over such a period, the CAPM would seem to be verified since funds with higher betas (since they have higher x_p) will also have higher realized returns. Sharpe's period 1953–1963 just happens to be a period when $r_M > r$. In contrast, 1937–1946 was a period in which $r_M < r$. Just looking at that period, Sharpe's approach would have rejected the CAPM since higher-beta funds would have experienced lower returns. West's criticism then shows that developing a statistical test that could reject the CAPM in the late 1960s remained an open problem.

1966   William Forsyth Sharpe, "Mutual Fund Performance," *Journal of Business* 39, No. 1, Part 2, Supplement (January 1966), pp. 119–138.

1966   Jack L. Treynor and **K.K. Mazuy**, "Can Mutual Funds Outguess the Market?," *Harvard Business Review* 44, No. 4 (July–August 1966), pp. 131–136.

CAPITAL ASSET PRICING MODEL (CAPM),
MUTUAL FUND PERFORMANCE, SHARPE RATIO,
MARKET TIMING VS. SECURITY SELECTION

To this point, investment performance had been measured simply by comparing realized returns to a market index, with no adjustment for risk. But with the development of the CAPM, a specific risk adjustment was now theoretically justified. Jack L. Treynor, in [Treynor (1965)] "How to Rate Management of Investment Funds," *Harvard Business Review* 43, No. 1 (January–February 1965), pp. 63–75, had proposed that mutual funds be evaluated using the ratio of the realized excess return (over the riskless return) to their realized beta $(\mu_p - r)/\beta_p$, while Sharpe (1966) proposes using the ratio $S_p \equiv (\mu_p - r)/\sigma_p$ on the grounds that funds should be penalized for incomplete diversification. This later ratio, which Sharpe called "the reward-to-variability ratio" is now widely known among professional investors as the Sharpe ratio.

Using this measure, Sharpe provides the first test of the persistence of mutual fund performance. Looking at the same 34 funds he examined in Sharpe (1965) he compares their performance over 1944–1953 with their performance over 1954–1963. He finds evidence of persistence: "An investor selecting one of the 17 best funds in the first period would have an 11:6 chance of holding one of the 17 best in the second period" (p. 127). However, relatively good performance is largely but not completely explained by low management fees, which ranged from .25 percent to 1.50 percent per year (he does not try to analyze the effects on performance of turnover and loads, which were a one-time charge of about 8.5 percent). Comparing the realized Sharpe ratios of his 34 funds (not including load charges) to the returns of the DJIA (without any trading costs), he concludes that "the odds are greater than 100 to 1 against the possibility that the average mutual fund did as well as the Dow Jones portfolio from 1954 to 1963" (p. 137).

Net of management expenses, 11 funds outperformed the DJIA in terms of their Sharpe ratios and 23 underperformed. However, adding back management expenses, this ratio was 19 to 15. So Sharpe concludes that management expenses are the major reason the average fund underperformed the DJIA and, absent these expenses, the average fund had about the same performance as the DJIA.

Sharpe reaches this conclusion as follows. He measures the average S_p over 10 years from 1954 to 1963 for each of his 34 funds. The standard deviation across the funds of S_p was 0.08057. Assuming a normal distribution for S_p, the standard deviation of the sample mean of the fund Sharpe ratios should then be $0.08057/\sqrt{34} = .01383$. The sample mean of the funds was 0.633 and the DJIA mean was 0.677. Therefore, the sample fund mean was 2.46 standard deviations below the DJIA mean. The odds, then, that the true fund mean was actually above the DJIA realized Sharpe ratio were 144 to 1.

Treynor-Mazuy (1966) is the first published test of the market-timing ability of mutual funds within the context of the CAPM. A fund presumably will invest relatively more of its total assets in the market at times it is bullish, and less when it is bearish. For a fund that cannot time the market, the graph of its "characteristic line," that is, its excess return as a function of the market's excess return, will be straight. For a fund that can successfully time the market, its characteristic line will be convex to the origin. Therefore, to isolate market timing, Treynor and Mazuy add a term, quadratic in the market return, to the market model regression equation of Sharpe (1963). The sign of this will indicate market timing, positive and significant for success, or insignificantly different from zero for no forecasting ability. Only one of the 57 mutual funds in their sample shows evidence of market timing ability at the 95 percent significance level. All the other funds seem to have linear characteristic lines. They end with a suitable quotation from Joseph de la Vega (1688):

Profits on the exchange are the treasures of goblins. At one time they may be carbuncle stones, then coals, then diamonds, then flint-stones, then morning dew, then tears.

1966 Benjamin F. King, "Market and Industry Factors in Stock Price Behavior," *Journal of Business* 39, No. 1, Part 2, Supplement (January 1966), pp. 139–190.

1967 **Kalman J. Cohen** and **Jerry A. Pogue**, "An Empirical Evaluation of Alternative Portfolio-Selection Models," *Journal of Business* 40, No. 2 (April 1967), pp. 166–193.

1974 **James L. Farrell Jr.**, "Analyzing Covariation of Returns to Determine Homogeneous Stock Groupings," *Journal of Business* 47, No. 2 (April 1974), pp. 186–207.

MULTIFACTOR MODELS, INDUSTRY FACTORS, SECTOR FACTORS, CLUSTER ANALYSIS

King (1966) examines 63 NYSE stocks between 1929 and 1960, drawn from a variety of industries. King shows that the return of an equity proxy for the market portfolio is strongly correlated with the returns of typical stocks, as Sharpe (1963) no doubt had in mind. However, in addition to the market proxy, there are other industry factors that were useful in explaining the co-movement of stock returns. This subsequently led to considerable interest in identifying other factors that could explain co-movement besides the market proxy. The search for factors was on and has continued ever since. Cohen-Pogue (1967) proposed multifactor extensions of the single-factor market model. The first assumes that the realized return of each stock is a linear function of the realized return of its industry or sector plus uncorrelated noise across securities. Then, the industry returns are assumed to be related by a general covariance matrix. The second extension is similar except the industry return is assumed to be a linear function of the realized market return plus uncorrelated noise across industries. These *realized* return models were at first presumed to be potentially consistent with the CAPM. The CAPM says there could be many sources of co-movement, but only one source, the market portfolio, is priced (that is, only the market portfolio affects *expected* portfolio returns). Somewhat heretically at the time, Merton (1973/September) and Ross (1976/December) in different ways then raised the possibility that other factors that could show up in a multifactor realized return model might end up being priced as well.

Another approach to determine the factors that determine stock returns is to let the data speak for themselves. Cluster analysis provides a simple and appealing way to do this. As this stepwise algorithm is described by Farrell (1974):

1. Identify n basic underlying variables (100 common stock monthly returns from 1961 to 1969).

2. Adjust these variables for known common factors and use these adjusted variables in place of the original basic underlying variables (ε_j = $r_j - a_j + \beta_j r_M$, where r_M is the monthly S&P 425 index).
3. Set $x \leftarrow n$.
4. Calculate $\frac{1}{2} x(x - 1)$ simple paired correlation coefficients.
5. *Stop* if all paired correlations are zero or negative.
6. Locate the two variables with the highest paired correlation.
7. Combine the two variables into a single composite variable.
8. Replace the two variables with the composite variable leaving a total of $x - 1$ variables.
9. Set $x \leftarrow x - 1$.
10. If $x \neq 1$, return to step 3; otherwise *stop*.

Eventually, this procedure produced four clusters:

Cluster 1: (Hewlett-Packard, Perkin Elmer, AMP, Maryland Cup, Burroughs, Ampex, Trane, ITT, MMM, Baxter Labs), (Zenith, Motorola, Polaroid, Texas Instruments), Becton Dickinson, National Cash Register, (Corning Glass, International Flavor and Fragrance, IBM, Avon, Xerox), Eastman Kodak, Harcourt Brace, (Pam Am, UAL, United Aircraft), Chesebrough-Ponds, NALCO, TRW, Honeywell, Merck.

Cluster 2: (Virginia Electric, American Electric, Central & Southwest, Florida Power, Columbia Gas), (Procter & Gamble, General Foods, Chase Manhattan, Coca-Cola, Transamerica, Household Finance, CIT, Northwest Bancorp, CPC International), (Gillette, Quaker Oats, Campbell Soup, Kellogg), (Hershey, Reynolds), American Home Products, (Kraftco, Sears, Federated Department Stores, National Biscuit).

Cluster 3: (American Metal Climax, Kennecott, American Smelting, Pullman), (Clark Equipment, International Harvester, Joy, International Paper, Alcoa), (Eaton, Borg Warner, Otis, National Lead), (Bethlehem Steel, National Steel, Gardner Denver, Rohm & Haas, Johns Manville, Ingersoll Rand, Goodyear), (Georgia Pacific, Weyerhaeuser), (Caterpillar, Timkin, Sunbeam, Deere), (American Can, Continental Can, Consolidated Freight, Cincinnati Milling, Babcock Wilcox, Square D), (American Standard, Monsanto, Burlington, Mohasco).

Cluster 4: Standard of California, Texaco, Jersey Standard, Mobil, Standard of Indiana, Gulf, Union Oil, Shell.

Items in parentheses are subclusters. For example, the three aircraft companies make a clear subcluster being more highly correlated with each other than any of the other stocks. Cursory examination of the stocks in each cluster suggests identifying cluster 1 with growth stocks, cluster 2 with stable stocks, cluster 3 with cyclical stocks, and cluster 4 with oil stocks. What makes this conclusion particularly compelling is that these cluster identifications were not assumed in advance, but the data automatically arranged themselves in these groups. The average computed percentage variations in monthly return for each cluster for the market factor and the cluster factor (created out of a value-weighted index of all stocks in a cluster) are:

Cluster	Market Factor	Cluster Factor
Growth stocks	31%	15%
Stable stocks	29	12
Cyclical stocks	33	9
Oil stocks	31	31

Farrell shows that standard stock classifications, with the addition of a separate oil category, are very useful artifices to explain the cross-sectional variation in stock returns and that the Markowitz (1959) and Sharpe (1963) market model with its single market factor index and assumed zero cross-sectional correlation of residual returns leaves a lot to be desired.

John D. Martin and Robert C. Klemkosky, in [Martin-Klemkosky (1976)] "The Effect of Homogeneous Stock Groupings on Portfolio Risk," *Journal of Business* 49, No. 3 (July 1976), pp. 339–349, suggest a way to measure the deficiency in the market model. Recall that the market model states that $r_j - r = \alpha_j + (r_M - r)\beta_j + \varepsilon_j$ where α_j and β_j are defined such that $E(\varepsilon_j) = \rho(r_M, \varepsilon_j) = 0$. To this tautological construction, the assumption is made that for any two different securities j and k, $\rho(\varepsilon_j, \varepsilon_k) = 0$. Consider any portfolio P with proportional composition $(x_1, x_2, \ldots, x_m)$ such that $\sum_j x_j = 1$. The variance of the portfolio return is:

$$\sigma_P^2 = \beta_P^2 \sigma_M^2 + \sum_j x_j^2 \omega_j^2$$

where $\beta_P \equiv \sum_j x_j \beta_j$, $\sigma_M^2 \equiv \text{Var}(r_M)$, and $\omega_j^2 \equiv \text{Var}(\varepsilon_j)$. Since $\rho(\varepsilon_j, \varepsilon_k) = 0$, many covariance terms do not appear. To the extent there are positive industry or sector cross-sectional correlation effects, if these are considered, σ_P^2 will be larger. So a way to consider the significance of extra-market covariation is to compare, for a given portfolio, σ_P^2 estimated from the market model using the earlier equation with either σ_P^2 estimated from a market model generalization that considers these effects or σ_P^2 estimated from the realized portfolio returns.

1967   John P. Shelton, "The Value Line Contest: A Test of the Predictability of Stock-Price Changes," *Journal of Business* 40, No. 3 (July 1967), pp. 251–269.

INDIVIDUAL INVESTOR PERFORMANCE

Most tests of the performance of investors have by necessity concerned financial intermediaries such as mutual funds. As much as we would like to examine the performance of individual investors on their private accounts, we simply have not had the information (until more recently). However, the 1965–1966 Value Line Contest provided a brief opportunity to examine the skill of 18,565 ordinary investors. Value Line ranks stocks from 1 to 5, with the stocks it expects to perform best ranked 1. Contestants were required to choose a portfolio of 25 stocks from the 350 stocks ranked 4 and 5 on November 25, 1965, investing an equal dollar amount in each stock. At the same time, Value Line selected a portfolio of 25 stocks from the 100 stocks it ranked 1. The winning contestant was to be the individual whose portfolio over the following six months had the best realized performance, and in particular, outperformed Value Line's portfolio. It turned out that only 20 investors were able earn higher returns than Value Line. But that was not the focus of Shelton (1967). He asked whether the average contestant was able to outperform the average of 18,565 randomly chosen 25-stock portfolios (each chosen from the 350-stock universe). Shelton concluded that the average randomly selected portfolio lost 5.95 percent of its value, while the average portfolio chosen by a contestant lost only 4.77 percent. Moreover, with such a large sample size, this difference (1.18 percent) was extremely statistically significant, about 49 standard deviations away from 0 percent.

Alas, positive empirical results of this sort, upon more careful analysis, are often overturned. Two years later, Warren H. Hausman, in [Hausman (1969)] "A Note on 'The Value Line Contest: A Test of the Predictability of Stock-Price Changes,'" *Journal of Business* 42, No. 3 (July 1969), pp. 317–330, argues that in effect the sample size was much smaller than 18,565 portfolios since the contestants did not choose their portfolios independently. They may have, for example, been influenced by the same news events or the same characteristics, such as high earnings per share (EPS) growth. Indeed, the data reveals that contestants concentrated their investments in the same stocks. Hausman concludes:

> *The fact that investors (or contest entrants) tend to agree with each other need not mean they know anything of value. Neither does the fact that, on a single occasion, they outperformed a random selection of stocks, especially if the degree of superiority was quite small when evaluated by means of the relevant measures of chance. As Shelton points out, there can be no substitute for additional observations made at different points of time. (p. 320)[22]*

1967   S. James Press, "A Compound Events Model for Security Prices," *Journal of Business* 40, No. 3 (July 1967), pp. 317–335.

1972   Peter D. Praetz, "The Distribution of Share Price Changes," *Journal of Business* 45, No. 1 (January 1972), pp. 49–55.

1972   Barr Rosenberg, "The Behavior of Random Variables with Nonstationary Variance and the Distribution of Security Prices," an unpublished but frequently cited working paper, Graduate School of Business, University of California at Berkeley (December 1972).

1982   Robert F. Engle (November 10, 1942–), "Autoregressive Conditional Heteroscadasticity with Estimates of the Variance of United Kingdom Inflation," *Econometrica* 50, No. 4 (July 1982), pp. 987–1008.

STABLE-PARETIAN HYPOTHESIS, VOLATILITY,
NONSTATIONARY VARIANCE, STOCHASTIC VOLATILITY,
FAT TAILS, EXCESS KURTOSIS, AUTOREGRESSIVE
CONDITIONAL HETEROSCEDASTICITY (ARCH)

Mandelbrot (1963) used stable-Paretian distributions to explain the fat tails observed by Osborne (1959) and Alexander (1961) in the frequency distributions of returns of stocks. However, financial economists were reluctant to adopt this model primarily because they would have to give up variance as their favored measure of risk (since the variance of a stable-Paretian random variable is infinite). In the end, the stable-Paretian hypothesis proved a dead end, particularly as alternative finite-variance explanations of stock returns were developed. Press (1967) was perhaps the first to propose such an alternative in what proved to be the first application of Poisson-jump processes to stock price behavior. He assumed that successive price changes behaved according to the following model:

$$\Delta P(t) \equiv \log P(t + 1) - \log P(t) = \Sigma_k Y_k + \varepsilon(t)$$

where the sum is taken $n(t - 1)$ to $n(t)$, and $\varepsilon(t)$ is a serially independent stationary normal random variable distributed as $N(0, \sigma_1^2)$; $Y_1, Y_2, \ldots, Y_k$, $\ldots$ is a sequence of mutually independent normally distributed random variables distributed as $N(\theta, \sigma_2^2)$; and $n(t)$ is a Poisson process with parameter λt representing the expected number of stock price–relevant events that occur between times t and $t + 1$. One is free to think of $n(t)$ as a number of trades, but it is not necessary to do this. It is easy to show then that the first two central moments of $\Delta P(t)$ are given by:

$$E[\Delta P(t)] = \lambda\theta \text{ and } Var[\Delta P(t)] = \sigma_1^2 + \lambda(\theta^2 + \sigma_2^2)$$

The first four cumulants are:

$$K_1 = E[\Delta P(t)], K_2 = Var[\Delta P(t)], K_3 = \lambda\theta(\theta^2 + 3\sigma_2^2),$$
$$K_4 = \lambda(\theta^4 + 6\theta^2\sigma_2^2 + 3\sigma_2^4)$$

Standardized skewness and kurtosis are:

$$\text{Skw}[\Delta P(t)] = \frac{K_3}{K_2^{3/2}} \text{ and } \text{Kurt}[\Delta P(t)] = \frac{K_4}{K_2^2}$$

Press claims that the sign of $\text{Skw}[\Delta P(t)]$ is the same as the sign of θ, the distribution of $\Delta P(t)$ is more peaked than the normal, there exists an extreme enough level of $\Delta P(t)$ such that the distribution has more probability than the normal after that level, and the smaller $|\theta|$, the less extreme this level needs to be.

To estimate the four parameters $(\lambda, \theta, \sigma_1^2, \sigma_2^2)$ from a time series, Press advises using the method of matching cumulants. To do this, suppose that $\Delta P(1), \Delta P(2), \ldots, \Delta P(t), \ldots, \Delta P(T)$ is the observed time series of log stock price differences, and the sample noncentral moments are defined as $m_r = (\Sigma_t [\Delta P(t)]^r)/T$ for $r = 1, \ldots, 4$. Press assumes that the time series consists of uncorrelated and identically distributed random variables. It then follows that the sample cumulants are (see Maurice G. Kendall, *The Ad-*

vanced Theory of Statistics, Volume I [New York: Hafner Publishing, 1958], p. 70):

$$\underline{K}_1 = m_1, \underline{K}_2 = m_2 - m_1^2, \underline{K}_3 = m_3 - 3m_1m_2 + 2m_1^3,$$
$$\underline{K}_4 = m_4 - 3m_2^2 - 4m_1m_3 + 12m_1^2m_2 - 6m_1^4$$

Then equate $K_r = \underline{K}_r$ for $r = 1, \ldots$ 4 and solve the four equations for the four parameter unknowns $(\lambda, \theta, \sigma_1^2, \sigma_2^2)$. Press shows that once θ is solved for implicitly, the remaining three parameters can be solved in closed form.

An alternative way to generate fat tails is to assume instead the variance of the distribution of log price differences is itself a random variable which can take a different value each time period. Praetz (1972) is the first to investigate this possibility. In this case,

$$\Delta P = \int f(\Delta P \mid \sigma^2)g(\sigma^2)d\sigma^2$$

where $\sigma^2 \equiv \mathrm{Var}(\Delta P)$, f and g are densities, and the integral is taken from 0 to ∞. For g, Praetz specifically proposes an inverted gamma distribution.

Unfortunately, this model has a serious problem. As Praetz himself notes, actual volatility clusters. There are often consecutive periods of abnormally high volatility and other consecutive periods of abnormally low volatility. But Praetz has assumed that the *level* of variance is random so that unusually high variance today is likely to be followed by normal variance. A much better hypothesis is to suppose that the *change in the level* of variance is an independent and identically distributed random variable. This allows for volatility clustering. The first to propose a model of this sort is Rosenberg (1972). Also, prior to Rosenberg, economists, including Press and Praetz, had assumed that individual price changes or (log) returns were serially identically distributed.

Using the 100-year history of serial changes in the logarithms of the monthly price levels of the S&P Composite Stock Price Index (1871–1971), Rosenberg calculates that the standardized kurtosis of the frequency distribution of the time series (the ratio of the fourth central moment to the square of the second central moment) is 14.79, much larger than 3 for a normal distribution. While maintaining the assumption that each individual price change is drawn from a normal distribution, Rosenberg argues that a potential explanation for the high kurtosis is nonstationarity of the variance of the normal distribution from which the price is drawn. He proposes a model where the price change is drawn in two steps. First, the variance is drawn from a given nonstationary distribution; second, the price change is drawn from a normal distribution with the updated variance.

He begins by showing that when the variance of a time series of random variables is nonstationary (perhaps even nonstochastic) then the population kurtosis will be greater than the kurtosis of the individual variables (3 in the case of the normal distribution).

Rosenberg's Proof That Nonstationary Variance Leads to Increased Kurtosis

Suppose that the changes in the natural logarithm of prices in the time series of a single security are distributed as: $z_t \equiv \log P_t - \log P_{t-1} = \mu_t + \sigma_t \varepsilon_t$, for $t = 1, 2, \ldots, n$, where ε_t are serially independent and identically distributed random variables with a mean 0, variance 1, and kurtosis γ. In general, ε_t can follow a stochastic process and, if so, σ_t is independent of ε_t. However, for now, assume that future values of σ_t are known even though they are time-dependent. Define y_t as the de-meaned version of z_t so that $y_t \equiv z_t - \mu_t = \sigma_t \varepsilon_t$. Then, $E(y_t) = 0$, $E(y_t^2) = \sigma_t^2$, and $E(y_t^4) = \gamma \sigma_t^4$ where $\gamma \equiv E(\varepsilon_t^4)$. Therefore, the standardized kurtosis of y_t is:

$$\frac{E(y_t^4)}{E(y_t^2)^2} = \gamma$$

Now, suppose that I calculate the expectations of the sample moments and $\underline{\mu}_1$, $\underline{\mu}_2$, and $\underline{\mu}_4$ of the time series of realized values of y_t:

$$E(\underline{\mu}_1) = E\left(\frac{\Sigma_t y_t}{n}\right) = 0$$

$$E(\underline{\mu}_2) = E\left(\frac{\Sigma_t y_t^2}{n}\right) = \Sigma_t \frac{E(y_t^2)}{n} = \frac{\Sigma_t \sigma_t^2}{n}$$

$$E(\underline{\mu}_4) = E\left(\frac{\Sigma_t y_t^4}{n}\right) = \Sigma_t \frac{E(y_t^4)}{n} = \frac{\gamma \Sigma_t \sigma_t^4}{n}$$

So the standardized kurtosis of the time series of realized values of y_t is:

$$\frac{E(\underline{\mu}_4)}{[E(\underline{\mu}_2)]^2} = \left[\frac{\gamma \Sigma_t \sigma_t^4 / n}{(\Sigma_t \sigma_t^2 / n)^2}\right] = \gamma \left[n \frac{\Sigma_t \sigma_t^4}{(\Sigma_t \sigma_t^2)^2}\right]$$

It is easy to see that if $\sigma_t = \sigma$, so that variance is stationary, then $n[\Sigma_t \sigma_t^4]/[\Sigma_t \sigma_t^2]^2 = 1$. But if σ_t varies at all from date to date, then $n[\Sigma_t \sigma_t^4]/[\Sigma_t \sigma_t^2]^2 > 1$, so $E(\underline{\mu}_4)/[E(\underline{\mu}_2)]^2 > \gamma$.

For example, suppose $n = 2$ and I set $a = \sigma_1^2$ and $b = \sigma_2^2$, then the standardized kurtosis of the time series is $2(a^2 + b^2)/(a + b)^2$. If $a = b$, then this ratio equals 1; but if $a \neq b$, then a little algebra shows that the ratio is greater than 1.

Rosenberg then employs a simple model of stochastic volatility: The predicted next-month squared price change (the current variance) equals a fixed linear function of the previous 10 squared monthly price changes:

$$y_t^2 = \alpha + \frac{\beta \Sigma_{k=2} y_{t-k}^2}{m-1}$$

where the sum is taken from $k = 2$ to $k = m = 11$ (the first 32 months from January 1871 to July 1873 were used to establish a sample size of 10 months). Regression estimates taken over the subperiod August 1873–December 1950 yield $\alpha = .001$ and $\beta = .666$, with the latter quite significantly different from 0 with a t-statistic of 10.06. This implies that simple as the variance forecasting model is, it works. This may be the first published evidence for security prices for what later became known as volatility clustering, that is, the tendency for variance to change stochastically but slowly over time so that there are extended periods of consistently low variance and extended periods of consistently high variance. This simple volatility model reduces the standardized kurtosis of ε_t to an upper bound between 4.61 and 6.19, a significant reduction in the sample kurtosis calculated from a constant volatility model. Moreover, for longer sampling intervals for two, three, four, five, and six months, this upper bound is reduced to between 2.17 and 4.45. Rosenberg emphasizes that this considerable reduction of kurtosis is achieved with a very simple model of predicted variance; presumably more sophisticated predictive models would bring this even closer to 3. Rosenberg prophetically concludes that this:

> *suggests that better forecasting models for the variance will explain virtually all of the nonnormality in the empirical frequency distribution of NYSE stock price changes. . . . The apparent kurtosis of the empirical frequency distribution is the result of mixing distributions with predictably differing variances. . . . The results of the experiment have widespread implications for financial management and the theory of security markets. Some of these are the following: (i) the requirements for forecasts of price variance; (ii) the opening of the study of the determinants of price variance as a field of economic analysis; (iii) the need to respond to fluctuations in variance in portfolio management; (iv) the role of fluctuations in variance, through their effect on the riskiness of investment and, hence, on the appropriate risk premium, as an influence on the price level. (pp. 39–40)*[23]

A decade later Engle (1982) labeled the model that Rosenberg had applied to stock prices, an autoregressive conditional heteroscedasticity (ARCH) model (see in particular p. 988). Though widely circulated and referenced, Rosenberg's working paper had never been published, and Engle seemed unaware of it since he does not mention or reference it. In 2003, Engle won the Nobel Prize in Economic Science "for methods of analyzing economic time series with time-varying volatility (ARCH)."

1968   Robert Wilson, "The Theory of Syndicates," *Econometrica* 36, No. 1 (January 1968), pp. 119–132.

AGGREGATION, PARETO-OPTIMAL SHARING RULES,
CONSENSUS INVESTOR, EXPONENTIAL UTILITY

Wilson (1968) is the classic aggregation paper under uncertainty. A group chooses a common action and nature chooses a state that together determine the total payoff for the group. The group then distributes this payoff to its members using a prespecified sharing rule that specifies how the total payoff is to be divided. It is assumed that each member evaluates potential payoffs in terms of his expected utility using his own subjective probabilities. Wilson's problem is to determine the circumstances under which a Pareto-optimal sharing rule can be defined such that the same common action is chosen as if the group were a single agent using its own utility function and subjective probabilities. Wilson shows that such an agent exists if and only if the sharing rule is linear in the total payoff or all agents have the same probability assessments. He also shows that if probability assessments are the same for all agents, concavity of the member utility functions implies concavity of the group utility function.

This anticipates subsequent work where the sharing rule is determined via a perfect and competitive securities market equilibrium. Rubinstein (1974) derives implications in this context of linear sharing rules and Constantinides (1982) derives implications in this context if instead all agents have the same probability assessments. Wilson's paper also highlights the unique aggregation properties of groups whose members all have exponential utility functions but have different probability assessments, a setting that is commonly used in many subsequent papers in finance.

1968 Jan Mossin, "Optimal Multiperiod Portfolio Policies," *Journal of Business* 41, No. 2 (April 1968), pp. 215–229.

1969 Paul Anthony Samuelson, "Lifetime Portfolio Selection by Dynamic Stochastic Programming," *Review of Economics and Statistics* 51, No. 3 (August 1969), pp. 239–246, reprinted in *The Collected Scientific Papers of Paul A. Samuelson,* Volume 3 (Cambridge, MA: MIT Press, 1972), pp. 883–890.

1969, 1970, and **1971 Nils H. Hakansson** (June 2, 1937–), "Optimal Investment and Consumption Strategies under Risk, an Uncertain Lifetime and Insurance," *International Economic Review* 10, No. 3 (October 1969), pp. 443–466; "Optimal Investment and Consumption Strategies under Risk for a Class of Utility Functions," *Econometrica* 38, No. 5 (September 1970), pp. 587–607; "Optimal Entrepreneurial Decisions in a Completely Stochastic Environment," *Management Science* 17, No. 7 (March 1971), pp. 427–449.

MULTIPERIOD PORTFOLIO SELECTION,
LONG-TERM INVESTMENT, PORTFOLIO REVISION, MYOPIA,
WORKING BACKWARDS, DYNAMIC PROGRAMMING,
INDIRECT OR DERIVED UTILITY, TIME-ADDITIVE UTILITY,
CONSTANT ABSOLUTE RISK AVERSION (CARA),
HYPERBOLIC ABSOLUTE RISK AVERSION (HARA),
LOGARITHMIC UTILITY, POWER UTILITY, TURNPIKES

Kelly (1956), Latané (1959), Markowitz (1959), and Breiman (1961) consider the problem of maximizing the utility of wealth after many periods of potential portfolio revisions where investors allocate their accumulated wealth in each period between a riskless and a risky security. They specifically restricted their analyses to terminal logarithmic utility. In contrast, Markowitz (1952/March), Roy (1952), and Tobin (1958) examine portfolio choice only over a single period and restrict themselves to mean-variance preferences. Mossin (1968) considers the multiperiod setting in which an investor maximizes the expected utility of his terminal wealth (at some preselected horizon date T), deliberately ignoring, for purposes of simplification, any intermediate withdrawals for consumption as in Phelps (1962).

Since, generally, the decision an investor makes in any period before the last depends on what his subsequent decisions can be, he solves the problem, as Markowitz (1959) originally suggested, using dynamic programming. That is, he starts at the penultimate date $T - 1$, and maximizes given terminal expected utility $E[U(W_T)|W_{T-1}]$ as a function of the wealth

W_{T-1} available at $T - 1$. This leads to an indirect or derived utility of wealth $V_{T-1}(W_{T-1}) = \max E[U(W_T)|W_{T-1}]$ at date $T - 1$, where the random wealth outcome W_T is the result of allocating wealth W_{T-1} between the riskless and risky security at date $T - 1$ to maximize expected utility. Continuing to work backward recursively, he solves for $V_{T-2}(W_{T-2}) = \max E[V_{T-1}(W_{T-1})|W_{T-2}]$, and so on, until he reaches date 1 when he can now determine the current optimal allocation between the riskless and risky security simply by maximizing $E[V_1(W_1)|W_0]$ based on the current known wealth W_0. Mossin makes the important simplifying random walk assumption that the security returns in each period are independent of the security returns available in other periods.

Decision making would be vastly simplified if the investor could choose myopically, that is, at each date treat his decision then as if it were his last. Mossin therefore asks: What class of terminal utility of wealth functions $U(W_T)$ is necessary and sufficient for myopia? He proves that only utility functions with constant relative risk aversion (CRRA) (logarithmic and power utility) have the myopia property. That is, at each date t, such investors optimally choose their allocation between the riskless and the risky security using $V_t(W_{t+1}) = U(W_{t+1})$. In other words, to make the optimal dollar allocation at each date, the investor need only know his wealth and the returns available over the current period; in particular, he does not have to consider the time remaining to his horizon date T or the available returns after the current period.

Proof of Sufficiency of CRRA for Myopia

Sufficiency of CRRA is easy to see. First consider an investor who maximizes the expected logarithmic utility of his date $T = 2$ wealth: $E[U(W_2)]$ $= E[\log(W_2)] = E[\log(W_0 r_{P1} r_{P2})]$ where W_0 is his known initial wealth, r_{P1} is the random return from his chosen portfolio over the first period (from date 0 to date 1), and r_{P2} is the random return from his possibly revised (at date 1) portfolio over the second period from date 1 to date 2. Observe that:

$$E[\log(W_0 r_{P1} r_{P2})] = E[\log(W_0 r_{P1}) + \log(r_{P2})]$$
$$E[\log(W_0 r_{P1}) + \log(r_{P2})] = E[\log (W_0 r_{P1})] + E[\log(r_{P2})]$$
$$E[\log(W_0 r_{P1})] + E[\log(r_{P2})] \sim E[\log(W_1)]$$

Proof of Sufficiency of CRRA for Myopia *(Continued)*

The notation ~ indicates "is equivalent up to an increasing linear translation to." In this case, in the third step, we simply have an additive constant $E[\log(r_{P2})]$ that we can omit without affecting our date 0 portfolio choices. This gives rise to utility of wealth W_1 at date 1. Therefore, $V_1(W_1)$ $= \log(W_1)$ and we have myopia. Notice that the myopia under logarithmic utility is quite robust since it will hold even if r_{P1} and r_{P2} were to end up correlated, say, due to changing but correlated investment opportunities. That is, even if these variables were correlated we would still have the second step since the expectation of the *sum* of two random variables equals the sum of their separate expectations, even if they are correlated.

Now consider power utility: $E[U(W_2)] = E[W_2^b] = E[(W_0 r_{P1} r_{P2})^b]$ for $0 < b < 1$. In this case:

$$E[(W_0 r_{P1} r_{P2})^b] = E[(W_0 r_{P1})^b r_{P2}^b]$$
$$E[(W_0 r_{P1})^b r_{P2}^b] = E(r_{P2}^b) E[(W_0 r_{P1})^b]$$
$$E(r_{P2}^b) E[(W_0 r_{P1})^b] \sim E(W_1^b)$$

In this case, the multiplicative constant $E[r_{P2}^b]$ can be omitted without affecting our date 0 portfolio choices. Again, we find myopia since $V_1(W_1)$ $= W_1^b$. However, note here that we need to assume r_{P1} and r_{P2} are not correlated random variables since otherwise step 2 would not go through. That is, the expectation of the *product* of two random variables equals the product of their separate expectations only if they are not correlated.

Moreover, Mossin shows that for constant relative risk aversion (CRRA), the optimal proportionate allocation between the two securities is even independent of the investor's wealth W_t, only being dependent on the current period's security returns.

Proof that CRRA Is Sufficient for Investment Choices to Be Independent of Initial Wealth

This is quite easy to see. Consider a single-period situation in which an investor maximizes his expected utility of his future wealth, $E[U(W_1)]$, where future wealth W_1 equals current wealth W_0 times portfolio return r_P so that $W_1 = W_0 r_P$. The investor therefore maximizes

(Continued)

Proof that CRRA Is Sufficient for Investment Choices to Be Independent of Initial Wealth *(Continued)*

$E[U(W_0 r_P)]$. In general, initial wealth W_0 cannot be separated from this objective. However, in the CRRA case of logarithmic utility, $U(W_1) = \log(W_1)$. Therefore, the investor maximizes:

$$E[U(W_1)] = E[\log(W_0 r_P)] = E[\log(W_0) + \log(r_P)]$$
$$= \log(W_0) + E[\log r_P] \sim E[\log r_P]$$

Because utility functions are "unique up to an increasing linear transformation," the choices of the investor are not changed by adding a constant to each outcome. Since, as we have seen, initial wealth enters as an additive constant, it will not affect choices.

Alternatively, consider the remaining CRRA utility functions, $U(W_1) = W_1^b$ for $0 < b < 1$:

$$E[U(W_1)] = E[(W_0 r_P)^b] = E[(W_0^b)(r_P^b)] = W_0^b E[r_P^b] \sim E[r_P^b]$$

Because utility functions are "unique up to an increasing linear transformation," the choices of the investor are not changed by multiplying each outcome by a positive constant. Since, as we have seen, initial wealth enters as a positive multiplicative constant, is will not affect choices. It is not hard to see that these utility functions exhaust the set of risk-averse utility functions for which initial wealth does not affect choices.

It follows that if these returns are stationary, the investor will rebalance at every date to the same portfolio proportions. Mossin defines "partial myopia" to permit some modest foresight about the future, namely, knowledge of future riskless returns and the time remaining to the horizon, but still no knowledge of the returns of the risky security after the current period. He shows that the hyperbolic absolute risk aversion (HARA) or "homothetic" class of utility functions is necessary and sufficient for partial myopia. While these results generally depend crucially on the independence assumption of security returns over time, Mossin neglects to mention that for the very special case of logarithmic utility, they do not.

This HARA class of utility functions plays an important role in subsequent research because the class has convenient myopia, separation (Hakansson 1969/December; Cass-Stiglitz 1970), and aggregation (Wilson 1968; Rubinstein 1974) properties, making it ideally suited for obtaining closed-form solutions to consumption and portfolio decision rules, and to equilibrium prices. The following utility functions belong to and exhaust the HARA class:

(1) $U(W_t) \sim (b/(1-b))(A + BW_t)^{1-b}$ $(B \neq 0, 1)$

(2) $U(W_t) \sim - Ae^{-W_t/A}$ $(B = 0)$

(3) $U(W_t) \sim \log(A + W_t)$ $(B = 1)$

where A and B are constants, $b \equiv B^{-1}$, and $\sim$ means "is equivalent up to an increasing linear transformation to." Utility functions (2) are the limit of (1) as $B \to 0$, and utility functions (3) are the limit of (1) as $B \to 1$. Logarithmic utility is bounded neither above nor below. Power utility with $b < 1$ is bounded from below but not from above, and with $b > 1$ is bounded from above but not from below. These functions are all the solutions to the differential equation:

$$\frac{-U'(W_t)}{U''(W_t)} = A + BW_t$$

The left-hand side of this equation is the inverse of absolute risk aversion, sometimes called "risk tolerance." So the HARA class is also termed the "linear risk tolerance" class. It is easy to see from this that utility functions (2) constitute all utility functions with constant absolute risk aversion (CARA), and utility functions (1) and (3) where $A = 0$ constitute all utility functions with constant relative risk aversion (CRRA). B (or b) is often referred to as "cautiousness."

Mossin ends the paper with some comments about portfolio "turnpikes," (a singularly appropriate appellation from Leland (1972): A portfolio has the turnpike property if in the limit as the investor's horizon recedes into the future, his current portfolio choice becomes independent of his horizon. He notes that the HARA class has this property since in this limit, HARA investors become CRRA investors, and he conjectures that these turnpike results may carry over even to a much wider class of utility functions than HARA.

Samuelson (1969), under the generalization of an additive utility function of consumption over time, redevelops the portion of Mossin's results that show the sufficiency of CRRA utility for myopia. In addition, he shows that the consumer/investor's portfolio proportions are also chosen independently of his consumption decisions, as does Hakansson (1970). He points out that any lingering belief that the logarithmic utility strategy is the only rational risk-averse investment rule for long-term investors has been permanently set to rest. CRRA, for example, even if it were the result of turnpike investing, only contains logarithmic utility as a special and not the only case.

Hakansson (1971) is the third and most general in a sequence of papers beginning with Hakansson (1970) and Hakansson (1969/October). Building on Phelps (1962) in this paper, an individual is assumed to maximize the expected utility of lifetime consumption with a final bequest, allocating his wealth among consumption, bequest, life insurance, many risky securities, and a riskless security (riskless over a single period). The individual is allowed to have state-dependent future preferences and an uncertain lifetime, and his investment opportunities including the riskless return are allowed to vary stochastically over time, with possible serial correlation. Specific results are derived for the case of time-additive utility with constant relative risk aversion and state-dependent rates of time preference.

Nils H. Hakansson, in [Hakansson (1974)] "Convergence to Isoelastic Utility and Policy in Multiperiod Portfolio Choice," *Journal of Financial Economics* 1, No. 3 (September 1974), pp. 201–224, follows Mossin's suggestion that the CRRA class of utility of terminal wealth functions may have significant turnpike properties. The first extension of Mossin's results is by Hayne Ellis Leland, in [Leland (1972)] "On Turnpike Portfolios," in *Mathematical Methods in Investment and Finance*, edited by G.P. Szego and K. Shell (Amsterdam: North-Holland, 1972), pp. 24–33. Hakansson weakens the turnpike conditions considerably (always under conditions of serial independence of security returns). He concludes that "the conditions for convergence are weakened further, to the point where they appear sufficiently broad to encompass perhaps most utility functions of practical interest." Stephen A. Ross, in [Ross (1974)] "Portfolio Turnpike Theorems for Constant Polices," *Journal of Financial Economics* 1, No. 2 (July 1974), pp. 171–198, also derives related turnpike results.

Further work by Barry Goldman, in [Goldman (1974)] "A Negative Report on the 'Near-Optimality' of the Max-Expected Log Policy As Applied to Bounded Utilities for Long-Lived Programs," *Journal of Financial Economics* 1, No. 1 (May 1974), pp. 97–103, shows that the most important special case of the CRRA class, logarithmic utility, is generally not a good turnpike strategy for investors with bounded terminal utility of wealth functions. Hakansson confirms that such investors never have turnpike utility functions that are logarithmic.

1968 Michael C. Jensen (1939–), "The Performance of Mutual Funds in the Period 1945–1964," *Journal of Finance* 23, No. 2 (May 1968), pp. 389–416.

MUTUAL FUND PERFORMANCE, ALPHA,
BETA, MARKET MODEL, LUCK VS. SKILL

Measurements of mutual fund performance not only are useful for determining the allocation of investors' funds among managers, but perhaps even more significant, they provide perhaps the best empirical test of whether securities are rationally priced. Compared to others, these tests have several advantages: (1) they are based on actual, not paper, profits and losses; (2) they are the results of strategies that were actually, and not imaginatively, implemented using coexisting investment technology and knowledge; (3) properly examined, the results are free from data-mining and survivorship bias; (4) they now cover more than 60 years of investing by thousands of different funds; (5) they summarize the success of a large number of smart and highly compensated managers who devoted most of their waking hours to detecting mispriced securities; and (6) they implicitly test a large number of strategies, including those that may be difficult to translate into a testable algorithm. If these funds, being relatively sophisticated investors, cannot outperform the simple buy-and-hold index fund strategy, then it must be very difficult, if not impossible, for normal investors to beat the market even if they devote several hours a day in the attempt.

Jensen (1968) argues that earlier measures of investment performance developed by others such as Treynor (1965) and Sharpe (1966), while they allow one to rank the performances of different portfolios, do not provide an absolute standard for comparison. Therefore, he suggests his now-famous "alpha" measure of performance. The Sharpe (1964), Lintner (1965/February), Mossin (1966), Treynor (1999) CAPM equation implies that in equilibrium, for any portfolio P:

$$\mu_P = r + (\mu_M - r)\beta_P$$

where r is the riskless return, μ_M is the expected return of the market portfolio, and μ_P and β_P are the expected return and beta of the portfolio. Jensen argues that if an investment manager can select a portfolio that outperforms the market, given its level of risk, then for that portfolio:

$$\mu_P = \alpha_P + r + (\mu_M - r)\beta_P \text{ where } \alpha_P > 0$$

This provides Jensen's absolute standard of performance. Jensen further argues that since it would be perverse for a manager to knowingly choose a portfolio for which alpha would be negative, if a manager has no skill, his alpha will be zero.

Of course, this is itself an internal contradiction to the CAPM since under its assumptions (in particular, all agents have the same beliefs), α_P must equal zero for all portfolios. Moreover, even if one were to imagine a plausible generalization of the CAPM that would allow mispricing so that alpha were positive for some held portfolios, it would seem that an adding-up constraint would mean that alpha would then have to be negative for other held portfolios (this was shown earlier in my discussion in the context of the market model). But moving on (such details never stop a determined empiricist), using the Markowitz (1959) and Sharpe (1963) diagonal or market model to convert this from expected to realized returns, Jensen proposes:

$$r_P - r = \alpha_P + (r_M - r)\beta_P + \varepsilon_P$$

where r_P and r_M are realized returns and $E(\varepsilon_j) = \rho(r_M, \varepsilon_j) = 0$. Underlying this, at the security level, for any two different securities j and k, $\rho(\varepsilon_j, \varepsilon_k) = 0$ and their returns r_j and r_k are assumed to be jointly normally distributed. Jensen argues that this equation can represent the realized returns of securities over time, as well as in the cross section, and that for the same held portfolio the serial correlation of its epsilon will be zero. If it were not, then the manager would use this information to earn additional expected returns, which would become part of the portfolio's alpha; so in the end, the serial correlation of epsilon must be zero.

Of course, any regression of portfolio returns against the market provides only an estimate of alpha, not the true alpha. Fortunately, the setup allows the machinery of the Gauss-Markov Theorem to apply, so that the sampling distribution estimate of alpha will conform to a t-distribution with $n_P - 2$ degrees of freedom, where n_P is the number of observations over time for portfolio P. Using this, we can determine the statistical significance of alpha.

Application of the market model, as outlined by Jensen, strictly requires that the beta of a portfolio β_P be an intertemporal constant, a condition that is not realistic. However, Jensen cleverly attempts to argue that this will mean that estimates of β_P will be biased downward, so that the estimates of α_P will be biased upward. Unfortunately (and this is not well-known), Jensen seems to have made a mathematical error, so that variation of the sample estimate of portfolio beta will instead be biased upward, and thus alpha will be biased downward.

An Apparent Error in Jensen's Analysis

To see this, Jensen argues that the performance of a portfolio derives from two sources: market timing and security selection. There will be a normal beta around which the manager, in attempting to exploit his market timing skill, will vary the actual beta of his portfolio. If β_N is the normal beta, if the manager is bullish at time t, he will choose $\beta_{Pt} > \beta_N$; and if he later becomes bearish at some other time t, he will then choose $\beta_{Pt} < \beta_N$. To capture this, we can suppose that $\beta_{Pt} = \beta_N + u_{Pt}$ where $E(u_{Pt}) = 0$ and u_{Pt} is normally distributed. Clearly, the manager will try to make u_{Pt} positively correlated with $\pi_t \equiv r_{Mt} - \mu_{Mt}$ so that we can suppose that $u_{Pt} = a_P\pi_t + w_{Pt}$ where $E(w_{Pt}) = 0$, $\rho(\pi_t, w_{Pt}) = 0$ and w_t is normally distributed. Jensen again argues that $a_P \geq 0$ since $a_P < 0$ would be consciously irrational; $a_P = 0$ then implies no market timing skill.

An Apparent Error in Jensen's Analysis *(Continued)*

The least squares estimate of the true β_N is $\underline{\beta}_N$ where

$$E(\underline{\beta}_N) = \frac{\text{Cov}\left[(r_{Pt} - r_t), (r_{Mt} - r_t)\right]}{\sigma_M^2} = \frac{\text{Cov}\left[(r_{Pt} - r_t), r_M\right]}{\sigma_M^2}$$

Successively substituting the market model for $r_{Pt} - r_t$, then $\beta_N + u_{Pt}$ for β_{Pt}, and then $a_P(r_{Mt} - \mu_{Mt}) + w_{Pt}$ for u_{Pt} leads to:

$$E(\underline{\beta}_N) = \frac{\text{Cov}\left(\begin{array}{c} \alpha_P + \beta_N r_{Mt} - \beta_N r_t + a_P r_{Mt}^2 - a_P r_{Mt} r_t \\ -a_P \mu_M r_{Mt} + a_P r_t \mu_M + r_{Mt} w_t - r_t w_t + \varepsilon_{Pt}, \; r_{Mt} \end{array}\right)}{\sigma_M^2}$$

Eliminating all constants in the covariance and setting some terms to zero due to zero-correlation assumptions:

$$E(\underline{\beta}_N) = \beta_N - a_P(\mu_M + r) + a_P \frac{\text{Cov}\left(r_{Mt}^2, \; r_{Mt}\right)}{\sigma_M^2}$$

It is easy to show that for any random variable x, $\text{Cov}(x^2, x) = E(x^3) - \mu\sigma^2 - \mu^3$. Also, it is easy to show that for any random variable x, $E[(x - \mu)^3] = E(x^3) - 3\mu\sigma^2 - \mu^3$. Now, if x is normally distributed (as r_{Mt} is), the skewness $E[(x - \mu)^3] = 0$. Putting this together, $\text{Cov}(x^2, x) = 2\mu\sigma^2$. Using this result and substituting above:

$$E(\underline{\beta}_N) = \beta_N - a_P(\mu_M + r) + a_P(2\mu_M) = \beta_N + a_P(\mu_M - r) > 0$$

However, this bias is not likely to be significant, at least for Jensen's sample. Recall that Treynor-Mazuy (1966) find very little evidence of market timing skill in their sample of mutual funds (that is, $a_P \approx 0$, in the earlier argument).

Jensen gathers annual prices and dividends covering 115 mutual funds from Wiesenberger's *Investment Companies* (Arthur Wiesenberger, *Investment Companies*, New York: Arthur Wiesenberger & Company, 1955 and

1965) during 1955–1964, and as much data as was available on these funds from 1945 to 1954. He measures the beta of each fund using natural logarithms of this time series from 1945 to 1964 using the market model. The average beta across all the funds was .840, so failing to adjust for risk would bias the funds' performance against the funds in any comparison with the market. The correlation coefficient of the market model regression was .930, indicating, as Sharpe had previously found, that most of the variance of the funds' returns can be explained by the market return. As in Sharpe (1966), load charges are ignored since the objective is to measure managerial forecasting skill rather than returns to investors. The average alpha from the market model regression of fund returns net of management expenses was –1.1 percent; 76 funds had a negative alpha, and 39 funds had a positive alpha. Using gross returns (with management expenses added back), the average alpha becomes –0.1 percent. Correcting further for the small amounts of cash held by the funds, the average alpha becomes –0.04 percent, virtually zero, and the funds split about evenly between negative and positive alphas.

Although there is no evidence that the average fund can outperform the market, there is still the possibility that at least one of the funds outperformed the market by skill. Using the time series regression for each fund and using returns net of management expenses, Jensen calculates the t-values of their alphas. Fourteen funds had negative alphas and three funds had positive alphas with significance at the 5 percent level. However, with 115 funds, assuming normally distributed residual returns ε_p in the market model regression, just by chance about five or six should have had positive alphas at the 5 percent significance level. Jensen concludes his paper with:

> The evidence on mutual fund performance discussed above indicates not only that 115 mutual funds were on average not able to predict security prices well enough to outperform a buy-the-market-and-hold policy, but also that there is very little evidence that any individual fund was able to do significantly better than that which we expected from mere random chance. It is also important to note that these conclusions hold even when we measure the fund returns gross of management expenses (that is, assume their bookkeeping, research, and other expenses except brokerage commissions were obtained free). Thus on average the funds were apparently not quite successful enough in their trading activities to recoup even their brokerage expenses. (p. 415)[24]

Unfortunately, one assumption that is untested in Jensen's paper is that the cross-sectional correlation of the residual returns of different fund portfolio returns is zero. Even if the market model assumption as applied to individual securities j and k that $\rho(\varepsilon_j, \varepsilon_k) = 0$ were correct—and we know from King (1966), for example, that is isn't—since mutual fund portfolios contain many of the same securities, for two such portfolios P and Q it would be very unlikely that $\rho(\varepsilon_P, \varepsilon_Q) = 0$. Jensen needs this assumption to interpret the cross-sectional significance of alpha. To see how this could in principle play out, if all 115 mutual funds held exactly the same portfolio, then cross-sectional differences in alpha would not be significant since they are really calculated from a sample of 1.

About 10 years later, Norman E. Mains in [Mains (1977)] "Risk, the Pricing of Capital Assets, and the Evaluation of Investment Portfolios: Comment," *Journal of Business* 50, No. 3 (July 1977), pp. 371–384, proved once again that even the most careful of empiricists often fails to take everything into consideration. In particular, Jensen assumed that fund dividends received over the year were reinvested in the fund at the end of the year (since he was using only annual returns). Jensen believed that the bias imparted by this would be negligible. Mains pointed out that in a period like Jensen's of significantly increasing stock returns, this bias could be important. Jensen also assumed that the fund betas were constant over his 20-year observation period but measured his alphas based on the last 10 years. In fact, according to Mains, the betas of most of the funds were lower in the last 10 years than in the first, imparting a downward bias to measured alphas. Redoing Jensen's alpha test with these corrections reversed Jensen's conclusions so that the average fund has about a zero, instead of negative, alpha on a net return basis. However, to correct for the problem of dividend reinvestment, Mains gathered monthly data, which had to be voluntarily supplied by the mutual funds, but only 70 of Jensen's original 115 funds supplied data. Unfortunately, the different sample not only prohibits a direct comparison with Jensen's results, but also could be biased since it may be that only the better-performing funds tended to supply their monthly data.

Jensen's paper is a landmark in the long history of testing investor performance—perhaps inaugurated by Cowles (1933)—convincing many financial economists that not only did the average U.S. equity mutual fund in his exhaustive sample not outperform a value-weighted market index, but also there was little evidence that even one fund outperformed this index other than by chance.

1968 Hayne Ellis Leland (July 25, 1941–), "Savings and Uncertainty: The Precautionary Demand for Saving," *Quarterly Journal of Economics* 82, No. 3 (August 1968), pp. 465–473.

UNCERTAIN ENDOWED INCOME,
SUBSTITUTION VS. INCOME EFFECTS,
PRECAUTIONARY SAVINGS,
ABSOLUTE RISK AVERSION

Consider the two-period exchange problem for the consumer under certainty:

$$\max_{C_0, C_1} U(C_0) + \rho U(C_1) \quad \text{subject to} \quad Y_0 + \frac{Y_1}{r} = C_0 + \frac{C_1}{r}$$

where Y_0 and Y_1 are endowed income at dates 0 and 1, r is the marketwide riskless return on investment, C_0 and C_1 are the consumer's consumption choices at dates 0 and 1, $U(\bullet)$ is the utility of consumption, and ρ is the patience factor; see Fisher (1930). One question of interest is what effect, other things being equal, increasing r has on future consumption. On the one hand, increasing r implies that the same current dollar consumption now permits more dollar consumption in the future so that to balance out utility over time—which the consumer likes to do since $U''(\bullet) < 0$—the consumer will choose to increase current consumption. This motivation is called the *substitution effect*. On the other hand, increasing r also implies that any sacrifice of current consumption for future consumption is more efficient since any savings earns higher interest. This opposing motivation is called the *income effect*.

Increasing future income Y_1, other things being equal, unambiguously decreases savings for future consumption out of current consumption. Generalizing the model to allow for uncertainty surrounding future income Y_1 introduces other questions of comparative statics. Leland (1968) asks the question: Under what circumstances, for a fixed mean of Y_1, does increasing the variance of Y_1 lead to increased saving for future consumption out of current income Y_0? Increased savings for this reason is called *precautionary savings*. Naively one might have supposed that risk aversion would lead to precautionary savings, but Leland shows this is not correct. By using a local Taylor series argument, which implies that risk is locally identified with variance, Leland concludes that increasing absolute risk aversion—see Pratt (1964)—is necessary and sufficient for a positive precautionary demand for savings.

1969 **Eugene F. Fama, Lawrence Fisher, Michael C. Jensen,** and **Richard Roll,** "The Adjustment of Stock Prices to New Information," *International Economic Review* 10, No. 1 (February 1969), pp. 1–21.

EVENT STUDIES, STOCK SPLITS, EARNINGS ANNOUNCEMENTS,
MARKET MODEL, WORLD EVENTS, ACCOUNTING CHANGES,
BLOCK TRADING, SECOND-HAND INFORMATION

James Clay Dolley in [Dolley (1933)] "Characteristics and Procedure of Common Stock Split-Ups," *Harvard Business Review* 11, No. 3 (April 1933), pp. 316–326, inaugurates hundreds of so-called event studies, a basic test of the rationality of market prices. If stock markets are working properly, stock prices should: (1) immediately increase with the publicity of good news, (2) immediately decrease with the publicity of bad news, and (3) thereafter not change at least in a predictable way as a result of the previously released news. In particular, Dolley studied the behavior of stock prices immediately after a stock split occurs and provided a simple count of stocks that increased and stocks that decreased in price. Over the next 35 years, event studies gradually increased in sophistication, controlling for general market price movements and other confounding events. In the late 1960s, two studies brought the technique to maturity: Ray Ball and Phillip Brown, in [Ball-Brown (1968)] "An Empirical Evaluation of Accounting Income Numbers," *Journal of Accounting Research* 6, No. 2 (Autumn 1968), pp. 159–178, on earnings announcements, and Fama-Fisher-Jensen-Roll (1969) on the response of stock prices to announcements of stock splits.

The authors of the latter study argue that stock splits per se should leave the total market value of the firm's equity unchanged. For example, if a firm splits its stock 2:1, its stock price should be cut in half. However, complicating the stock market response is the signal conveyed by a split. In particular, firms often increase total dividends in conjunction with splits by not cutting dividends in proportion to the split. Since John Lintner's article, [Lintner (1956)] "Distribution of Incomes of Corporations among Dividends, Retained Earnings, and Taxes," *American Economic Review* 46, No. 2 (May 1956), pp. 97–113, it has been known that once firms raise dividends, they are very reluctant to lower them. Therefore, raising dividends tends to signal that the management of the firm is optimistic about its future prospects. As a result, the announcement of split, if accompanied by a dividend increase, should tend to move stock prices up.

The authors use a version of the Markowitz (1959) and Sharpe (1963) market model:

$$\log r_{jt} = \alpha_j + \beta_j \log r_{Mt} + \varepsilon_{jt}$$

where r_{jt} is the return of stock j for month t, r_{Mt} is similar to the return of the S&P 500 index for month t, and ε_{jt} obeys the standard restrictions of the market model. Least squares estimates ($\underline{\alpha}_j$, $\underline{\beta}_j$) were calculated for 622 stocks over the period 1926–1960, which included 940 splits (of 25 percent or more). For each split, define month $t = 0$ as the month in which the split occurs, $t = -1$ as one month before the split, $t = 1$ as one month following the split, and so on. Now, for month k define ε_k as the cross-sectional average of the residuals:

$$\varepsilon_k \equiv \frac{\Sigma_j \varepsilon_{jk}}{n_k}$$

where n_k is the number of splits with data available in month k. Note that this sum is taken over residual returns measured over different calendar months for different splits. Finally, define the cumulative average residual as:

$$E_m \equiv \Sigma_k \varepsilon_k$$

where the sum is taken from –29 (29 months before the splits) to month m.

For all splits in the database, the cumulative average residuals rise steadily as m goes from –29 to 0 and levels off from $m = 0$ to $m = 30$. The authors argue this is just what one would expect from a rational market. Prior to the split date, stocks to be split should on average have experienced rising prices (in part because increases in dividends are expected), but after that date there should be no further information in the split that is not reflected in the stock price at the end of the split month. However, if the sample is divided between splits followed by dividend increases and those followed by dividend decreases, it turns out that the stocks with increases continue to have slightly increasing cumulative average residuals after the split, and stocks with dividend decreases have sharply declining cumulative average residuals after the split. But since most stocks have dividend increases following splits, the sum of the cumulative average across both stocks with dividend increases and decreases is approximately zero. The authors take the whole of this evidence to be consistent with rational markets.

Two years later, Victor Niederhoffer published another event study in [Niederhoffer (1971)] "The Analysis of World Events and Stock Prices," *Journal of Business* 44, No. 2 (April 1971), pp. 193–219. If stock markets are rational, then stock market indexes should tend to have greater changes after significant marketwide events. To test this, Niederhoffer creates a list of 432 world events over the period 1950–1966, defined as events described by headlines in the late city edition of the *New York*

Times (news usually happening before 9:00 P.M. of the previous day) that span five to eight columns across the front page. As one would have expected, the price change of the S&P Composite Index on the next day tended to be much greater in absolute magnitude than usual. Moreover, the Mandelbrot (1963) prediction that large price changes tend to be followed by large price changes is also confirmed, but Mandelbrot's other prediction that these subsequent price changes will be of random sign is not confirmed. Indeed, Niederhoffer notes that the Fama (1965) confirmation of this relates to individual stocks and not a stock index. For the index, Niederhoffer finds that index continuations are more likely than index reversals, so that the market would appear typically to underreact to world events over the first succeeding day. Unfortunately, the result could be spurious since, as Niederhoffer readily admits, he has not corrected for the index staleness problem first noted by Cowles (1960).

In 1972, Robert S. Kaplan and Richard Roll, in [Kaplan-Roll (1972)] "Investor Evaluation of Accounting Information: Some Empirical Evidence," *Journal of Business* 45, No. 2 (April 1972), pp. 225–257, report the results of another event study using the same methodology as Fama, Fisher, Jensen, and Roll. They test the widely believed view, at least among corporate executives, that changes in external accounting methods that affect reported earnings per share affect share price. Until the Kaplan-Roll study, this view had never been tested systematically. They test two changes. In 1964, many firms shifted from gradually amortizing to immediately crediting the benefits of the investment tax credit. Second, from 1962 to 1968 a number of firms shifted from accelerated to straight-line depreciation. Using cumulative average residuals, they find little evidence that these changes (although they clearly impacted reported earnings per share) affect share prices; any such effects were short-lived and quickly reversed. One problem with this study, however, is that firms that make these changes to prop up their reported earnings may be self-selected to be firms that insiders believe are expected to perform poorly in the future.

Fama, Fisher, Jensen, and Roll provide empirical evidence supporting a key implication of efficient markets: Stock prices respond to new relevant information. The opposite side of this implication is that stock prices do *not* respond to irrelevant information. Myron Scholes, in [(Scholes (1972)] "The Market for Securities: Substitution versus Price Pressure and Effects of Information on Stock Prices," *Journal of Business* 45, No. 2 (April 1972), pp. 179–211, provides perhaps the first study to provide evidence in support of this. He shows that when sellers dispose of a large block of stock, although the price typically falls in response, it quickly bounces most of the way back as investors apparently arbitrage between it and close substitutes.

As a final example of an event study, Peter Lloyd Davies and Michael Canes, in [Davies-Canes (1978)] "Stock Prices and the Publication of Second-Hand Information," *Journal of Business* 51, No. 1 (January 1978), pp. 43–56, examine the effects of buy and sell recommendations for New York Stock Exchange (NYSE) stocks that appeared in the "Heard on the Street" column in the *Wall Street Journal* during 1970–1971. The authors presume that these recommendations are based only on public information and therefore represent a second-hand opinion or analysis of already available information. In a fully rational market, where all information is immediately reflected in stock prices the moment it becomes public, there should be no price reaction to second-hand information. Despite this, the authors calculate an average abnormal return on the day of the column of about 1 percent for buy recommendations and about –2 percent for sell recommendations. However, considering trading costs, the authors conclude that even these changes do not lead to a profitable trading rule, so in that weak sense the predictions of a rational market are not overturned. Unfortunately, the authors cannot really be sure that the news column does not contain previously unreleased information, and if occasionally some of the information in the column were really new to the market, then the predictions of a rational market might remain unrefuted even in a strong sense.

1970 Eugene F. Fama, "Multiperiod Consumption-Investment Decisions," *American Economic Review* 60, No. 1 (March 1970), pp. 163–174; "Multiperiod Consumption-Investment Decisions: A Correction," *American Economic Review* 66, No. 4 (September 1976), pp. 723–724.

1974 Eugene F. Fama and **James D. MacBeth,** "Tests of the Multiperiod Two-Parameter Model," *Journal of Financial Economics* 1, No. 1 (May 1974), pp. 43–66.

STATE-DEPENDENT UTILITY,
INTERTEMPORAL CONSUMPTION AND INVESTMENT,
WORKING BACKWARDS,
IMPLIED OR DERIVED UTILITY, RISK AVERSION

A utility function is state-dependent if in addition to depending on dollar consumption and/or wealth, it also depends on other initially uncertain aspects of the state. There are at least six important ways the utility function can have this dependency: (1) it can depend on other exogenous, initially uncertain aspects of the state, such as health or the weather; (2) it can depend on the uncertain future prices of physical commodities on which dollar consumption will be spent; (3) it can depend stochastically on the value of incompletely marketable assets such as human capital; (4) it can depend directly on the choice of other economic agents created, for example, by production externalities or keeping up with the Joneses; (5) it can depend on the results of as yet unperformed calculations or an incomplete self-knowledge that is gradually revealed over time; and (6) in a multiperiod model, it can depend on state variables that summarize what is known about the way the opportunity set of investments or the opportunity set of unmarketable human capital is changing over time.

Fama (1970/March) first shows that if a consumer/investor's utility of lifetime consumption function, $U(C_0, C_1, C_2, \ldots, C_{T-1}, W_T)$, where C_t is dollar consumption at date t and W_T is a bequest at death at date T, is strictly increasing and strictly concave in the stream of consumption over his lifetime, then working backwards—as, for example, in Mossin (1968)—his single-period (two-date) date t derived utility function $V_t(C_t, W_{t+1}|S_t)$ will also be strictly increasing and strictly concave in contemporaneous consumption C_t and end-of-period wealth W_{t+1}, where S_t is the dated event at date t. So the consumer/investor's sequential single-period decisions inherit risk aversion from his utility function of lifetime consumption. Fama then derives the key condition for the standard finance single-period (two-date) risk-averse model of consumption and portfolio choice to be embedded in a multiperiod consumption model, where the investor is risk-averse over his lifetime consumption. Fama shows that this requires that the derived single-period utility function be state-independent, so that $V_t(C_t, W_{t+1}|S_t) = V_t(C_t, W_{t+1})$. This generally requires that the opportunity set of security prices follow a (possibly nonstationary) random walk.

Of course, Fama's results should not be taken to show that with state independence, the derived single-period utility function is myopic and therefore that the same function is simply used repeatedly over time. Indeed, his results allow for this function to depend on past levels of consumption, perhaps building in habit formation, and on the time $T - t$ remaining until his death.

Fama-MacBeth (1974) empirically tests a special case of this requirement: that attempts to hedge against anticipated future changes in expected returns not affect contemporaneous returns. Their empirical results support this. In particular, they examine whether next-period returns on market portfolio and riskless return proxies depend on the returns of these proxies in the earlier period; these are chosen to summarize the investor's opportunity set since they are suggested as sufficient statistics by the portfolio separation property of the mean-variance equilibrium model—see Sharpe (1964), Lintner (1965/February), Mossin (1966), and Treynor (1999). They conclude that there is no evidence of any change in the expected returns of these proxies over their sample period, 1953–1972, so obviously there is no serial dependence. In particular, although nominal interest rates fluctuate, almost all change comes from changes in the anticipated rate of inflation, rather than changes in the real rate. A by-product of this analysis is the observation that the expected rate of inflation extractable from one-month U.S. Treasury bill rates at date t is a useful predictor of the realized rate of inflation between dates t and t plus one month, and therefore a strategy of rolling over one-month T-bills will be a useful hedge against inflation. By contrast, common stocks, often thought to be an inflation hedge, are in the short run, at least, overwhelmed by other factors affecting their returns, making them difficult in practice to use as a short-term hedge against inflation.

Theoretical models explicitly including more complex state-variables than merely wealth or consumption include [Roll (1973/November)] Richard Roll, "Assets, Money and Commodity Price Inflation under Uncertainty," *Journal of Money, Credit and Banking* 5, No. 4 (November 1973), pp. 903–923. In the context of a single-period economy, Roll extends the standard finance model to uncertain prices for consumption goods (commodities). John B. Long, Jr., in [Long (1974)] "Stock Prices, Inflation and the Term Structure of Interest Rates," *Journal of Financial Economics* 1, No. 2 (July 1974), pp. 131–170, extends this to a multiperiod economy allowing both for uncertain prices of consumption goods and investment opportunities that are intertemporally stochastically dependent.

1970   **Eugene F. Fama**, "Efficient Capital Markets: A Review of Theory and Empirical Work," *Journal of Finance* 25, No. 2 (May 1970), pp. 383–417.

1970   **Charles P. Jones** and **Robert H. Litzenberger**, "Quarterly Earnings Reports and Intermediate Stock Price Trends," *Journal of Finance* 25, No. 1 (March 1970), pp. 143–148.

EFFICIENT MARKETS, RANDOM WALK,
WEAK VS. SEMISTRONG VS. STRONG FORM EFFICIENCY,
FULLY REFLECT INFORMATION,
MINIMALLY VS. MAXIMALLY RATIONAL MARKETS,

PROPERLY ANTICIPATED PRICES, MARTINGALES, EARNINGS ANNOUNCEMENTS

Fama (1970/May) is probably the most widely cited review ever published in financial economics. The paper popularizes the term "efficient markets" to describe markets in which prices "fully reflect" all available information. Following a suggestion from Harry V. Roberts, it also inaugurates the now-familiar nested trichotomy of hypotheses: "weak form efficient" (prices fully reflect historical prices), "semistrong form efficient" (prices fully reflect all publicly available information, including historical prices), and "strong form efficient" (prices fully reflect all private as well as public information). Many financial economists would now amend this distinction to say that "weak form efficiency" means that prices fully reflect all publicly available technical or market-generated information, such as past prices, trading volume, short sales, and so on, while "semistrong form efficient" means that prices additionally fully reflect all publicly available fundamental information.

What is more, this tripartite distinction as originally designed is clearly a concoction of the empirical mind. A theorist would never have dreamed it up; yet like lemmings, most financial economists have accepted it uncritically. By contrast, Rubinstein (2001) claims that a theoretically fundamental distinction should be made between (1) markets that are maximally rational in that all agents are rational—the usual assumption in most theoretical research, (2) markets that are rational in the sense that prices are set *as if* all agents were rational, and (3) markets that are only minimally rational in the sense that although markets are not rational, there are nonetheless no profit opportunities. For example, if I tell you stock prices are too volatile relative to fundamentals, the market may not be rational, but it still may be minimally rational since there may be no way for you to profit from that observation.

Clearly the phrase "fully reflect" needs to be carefully defined to place the efficient markets hypothesis on firm footing. Unfortunately, Fama's attempt to do so leaves much to be desired and has confused many readers. The current date 0 price P_0 of a security is said to fully reflect the information set Φ available at date 0 if:

$$E(P_1|\Phi) = E(r_1|\Phi)P_0$$

where r_1 is the (random) return of the security between dates 0 and 1, P_1 is the (random) price of the security at date 1, and $E(x|\Phi)$ is the expected value of the random variable x fully utilizing the information contained in Φ. This appears to be a tautology, and therefore is not a useful definition.

Although Fama is far from clear and this may be putting words into his mouth, the definition can be interpreted nontautologically as discussed in Rubinstein (1975), slightly rephrased:

> *Using information set Φ, forecast the probability distribution of prices (P_1) that will be realized at date 1. Input this data into a model of market equilibrium determining expected returns. From these and the expected date 1 prices, the date 0 security value, given the information set Φ and the market equilibrium model, can be computed. Compare this computed value with the price (P_0) actually observed in the marketplace. If these are the same, then the actual security price is said to "fully reflect" Φ.*[25]

As Fama himself concedes, this definition is limited only to expected returns, while a more encompassing definition would have the whole probability distribution forecast from Φ fully reflected in the current price; but he argues that couching the definition only in terms of expected returns is more empirically operational. For example, the random walk model, which requires that the time series of returns be independently and identically distributed, is a much stronger notion of efficiency. Fama also points out there is no inconsistency between the random walk model and the use of past information in assessing the distributions of future returns (say for forecasting future means and variances); however, the model does say that the *sequence* (or order) of past returns is not relevant to these forecasts.

Five years earlier, Paul Anthony Samuelson, in [Samuelson (1965)] "Proof That Properly Anticipated Prices Fluctuate Randomly," *Industrial Management Review* 6, No. 1 (Spring 1965), pp. 321–351, reprinted in *The Collected Scientific Papers of Paul A. Samuelson*, Volume 3 (Cambridge, MA: MIT Press, 1972), pp. 782–790, drew an important distinction between a random walk and expectationally driven definitions of market efficiency. Suppose there is a security with a single payoff X_T at date T where X_T is a random variable. Suppose the time series of prices of a security with this payoff is $\ldots . P_{t-2}, P_{t-1}, P_t, P_{t+1}, P_{t+2}, \ldots .$ Finally, define the price change $\Delta P_{t+1} \equiv P_{t+1} - P_t$ for any pair of dates t and $t + 1$. Samuelson begins by defining "properly anticipated prices" as prices that, at every date $t \leq T$ have the property that, based on the information available at Φ_t at date t (which, in particular, includes the present and all past price realizations for that security, $\ldots P_{t-2}, P_{t-1}, P_t$), equal the expected value of X_T. That is, for all $t \leq T$:

$$P_t = E(X_T | \Phi_t)$$

In particular, $P_T = X_T$. He then proves that the "prices fluctuate randomly" since it follows that for all $t \leq T$, $P_t = E(P_{t+1}|\Phi_t)$ or alternatively that $E(\Delta P_{t+1}|\Phi_t) = 0$, and $E(\Delta P_{t+1} \Delta P_{t+2} \cdots \Delta P_T|\Phi_t) = E(\Delta P_{t+1}|\Phi_t) E(\Delta P_{t+2}|\Phi_t) \cdots E(\Delta P_T|\Phi_t) = 0$. In words, prices follow a martingale, and successive price changes are mutually uncorrelated.

Proof of Samuelson's Result on "Properly Anticipated Prices"

Proof of the martingale property follows trivially from the law of iterated expectations. By the assumption of "properly anticipated prices," $P_t = E(X_T|\Phi_t)$ and $P_{t+1} = E(X_T|\Phi_{t+1})$. Therefore, $E(P_{t+1}|\Phi_t) = E[E(X_T|\Phi_{t+1})|\Phi_t] = E(X_T|\Phi_t) = P_t$, where the second equality follows from the law of iterated expectations since $\Phi_t \subset \Phi_{t+1}$.

Proof that successive price changes are mutually uncorrelated starts with the observation that $\text{Cov}(\Delta P_T, \Delta P_{t+1} \Delta P_{t+2} \cdots \Delta P_{T-1}) < > 0$ implies that for at least one possible realization of Φ_{T-1}, since $\Delta P_{t+1} \Delta P_{t+2} \cdots \Delta P_{T-1} \subset \Phi_{T-1}$, then $E(\Delta P_T|\Phi_{T-1}) \neq 0$. By the contrapositive, the first conclusion, $E(\Delta P_T|\Phi_{T-1}) = 0$, then implies $\text{Cov}(\Delta P_T, \Delta P_{t+1} \Delta P_{t+2} \cdots \Delta P_{T-1}) = 0$. Since for general random variables $E(XY) = \text{Cov}(X, Y) + E(X)E(Y)$, we must have:

$$E(\Delta P_T \Delta P_{t+1} \Delta P_{t+2} \cdots \Delta P_{T-1}|\Phi_t) = \text{Cov}(\Delta P_T, \Delta P_{t+1} \Delta P_{t+2} \cdots \Delta P_{T-1})$$
$$+ E(\Delta P_T| \Phi_t) E(\Delta P_{t+1} \Delta P_{t+2} \cdots \Delta P_{T-1}|\Phi_t)$$
$$= E(\Delta P_T| \Phi_t) E(\Delta P_{t+1} \Delta P_{t+2} \cdots \Delta P_{T-1}|\Phi_t)$$

By induction, the second conclusion above follows.

This implies that if "prices are properly anticipated," all the information in the past price series that is useful for forecasting next period's *expected* price is contained in the current price. In the distinction that Fama emphasizes, observe that this is a much weaker assertion than to say all information in the past price series that is useful for forecasting the *probability distribution* of next period's price is contained in the current price, or even in a knowledge of the current price and the probability distribution of the past period's return (this would be a conclusion from a random walk model, as Fama defines it).

Following his tripartite division of versions of efficient markets, Fama begins his empirical survey by reviewing papers dealing with "weak form efficiency," including Fama (1965), Alexander (1961), Alexander (1964),

Fama-Blume (1966), and Victor Niederhoffer and M.F.M. Osborne in [Niederhoffer-Osborne (1966)] "Market Making and Reversal on the Stock Exchange," *Journal of the American Statistical Association* 61, No. 316 (December 1966), pp. 897–916. Niederhoffer and Osborne are perhaps the first to take systematic tests of the random walk hypothesis to the transaction level. They note that reversals occur several times more frequently than continuations. But this does not provide an opportunity for profits for public investors since the extra reversals are typically fluctuations across the market makers' best bid and ask prices. Fama's examples of papers dealing with semistrong efficiency include Fama-Fisher-Jensen-Roll (1969) on stock splits, Ball-Brown (1968) on earnings announcements, Roger N. Waud, in [Waud (1970)] "Public Interpretation of Federal Reserve Discount Rate Changes: Evidence on the 'Announcement Effect,' " *Econometrica* 38, No. 2 (March 1970), pp. 231–250, and Scholes (1972). Fama's discussion of strong form efficiency focuses on Jensen (1968). In 1970, Fama could conclude:

> *In short, evidence in support of the efficient market model is extensive, and (somewhat uniquely in economics) contradictory evidence is sparse. (p. 416)*

Just as Fama (1970/May) was declaring the victory of the efficient markets hypothesis, the first significant crack in its edifice appeared. In another event study, Jones-Litzenberger (1970) uncovers one of the earliest market anomalies seeming to violate market rationality, even to the extent of providing economically and statistically significant abnormal profit opportunities. They hypothesize that investors may react slowly to the release of fundamental information. In particular, they form a portfolio of firms that experience a quarterly earnings announcement that is unexpectedly very high (relative to earnings trends over the past eight quarters). They compare the return of this portfolio from the second month of the 10th quarter (which gives ample time for the earnings to have been public information) to the second month of the 12th quarter to a risk-adjusted market return. They find that in every one of the 10 overlapping periods from 1964 to 1967 that they examine, the selected portfolio outperforms the market, with economically significant excess returns.

1970   David Cass (July 19, 1937–) and **Joseph E. Stiglitz** (February 9, 1943–), "The Structure of Investor Preferences and Asset Returns, and Separability in Portfolio Allocation: A Contribution to the Pure Theory of Mutual Funds," *Journal of Economic Theory* 2, No. 2 (June 1970), pp. 122–160.

HYPERBOLIC ABSOLUTE RISK AVERSION (HARA), PORTFOLIO SEPARATION, QUADRATIC UTILITY, CONSTANT RELATIVE RISK AVERSION (CRRA), NORMAL DISTRIBUTION

That the hyperbolic absolute risk-averse class of utility functions (which includes logarithmic, quadratic, and exponential utility) is sufficient for portfolio separation (two funds where one is riskless) had been already demonstrated, for example, in [Hakansson (1969/December)] Nils H. Hakansson, "Risk Disposition and the Separation Property in Portfolio Selection," *Journal of Financial and Quantitative Analysis* 4, No. 4 (December 1969), pp. 401–416. In the absence of restrictions placed on probability distributions of returns, Cass-Stiglitz (1970) show these conditions are necessary as well. Moreover, they also show that quadratic utility or constant relative risk aversion (CRRA) is necessary and sufficient for portfolio separation with one or two portfolios where neither is riskless; they also derive more general conditions for portfolio separation if there is a complete market.

A related problem is to discover the class of joint probability distributions of security returns that, in the absence of restrictions on utility functions beyond risk aversion, leads to portfolio separation. From Tobin (1958), normal distributions were known to be sufficient. Stephen A. Ross, in [Ross (1978/April)] "Mutual Fund Separation in Financial Theory—The Separating Distributions," *Journal of Economic Theory* 17, No. 2 (April 1978), pp. 254–286, characterizes a somewhat broader class that are necessary and sufficient for two-fund separation with a riskless security.

In 2001, Stiglitz won the Nobel Prize in Economic Science for his analysis of markets with asymmetric information.

1970   George A. Akerlof (June 17, 1940–), "The Market for 'Lemons': Quality Uncertainty and the Market Mechanism," *Quarterly Journal of Economics* 84, No. 3 (August 1970), pp. 488–500.

ADVERSE SELECTION, ASYMMETRIC INFORMATION, RATIONAL EXPECTATIONS

Akerlof (1970) explains one of the reasons complete markets do not exist. Consider the market for second-hand cars that contains a continuous range of quality from very good to very bad cars. Suppose the seller knows the quality of his car, but the buyer doesn't. The buyer knows the probability distribution of car qualities but not the quality of any individual car. The buyer will then expect to buy a car of average quality and will pay only enough for a car of average quality. Sellers of better than average cars will then not receive enough for their cars and will withdraw them from the market. This reduces the average quality of the remaining pool. Buyers will then lower their purchase price to the average of the remaining cars. In turn, sellers with better than average cars in this new pool will withdraw from the market. This process will continue until there is virtually no car left in the market. Thus the market self-destructs and disappears. Akerlof gives perhaps a better example: the absence of a market for medical insurance for people over 65 who do not already have it. Although the paper's emphasis is on adverse selection, less remarked but still important is that this is one of the first to use the observation that prices convey information (in this case, private information known by the seller about the quality of the commodity being sold) that helps agents make decisions.

When markets are faced with self-destruction, special mechanisms often come into play to shore them up. The first line of defense is techniques to reduce information asymmetries such as repeat purchasing from the same seller, product labeling, published reviews by third parties, such as *Consumer Reports*, and third-party certification such as the Good Housekeeping Seal. Other more drastic measures include making sellers liable for defects and imposing minimum quality standards. This last method is examined by Hayne Ellis Leland, in [Leland (1979)] "Quacks, Lemons, and Licensing: A Theory of Minimum Quality Standards," *Journal of Political Economy* 87, No. 6 (December 1979), pp. 1328–1346, which includes a mathematically formal model of Akerlof's lemons example.

In 2001, Akerlof won the Nobel Prize in Economic Science for his analysis of markets with asymmetric information.

1970   William H. Beaver, Paul Kettler, and **Myron Scholes** (July 1, 1941–), "The Association between Market Determined and Accounting Determined Risk Measures," *Accounting Review* 45, No. 4 (October 1970), pp. 654–682.

1988   Laxmi Chand Bhandari, "Debt/Equity Ratio and Expected Common Stock Returns: Empirical Evidence," *Journal of Finance* 43, No. 2 (June 1988), pp. 507–528.

ACCOUNTING BETA, FINANCIAL LEVERAGE, OPERATING LEVERAGE

Beaver-Kettler-Scholes (1970) is the first study to measure security beta from fundamental risk factors such as numbers derived from accounting statements. The authors find that dividend payout, financial leverage, and measures of earnings yield instability not only are correlated with beta, but can predict the next period's beta better than the last period's beta "naively" measured by the Markowitz (1959) and Sharpe (1963) market model.

Robert S. Hamada, in [Hamada (1969)] "Portfolio Analysis, Market Equilibrium, and Corporation Finance," *Journal of Finance* 24, No. 1 (March 1969), pp. 13–31, was the first to develop a theoretical connection between beta and a firm's debt-equity ratio. Let B_j and S_j be the current market values of the debt and equity of firm j, and let β_j^* be the beta of an otherwise identical unlevered firm. If the debt is riskless, it is easily shown that

$$\beta_j = \beta_j^*\left(1 + \frac{B_j}{S_j}\right)$$

Mark Rubinstein, in [Rubinstein (1973/March)] "A Mean-Variance Synthesis of Corporate Financial Theory," *Journal of Finance* 28, No. 1 (March 1973), pp. 167–181, carries this the next step further showing how beta depends as well on operating leverage (that is, the difference between output selling price and variable cost) as well as financial leverage.

For many years, as a matter of theory, other things being equal, beta was expected to be an increasing function of corporate leverage, as justified, for example, by Hamada and Rubinstein. While the CAPM of Sharpe (1964), Lintner (1965/February), Mossin (1966), and Treynor (1999) implies that corporate leverage should influence expected returns indirectly though beta, leverage should have no separate influence on expected returns. Bhandari (1988) tests these assertions and obtains two principal results. Looking at all stocks traded on the NYSE from 1948 to 1981, he examines 17 two-year intervals using real returns (deflated for inflation). He measures beta by regressing returns on samples taken two years before and two years after each sampling period, and measures leverage by the debt-equity ratio at the beginning of each two-year sample, defined as the ratio of the (difference between the book value of assets minus the book value of equity) divided by the market value of equity. First, looking at only manufacturing firms, a cross-section regression of beta against leverage has an average .51 correlation, varying in a narrow range from a low of .35 during the subperiod 1958–1959 and .69 during the subperiod

1952–1953. This is supportive of the CAPM theory. Second, after accounting for beta and firm size, leverage seems to be a third factor that explains realized returns, implying a difference of 5.83 percent per annum rate of return between the maximum and minimum leverage portfolios in the manufacturing subsample. So, apart from its influence on beta, leverage tends to increase realized returns, a new anomaly heretofore unexplained by theory.

1971   Robert C. Merton (July 31, 1944–), "Optimal Consumption and Portfolio Rules in a Continuous-Time Model," *Journal of Economic Theory* 3, No. 4 (December 1971), pp. 373–413; reprinted in Robert C. Merton, *Continuous-Time Finance*, Chapter 5 (Malden, MA: Blackwell, 1990), pp. 120–165.

1973   Robert C. Merton, "An Intertemporal Asset Pricing Model," *Econometrica* 41, No. 5 (September 1973), pp. 867–887; reprinted with updated footnotes in Robert C. Merton, *Continuous-Time Finance*, Chapter 15 (Malden, MA: Blackwell, 1990), pp. 475–523.

> INTERTEMPORAL CONSUMPTION AND INVESTMENT, HARA,
> CRRA, CARA, CONTINUOUS-TIME, CONTINUOUS-STATE CAPM,
> INTERTEMPORAL ASSET PRICING, STOCHASTIC CALCULUS,
> STATE-DEPENDENT UTILITY, STOCHASTIC OPPORTUNITY SET

Robert C. Merton, in [Merton (1969)] "Lifetime Portfolio Selection under Uncertainty: The Continuous-Time Case," *Review of Economics and Statistics* 51, No. 3 (August 1969), pp. 247–257, reprinted with updated footnotes in Robert C. Merton, *Continuous-Time Finance*, Chapter 4 (Malden, MA: Blackwell, 1990), pp. 97–119, introduces stochastic calculus (Ito's lemma) into the theory of finance to solve in continuous time the problem posed by Samuelson (1969) and Hakansson (1970). Merton (1971) extends his earlier results to more general utility functions. Mean-variance results in discrete time are justified by either multivariate normality of security returns (which is inconsistent with limited liability) or quadratic utility (which is inconsistent with nonsatiation beyond some level of wealth and implies increasing absolute risk aversion). Both of these assumptions have serious problems for some purposes. Merton's key result is to show yet a third scenario in which optimal portfolio choices can be reduced to choices over mean and variance: (1) all security returns follow geometric Brownian motion (that is, they are lognormal over all time intervals), and (2) consumer/investors trade in continuous time.

An intuitive way to see why this works is to examine the logarithm of a lognormally distributed security return log r_j. It is commonplace to approximate this with log $r_j \cong r_j - 1$. Since log r_j is normally distributed, if this approximation were exact, r_j itself would be normally distributed. This approximation, of course, gets better as r_j gets closer to 1. Merton makes exactly the assumptions needed for the approximation to work: r_j is measured over an infinitesimal interval, and there are no jumps between successive price changes, so that r_j measured over this interval is always close to 1. In other words, in his continuous-time, continuous-state model we lose nothing by regarding the continuously observed returns as normal, even though cumulated over any finite interval they are not (that is, they are lognormal over any finite interval and the normal approximation is not accurate). Therefore, mean-variance portfolio choice is optimal at each moment in time as long as the investor can continuously revise his choices. So the new justification for mean-variance analysis does not come for free: continuous-time trading with continuous-state returns. Whether or not we may want to pay that price depends on the circumstances.

Merton also derives closed-form consumption/portfolio results for hyperbolic absolute risk aversion (HARA) utility, which include as special cases constant relative risk aversion (CRRA) and constant absolute risk aversion (CARA) (e.g., exponential utility) that he derived in his earlier paper. One of the nice features of these results is that the consumption and portfolio decision rules are expressed as simple functions of the first and second moments of security returns.

Just as Sharpe (1964) had asked what would happen if all investors followed the advice of Markowitz (1952/March), so too Merton (1973/September) asks what are the implications of all investors following the prescriptions of Merton (1971). He derives an equilibrium by supposing that all consumer/investors in the economy follow the optimal consumption and portfolio decision rules that he derived in Merton (1971) and that markets clear at each date and state. As would be expected, he finishes with a version of the capital asset pricing model, applying over an instantaneous time interval, under continuous time and continuous states. The model takes a significant step forward since this version of the single-period CAPM is clearly embedded in a multiperiod consumption and investment economy.

Equally important, Merton derives an extension of the CAPM where the opportunity set of security returns evolves over time as a function of the evolution of the riskless local return. Merton shows that this leads to an additional CAPM term resulting from the extent a security is a hedge against future shifts in the opportunity set. Corresponding to this result is a three-fund separation theorem: All investors divide their wealth among the same three mutual funds: a riskless security, the market portfolio, and a third fund that hedges them against shifts in the opportunity set over time. Merton is careful to choose as his extra source of risk something that results directly from his embedding of his generalized CAPM in a multiperiod economy, showing that the single-period discrete-time model of Sharpe (1964), Lintner (1965/February), Mossin (1966), and Treynor (1999) need not be simply reinterpreted as holding over an instantaneous interval. However, it is easy to see that, more generally, the addition of another source of risk, in effect, makes utility functions state-dependent so that consumer/investors will want to hedge this new risk. This state-dependence could come from a variety of sources (see my discussion under Fama (1970/ March)) such as uncertain contemporaneous inflation as in Long (1974), not only from shifts in opportunity sets, although that is certainly potentially an important source of nonwealth risk.

1972   Jack Hirshleifer (August 26, 1925–July 26, 2005), "Liquidity, Uncertainty and the Accumulation of Information," in *Uncertainty and Expectations in Economics*, edited by Carter and Ford (Oxford: Basil Blackwell, 1972), pp. 136–147.

TERM STRUCTURE OF INTEREST RATES, IRREVERSIBILITY

A frequently made empirical observation is that the term structure of interest rates is typically upward sloping. In an effort to explain this bias, Hirshleifer (1972) looks behind financial markets to the markets for real assets that underlie them. He argues that necessary conditions for the bias are uncertainty about future interest rates and the ability to defer decisions about future consumption until the future when some of the uncertainty will be resolved. This, in itself, does not create a bias but sets the scene for it. The bias fundamentally stems from the physical irreversibility of production. If forward and reverse storage were both equally possible, then there would be no bias to the term structure. But in real life, while it is possible to store commodities forward in time, it is generally not possible to store commodities backward ("reverse storage")—somewhat like the impossibility of traveling backwards in time. In Hirshleifer's three-date model, consumption can be transferred from date 0 to date 2 in two ways: (1) by committing resources to date 2 in a way that cannot be reversed (these are long-term assets); (2) by storing consumption from date 0 to date 1, and then, depending on the information that then becomes available, storing consumption from date 1 to date 2 (these are short-term assets). The second technology is more flexible or liquid since it can take advantage of enfolding information. The market for real assets then passes this liquidity advantage to the financial market so that in equilibrium the marginal demands for shorter- and longer-term bonds are equal: In compensation for their valued liquidity, shorter-term bonds must have yields lower than longer-term bonds.

1972   Merton Howard Miller and **Myron S. Scholes,** "Rates of Return in Relation to Risk: A Re-Examination of Some Recent Findings," in *Studies in the Theory of Capital Markets*, edited by Michael C. Jensen (New York: Praeger, 1972), pp. 47–78.

1972   Fischer Sheffey Black, Michael C. Jensen, and **Myron S. Scholes,** "The Capital Asset Pricing Model: Some Empirical Tests," in *Studies in the Theory of Capital Markets*, edited by Michael C. Jensen (New York: Praeger, 1972), pp. 79–121.

CAPITAL ASSET PRICING MODEL (CAPM),
GROUPING DATA, ALPHA, BETA, ZERO-BETA CAPM

Black-Jensen-Scholes (1972) is the best-known early test of the Sharpe-Lintner-Mossin-Treynor capital asset pricing model (CAPM) where great care is taken to deal with a number of statistical issues that called earlier tests into question. Most of these earlier tests were *cross-sectional tests* regressing $R_j = \gamma_0 + \gamma_1 \beta_j + \varepsilon_j$ for $j = 1, 2, \ldots, m$, the total number of securities in the sampled universe; the excess realized returns are $R_j \equiv r_j - r$ and $R_M \equiv r_M - r$, and $\beta_j \equiv \mathrm{Cov}(R_j, R_M)/\mathrm{Var}(R_M)$ is the estimated measure of the true systematic risk β_j. The CAPM makes the clear prediction that $\gamma_0 = 0$ and $\gamma_1 = R_M \equiv r_M - r$.

Perhaps the earliest test of this sort is by George W. Douglas, in [Douglas (1969)] "Risk in the Equity Markets: An Empirical Appraisal of Market Efficiency," *Yale Economic Essays* 9, No. 1 (Spring 1969), pp. 3–45. He finds that the prediction of the CAPM that covariance with all other securities should swamp their own variance as a determinant of realized return—see discussion under Sharpe (1964)—is not supported by the data. Indeed, returns are related to variance, not covariance. In addition, in a related finding from unpublished tests by John Lintner that are reported by Douglas, Lintner finds that market model residual risk is an economically and statistically significant determinant of realized returns, again contrary to the CAPM. Miller-Scholes (1972) reexamine these tests very carefully considering potential biases created by changing interest rates, sources of possible nonlinearity in the return-beta relation, heteroscedasticity of the residual (that is, correlation of the variance of the residual with the level of returns), measurement errors in beta, correlation of residual risk with beta, an inadequate proxy for the market return, and nonnormality or skewness of returns. Even with this more careful analysis, they are unable to clearly overturn the Douglas and Lintner results. In addition, Miller and Scholes present evidence that the alphas of individual securities seem to be negatively correlated with their betas, further evidence that the CAPM is incorrect or its empirical tests misspecified.

Following Miller and Scholes, Black, Jensen, and Scholes argue that cross-sectional tests suffer from a number of difficulties and propose instead an alternative *time-series* test similar to Jensen (1968). This test regresses $R_{jt} = \alpha_j + \beta_j R_{Mt} + \varepsilon_{jt}$ where the residual return is assumed to be serially uncorrelated and normally distributed, constructed to have a zero mean and zero correlation with the market return. In this regression, the CAPM has the clear prediction that $\alpha_j = 0$. Note that so far as proposed by the active assumption of the Markowitz (1959) and Sharpe (1963) market model, for any two securities j and k, the correlation $\rho(\varepsilon_{jt}, \varepsilon_{kt}) = 0$ has not been made.

Unfortunately, this simple time-series test gives no way to aggregate tests across different securities and so uses the available information very inefficiently. The Jensen (1968) solution to this problem is to interpret j as a mutual fund portfolio and to make the questionable assumption that the residual returns ε_{jt} have zero cross-correlation. Black, Jensen, and Scholes do not do this; instead they adopt a clever and now classic device to overcome this problem: grouping data into systematic risk classes. In particular, securities are grouped into 10 beta classes, with the lowest beta securities in the first class ($K = 1$) to the highest beta securities in the tenth class ($K = 10$), with 10 percent of the universe in each class. They then run the regression $R_{Kt} = \alpha_K + \beta_K R_{Mt} + \varepsilon_{Kt}$ for $K = 1, 2, \ldots, 10$ where α_K and β_K are the portfolio alpha and beta of the Kth group. This procedure also accomplishes the goal of providing a large dispersion of observations across beta, which makes the regression less sensitive to measurement errors in beta.

Another potential problem would arise if the betas used to allocate securities to different groups were measured over the same time period used to estimate the group alpha. Clearly, the security beta will be measured with a random error, causing at least some of the securities, say in the lowest (or highest) beta group, to have a spuriously measured low (or high) beta. This would mean that β_1 (or β_{10}) would be biased low (or high). In turn, in the regression, this would cause α_1 (or α_{10}) to be biased high (or low). To avoid this, Black, Jensen, and Scholes measure the beta used to allocate stocks to groups from an earlier (five-year) period than the subsequent (one-year) period covered by the regression. Although this earlier beta is measured independently of the beta measured in the regression, the known stationarity of beta, especially for portfolios—see Marshall E. Blume, in [Blume (1971)] "On the Assessment of Risk," *Journal of Finance* 26, No. 1 (March 1971), pp. 1–10—means that the earlier beta will be highly correlated with the beta in the subsequent regression period and so will still do a good job in dividing up the universe of securities into distinct risk classes.

The study covered all NYSE stocks from 1926 to 1965 using monthly returns resulting in 10 estimated alpha-beta pairs, a pair for each group. Group betas ranged from a low of .499 to a high of 1.561 (of course, centered around a beta of 1 for the universe). In contradiction to the CAPM, like Miller and Scholes before them, in the time-series regression the alphas were negative for the highest-beta portfolios and positive for the lowest-beta portfolios, with most of the alpha coefficients statistically significant. Black (1972) sees the negative correlation of alpha with beta as evidence of borrowing constraints that prompt less risk-averse investors to hold high-beta stocks as a substitute for leverage, thereby pushing up their prices and lowering their expected return. However, the Douglas and Miller-Scholes finding that residual volatility contributes to explain realized group returns is not confirmed. The grouping procedure produced a correlation $\rho(R_{Kt}, R_{Mt}) > .950$ for all but the highest-beta ($K = 10$) group. As a result, another advantage of the grouping procedure is to considerably reduce the standard deviation of the residual ε_{Kt} and thereby make the measured group alphas more likely to be statistically significantly different from zero, if in fact the alphas are.

Black, Jensen, and Scholes also revisit the cross-sectional test, but modified so as to allow for a random intercept. One justification for this comes from the Black (1972) and Rubinstein (1973/January) zero-beta generalization of the CAPM, which does not assume that riskless borrowing and lending is possible. This results in a pricing equation of the form:

$$\mu_j = (1 - \beta_j)\mu_Z + \beta_j\mu_M$$

where r_Z is the return of a portfolio with zero beta (and μ_Z is its expectation), ideally for purposes of coefficient estimation, the return of the *minimum variance* zero-beta portfolio.

This is tested using a two-factor market model:

$$r_{Kt} = (1 - \beta_K)r_{Zt} + \beta_j r_{Mt} + \varepsilon_{Kt} = r_{Zt} + \beta_K(r_{Mt} - r_{Zt}) + \varepsilon_{Kt}$$

Black, Jensen, and Scholes conclude, again using their grouping procedure, that this model is supported by the data in the following sense: Over the entire 35-year period, the average r_K (averaged over time) is a linear function of β_K (as K is spanned from $K = 1$ to 10) with intercept γ_0 and slope equal to the average r_M (averaged over time) minus γ_0. Furthermore, the slope is positive, consistent with the generalized model, which would predict that on average $r_M > r_Z$. However, since the intercept $r_Z > r_F$ (averaged over the entire period) and the slope is less than $r_M - r_F$, the standard CAPM is rejected. In addition, over each of the three nonoverlapping nine-year subperiods and one last eight-year subperiod, the substantial linearity is evident, but the intercept and slope vary depending on the subperiod. Indeed, in the last subperiod (April 1957–December 1965) the slope is actually negative (consistent with the two-factor model but not consistent with the standard CAPM).

Unfortunately, a serious weakness of these tests is failure to identify the intercept. Although theory, as I have noted, suggests that the intercept could be the realized return of a zero-beta portfolio, since the return on this portfolio is elusive, Black, Jensen, and Scholes do not confirm this correspondence. Therefore, in the two-factor regressions, r_{Zt} is little more than a plug factor that helps to make the regressions come out linear.

1972 Fischer Sheffey Black (January 11, 1938–August 31, 1995), "Capital Market Equilibrium with Restricted Borrowing," *Journal of Business* 45, No. 3 (July 1972), pp. 444–455.

1973 Mark Rubinstein (June 8, 1944–), "The Fundamental Theorem of Parameter-Preference Security Valuation," *Journal of Financial and Quantitative Analysis* 8, No. 1 (January 1973), pp. 61–69.

ZERO-BETA CAPM, PORTFOLIO SEPARATION,
JOINT NORMALITY COVARIANCE THEOREM,
AGGREGATE RISK AVERSION,
SKEWNESS PREFERENCE CAPM, COSKEWNESS

Black (1972) generalizes the capital asset pricing model (CAPM) for the absence of a riskless security. He shows that a zero-beta risky portfolio, in this case, plays the same role as the riskless return. This result was also contemporaneously and independently derived by others, but is known as the Black model (perhaps because Black was the only one who chose to devote an entire paper to it). He also shows that a version of the two-fund portfolio separation property continues to hold even in the absence of a riskless security; for jointly normally distributed returns, this parallels the Cass-Stiglitz (1970) earlier result for quadratic utility.

Rubinstein (1973/January) independently derives the zero-beta version of the CAPM using a transparent proof.

Rubinstein's Derivation of the Zero-Beta CAPM

One way to derive the zero-beta CAPM equation follows. Each investor $i = 1, 2, \ldots, I$ is assumed to solve the following portfolio selection problem:

$$\max_{\{x_{ij}\}} E[U_i(W_1^i)] \quad \text{subject to} \quad W_1^i = W_0^i \Sigma_j x_{ij} r_j \quad \text{and} \quad \Sigma_j x_{ij} = 1$$

by choosing portfolio proportions x_{ij} for different *risky* securities $j = 1, \ldots, m$. Using the technique of Lagrangian multipliers, this can be restated as:

$$\max_{\{x_{ij}\}} E[U_i(W_0^i \Sigma_j x_{ij} r_j)] - \xi_i(\Sigma_j x_{ij} - 1)$$

The first-order conditions, which are guaranteed to describe a maximum since $U'(W_1^i) > 0$, $U''(W_1^i) < 0$, are:

$$W_0^i E[r_j U'(W_1^i)] = \xi_i \text{ (all } i \text{ and } j)$$

By multiplying through by a set of x_{ij} (that sum to 1) that define an *arbitrary* portfolio return $r_P \equiv \Sigma_j x_{ij} r_j$, and summing over all securities, I have:

$$W_0^i E[r_P U'(W_1^i)] = \xi_i \text{ (all } i \text{ and } P)$$

Combining these two equations, for any security j and any arbitrary portfolio P, I can substitute out the Lagrangian multiplier and obtain:

$$E[r_j U'(W_1^i)] = E[r_P U'(W_1^i)]$$

Therefore,

$$\mu_j E[U'(W_1^i)] + \text{Cov}[r_j, U'(W_1^i)] = \mu_P E[U'(W_1^i)] + \text{Cov}[r_P, U'(W_1^i)]$$

From Tobin (1958), one way to justify mean-variance preferences is to assume all securities have returns r_j which are jointly normally distributed. Since weighted sums of jointly normally distributed random variables, in particular W_1^i, are themselves normal, it follows that $(r_j$ and $W_1^i)$ are also jointly normal. The joint normality covariance theorem, as derived by Rubinstein (1973/October) and Stein (1973) states: If x and y

(Continued)

Rubinstein's Derivation of the Zero-Beta CAPM *(Continued)*

are jointly normal, $g(y)$ is any differentiable function of y, and $E|g'(y)| < \infty$, then $\text{Cov}[x, g(y)] = E[g'(y)]\text{Cov}(x, y)$. Using this:

$$\mu_j E[U'(W_1^i)] + E[U''(W_1^i)]\text{Cov}(r_j, W_1^i) = \mu_P E[U'(W_1^i)] + E[U''(W_1^i)]\text{Cov}(r_P, W_1^i)$$

Now divide both sides by $E[U'(W_1^i)]$, define $\theta_i \equiv -E[U''(W_1^i)]/E[U'(W_1^i)] > 0$, and reorganize the order of the terms:

$$(\mu_j - \mu_P)\theta_i^{-1} = \text{Cov}(r_P, W_1^i) + \text{Cov}(r_k, W_1^i)$$

Aggregating this over all investors (following the earlier approach in my CAPM derivation under Sharpe (1964)):

$$\mu_j = [\mu_P - \theta\text{Cov}(r_P, r_M)] + \theta\text{Cov}(r_j, r_M) \text{ with } \theta \equiv W_0^M(\Sigma_i\theta_i^{-1})^{-1} > 0$$

(for all securities j and for arbitrary portfolios P).

As long as two different securities exist (and one can be short sold), then it is possible to construct a portfolio Z with a zero beta (but positive variance). For such a portfolio since $\text{Cov}(r_Z, r_M) = 0$, we have finally:

$$\mu_j = \mu_Z + \theta\text{Cov}(r_j, r_M)^{26}$$

The paper is also the first to interpret the risk-aversion parameter θ in the CAPM, $\mu_j = r + \theta\text{Cov}(r_j, r_M)$, in terms of general expected utility. It is shown that this parameter is an aggregation of the risk aversions of all investors, where each investor's risk aversion is measured by something quite similar to absolute risk aversion. In [Rubinstein (1973/October)] "A Comparative Statics Analysis of Risk Premiums," *Journal of Business* 46, No. 4 (1973/October), pp. 605–615, Rubinstein shows that in discrete time under joint normality of security returns the risk measure is an aggregation of $-E[U''(W_1)]/E[U'(W_1)]$ (as I have reproduced earlier here in my CAPM proof). In continuous time, Merton (1973/September) derives a similar result for each agent, but where the risk measure is exactly absolute risk aversion in terms of initial wealth—which is the limit as the time interval between trades approaches zero of the discrete-time measure.

The emphasis of Rubinstein's paper, however, is on generalizing the capital asset pricing model for preference toward higher-order moments of portfolio returns, such as skewness and kurtosis. In particular, Rubinstein derives the logical extension of the CAPM for skewness preference under cubic utility with the separation property. The net result is an additional term in the CAPM formula that accounts for the extent to which a security adds skewness to the market portfolio:

$$\mu_j = r + \theta_1 \text{Cov}(r_j, r_M) + \theta_2 \text{Cos}(r_j, r_M, r_M)$$

where $\text{Cos}(r_j, r_M, r_M) \equiv E[(r_j - \mu_j)(r_M - \mu_M)^2]$ and risk aversion and skewness preference tend to imply that $\theta_1 > 0$ and $\theta_2 < 0$.

Very little interest was shown in the skewness model for the next 27 years. Then, Campbell R. Harvey and Akhtar Siddique, in [Harvey-Siddique (2000)] "Conditional Skewness and Asset Pricing Tests," *Journal of Finance 55*, No. 3 (June 2000), pp. 1263–1295, empirically test the model, where it is assumed to hold over each successive period, and where its parameters are nonstationary, being conditional on information at the beginning of each period. They show that conditional skewness helps to explain the cross-sectional variation of security returns, even in the presence of factors based on size and book-to-market ratio. They find that systematic skewness has a surprisingly large risk premium of 3.6 percent per annum over their sample period. In addition, they show that skewness picks up much of the effect on returns previously attributed to momentum.

1973 Jack L. Treynor and **Fischer Sheffey Black**, "How to Use Security Analysis to Improve Portfolio Selection," *Journal of Business* 46, No. 1 (January 1973), pp. 66–86.

PORTFOLIO SELECTION,
CAPITAL ASSET PRICING MODEL (CAPM), MARKET MODEL,
PORTFOLIO SEPARATION, MARKET PORTFOLIO,
RISKLESS SECURITY, ALPHA, BETA,
RESIDUAL VS. SYSTEMATIC RISK,
MARKET TIMING VS. SECURITY SELECTION, SHORT SALES

The Markowitz (1952/March) and Roy (1952) mean-variance portfolio choice problem with many risky securities, supplemented by a riskless security (Tobin 1958), seems to require solution by numerical analysis. However, Treynor-Black (1973) ingeniously show how, in combination with the Markowitz (1959) and Sharpe (1963) diagonal or market model, $r_j - r = \alpha_j + (r_M - r)\beta_j + \varepsilon_j$, the solution can be derived in closed form. In particular, their solution shows how the trade-off between security alpha (α_j) and security residual variance, $\omega_j^2 \equiv \text{Var}(\varepsilon_j)$, affects the optimal allocation of an investor's portfolio. By inspection of their solution, it is easy to derive the portfolio separation property of this type of model (the optimal proportional composition of the risky security portfolio is independent of investor risk aversion), to see how differences in beliefs of investors, captured by the alphas an investor assigns to securities, lead to portfolios that depart from the market portfolio, and to sort out security selection and market timing motivations for portfolio positions.

Their solution technique is motivated by the structure of the market model and is reminiscent of the simplifications created by the use of state-securities. A \$1 out-of-pocket investment in security j is divided into three parts: (1) $1 - \beta_j$ dollars in the riskless security (with return r), (2) β_j dollars in the market portfolio (with return r_M), and (3) one dollar invested in the security j but completely financed by borrowing $1 - \beta_j$ dollars and selling β_j dollars of the market portfolio. Although this latter investment costs nothing, it will have a random return equal to the security's residual return, ε_j. An investor can then think of constructing his portfolio with proportions γ invested in the riskless security, β invested in the market portfolio, and h_j invested in the residual return of risky security j, so that his portfolio return $r_p = \gamma r + \beta r_M + \Sigma_j h_j \varepsilon_j$ where $\Sigma_j h_j = 1$. β can be interpreted as the passive investment plus potentially a market-timing component (which is later sorted out by their analysis) and the h_j can be interpreted as "active bets." This way of breaking down security returns effectively inverts a matrix early, and permits closed-form solutions for γ, β, and $\{h_j\}$ that are then translated back into closed-form solutions for the proportions held of the actual securities.

Their solution is:

$$x_0 = 1 - \lambda^{-1}\left[\left(\frac{\mu_M - r}{\sigma_M^2}\right) + \Sigma_j(1 - \beta_j)\left(\frac{\alpha_j}{\omega_j^2}\right)\right]$$

$$x_j = \lambda^{-1}\left[\chi_j\left\{\left(\frac{\mu_M - r}{\sigma_M^2}\right) - \Sigma_j\beta_j\left(\frac{\alpha_j}{\omega_j^2}\right)\right\} + \left(\frac{\alpha_j}{\omega_j^2}\right)\right] \quad \text{for all } j = 1, \ldots, m$$

where $x_0 \equiv$ the proportion of the portfolio P value invested in the riskless security

$x_j \equiv$ the proportion of the portfolio P value invested in risky security $j(\Sigma_{j=0,\ldots,m} x_j = 1)$

$\chi_j \equiv$ the market value proportion of security j in the portfolio M of all available securities so that $\Sigma_j \chi_j = 1$

$\lambda \equiv$ measures the investor's risk aversion (the higher λ, the more risk averse the investor)

$\mu_M, \sigma_M^2 \equiv$ mean and variance of return of portfolio M[27]

Several sensible conclusions follow:

1. *Index fund condition.* If $\alpha_j = 0$ for all j, then the investor divides his investable wealth between the riskless security and an index fund M.
2. *Market timing condition.* The market timing component of the investment is determined by the ratio $(\mu_M - r)/\sigma_M^2$; as the investor's opinion about this ratio changes over time, he will invest more or less in the market component M.
3. *Security selection condition.* If $\alpha_j > 0$, the investor tends to concentrate more than the market proportion χ_j in security j.
4. *Avoidance of diversifiable risk.* The greater the residual risk ω_j^2 (other things held constant), the less the investor holds of security j.
5. *Portfolio separation.* The proportionate composition of the investor's holdings of risky securities is easily shown to be independent of the investor's risk aversion λ; to see this, consider the proportions for any two risky securities x_j and x_k and calculate the ratio x_j/x_k.

Unfortunately, the introduction of short-selling restrictions will destroy the closed-form nature of these results. Indeed, the optimal solution can easily involve extremely large long positions offset by extremely large short positions, and therefore the solution will generally be impractical in the presence of even modest trading costs or uncertainty about estimates of expected return and risk. To see this intuitively, in an extreme case, suppose that two of the securities have almost perfectly positively correlated returns but somewhat different prices. Although this is not an arbitrage opportunity, in the absence of trading costs, the investor may want to take advantage of this by taking a hugely long position in one of the securities offset by a similar-sized short position in the other security. Edwin J. Elton, Martin J. Gruber, and Manfred W. Padberg in [Elton-Gruber-Padberg (1976)] "Simple Criteria for Optimal Portfolio Selection," *Journal of Finance* 31, No. 5 (December 1976), pp. 1341–1357, find a relatively simple solution *algorithm* in a context similar to Treynor-Black but when no short selling is allowed.

1973 **Robert C. Merton,** "The Relationship between Put and Call Option Prices: Comment," *Journal of Finance* 28, No. 1 (March 1973), pp. 183–184.

DERIVATIVES, OPTIONS, ARBITRAGE,
PUT-CALL PARITY RELATION,

EUROPEAN VS. AMERICAN OPTIONS, PAYOUT PROTECTION, OPTION EARLY EXERCISE

It is still popularly believed that investor optimism, even if the underlying asset price remains unchanged, will tend simultaneously to push call prices up and put prices down. However, the long-practiced strategy of conversion—buying a call, selling short its underlying asset, and lending the call's strike price—is a way of creating the same payoff as a put (and a way used in practice to create puts from calls, when no puts are being traded). Although this strategy had been known certainly as early as 1688, at least for options on forward contracts, in [de la Vega (1688)] Joseph de la Vega, *Confusion de Confusiones*, reprinted in Martin Fridson, editor, *Extraordinary Popular Delusions and the Madness of Crowds; and Confusion de Confusiones* (New York: John Wiley & Sons, 1996), Hans R. Stoll, in [Stoll (1969)] "The Relationship between Put and Call Option Prices," *Journal of Finance* 24, No. 5 (December 1969), pp. 801–824, may have been the first to express this relation algebraically, proving that it holds under the twin assumptions of no arbitrage and perfect markets.

Arguably the most important arbitrage relation for options, the put-call parity relation states:

$$P_0 = C_0 - S_0 d^{-t} + K r^{-t}$$

where P_0 and C_0 are the contemporaneous values of an otherwise identical put and call, with common strike price K, common years to expiration t, written on an underlying asset with concurrent price S_0 and

---

Proof of the Put-Call Parity Relation

To see this, the payoff from the call may be written $\max(0, S_t - K)$ where S_t is the (random) underlying asset price at expiration. The payoff from the put is then $\max(0, K - S_t)$. Observe that for every value of S_t at expiration:

$$\max(0, K - S_t) = \max(0, S_t - K) - S_t + K$$

If I now take present values of each side of this equation, we will have the put-call parity relation stated earlier.

annualized payout return d, and where the annualized riskless return is r.

As Cox points out in Cox-Rubinstein (1985), given the underlying asset price and the riskless return (as well as the payout return), put-call parity implies that the difference between otherwise identical call and put values cannot depend on the expected return of the underlying asset. To prove this, he simply observes that the put-call parity relation can be written:

$$C_0 - P_0 = S_0 d^{-t} - Kr^{-t}$$

Therefore, the difference $C_0 - P_0$ can depend only on S_0, r, d, K, and t. Although the independence of this difference from the expected return contradicts common belief, if it were not so there would be an arbitrage opportunity.

In his comment, Merton (1973/March) points out that while true for European options (that is, options that cannot be exercised early), the put-call parity relation will not hold for American options because it may be optimal to exercise the call or the put early. Samuelson-Merton (1969) had already pointed out that payout-protected calls should never be exercised early, but absent payout protection, it may pay to do so. In his comment, Merton argues that puts (with or without payouts) may be optimally exercised early.

Merton further argues that it will generally pay to exercise many (if not most) in-the-money puts early, so this is of considerable practical relevance.

Optimal Early Exercise of American Puts: An Extreme Example

An easy way to see this is to consider an extreme case: an American put with one year to expiration and a strike price equal to $100. Now suppose its underlying asset price falls immediately almost to zero. If you now exercise the put, you will receive almost $100, close to the most you could ever receive from the put (assuming the underlying asset price cannot fall below $0). You can either receive (almost) $100 now, or wait and receive at most $100 later. Clearly, as long as interest rates are positive, you would prefer to exercise now so as to be able to reinvest the $100 and earn interest.

1973   Marshall E. Blume and Frank Husic, "Price, Beta and Exchange Listing," *Journal of Finance* 28, No. 2 (May 1973), pp. 283–299.

1974   Marshall E. Blume and Irwin Friend, "Risk, Investment Strategy and the Long-Run Rates of Return," *Review of Economics and Statistics* 56, No. 3 (August 1974), pp. 259–269.

1977   S. Basu, "Investment Performance of Common Stocks in Relation to Their Price-Earnings Ratios: A Test of the Efficient Market Hypothesis," *Journal of Finance* 32, No. 3 (June 1977), pp. 663–682.

1981   Rolf W. Banz in "The Relationship between Returns and Market Value of Common Stocks," *Journal of Financial Economics* 9, No. 1 (March 1981), pp. 3–18.

SIZE EFFECT, BETA, PRICE EFFECT, MARKET-TO-BOOK ANOMALY

Blume-Husic (1973) is an unrecognized classic in empirical financial economics since it is probably the first evidence for what later has become known as the "size effect," one of the most puzzling anomalies. Using monthly data from 1932 to 1971 on NYSE stocks, each month stocks are sorted by month-end price into quintiles, and stocks are also sorted into quintiles based on beta measured from a regression of the prior 60-month returns. Then, each month 25 portfolios are formed from the Cartesian product of these two quintiles. Monthly returns of these 25 portfolios are then regressed against price and beta with the result that over the whole period return was positively and insignificantly related to beta but negatively and significantly related to price. However, if instead returns are regressed against price and the *future* beta of the portfolio (measured over the next 60 months), then though the coefficient on price continues to be negative, it is smaller in absolute value than in the first regression using *past* beta. Taken together, these regression results suggest a "price effect" where low-priced stocks tend to have higher future returns than measured beta would suggest, whether beta is measured over the prior 60 months or over the future 60 months. In addition, beta changes over time, and using the past 60 months of data to measure current beta contains measurement error that is correlated with price: For low-priced stocks, future betas will tend to be higher than past betas. For example, for stocks priced in January 1967, the portfolio with the highest-past-beta stocks and the lowest-priced-stocks had a future beta of 1.49, while the portfolio with the highest-past-beta stocks and the highest-priced stocks had a future beta of 1.24.

It appears from the article that this directional discrepancy is consistent over subsamples taken every five years; that is, holding past beta constant, lower-priced stocks had very consistently higher future betas.

The paper raises two questions: (1) why does price anticipate changes in beta? and (2) why should price predict returns, even after considering the effect of price on future beta? At this point, in 1973, one could have proposed the following answer for question (1). Among the stocks in the portfolio of low-priced stocks are recent arrivals. These are stocks whose prices have recently fallen. Since firms rebalance their capital structures only periodically, the fall in stock price will cause an automatic increase in their debt/equity ratios measured in market value terms. In turn, this will cause their betas to be higher in the future than in the past.

Although, strictly speaking, Blume and Husic are measuring a price effect and not a size effect, clearly the two are closely related. Not only, as a matter of fact, do low-priced stocks tend to be smaller in terms of market capitalization than high-priced stocks, but many of the low-priced stocks at a given time have presumably only recently become low-priced, so they are smaller in terms of market capitalization than they used to be.

A subsequent paper, Blume-Friend (1974), tests for the size effect more directly. This paper examines stock returns covering nonoverlapping five-year periods from 1938 to 1968. Stocks are assigned to beta deciles in each five-year period. Five-year returns are compared for equally weighted versus proportionally weighted portfolios. Equally weighted portfolios are proxies for small stocks and proportionally weighted portfolios for large stocks. Breaking the entire period into three decades, the averages of the two five-year returns in each decade are:

Five-Year Stock Returns, Sorted by Size

Beta Decile	1938–1948		1948–1958		1958–1968	
	Equal	Proportional	Equal	Proportional	Equal	Proportional
Lowest	62%	44%	85%	75%	103%	92%
2	96	54	96	112	101	91
3	93	71	105	130	101	84
4	93	69	97	204	101	56
5	94	73	90	126	124	90
6	119	86	103	101	104	88
7	108	76	104	125	142	78
8	105	66	94	107	130	116
9	128	109	102	162	153	108
Highest	96	74	77	145	137	101

Although the authors do not provide measures of statistical significance, casual empiricism suggests that the size effect documented here is both statistically and economically significant, but not temporally consistent. While small firms appear on average to outperform large firms (even while holding beta constant), there can be significant periods of time when this normal relation is reversed.

The authors conclude:

> *These substantial period-dependent differences in performance between equally weighted and proportionally weighted portfolios, or equivalently between large and small stock issues, may indicate that there is another (or more than one) important factor affecting returns which is not allowed for in current return generating functions. . . . The gap in performance between equally weighted and proportionally weighted portfolios appears too great to be explained by the greater liquidity risks attached to equal weighting but of the wrong sign (in two out of three instances) if greater unique risks are attached to proportional weighting. Additional testing will be required to confirm whether a size-related factor is necessary in explaining returns of individual securities. (p. 267)[28]*

The more definitive research that Blume and Friend called for was published seven years later in Banz (1981), the paper commonly credited with the discovery of the size effect. Surprisingly, this paper fails to discuss or cite the earlier related work of Blume and Husic or Blume and Friend. The paper follows the methodology established by Black and Scholes (1974) of stratifying the universe of securities (in this case, monthly price data on all NYSE stocks between 1926 and 1975) into quintile portfolios sorted on the basis of the key variable—market value proportion—and then each quintile portfolio is itself subdivided into five subportfolios sorted by beta. Then, each month, the realized returns of 25 portfolios are regressed against beta and the key variable, in this case a measure of size:

$$r_{jt} = \gamma_{0t} + \gamma_{1t}\beta_{jt} + \gamma_{2t}\left(\frac{\varphi_{jt} - \varphi_{Mt}}{\varphi_{Mt}}\right) + \varepsilon_{jt}$$

with φ_{jt} defined as the market value proportion of security j and φ_{Mt} as the average market value proportion. Similar to Blume and Husic, Banz concludes that although size does anticipate changes in beta, in addition it has an independent effect on returns: Other things being equal, smaller firms tend to have higher realized rates of return. Banz finds the size effect to be highly economically significant. To dramatize his results, he considers a zero-beta portfolio, formed by going long the smallest 10 (or 50) firms and going short the largest 10 (or 50) firms, which earns about 20 percent (or 12 percent) per annum on average from 1931 to 1975!—and both these returns are statistically significant. Returns on zero-beta portfolios that replace the largest 10 (or 50) firms with medium-size firms give about the same results. This shows that by far the largest impact on the results comes from the smallest firms, which seem to be underpriced, not mispricing of the larger firms. Breaking this up into nonoverlapping five-year intervals, the smallest stocks outperform larger stocks in seven of the nine subperiods. Notably, the size effect, as strong as it is on average, is nonetheless reversed in each of the two five-year periods between 1946 and 1955: During that decade, larger stocks outperformed the smallest stocks. This closely confirms the earlier findings by Blume and Friend. Banz concludes:

There is no theoretical foundation for such an effect. We do not even know whether the factor is size itself or whether size is just a proxy for one or more true but unknown factors correlated with size. (p. 16)

At the time of Banz's study, candidates for this missing factor included price-earnings (P/E) ratios, book-to-market ratios, and the extent to which different stocks are held in widely diversified portfolios. For example, Roger W. Klein and Vijay S. Bawa, in [Klein-Bawa (1977)] "The Effect of Limited Information and Estimation Risk on Optimal Portfolio Diversification," *Journal of Financial Economics* 5, No. 1 (August 1977), pp. 89–111, argue theoretically that if investors face relatively high costs of gathering information for some firms, this will increase the estimation risk for these securities. Investors will then have less demand for these securities, which will decrease their prices and correspondingly tend to increase their realized returns. So if the smallest firms have the highest information costs, they will seem riskier to most investors, and hence have lower prices and tend to have higher realized returns.

A related anomaly concerns the market-to-book ratio (or in per-share terms, the P/E ratio). Popular market wisdom often comes down on the side of low-P/E-ratio stocks. It is said that the potential of these stocks is unappreciated by the market and that a portfolio of low-P/E stocks will tend to outperform the market portfolio. While the prior large-sample studies of several other researchers had tended to support this hypothesis, Basu (1977) was the first to provide persuasive evidence since earlier studies were questionable because of either survivorship bias, failure to adjust for risk, trading costs, differential taxation, or use of a trading strategy based on earnings before they were known.

Basu examined 753 NYSE stocks from April 1957 to March 1971. At the end of each year, the P/E ratio of each stock was calculated by dividing the total market value of the stock on December 31 by its reported annual earnings (before extraordinary items). These stocks were then placed into five ranked portfolios, with the highest-P/E-ratio stocks in the first portfolio, and so on. The portfolios were assumed to be purchased on April 1 of the succeeding year (by which time the earnings would surely have been reported) and held for the next 12 months. On April 1 of the next year, the proceeds from each of the portfolios were reinvested in the new revised portfolio of the same rank. The highest- and lowest-P/E-ratio portfolios had per-annum compound rates of return of 9.3 percent and 16.3 percent, respectively, a difference that was both statistically and economically significant. Moreover, none of the potential explanations mentioned earlier (risk, trading costs, etc.) was capable of changing this conclusion.

1973 **Fischer Sheffey Black** and **Myron S. Scholes**, "The Pricing of Options and Corporate Liabilities," *Journal of Political Economy* 81, No. 3 (May–June 1973), pp. 637–659.

1973 **Robert C. Merton**, "Theory of Rational Option Pricing," *Bell Journal of Economics and Management Science* 4, No. 1 (Spring 1973), pp. 141–183, reprinted with updated footnotes in Robert C. Merton, *Continuous-Time Finance*, Chapter 8 (Malden, MA: Blackwell, 1990), pp. 255–308.

1974 **Robert C. Merton**, "On the Pricing of Corporate Debt: The Risk Structure of Interest Rates," *Journal of Finance* 29, No. 2 (May 1974), pp. 449–470, reprinted in Robert C. Merton, *Continuous-Time Finance*, Chapter 12 (Malden, MA: Blackwell, 1990), pp. 388–412.

1976 **Henry A. Latané** (1907–1984) and **Richard J. Rendleman Jr.** (1949–), "Standard Deviations of Stock Prices Ratios Implied in Option Prices," *Journal of Finance* 31, No. 2 (May 1976), pp. 369–381.

1977 **Robert C. Merton**, "On the Pricing of Contingent Claims and the Modigliani-Miller Theorem," *Journal of Financial Economics* 5, No. 2 (November 1977), pp. 241–249, reprinted with updated footnotes in

Robert C. Merton, *Continuous-Time Finance*, Chapter 13 (Malden, MA: Blackwell, 1990), pp. 413–427.

DERIVATIVES, OPTIONS, OPTION PRICING,
BLACK-SCHOLES FORMULA, LOGNORMAL DISTRIBUTION,
VOLATILITY, DYNAMIC STRATEGIES,
SELF-FINANCING STRATEGIES, ARBITRAGE,
PORTFOLIO REVISION, REPLICATING PORTFOLIO,
DYNAMIC COMPLETENESS, DOWN-AND-OUT OPTIONS,
HEDGE RELATION, BULL SPREAD RELATION,
BUTTERFLY SPREAD RELATION, TIME SPREAD RELATION,
PAYOFF FUNCTION, IMPLIED VOLATILITY,
CORPORATE SECURITIES AS OPTIONS,
DEFAULT OPTION, STATE-PRICES

Black-Scholes (1973) is the classic paper on derivatives pricing. Black and Scholes assume the return of the asset underlying a standard European call or put follows geometric Brownian motion as first described in a finance context by Osborne (1959). Therefore, (1) the local return of the underlying asset is continuous; that is, its price can go from S_0 to S_t only if it traverses all the prices in between; and (2) the local volatility of the underlying asset return is constant. They then offer two proofs of their pricing formula for the option, one based on the Merton (1973/September) intertemporal CAPM and one based, apparently at Merton's suggestion, on the idea that a self-financing dynamic strategy in an option and its underlying asset is locally riskless. Each proof leads to the same stochastic partial differential equation. The solution of this equation, subject to the boundary condition of the value of the option at its expiration $\max(0, S_t - K)$ is the celebrated and widely used Black-Scholes formula for the current value of a call C_0 in terms of the current price S_0, payout return d (not included in the original formula) and volatility σ of its underlying asset, the riskless return r, and the strike price K and current time to expiration t of the call:

$$C_0 = S_0 d^{-t} N(x) - K r^{-t} N(x - \sigma\sqrt{t}) \quad \text{with} \quad x \equiv \left[\frac{\log(S_0 d^{-t} / K r^{-t})}{\sigma\sqrt{t}} \right] + \frac{1}{2}\sigma\sqrt{t}$$

where $N(\bullet)$ is the standard normal distribution function. A key feature of this formula is the dog that didn't bark: Given the six variables that determine the value of a call, it is not necessary to know as well the expected return of the underlying asset over the life of the call.

The real significance of the formula to the financial theory of investments lies not in itself, but rather in how it was derived. Ten years earlier the same formula had been derived by Case M. Sprenkle, in [Sprenkle (1962)] "Warrant Prices as Indicators of Expectations and Preferences," *Yale Economic Essays* 1 (1962), pp. 178–231, reprinted in *The Random Character of Stock Market Prices*, edited by Paul H. Cootner (London: Risk Publications, 2000), pp. 504–578, and A. James Boness, in [Boness (1964)] "Elements of a Theory of Stock-Option Value," *Journal of Political Economy* 72, No. 2 (April 1964), pp. 163–175. Sprenkle derived the current value of a call by integrating the option payoff assuming a lognormal distribution for the underlying asset price. The result contains the expected underlying asset rate of return m and an unspecified option payoff risk-adjusted discount rate x. Boness specialized Sprenkle's formula for the case when investors are assumed to have "risk-neutral preferences," setting the expected underlying asset rate of return equal to the option payoff discount rate ($m = x$). He then obtains exactly what later became known as the Black-Scholes formula. Despite his statement that "investors in puts and calls are indifferent to risk" and the fact that he used the same discount rate for options to different stocks, he did not interpret this as the riskless rate of return $r - 1$. Indeed, he calculated this parameter by choosing the value of x that caused the best fit between option values (as computed by his formula) and market prices. The first person to interpret x as the riskless rate of return $r - 1$ may well have been Edward O. Thorp, then a mathematician at the University of California, Irvine, although he never published this result. But neither Boness nor Thorp understood the crucial idea that continuous-time, continuous-state arbitrage arguments could be used to justify equating this discount rate to the riskless rate of return— although Thorp came close since he clearly understood the idea of dynamically hedging an option with a position in its underlying asset, as can be seen from his article, [Thorp (1969)] "Optimal Gambling Systems for Favorable Games," *Review of the International Statistical Institute* 37, No. 3 (1969), pp. 273–293, and his book with Sheen T. Kassouf [Thorp-Kassouf (1967)], *Beat the Market* (New York: Random House, 1967), particularly pages 81–83.

In their second and more enduring proof, apparently suggested by Robert C. Merton, Black and Scholes show that a hedge position in the underlying asset and the call can be chosen to be locally riskless, and that no knowledge of the asset's expected return is required to know the correct hedge ratio. By continually revising the hedge as the underlying asset price moves using only accumulated profits and losses from the hedge, the hedge can be maintained as locally riskless through the option's expiration date. In subsequent work, this argument is typically turned around to say that by continually revising a "self-financing" portfolio containing the underlying asset and cash over the life of the option, it is possible to replicate the expiration-date payoff of the option. Therefore, if there is no arbitrage, the initial cost of establishing the hedge must equal the concurrent value of the option. Indeed, as Cox may have pointed out for the first time, in [Cox-Rubinstein (1985)] John C. Cox and Mark Rubinstein, *Options Markets* (Englewood Cliffs, NJ: Prentice-Hall, 1985), the Black-Scholes formula itself says what the initial hedge components must be: buy $d^{-t}N(x)$ units of the underlying asset, each worth S_0, financed by risklessly borrowing Kr^{-t} $N(x - \sigma\sqrt{t})$.

This reversal of the initial Black and Scholes proof (from stock and option replicating cash to stock and cash replicating option) first appears in Merton (1977). He points out that this way of looking at the problem makes it clear that the value of the call is not assumed to follow an Ito process, but can rather be proven to do so (since its own stochastic process can be replicated by correctly managing a portfolio containing only its underlying asset and cash). Moreover, one can determine the value the option would need to have even if it does not exist.

Revisiting Arrow (1953), Arrow was troubled: As I remarked earlier, if one took full account of the number of decision-relevant states, the number of securities required to complete the market would be vast. Somewhat overshadowed by the idea of state-securities, Arrow's 1953 paper also contains his principal solution to this difficulty: the first published occurrence of the idea that an initially incomplete market can be effectively completed by opportunities for portfolio revision over time—the key idea behind many subsequent models of intertemporal equilibrium as well as modern option pricing theory.

Let's take a simple example and consider the evolution of states over just three future dates. In the diagram, the state at the current date (0) is assumed known. Three states, A, B, and C can occur at date 1. Each of these gives birth to three more states at date 2, and in turn each of these gives birth to three more states at date 3, for a total of 27 possible states at date 3. As in the Problem of Points, knowing what state occurs at an earlier date limits the possible states that can occur at subsequent dates. So if A occurs, then only the states emerging out of that node can occur at date 2; in that case, the states emerging out of B and C will not occur.

State-Space Evolution

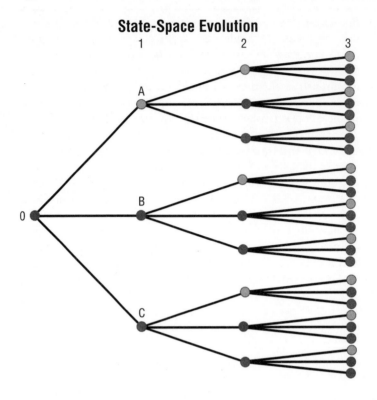

Suppose we consider an economy in which investors purchase securities at date 0 with the ultimate goal of accumulating wealth at date 3. Analogous to Pascal and Fermat, Arrow considers two ways markets for securities could be organized. One possibility is that at date 0, 27 securities are available that have different payoffs at date 3. With 27 states and 27 different securities, we have a complete market. Investors can distinguish among all 27 states at date 3 by investing in a buy-and-hold portfolio of the 27 securities in the market at date 0. To conserve on the number of securities, Arrow proposes instead that only three securities be available at date 0, which will have different values at date 1 covering the three states, A, B, and C, that can occur; so the market is initially incomplete. Now if state A occurs, Arrow supposes that a *new market* with three securities becomes available at date 1 that will have different values over the three possible states that could then occur at date 2. Investors can liquidate their portfolios and reinvest in the new securities that then become available. Similarly, at date 2, given the state that occurs, again a new market with three securities becomes available with different values (or payoffs) over the three possible states that could then occur at date 3. In this second way of organizing the market for securities, the total number of securities required would be only three at each date, or $3 + 3 + 3 = 9$ securities in total. The second way has miraculously conserved on the number of securities or markets that would be needed to complete the market. Instead of 27 securities, we can accomplish this with 9. To distinguish these two ways of organizing the market, financial economists say that that second method is a *dynamically* complete market, since investors must revise their portfolios over time to achieve the effects of completeness.[29]

Note, however, that in this case markets to commodities open up at date 1 that were not available at date 0. In contrast, Black and Scholes show how opportunities to trade over time in the same "long-lived" securities (the securities initially available at date 0) will dynamically complete the market. Although the number of *markets* that must be opened over time is essentially the same as in Arrow, the number of *eventually traded instruments* that must be created is not. Indeed, Black and Scholes show how just two securities are sufficient to dynamically complete the market! So the real significance of the Black-Scholes model for general work in asset pricing, to the extent it pushes beyond Arrow, is its demonstration of the role of *long-lived* securities in completing the market.

Other than this, the situations envisioned by Arrow and Black-Scholes are at core very similar. To see this intuitively, imagine that you are trying to decide what securities to hold now. Suppose the market is incomplete in the sense that there are insufficient securities to tailor-make a buy-and-hold portfolio that will deliver the most preferred outcomes in the distant future; instead you plan to rely on revising the portfolio you choose today in intermediate markets to make up for the missing securities. But to know what to do today, you need to know now, for each intermediate state, on what terms you will be able to revise your portfolio in these intermediate markets.[30]

So Arrow's solution does not really reduce the information investors need to make their current decisions compared with a complete market. How can investors know what future state-prices will be without convening the markets? Arrow's solution is not ultimately satisfactory.

The same criticism can be made of the Black-Scholes (1973) option pricing model. That model assumes the volatility of the underlying security and future interest rates can be predicted in advance (and indeed remain constant). But knowing future volatility and interest rates is tantamount to knowing in advance the state-prices to be established in future markets.[31] More generally, financial economists are often keen to adopt this method of solving Arrow's problem when they assume that investors know aspects of the stochastic process of the behavior of security prices into the future, even though the markets for these securities have yet to convene. For example, even to assume that the return over time of the market portfolio follows a random walk has implications for the evolution of future state-prices, which, since these are determined by future subjective probabilities and risk aversion, has implications for the evolution of these fundamental variables. If social risk aversion changes as total market wealth changes, then it will be difficult for the return of the market portfolio to have the same risk-neutral probability distribution over time, making it unlikely for the return of an arbitrary stock to have the same risk-neutral distribution, violating a key assumption of the Black-Scholes model.[32]

Merton (1973/Spring) is a complementary paper to Black-Scholes (1973) that extends the new option pricing theory in a number of ways. He shows that with predictably changing interest rates, European options should be valued using the interest rate on a zero-coupon bond maturing on the option expiration date. He adds predictable payouts on underlying assets and devises a generalized formula incorporating uncertain future riskless returns. He also produces perhaps the first closed-form formula for an exotic option, namely for "down-and-out" barrier calls (similar to standard calls except if, during the life of the call, its underlying asset price falls below a prespecified barrier level, the option becomes worthless).

In addition, in a more general setting than Black and Scholes, assuming only no arbitrage and perfect markets, Merton derives a number of "general arbitrage inequalities" relating the price of a call or a put to its concurrent underlying asset price ("the hedge relation"), the relation between the values of two otherwise identical options differing only by strike price ("the bull spread relation"), the relation among the values of three otherwise identical options differing only by strike price ("the butterfly spread relation"), and the relation between two otherwise identical options differing only by time to expiration ("the time spread relation"):

For American calls:

- *Hedge relation:* $S_0 \geq C_0 \geq \max(0, S_0 - K, S_0 d^{-t} - Kr^{-t})$.
- *Bull spread relation* (for two otherwise identical calls with $K_1 < K_2$): $C(K_1) > C(K_2)$ and $C(K_1) - C(K_2) \leq K_2 - K_1$.
- *Butterfly spread relation* (for three otherwise identical calls with $K_1 < K_2 < K_3$): $C(K_2) \leq \lambda C(K_1) + (1 - \lambda)C(K_3)$ where $\lambda \equiv (K_3 - K_2)/(K_3 - K_1)$.
- *Time spread relation* (for two otherwise identical calls with $t_1 < t_2$): $C(t_2) \geq C(t_1)$.

If the calls are European, then the hedge relation formula is changed to $S_0 d^{-t} \geq C_0 \geq \max(0, S_0 d^{-t} - Kr^{-t})$, the bull spread relation is changed to $C(K_1) > C(K_2)$ and $C(K_1) - C(K_2) \leq (K_2 - K_1)/r^{-t}$, and the time spread relation need not hold as long as the underlying asset has payouts prior to the calls' expiration dates.

Proof of the Butterfly Spread Relation for Standard Options

To illustrate how these are proven, examine the butterfly spread relation, where to simplify suppose the strike prices are equally spaced so that $K_3 - K_2 = K_2 - K_1$, and the options are all European. Consider the payoff of a butterfly spread where one call is purchased with strike price K_1, two calls are sold with strike price K_2, and one call is purchased with strike price K_3. The payoff from this position is:

$$\max(0, S_t - K_1] - [2 \max(0, S_t - K_2)] + \max(0, S_t - K_3)$$

Now consider all possible realizations of S_t ranging from zero to infinity. It is easy to see that this payoff can never be negative (and could be positive). Therefore, if there is no arbitrage, the present value of the position, $C(K_1) - 2C(K_2) + C(K_3)$, must also be nonnegative. This inequality then can be rewritten to give the butterfly spread relation.

Mark B. Garman, in [Garman (1976)] "An Algebra for Evaluating Hedge Portfolios," *Journal of Financial Economics* 3, No. 4 (October 1976), pp. 403–427, shows that, in the absence of restrictions on the probability distribution of the underlying asset price and provided the underlying asset is itself considered a payout-protected call with a zero strike price, these conditions are *necessary and sufficient* for there to be no buy-and-hold arbitrage opportunities among all coexisting calls to the same underlying asset. Yaacov Z. Bergman, Bruce D. Grundy, and Zvi Wiener, in [Bergman-Grundy-Wiener (1996)] "General Properties of Option Prices," *Journal of Finance* 51, No. 5 (December 1996), pp. 1573–1610, ask to what extent these arbitrage characteristics derived from option payoff functions are inherited by the option pricing function prior to expiration. They show that given a constant riskless return and a univariate diffusion process for the underlying asset price (a continuous-time, continuous-state process where the local volatility is a continuous function only of the concurrent asset price and time), any European derivative (with an arbitrary continuous payoff function and therefore not limited to standard calls and puts) inherits at all times in its life the key features of its payoff function: upper and lower delta bounds and monotonicity and convexity or concavity with respect to the underlying asset price.

Merton also shows that the value of an option on a portfolio of underlying assets will be less than the value of the corresponding portfolio of options, each on a single one of the same underlying assets.

An important application of the Black-Scholes formula has been to recover the risk-neutral distribution of the asset underlying the option from the option's price. Since Black and Scholes assume a *risk-neutral* lognormal distribution, this amounts to recovering its standard deviation. Both academics and practitioners term this the option's "implied volatility." This is done by implicitly inverting the Black-Scholes formula, taking the current option price (C_0) as given and solving for the unknown volatility (σ). As restrictive as this is, this nonetheless may be the first practical method to recover state-prices from the prices of ordinary securities. The first to publish this was Latané-Rendleman (1976).

As Black and Scholes point out in their paper and its very title, the theory can be applied to corporate securities (stocks and bonds) since they can be interpreted as options. To see this, consider a firm financed completely by stock and a single issue of zero-coupon debt. The shareholders then have a "default option": that is, at the maturity of the debt, they can choose to pay off the debt principal or to default. In the former case, they then own what remains of the firm after paying off the debt, and in the latter case they forfeit their ownership to the bondholders and end up with nothing. The stockholders will exercise their option to default whenever the value of the firm at the maturity date is less than the debt principal. Therefore, the stock can be interpreted as a call option on the value of the firm with a strike price equal to the debt principal and a time to expiration equal to the time to maturity of the debt. Similarly, the debt can be interpreted as a portfolio containing a default-free zero-coupon bond with the same principal and maturity as the debt and a sold put option on the value of the firm with a strike price equal to the debt principal and a time to expiration equal to the time to maturity of the debt; see the payoff representations of stock and bonds in my arbitrage proof of the Law of the Conservation of Investment Value in connection with Modigliani-Miller (1958).

Merton (1974) applies this idea to the pricing of zero-coupon corporate debt and shows how the default premium is a function of underlying firm volatility, bond maturity, and the ratio of promised principal repayment to the concurrent value of the firm. In subsequent years, this model has been extended by others to encompass callable and convertible corporate debt with coupons, junior debt, safety covenants, and the interaction between corporate choice of the risk of its assets and the composition of its capital structure, leading to the endogeneity of bankruptcy. Indeed, as subsequent work has shown, option pricing methods are the key to the valuation of a very wide range of securities.

Yet another way to view the contribution of Black, Scholes, and Merton is to see the Black-Scholes model as opening the door to operationalizing the abstract results of Arrow (1953). Until 20 years later in 1973, it was hard to see how the idea of state-securities was anything more than a very useful theoretical abstraction. As long as state-prices could not be measured, their practical applications were clearly severely limited. But after 1973, with the subsequent refinements of Breeden-Litzenberger (1978) and Rubinstein (1994) and with the simultaneous expansion of the market for exchange-traded options, it now became possible to estimate the state-price distribution (and even its stochastic process over time) used by the market. This new linkage between fundamental finance theory and practice remains an area of considerable promise.

Perhaps no other invention in economics or finance has had such widespread application in so short a time. Within a year or two after its publication, the Black-Scholes formula became the valuation standard for the first U.S. exchange-traded options on the newly formed Chicago Board Options Exchange. The exchange first opened its doors for trading on April 23, 1973, nearly coincident with the publication of the Black and Scholes paper. Indeed, along with its binomial generalization (Cox-Ross-Rubinstein 1979) and Rendleman-Bartter 1979), the Black-Scholes formula may now be the most widely used algorithm with embedded probabilities in human history. As Gerald R. Faulhaber and William J. Baumol, in [Faulhaber-Baumol (1988)] "Economists as Innovators Theoretical Research," *Journal of Economic Literature* 26, No. 2 (June 1988), pp. 577–600, point out, economic inventions with the shortest time between discovery and implementation tend to be those (1) that help cope with future uncertainty and (2) that are used in markets that are easy to enter and exit so that competitive pressures are particularly powerful—conditions that were particularly well met for the new option pricing theory.

Merton and Scholes won the 1997 Nobel Prize in Economic Science "for a new method to determine the value of derivatives" (Black had died prematurely in 1995).

1973 Stephen E. LeRoy, "Risk Aversion and the Martingale Property of Stock Prices," *International Economic Review* 14, No. 2 (June 1973), pp. 436–446.

EFFICIENT MARKETS, RANDOM WALK, MARTINGALES,
RISK AVERSION, CONSTANT RELATIVE RISK AVERSION (CRRA)

Early attempts to formalize the notion of efficient markets by Samuelson (1965) define efficient markets in terms of a martingale: The expected next price of any security conditional on information set Φ equals (a possibly time-dependent) constant times the current price: $E(P_{t+1}|\Phi) = kP_t$. The crucial part of this is that k is nonstochastic; otherwise, it would be a tautology. In particular this should hold if Φ equals the history of the past returns of the security so $\Phi = r_{t-1}, r_{t-2}, r_{t-3}, \ldots$ An equivalent way to write Samuelson's definition is in terms of returns, where $r_t = P_{t+1}/P_t$ and k is identified as the *unconditional* expected return $E(r_t)$:

$$E(r_t|r_{t-1}, r_{t-2}, r_{t-3}, \ldots) = E(r_t)$$

This implies that, given the current price, knowledge of the past realized returns of a security is of no help in forecasting expected future returns. Why? Because to the extent they might have been of some help, their influence has already been factored into the current price of the security (Bachelier 1900; Working 1949/May; Working 1958).

Under risk neutrality, the martingale result should hold since then $E(r_t|r_{t-1}, r_{t-2}, r_{t-3}, \ldots) = r$, the riskless return. Under risk aversion, for most securities, the CAPM suggests $E(r_t) > r$. Moreover, LeRoy (1973) claims that under risk aversion the conditional expected return will be random and therefore not equal its unconditional value. Consider the market portfolio: Samuelson's definition implies $E(r_{Mt}|r_{Mt-1}, r_{Mt-2}, r_{Mt-3}, \ldots) = E(r_{Mt})$. Suppose the previous market portfolio return r_{Mt-1} had been high; then the representative investor might become less risk averse and therefore demand a lower risk premium in the next period. Thus $E(r_{Mt}|r_{Mt-1})$ would fall in equilibrium, so that $E(r_{Mt}|r_{Mt-1}) \neq E(r_{Mt})$. This makes the conditional return a random variable since it is a function of the random variable r_{Mt-1}. Likewise, any security with return correlated with the return of the market portfolio will also have $E(r_t|r_{t-1}) \neq E(r_t)$. So Samuelson's definition of efficient markets does not make sense under risk aversion.

Rescuing Samuelson slightly, from the perspective of an intertemporal additive utility of consumption equilibrium, Rubinstein (1976/Autumn) shows that, while LeRoy's result generally holds under risk aversion, it need not. In particular, if the representative agent has constant relative risk aversion (CRRA) and aggregate consumption follows a random walk, then the value of the market portfolio will follow a random walk. Therefore, $E(r_{Mt}|r_{Mt-1}, r_{Mt-2}, r_{Mt-3}, \ldots)$ will be a constant independent of past returns.

The assumption that security prices follow a random walk is much stronger than the martingale restriction, for then the entire distribution of next period's return, not just its mean, is independent of realized past returns. If $f(\bullet)$ is the subjective probability distribution of returns, a random walk requires: $f(r_t|r_{t-1}, r_{t-2}, r_{t-3}, \ldots) = f(r_t)$. Clearly, security returns can obey the martingale restriction, even if they do not follow a random walk.

For example, consider a two-period default-free zero-coupon bond. Knowing its initial date 0 price, its return between dates 0 and 1 completely determines its return between dates 1 and 2 (its maturity). So the bond price does not follow a random walk. But it does obey the martingale restriction since knowing its price at date 1, irrespective of its previous returns, fully determines its return between dates 1 and 2. Alternatively, if the martingale restriction does not hold, then security prices cannot follow random walk.

1974 Fischer Sheffey Black and **Myron S. Scholes**, "The Effects of Dividend Yield and Dividend Policy on Common Stock Returns and Prices," *Journal of Financial Economics* 1, No. 1 (May 1974), pp. 1–22.

DIVIDENDS, PRICED VS. NONPRICED FACTORS

Black-Scholes (1974), the very first article in the maiden issue of the *Journal of Financial Economics*, provides evidence that dividend yield cannot be shown with confidence to be a priced factor, after considering normal CAPM risk adjustments, with returns measured either before or after taxes. Black and Scholes interpret their results as implying that investors should ignore distinctions between income in the forms of dividends or capital gains since it is not clear if the investor will benefit from this consideration, while if he concentrates his investment, say, in low- or in high-dividend-paying stocks, he is sure to lose some of the benefits of diversification. As a corollary, in a world in which investors optimally ignore dividends, corporations cannot use dividend policy to influence their stock prices (apart from information signaling effects).

To examine these issues, Black and Scholes develop a new empirical methodology. Their goal is to estimate γ_{2t} in the following regression equation:

$$r_{jt} = \gamma_{0t} + \gamma_{1t}\beta_{jt} + \gamma_{2t}\left(\frac{\delta_{jt} - \delta_{Mt}}{\delta_{Mt}}\right) + \varepsilon_{jt}$$

with δ_{jt} defined as the dividend yield of security j and δ_{Mt} as the dividend yield on the market portfolio. Their first step, for each month, is to divide the security universe into 5 portfolios stratified by dividend yield and then to subdivide each of these into 5 portfolios stratified by beta (measured over the previous five years), for a total of 25 portfolios. Each month these 25 portfolios are reconstituted. In the second step, each month, out of these 25 intermediate portfolios, a final portfolio P is constructed where the weights across the 25 intermediate portfolios are chosen to minimize the variance of return of the final portfolio. The final portfolio tends to consist of long positions in high-yield stocks and short positions in low-yield stocks with an overall beta near zero and a low variance of return. In the third step, even though β_P should turn out to be near zero, to eliminate any effect from nonzero betas, the following time-series regression over different subperiods is used to estimate a single γ_2 for each subperiod from each regression:

$$r_{Pt} - r_t = \gamma_2 + \beta_P(r_M - r) + \varepsilon_{Pt}$$

It turns out that for the entire period, and every subperiod, the estimate of γ_2 is not statistically significant.

1974   Mark Rubinstein, "An Aggregation Theorem for Securities Markets," *Journal of Financial Economics* 1, No. 3 (October 1974), pp. 225–244.

1982   George M. Constantinides, "Intertemporal Asset Pricing with Heterogeneous Consumers and without Demand Aggregation," *Journal of Business* 55, No. 2 (April 1982), pp. 253–267.

1985   Hal R. Varian, "Divergence of Opinion in Complete Markets: A Note," *Journal of Finance* 40, No. 1 (March 1985), pp. 309–317.

AGGREGATION, HETEROGENEOUS BELIEFS,
MARKET-EQUIVALENCE THEOREM, PORTFOLIO SEPARATION,
STATE-SECURITIES, CONSENSUS VS. COMPOSITE INVESTOR,
LOGARITHMIC UTILITY, AVERAGE OR REPRESENTATIVE MAN

Rubinstein (1974) specializes the very general group decision-making setting of Wilson (1968) to an explicit securities market equilibrium context. Rubinstein derives conditions for the standard finance model under many states in which, although consumer/investors may have heterogeneous levels of wealth, patience, risk aversion, and beliefs, prices are set as if there were a single representative consumer/investor whose wealth, patience, risk aversion, and/or beliefs are simple aggregates of those characteristics for the individual consumer/investors.

This is the first paper to use the market-equivalence theorem in the context of apparently incomplete markets but which have the property of universal portfolio separation (all investors choose optimally from the same two mutual funds, one of which is riskless); in that context optimal choices and equilibrium prices will be the same if it is assumed that a full set of state-securities exists (complete markets).

Simplifying the Portfolio Selection Problem with State-Securities

Consider the standard portfolio selection problem:

$$\max_{\{x_j\}} \Sigma_s p_s [U(W_0 \Sigma_j x_j r_{sj})] \quad \text{subject to} \quad \Sigma_j x_j = 1$$

where W_0 is current wealth, r_{sj} is the return on security $j = 0, 1, 2, \ldots, m$ in state s, p_s is the subjective probability of state s, and x_j is the proportion of the investor's portfolio devoted to security j. $x_j > 0$ indicates a purchase, $x_j < 0$ indicates a (short) sale, and all wealth is allocated to securities so that $\Sigma_j x_j = 1$. $W_{s1} \equiv W_0 \Sigma_j x_j r_{sj}$ can be interpreted as random future wealth—the combined result from the investor making choices (x_j) and from nature choosing which state occurs. $U(W_{s1})$ is utility given future wealth W_{s1}. To find the optimal portfolio choices, I usually use a Lagrangian multiplier λ, setting up the problem as:

$$\max_{\{x_j\}} \Sigma_s p_s [U(W_0 \Sigma_j x_j r_{sj})] - \lambda(\Sigma_j x_j - 1)$$

Differentiate this with respect to x_j and set the derivative equal to 0. This leads to the condition: $\Sigma_s p_s [U'(W_{s1}) r_{sj})] = \lambda/W_0$. This says that at the optimal set of portfolio proportions, the expected marginal utility of earning return from each security is identical for all securities and moreover equal to λ/W_0. In general, this problem cannot be solved in closed form. To see the problem, suppose there are three states ($s = 1, 2, 3$) and three securities ($j = 1, 2, 3$), writing this out in longhand where r_{sj} represents the return on security j in state s:

$$p_1 \{U'[W_0(x_1 r_{11} + x_2 r_{12} + x_3 r_{13})] r_{11}\}$$
$$+ p_2 \{U'[W_0(x_1 r_{21} + x_2 r_{22} + x_3 r_{23})] r_{21}\}$$
$$+ p_3 \{U'[W_0(x_1 r_{31} + x_2 r_{32} + x_3 r_{33})] r_{31}\} = \frac{\lambda}{W_0}$$

$$p_1 \{U'[W_0(x_1 r_{11} + x_2 r_{12} + x_3 r_{13})] r_{12}\}$$
$$+ p_2 \{U'[W_0(x_1 r_{21} + x_2 r_{22} + x_3 r_{23})] r_{22}\}$$
$$+ p_3 \{U'[W_0(x_1 r_{31} + x_2 r_{32} + x_3 r_{33})] r_{32}\} = \frac{\lambda}{W_0}$$

(Continued)

Simplifying the Portfolio Selection Problem
with State-Securities *(Continued)*

$$p_1\{U'[W_0(x_1r_{11}+x_2r_{12}+x_3r_{13})]r_{13}\}$$
$$+p_2\{U'[W_0(x_1r_{21}+x_2r_{22}+x_3r_{23})]r_{23}\}$$
$$+p_3\{U'[W_0(x_1r_{31}+x_2r_{32}+x_3r_{33})]r_{33}\}=\frac{\lambda}{W_0}$$

$$x_1 + x_2 + x_3 = 1$$

We have four equations in four unknowns, λ and (x_0, x_1, x_2). But since generally $U'(W_1)$ is a nonlinear function of W_1 (to build in risk aversion), these equations cannot be analytically solved. That is, each unknown cannot be isolated on the left-hand side of an equation whose right-hand side does not contain the other unknowns.

Now, suppose there is a complete market, where the investor can buy a full set of state-securities. In that case, the portfolio selection problem can be stated as:

$$\max_{\{x_s\}} \Sigma_s p_s[U(W_0 x_s r_s)] - \lambda(\Sigma_s x_s - 1)$$

where x_s is the proportion of the investor's portfolio devoted to state-securities that pay off only in state s. r_s is the return on state security s (which, of course, is only nonzero if state s occurs). Thus, $W_{s1} \equiv W_0 x_s r_s$ can be interpreted as the investor's future wealth in state s. As before, but differentiating by x_s, we derive: $p_s U'(W_0 x_s r_s)r_s = \lambda/W_0$. Again, with three states, writing this out in longhand, we need to solve:

$$p_1 U'(W_0 x_1 r_1)r_1 = \frac{\lambda}{W_0}, \quad p_2 U'(W_0 x_2 r_2)r_2 = \frac{\lambda}{W_0}, \quad p_3 U'(W_0 x_3 r_3)r_3 = \frac{\lambda}{W_0}$$

$$x_1 + x_2 + x_3 = 1$$

for λ and (x_1, x_2, x_3). Clearly, these equations are much easier to solve.

The paper draws a distinction between consensus and composite economic characteristics. In each case, equilibrium prices are set as if there were a single representative agent with the consensus or composite characteristics. Composite characteristics depend only on exogenously specified parameters (in particular, they do not depend on prices), while consensus characteristics can depend as well on variables such as prices that are endogenous to the economy.

Michael John Brennan and Alan Kraus, in [Brennan-Kraus (1978)] "Necessary Conditions for Aggregation in Securities Markets," *Journal of Financial and Quantitative Analysis* 13, No. 3 (September 1978), pp. 407–418, define the aggregation problem as the derivation of equilibrium security prices that are independent of the allocation of initial wealth across investors. This is a stronger assumption than that of Wilson (1968), so the result must be a subset of his derived conditions. While Rubinstein derived a set of sufficient conditions for aggregation, Brennan and Kraus show that these are also necessary. Earlier papers that provide pieces of a similar result for an economy under certainty include: (1) [Gorman (1953)] W.M. Gorman, "Community Preference Fields," *Econometrica* 21, No. 1 (January 1953), pp. 63–80, who shows that a necessary condition for aggregation, as defined by Brennan and Kraus, is that the Engle curves of investors be parallel straight lines. These conditions were apparently first discovered by Giovanni Battista Antonelli, privately published in 1886 in [Antonelli (1886)] "Sulla teoria matematica della economia politica," translated from Italian into English as "On the Mathematical Theory of Political Economy," in *Preferences, Utility and Demand*, edited by J.S. Chipman, L. Hurwicz, M.K. Richter, and H.F. Sonnenschein (Harcourt Brace, 1971), pp. 333–360; and (2) [Pollack (1971)] Robert A. Pollack, "Additive Utility Functions and Linear Engle Curves," *Review of Economic Studies* 38, No. 4 (October 1971), pp. 401–414, who shows that a necessary and sufficient condition for an investor to have linear Engle curves is HARA utility.

Rubinstein (1974) also contains a new result concerning aggregation of heterogeneous probability beliefs in the context of perhaps the simplest rational competitive equilibrium model with risk aversion embodying this form of heterogeneity.

Illustration of an Economy with Heterogeneous Beliefs

In particular, let:

$s = 1, \ldots, S$ enumerate the exhaustive set of possible states, only one of which can occur at date 1.

π_s be the date 0 price to a dollar received at date 1 if and only if state s occurs.

$i = 1, \ldots, I$ enumerate the set of different investors in the economy, who differ only with respect to the subjective probabilities they assign to states.

p_s^i be the subjective probability believed by investor i that state s will occur.

C_s^i be the number of dollars chosen by investor i to be consumed in state s.

W_0 be the initial wealth of each investor at date 0; initially before exchange this is composed of given endowments to date 1 consumption $\underline{C}_s$ to be divided among claims to consumption at date 1 such that each investor i's state-by-state choices of consumption are constrained so that their present value equals his initial wealth (that is, $W_0 \equiv \Sigma_s \pi_s \underline{C}_s = \Sigma_s \pi_s C_s^i$).

Each investor is assumed to maximize his expected logarithmic utility of date 1 consumption, $\Sigma_s p_s^i \log(C_s^i)$. Therefore, we can concisely summarize each investor's problem as:

$$\max_{\{C_s^i\}} \Sigma_s p_s^i \log(C_s^i) - \lambda_i (\Sigma_s \pi_s C_s^i - W_0)$$

where λ_i is the Lagrangian multiplier for investor i. Differentiating by C_s^i, the first-order condition for a maximum is:

$$\frac{p_s^i}{C_s^i} = \lambda_i \pi_s$$

Illustration of an Economy with
Heterogeneous Beliefs *(Continued)*

Summing this over all states, using the property $\Sigma_s p_s^i = 1$, and substituting in the wealth constraint, it is quite easy to see that $\lambda_i = 1/W_0$. Now using the first-order condition, we have:

$$C_s^i = W_0 \left(\frac{p_s^i}{\pi_s} \right)$$

This has the very sensible and transparent implications that any investor's optimal holdings of claims to state s consumption, other things being equal, increases with his current wealth (W_0), increases with the probability he assigns to state s, and decreases with the cost of claims to state s.

What is more, summing the above equation over all investors, we have:

$$C_s^M = W_0 \left(\frac{p_s^M}{\pi_s} \right)$$

where $C_s^M \equiv (\Sigma_i C_s^i)/I$ and $p_s^M \equiv (\Sigma_i p_s^i)/I$. C_s^M has the natural interpretation of per-capita consumption. Rearranging this, we can say that in equilibrium, state-prices are set as if there exists a representative agent with subjective beliefs p_s^M that are a simple arithmetic average of the separate beliefs of all investors in the economy. That is,

$$\pi_s = p_s^M \left(\frac{W_0}{C_s^M} \right)$$

Other things being equal, state-prices will be higher the higher this average belief.[33]

We are now in position to ask a critical question: To what extent do heterogeneous beliefs across investors affect equilibrium prices? In particular, does increasing dispersion of beliefs across different investors have any systematic effect on security prices? To isolate a pure dispersion effect, suppose for a given state we consider a "mean-preserving spread" of beliefs across different investors. Such a change leaves the arithmetic average (mean) belief the same. For example, suppose there are just two investors $i = 1, 2$, and for a given state s, $p_s^1 = .3$ and $p_s^2 = .5$. The average belief $p_s^M = (.3 + .5)/2 = .4$. An example of an increase in belief dispersion with a mean-preserving spread would be a change in beliefs to $p_s^1 = .1$ and $p_s^2 = .7$, thus preserving the mean of $(.1 + .7)/2 = .4$. Trivially, for our example, it is only the mean that matters; pure belief dispersion has no effect. So I conclude that in the case of logarithmic utility, moving from homogeneous to heterogeneous beliefs has no effect on current prices since the only property of investor beliefs that affects prices is their mean across investors for each state.

However, Varian (1985) shows that logarithmic utility is a knife-edge case (as it is in so many other situations). For example, if we suppose more generally that all investors have utility functions with constant relative risk aversion (of which logarithmic utility is but a special case), for economies in which investors are more (or less) risk averse than logarithmic utility, pure increases in the dispersion of beliefs will tend to reduce (or increase) current security prices. Varian concludes that since several pieces of empirical evidence suggest investors are more risk averse than logarithmic utility, pure increases in dispersion of beliefs will tend to reduce security prices.

Intuitive Explanation of Varian's Result on Heterogeneous Beliefs

To understand the intuition behind Varian's analysis, first reconsider the logarithmic utility case where optimal consumption choice for state s by investor i is:

$$C_s^i = \gamma_s p_s^i \quad \text{with} \quad \gamma_s \equiv \frac{W_0}{\pi_s}$$

Following our two-investor example, where belief dispersion is increased as p_s^1 changes from .3 to .1, and p_s^2 changes from .5 to .7, the first investor can decrease his consumption and by $\Delta C_s^1 = \gamma_s(.1 - .3) = -.2\gamma_s$ while second investor 2 can increase his consumption by $\Delta C_s^2 = \gamma_s(.7 - .5) = .2\gamma_s$, an exactly offsetting amount, with no pressure on γ_s (that is, state-prices) to change as well. However, suppose instead the two investors have more general power utility functions $[1/(1-b)](C_s^i)^{1-b}$. Here b measures (proportional) risk aversion, with a minimum of $b = 0$ signifying risk neutrality, and increases in b implying greater and greater risk aversion. In the limiting case of $b = 1$, this can be shown to imply logarithmic utility.

Intuitive Explanation of Varian's Result on Heterogeneous Beliefs *(Continued)*

Therefore, for $b > 1$, the investors are more risk averse than logarithmic utility investors. Using this utility function, the first-order condition that replaces the earlier one can be written:

$$C_s^i = \gamma_s^i (p_s^i)^{1/b} \quad \text{with} \quad \gamma_s^i \equiv \left(\frac{1}{\lambda_i \pi_s}\right)^{1/b}$$

Now for, say, $b = 2$, consider the same change in belief dispersion: If state-prices remain unchanged, the two investors will want to change their state s consumption by:

$$\Delta C_s^1 = \gamma_s^1 (\sqrt{.1} - \sqrt{.3}) = -.231\gamma_s^1 \quad \text{and}$$
$$\Delta C_s^2 = \gamma_s^2 (\sqrt{.7} - \sqrt{.5}) = .130\gamma_s^2$$

Since these changes tend not to be exactly offsetting, the state-price for s must change. In fact, if this price does not change, since the increasingly pessimistic investor 1 will want to sell more than the increasingly optimistic investor 2 will want to buy, to the contrary, the state s price will need to fall to cause these changes in state s consumption for the two investors to exactly offset.

Constantinides (1982) also specializes the very general group decision-making setting of Wilson (1968) to an explicit securities market equilibrium context. Constantinides derives the following theorem as a justification for assuming a representative investor. In an exchange economy with perfect, competitive, and complete markets, assume all investor/consumers have the same beliefs and potentially different time-additive, state-independent utility functions that are increasing, strictly concave, and differentiable. Then there is another otherwise identical economy (with the same equilibrium state-prices) with just one representative agent (endowed with aggregate consumption) who has the same beliefs and also has a time-additive utility function that is increasing, strictly concave, and differentiable. Constantinides shows that the Rubinstein (1976/Autumn) aggregation assumptions are much more restrictive than necessary to obtain a representative investor. However, in general it will not be easy to show explicitly how the characteristics of the representative investor are an aggregation of the traits of individual investors, and for this, Rubinstein's special cases are useful.

1975   Marshall E. Blume and **Irwin Friend**, "The Asset Structure of Individual Portfolios and Some Implications for Utility Functions," *Journal of Finance* 30, No. 2 (May 1975), pp. 585–603.

1975   Marshall E. Blume and **Irwin Friend**, "The Demand for Risky Assets," *American Economic Review* 65, No. 5 (December 1975), pp. 900–902.

DIVERSIFICATION, RISK AVERSION,
CAPITAL ASSET PRICING MODEL (CAPM)

Blume-Friend (1975/May) document one of the first pieces of anomalous evidence standing against the hypothesis of rational investor behavior. Using databases containing information about the composition and size of portfolios held by individual taxpayers in the United States (partially derived from income tax returns, which require individuals to list their sources of dividend income), they find that individuals are surprisingly undiversified, with the median household receiving income from only two payers. Modern investment theory, of course, suggests that individuals should instead be highly diversified. Even large net worth households (in excess of $1,000,000 exclusive of homes) typically receive payments from only 14 sources. The Sharpe-Lintner-Mossin-Treynor CAPM implies that *every firm* must have the same number of shareholders; in particular, every investor must be a shareholder. Potential explanations—holdings in mutual funds, trading costs, locked-in capital gains, and heterogeneous expectations—cannot explain this anomaly. However, the results of John L. Evans and Stephen H. Archer, in [Evans-Archer (1968)] "Diversification and the Reduction of Dispersion: An Empirical Analysis," *Journal of Finance* 23, No. 5 (December 1968), pp. 761–767, suggest that portfolios with even just 10 randomly selected stocks are expected to have a standard deviation of return almost as small as the standard deviation of portfolios containing hundreds of stocks. Indeed, K.H. Johnson and D.S. Shannon, in [Johnson-Shannon (1974)] "A Note on Diversification and the Reduction of Dispersion," *Journal of Financial Economics* 1, No. 4 (December 1974), pp. 365–372, show that given the randomly selected securities, if instead of investing in an equally dollar-weighted portfolio, the weights are chosen to minimize risk taking into account the estimated correlations of their returns, the number of securities can be reduced even further.

In Blume-Friend (1975/December), the authors use their wealth composition information regarding relatively riskless and risky assets to infer properties of investor utility functions (assuming, of course, that investors have utility functions). They find that the typical investor has approximately constant relative risk aversion (CRRA) with a relative risk aversion coefficient of 2, somewhat more risk averse than would be implied by logarithmic utility.

Virtually all empirical studies of modern asset pricing models have used the realized frequency distributions of security prices as proxies for the expectational distributions that actually appear in the theories. So, should a model be rejected, one can never be sure that the problem lies with the model and not with this proxy. John G. Cragg and Burton G. Malkiel, in [Cragg-Malkiel (1982)] *Expectations and the Structure of Share Prices* (Chicago: University of Chicago Press, 1982), make the first extensive study of asset pricing models that attempts to measure investor expectations directly. In particular, they collect forecasts from 19 investment management firms, covering 175 firms over the period 1961–1969. They conclude that the models perform better using these forecasts as proxies for expectations compared to using historical realizations. Perhaps most interesting is the result that the dispersion of growth forecasts across the investment firms concerning the same event provides a better measure of security risk than either the historically realized variance or beta.

1975   Eugene F. Fama, "Short-Term Interest Rates as Predictors of Inflation," *American Economic Review* 65, No. 3 (June 1975), pp. 269–282.

1981   Eugene F. Fama, "Stock Returns, Real Activity, Inflation, and Money," *American Economic Review* 71, No. 4 (September 1981), pp. 545–565.

FISHER EFFECT, NOMINAL VS. REAL INTEREST RATE,
INFLATION, STOCK PRICES AND INFLATION

The Fisher effect relates the nominal interest rate to the real interest rate and the rate of inflation; see Fisher (1930). In a perfect market with no arbitrage and predictable inflation, it is quite easy to see that the nominal riskless return (r) equals the real riskless return (ρ) times the inflation return (i): $r = \rho i$. Actually, since the nominal return cannot fall below 1 because of the "mattress strategy," the corrected relation is $r = \max(1, \rho i)$. Generalizing this to uncertain inflation, this relation suggests that $r = \rho E(i)$. Fama (1975) actually examines an almost equivalent version of this hypothesis that the nominal riskless *rate* of return equals the sum of the real riskless *rate* of return plus the expected *rate* of inflation. So buried inside the current nominal riskless return over period Δ is the market's expectation of inflation over the same time interval. This is an important example of the implication of a well-functioning market: The prices of securities set in such a market contain valuable forecasts of future economic events, in this case the future rate of inflation. Moreover, if the market is rational, it should build into prices all relevant information that is humanly cost-effective to gather. Therefore, if we can find an inexpensive method to extract this prediction from the prices of riskless securities, there is no reason to hire a financial economist to do a study of the economy to forecast inflation.

Earlier attempts to extract useful predictions of inflation from observed nominal interest rates were not promising. Fama is perhaps the first to show that this could be done, at least over the period January 1953 to July 1971 using one- to six-month U.S. Treasury bills to measure nominal interest rates and the consumer price index (CPI) to measure inflation. His key idea is to assume that the real rate is constant over this period so that *all* variation in nominal rates can be attributed to changes in the market's prediction of the expected rate of inflation. Fama regresses: $i_t = -\alpha_0 + \alpha_1 r_t + \alpha_2 i_{t-1} + \varepsilon_t$, where i_t, r_t, and i_{t-1} (past rates of inflation) in this equation are interpreted as observed *rates* over the subscripted periods. His model predicts α_0 = the real rate, $\alpha_1 = 1$, $\alpha_2 = 0$, and the serial correlation of ε_t is zero. Making a long story short, his results confirm these predictions including the constancy of the real rate. In addition, he estimates that variation in r_t explains about 30 percent of the variance of i_t for one-month bills, and about 65 percent of the variance of i_t for five- and six-month bills.

Subsequently, in [Fama-Gibbons (1984)] "A Comparison of Inflation Forecasts," *Journal of Monetary Economics* 13, No. 2 (May 1984), pp. 327–348, Fama and Michael R. Gibbons improve Fama's earlier model to allow the real rate intercept to follow a slow-moving random walk. Fama (1981) uses this refined model to estimate expected $(-\alpha_0 + \alpha_1 r_t)$ and unexpected (ε_t) inflation by constraining the regression coefficients $\alpha_1 = 1$ and $\alpha_2 = 0$. With this in hand, Fama then tests the relation between stock market returns and inflation. Naively, one might have expected that like Treasury bills, nominal stock returns should be higher in times of high rates of inflation, and it may be that their underlying risk-adjusted real return is a slow-moving random walk. One would think that stocks should be good hedges against inflation. Disturbingly, at least during the period 1953–1980, just the opposite seems to be true. See, for example, John Lintner, in [Lintner (1975)] "Inflation and Security Returns," *Journal of Finance* 30, No. 2 (May 1975), pp. 259–280, Presidential Address to the American Finance Association.

Fama attempts to explain this by a "proxy argument." He argues that (1) stock returns are positively correlated with favorable real economic fundamental variables such as industrial production, and (2) inflation (particularly expected inflation) is negatively correlated with these real variables, and therefore (3) stock returns can reasonably be negatively correlated with inflation. Thus, Fama again, as he did with Treasury bill returns and inflation, rescues the rational market hypothesis from a serious challenge. On the way he picks up further evidence, showing empirically that stock returns lead other economic variables. But why should industrial production, for example, be negatively correlated with inflation? Fama's quantity theory story is that expected increases in industrial production lead to increasing real demand for money, which because money does not usually grow sufficiently, requires accommodation through reduced inflation.

1975 Mark Rubinstein, "Securities Market Efficiency in an Arrow-Debreu Economy," *American Economic Review* 65, No. 5 (December 1975), pp. 812–824.

EFFICIENT MARKETS, FULLY REFLECT INFORMATION,
NO TRADE THEOREMS, STATE-SECURITIES,
CONSENSUS BELIEFS, PARETO OPTIMALITY

Rubinstein (1975) tries to give specific meaning to the phrase "equilibrium prices reflect information," which heretofore had been used very loosely in the literature despite its importance. The key idea is to link this concept with portfolio revision. Consider an economy of many consumer/investors with arbitrarily different beliefs and preferences (except all are risk averse and have additive utility functions of consumption). At date 0, long-lived state-securities are available for consumption at dates 1 and 2. At date 1, no new state-securities become available, but new information does and is heterogeneously distributed to investors, potentially changing the beliefs of all consumer/investors as well as the equilibrium prices of state-securities to date 2 consumption. This setup is designed so that at date 1 the only reason agents have to change their previously purchased claims to date 2 consumption stems from the arrival of the new information. If an agent does not revise his portfolio of these claims, but is happy to continue holding his prior claims, then it makes sense to say that despite whatever change in prices may have occurred, he sees his new information reflected in the revised prices.

The paper then derives an intuitively plausible and specific condition governing the intertemporal structure of the evolution of prices, which turns out not to depend on preferences and endowments (despite the agnosticism about these in its assumptions), that is necessary and sufficient for an investor not to revise his portfolio. If this condition holds, with all expectations assessed by an investor at date 0, his expected compound return of any state-security from date 0 to date 2 divided by the riskless return from date 0 to date 1 equals his expected return of the state-security between date 1 and date 2—a sort of "unbiased state-price" condition.

This, then, is a *necessary* condition for the investor to perceive his new information that he is to receive at date 1 reflected in the revised equilibrium prices to date 2 consumption. Among other implications, this condition, for example, is actually inconsistent with zero correlation in successive returns of state-securities to consumption at date 2, suggesting that simple random walk models are not the natural outcome of equilibrium even when prices fully reflect all information.

This approach may be contrasted with Grossman's (1976) notion of prices fully reflecting information. His model is more about how dispersed information gets into prices. To show this meaningfully, he is forced to examine a very restrictive economy (compared to the one here), to assume that investors somehow know enough about the structure of the economy (the preferences and endowments of other investors) to infer the information they are missing from current prices, and to know that all investors are equally well informed. This paper, in contrast, is agnostic about the process investors use to form their beliefs. It is perfectly possible, for example, for them to have followed the exercise that Grossman outlines. However their beliefs are formed, the pricing condition developed in the paper is nonetheless necessary and sufficient for their *new* information to be fully reflected in prices.

For *all* information at dates 0 and 1 to be reflected in prices, Rubinstein uses the idea of "consensus beliefs": the set of identical beliefs all consumer/investors would need so that in an otherwise identical economy all prices (at dates 0 and 1) would remain unchanged. All information is said to be fully reflected in prices if this condition is met: if all the agents were to share their information to the point that they would reach complete agreement, and their new beliefs would happen to be the consensus beliefs. Unfortunately, the paper leaves the issue at this point and does not show how to operationalize such an experiment. Grossman takes this a step further by describing a mechanism whereby the disparate information of different investors becomes shared among investors so that it is reflected in prices. But his notion of efficiency is much too restrictive to be taken as an empirical possibility. By contrast, the notion of consensus beliefs, for example, permits the market to be informationally efficient even if all investors do not end up having the same beliefs, whether they fail to start that way, or fail to infer the relevant information of all other investors from prices in the process of forming rational expectations.

Notice that Rubinstein's notion of efficient markets is closely related to what later became known as the Milgrom-Stokey "no trade theorem" developed in [Milgrom-Stokey (1982)] Paul Milgrom and Nancy Stokey, "Information, Trade and Common Knowledge," *Journal of Economic Theory* 26, No. 1 (February 1982), pp. 17–27. Traders have moved to their Pareto-optimal positions in the first period, new information then becomes available, and the absence of trade is identified with prices having immediately adjusted the reflect to new information.

In a 1975 working paper that remained unpublished until 1987 (despite several attempts to publish it), [Jaffe-Rubinstein (1987)] "The Value of Information in Personal and Impersonal Markets" in *Modern Finance and Industrial Economics*, edited by Tom Copeland (Oxford: Basil Blackwell, 1987), Jeffrey Jaffe and Mark Rubinstein clearly anticipate Milgrom-Stokey (1982). This paper considers a "completely personal market" in which, in addition to his own resources, tastes, and beliefs, each investor knows the resources and tastes of all other consumers, and knows the "knowledge type" of the information he and all others have. That is, investors agree on the ranking of informativeness of all investors, although they do not know the content of the information other investors possess. The paper then proves that in such a market, investors can identify Pareto-optimal allocations independent of their beliefs. This implies the "no trade" corollary that in such a market, if the endowed allocation is Pareto-optimal, then no investor will trade and the private value of information is zero.

1973 **Richard Roll**, "Evidence on the 'Growth-Optimum' Model," *Journal of Finance* 28, No. 3 (June 1973), pp. 551–566.

1975 **Alan Kraus** and **Robert H. Litzenberger**, "Market Equilibrium in a Multiperiod State-Preference Model with Logarithmic Utility," *Journal of Finance* 30, No. 5 (December 1975), pp. 1213–1227.

1976 **Mark Rubinstein**, "The Strong Case for the Generalized Logarithmic Utility Model as the Premier Model of Financial Markets," *Journal of Finance* 31, No. 2 (May 1976), pp. 551–571; the full version of this paper appears in *Financial Decision Making under Uncertainty*, edited by Haim Levy and Marshall Sarnat (New York: Academic Press, 1977).

LOGARITHMIC UTILITY, LOGARITHMIC UTILITY CAPM,
AGGREGATION, HETEROGENEOUS BELIEFS,
CONSENSUS BELIEFS, LIMITED LIABILITY,
DEFAULT-FREE ANNUITY,
INTERTEMPORAL PORTFOLIO SEPARATION

Roll (1973/June) develops and empirically tests an alternative to the CAPM based on maximizing logarithmic utility of wealth at the end of one period.

$$\mu_j = r + \mathrm{Cov}\left(r_j, \ -\frac{r}{r_M}\right)$$

replaces the somewhat more complex CAPM formula of Sharpe (1964), Lintner (1965/February), Mossin (1966), and Treynor (1999): $\mu_j = r + \theta\text{Cov}(r_j, r_M)$. If simplicity is a desideratum for theory, it is hard to beat this.

Kraus-Litzenberger (1975) extend Roll's model to consumption over many periods, showing that it continues to lead to very simple portfolio decision rules and equilibrium pricing relations. They also show that the model can easily accommodate heterogeneous consumer beliefs, also shown in Rubinstein (1974). They argue that the model is a serious competitor to the CAPM since it is even simpler to state and derive and can easily permit heterogeneous beliefs while also making no exogenous assumptions about probability distributions, such as joint normality. Even if investment opportunities are stochastic, as shown before by Merton (1973/September) in continuous time, these will not complicate the single-period pricing relation. Moreover, the CAPM, if justified by joint normality, is inconsistent with limited liability of the market portfolio (although this is not true of the continuous-time version), while the log model implies that the market portfolio will always have positive value.

It is convenient to have at hand as rich an example as possible of the "standard finance model" that still permits closed-form solutions for all decision variables and prices. Rubinstein (1976/May) argues that a complete markets model based on time-additive utility terms of the form $\log(A + C_t)$ is just such an example. This multiperiod consumption/portfolio equilibrium model has the following properties: (1) it requires decreasing absolute risk aversion while permitting increasing, constant, or decreasing relative risk aversion across different agents; (2) it assumes no exogenous specification of the contemporaneous or intertemporal stochastic process of security returns; (3) it permits heterogeneity with respect to initial wealth, lifetime, and time and risk preferences and beliefs; (4) it results in a complete specification of consumption/portfolio decision and sharing rules; (5) it explains the demand for default-free bonds of various maturities and options; (6) it solves the aggregation problem; and (7) it results in a complete endogenous specification of the contemporaneous and intertemporal process of security prices that includes simple necessary and sufficient conditions for an unbiased term structure and a random walk in the market portfolio.

One of the features of equilibrium first observed in this paper is an intertemporal separation theorem in which one of the funds is a default-free annuity (that is, an equally weighted portfolio of zero-coupon bonds of every maturity). This replaces the riskless security in single-period models or in multiperiod models that impose (as this model does not) exogenous restrictions on future riskless returns. And so this is the first equilibrium model that explains the demand for default-free bonds of different maturities and suggests that in addition to the market portfolio, one of the first portfolios an economy will want to make available to its agents is a default-free annuity. To connect this with earlier literature, in the Merton (1973/September) generalized CAPM, investors hold an unidentified portfolio to hedge themselves against shifts in the opportunity set. Rubinstein identifies this as a portfolio that contains zero-coupon bonds of different maturities. These multiperiod separation results are extended further in [Rubinstein (1981)] Mark Rubinstein, "A Discrete-Time Synthesis of Financial Theory," *Research in Finance* 3, (Greenwich, CT: JAI Press, 1981), pp. 53–102. There it is shown, for example, in a three-date similar economy but with exponential utility, that all consumer/investors will divide their wealth between three mutual funds: (1) the market portfolio, (2) a default-free annuity, and (3) a third fund holding long-term bonds (maturing at date 2) and at the same time shorting short-term bonds (maturing at date 1). Demand for the third fund comes from heterogeneous time preference toward consumption at date 2. Consumer/investors with more (or less) patience than average for date 2 consumption will buy (or sell) this fund, since they will be more (or less) eager to hedge themselves against shifts in investment opportunities.

1976 **Fischer Sheffey Black,** "Studies of Stock Price Volatility Changes," *Proceedings of the 1976 Meetings of the American Statistical Association,* Business and Economics Section (August 1976), pp. 177–181.

1979 **Robert Geske** (July 7, 1944–), "The Valuation of Compound Options," *Journal of Financial Economics* 7, No. 1 (March 1979), pp. 63–81.

1983 **Mark Rubinstein,** "Displaced-Diffusion Option Pricing," *Journal of Finance* 38, No. 1 (March 1983), pp. 213–217.

1996 **John C. Cox,** "Notes on Option Pricing I: Constant Elasticity of Variance Diffusions," unpublished notes, Stanford University (September 1975) and finally published as "The Constant Elasticity of Variance Diffusion Option Pricing Model," *Journal of Portfolio Management,* Special Issue: A Tribute to Fischer Black (December 1996), pp. 15–17.

VOLATILITY, STOCHASTIC VOLATILITY,
COMPOUND OPTIONS, CONSTANT ELASTICITY

OF VARIANCE (CEV) DIFFUSION MODEL,
FINANCIAL LEVERAGE, OPERATING DIVERSIFICATION,
MYOPIA, CONTINUOUS-TIME CONTINUOUS-STATE CAPM

Black (1976) is perhaps the first paper to verify empirically that in the time series of stock prices, stock return volatility tends to vary inversely with stock price changes. In particular, if a stock price rises (or falls) quickly, its volatility or return will tend to fall (or rise). A theoretical model with this property is proposed by Cox (1996).

While Cox simply assumes that volatility and price are inversely related, another option pricing model with this inverse relation built in rather than simply asserted is developed in Geske (1979). As in Merton (1974), Geske assumes that the market value of all the securities of a firm follows geometric Brownian motion (that is, follows a lognormal random walk).[34] In that case, if the firm has debt, as the stock price rises, although the debt perhaps becomes more valuable, the firm's stock rises in value even faster. This will reduce the debt-equity ratio of the firm, measured in terms of market values. This reduction in leverage will reduce the subsequent risk (hence volatility) of owning the firm's stock. So we have stock prices rising and volatility falling.

This model is carried yet another step further in Rubinstein (1983). Rubinstein shows that a deeper analysis of corporate determinants of stock price volatility can produce either positive or negative correlation between stock price changes and stock return volatility. He supposes that the assets of the firm can be divided roughly into two categories: relatively low-risk assets in place as a result of previous investments and the present value of relatively high-risk opportunities to make profitable investments in the future. As the stock price of the firm rises quickly, typically it will be the second class of assets that rises relatively more in value than the first class of assets. This will move the composition of the firm's asset portfolio further in the direction of the risky asset category. In turn this will increase the volatility of the stock. If the asset composition effect is stronger than the leverage effect considered by Geske, the net effect will be to see stock return volatility moving in the same direction as the stock price. This research predicts that the sign as well as size of the correlation between stock price and volatility will differ across firms not only depending on the degree of their financial leverage but also depending on their asset composition between relatively low-risk and relatively high-risk assets.

1976 **Barr Rosenberg** and **James A. Ohlson**, "The Stationary Distribution of Returns and Portfolio Separation in Capital Markets: A Fundamental Contradiction," *Journal of Financial and Quantitative Analysis* 11, No. 3 (September 1976), pp. 393–402.

PORTFOLIO SEPARATION, STATIONARITY

Rosenberg-Ohlson (1976) is one of the first articles to point out the perils of imposing exogenous assumptions on the intertemporal process of security prices in an equilibrium model. This runs the danger that aspects of this process that will be determined by the equilibrium may render the exogenous assumptions inconsistent. Such an example is models that assume there exist many *different* risky securities that have returns that are serially independent and identically distributed (i.i.d.) over time, with a constant cross-correlation structure. Clearly, it is possible to have an equilibrium consistent with this. But, if other assumptions are additionally made that result in portfolio separation (with a riskless security and the market portfolio), then the equilibrium is inconsistent. Rosenberg and Ohlson show that the combination of i.i.d. returns over time and portfolio separation forces *all risky securities* to have exactly the same returns over the same period—in essence, then, these are models with just one risky security.

The Merton (1973/September) intertemporal asset pricing model, with two-fund separation, is a good example of a model that falls into this trap. This degeneracy can be easily explained. In the model, at each date the only state-variables that affect portfolio choice are available wealth and the rates of return on available securities. With portfolio separation, the proportionate composition of a consumer/investor's optimal portfolio of risky securities is dependent on only the joint distribution of security returns; but if this distribution is identical at each date, then this proportionate composition must also be identical at each date. Since all agents hold the same risky portfolio, this must be the market portfolio. Therefore, the proportionate composition of the market portfolio must be identical at each date. But for this to be true, with constant numbers of shares, the relative prices of each security compared to each other must remain the same over time. The only way this can occur is if, at each date, the returns of all risky securities are the same.

1976 Mark Rubinstein, "The Valuation of Uncertain Income Streams and the Pricing of Options," *Bell Journal of Economics and Management Science* 7, No. 2 (Autumn 1976), pp. 407–425.

CRRA INTERTEMPORAL CAPM, PRICING UNCERTAIN INCOME STREAMS,

SINGLE-PRICE LAW OF MARKETS, ARBITRAGE, STATE-PRICES,
CONSUMPTION-BASED CAPM,
LOCAL EXPECTATIONS HYPOTHESIS,
UNBIASED TERM STRUCTURE, RANDOM WALK,
OPTION PRICING, TIME-ADDITIVE UTILITY,
LOGARITHMIC UTILITY, BLACK-SCHOLES FORMULA,
EQUITY RISK PREMIUM PUZZLE,
JOINT NORMALITY COVARIANCE THEOREM

Rubinstein (1976/Autumn) develops the general formulation for asset pricing from stochastic discount factors and the special case of the CRRA discrete-time intertemporal equilibrium model that in subsequent years was to replace the CAPM as the generator of new discrete-time financial theory and became the basis for the first paper, Mehra-Prescott (1985), to emphasize the "risk-premium puzzle."

Rubinstein's paper appears to contain the first statement that, even in an incomplete market, assuming the single-price law of markets and investor nonsatiation (which imply no arbitrage), price equals the expected value of future weighted cash flows where the weightings of the cash flows are the same weights used for all securities: that is, $P_j = E(X_j Z)$ where P_j is the current price of security j, X_j are its cash flows, Z is the stochastic discount factor (the same for all securities), and E is an expectation operator. This is frequently written as $1 = E(r_j Z)$ where $r_j \equiv X_j/P_j$.

In the early 1970s, previous research had led to the idea of state-prices, the use of the concept of complete markets to solve for investor portfolio choices and equilibrium prices, and the identification of state-prices with products of subjective probabilities and an adjustment factor for risk aversion divided by the riskless return. But the question of the minimal conditions for the existence of state-prices had not been worked out in its full generality, particularly in the context of incomplete markets.

Rubinstein derives the existence of state-prices from the single-price law, which states that two securities (or portfolios of securities) with the same payoffs across states must have the same current price. Clearly, if this fails, a very simple form of arbitrage is possible: (short) sell the high-priced security, use part of the proceeds to buy the low-priced security, and pocket the difference. Suppose I define "pseudo state-prices" as real numbers λ_s, the same for any security (or portfolio), such that the price P of the security is related to its payoffs (X_s) according to: $P = \Sigma_s \lambda_s X_s$. Unlike state-prices π_s, the numbers λ_s can be negative as well as positive. I can now state a simple condition for the existence of such numbers:

The single-price law holds if and only if pseudo state-prices exist.

Proof of the Relation between the
Single-Price Law and Pseudo State-Prices

The theorem makes two separate claims:

1. If the single-price law holds, then pseudo state-prices exist.
2. If pseudo state-prices exist, then the single-price law holds.

To prove the second claim, consider two securities (or portfolios) with respective payoffs X_{s1} and X_{s2}. If pseudo state-prices exist, then there exist λ_s such that their prices $P_1 = \Sigma_s \lambda_s X_{s1}$, and $P_2 = \Sigma_s \lambda_s X_{s2}$. Clearly, if for all states $X_{s1} = X_{s2}$, then $P_1 = P_2$, so the single-price law holds.

To prove the first claim, it is well-known from the theory of simultaneous linear equations that a necessary and sufficient condition for a solution to exist is that any linear combination of the equations (this, in effect, makes a new portfolio out of the original tableau of securities) which reproduces the same coefficients X_s as a preexisting equation must have the same left-hand side value P as that equation. Translated into the language of securities, this implication is the single-price law of markets.

In particular, if there are m equations in n unknowns and $m > n$, for a solution to exist, it must be possible to create $m - n$ of the equations from linear combinations of the remaining n equations. Stating this analogously in finance terminology, with m securities and n states such that $m > n$, for state-prices to exist, for any of $m - n$ securities it must be possible to create a portfolio from the other n securities that has the same payoffs, and such a portfolio must have the same price as the security. In this sense, $m - n$ of the securities must be redundant. For example:

$$P_1 = 1\lambda_1 + 2\lambda_2 + 3\lambda_3$$

$$P_2 = 1\lambda_1 + 1\lambda_2 + 1\lambda_3$$

$$P_3 = 1\lambda_1 + 1\lambda_2 + 0\lambda_3$$

This reproduces our earlier example of the asset, cash, and derivative—see the discussion under Arrow (1953). These equations are linearly independent since no linear combination of any two of them can reproduce the payoffs of the remaining third. In this case, pseudo state-prices exist (indeed, since there are as many securities as states, they will be unique). Suppose now a fourth security also exists:

$$P_4 = 0\lambda_1 + 1\lambda_2 + 4\lambda_3$$

(Continued)

Proof of the Relation between the
Single-Price Law and Pseudo State-Prices *(Continued)*

To check if pseudo state-prices $(\lambda_1, \lambda_2, \lambda_3)$ still exist, I first form a portfolio out of the first three securities that replicates the payoff of the new security. Note that if we buy 1 unit of security 1, buy 1 unit of security 2, and sell 2 units of security 3, we will have the same payoff in every state as security 4:

$$[0\ 1\ 4] = [1\ 2\ 3] + [1\ 1\ 1] - 2[1\ 1\ 0]$$

So if the single-price law holds, the price of the new security must be $P_4 = P_1 + P_2 - 2P_3$.

Notice that this result does not require any of the more stringent assumptions commonly used in finance such as investor rationality, risk aversion, aggregation, complete markets, normality, and so on. But the single-price law does not by itself imply that there is no arbitrage. For example, the single-price law is consistent with two securities with payoffs [1, 2] and [3, 4] selling for the same price. But in this case, either λ_1 or λ_2 must be negative. That is, the single-price law does not by itself imply that $\lambda_s > 0$. To deliver positive state-prices, Rubinstein makes the additional assumption that, ceteris paribus, the larger its payoff for any state, the greater the current price of the security. Under this assumption, the λ_s must be positive and hence equivalent to the state-prices π_s.

This paper also foreshadows several developments in asset pricing theory: (1) the consumption-based intertemporal asset pricing model (Breeden 1979); (2) the equity risk premium puzzle (Mehra-Prescott 1985); and (3) the special role of constant relative risk aversion (CRRA) in leading to an unbiased term structure defined in terms of the "local expectations hypothesis"—the expected next period returns are the same for all bonds, irrespective of their maturities—the definition of an unbiased term structure advocated later in Cox-Ingersoll-Ross (1981). Rubinstein also derives necessary and sufficient equilibrium conditions for the value of the market portfolio to follow a random walk.

With respect to (1), Rubinstein shows that if at each date cash flows (X_{jt}) of security j and aggregate per capita consumption (C_t) are bivariate normal (but the time-series structure of stochastic security cash flows is otherwise unrestricted), in the standard finance model with additive utility of consumption over time, the current date 0 price P_j of security j is:

$$P_j = \Sigma_{t=1} \frac{E(X_t) - \theta_t \text{Cov}(X_{jt}, C_t)}{R_{Ft}}$$

a certainty-equivalent formulation of present value, where $1/R_{Ft}$ is the current price of a default-free zero-coupon bond maturing at date t, and θ_t is the marketwide measure of risk aversion for cash flows at date t.

With respect to (2), the paper shows that relying only on utility restrictions, namely CRRA, in the standard finance model with additive utility of consumption over time: If the rate of growth r_C of aggregate consumption follows a random walk (this presumption is not required under the special case of log utility), then the return on the market portfolio (r_M) and the growth rate of aggregate consumption (r_C) are perfectly positively correlated, differing only by a positive multiplicative constant; that is, at date t the random outcome $r_{Mt} = k_t r_{Ct}$ where k_t is most generally a time-dependent positive constant. From this, it is an easy step to see that the logarithmic variances of r_{Mt} and r_{Ct}, $\sigma_{Mt}^2 = \text{Var}_t(\log r_M)$ and $\sigma_{Ct}^2 = \text{Var}_t(\log r_C)$ must be equal at all dates; that is, $\sigma_{Mt}^2 = \sigma_{Ct}^2$. This is the essence of what was later dubbed the equity risk premium puzzle. We can see here that in the standard model, at a deeper level, it derives from the property that $\rho(r_{Mt}, r_{Ct}) = 1$.

With respect to (3), Rubinstein shows that in the standard finance model with CRRA and additive utility of consumption over time: If the rate of growth of aggregate consumption follows a random walk, then (1) the market portfolio follows a (possibly nonstationary) random walk, and (2) the term structure of interest rates is unbiased in the sense that at each date the next period expected returns of default-free zero-coupon bonds of all maturities are the same. The random walk observation is immediate from the argument in the previous paragraph. This may be the first time in the academic literature that (1) a random walk for the market portfolio or (2) the unbiasedness of the term structure was derived as an outcome of equilibrium instead of simply assumed to be a property of the equilibrium.

John C. Cox, Jonathan E. Ingersoll Jr., and Stephen A. Ross, in [Cox-Ingersoll-Ross (1981)] "A Re-Examination of Traditional Hypotheses about the Term Structure of Interest Rates," *Journal of Finance* 36, No. 4 (September 1981), pp. 769–799, describe four potentially incompatible definitions of an unbiased term structure. They show that in continuous time with uncertain interest rates only one is consistent with equilibrium: the local expectations hypothesis that all default-free bonds have the same local expected return irrespective of their maturities. For example, the hypotheses

(1) that expected future spot rates equal today's corresponding forward rates, or (2) that the expected terminal return of rolling over a portfolio of short-term bonds has the same return as a currently purchased bond of the same maturity, are not consistent with the equilibrium. Although the local expectations hypothesis is potentially consistent with equilibrium, it need not be. Special cases in which it is consistent with equilibrium are developed, as we have seen, in Rubinstein (1976/Autumn).

Rubinstein includes the first simple formula (relying on a special case on additive logarithmic utility of consumption over time) consistent with equilibrium and risk aversion for valuing an uncertain stream of income received over many dates. This can most simply be stated as:

$$PV_0[X_0, (X_1), (X_2), \ldots, (X_T)]$$
$$= X_0 + E\left(\frac{X_1}{R_{M1}}\right) + E\left(\frac{X_2}{R_{M2}}\right) + \cdots + E\left(\frac{X_T}{R_{MT}}\right)$$

where $R_{Mt} \equiv r_{M1} r_{M2} \cdots r_{Mt}$ is the return on the market portfolio cumulated to date t, (X_t) are the set of possible cash flows that can be received at date t, $PV_0(\bullet)$ is the present value at date 0 of all future cash flows, and expectations E are assessed with respect to date 0 subjective beliefs about future cash flows. This result is just about as simple as one could reasonably imagine: Intertemporal *time and risk* adjustments are made to cash flows simply by deflating (that is, dividing) by the corresponding cumulated return of the market portfolio, taking expected values, and adding them up. Despite its simplicity, no probabilistic restrictions, serial or cross-sectional (other than limited liability for the market portfolio), are required on the cash flows or on the market portfolio return.

Some of the results of the paper rely on a special mathematical property of jointly normal random variables borrowed from Rubinstein (1973/October). This property substantially simplifies many results derived in finance both here and in much subsequent research. The joint normality covariance theorem states: If x and y are jointly normal, $g(y)$ is any differentiable function of y, and $E|g'(y)| < \infty$, then $\text{Cov}[x, g(y)] = E[g'(y)]\text{Cov}(x, y)$. This is frequently called "Stein's lemma" since it was independently and contemporaneously derived by C. Stein, in [Stein (1973)] "Estimation of the Mean of a Multivariate Normal Distribution," *Proceedings of the Prague Symposium on Asymptotic Statistics* (September 1973).

Rubinstein (1976) is also known for its linkage of discrete-time asset and option pricing models. Samuelson-Merton (1969) had already shown that another route to the Black-Scholes formula, but in discrete time and for an option on the *market portfolio*, was to assume a representative investor with CRRA utility of wealth on the expiration date of the option and that the return of the market portfolio is lognormally distributed. Rubinstein shows more generally that a formula identical to Black-Scholes (1973) will hold in that context (even including consumption over time in the model) for options on *any* underlying asset with return jointly lognormal with the market portfolio.

With this, it became apparent that because of the myopia properties of CRRA (Mossin 1968), discrete-time CRRA models and continuous-time models are in an important sense equivalent. Myopia means that portfolio decisions do not depend on the length of the holding period. Therefore, as the time to the next opportunity to revise a portfolio approaches zero, a CRRA investor sees no reason to alter his portfolio; therefore, he will make the same portfolio decision in continuous time that he does in discrete time. Any result, then, that relies on continuous trading and does not depend on investor preferences (such as the Black-Scholes formula) will not be changed in discrete-time under CRRA. Given this, it is hardly surprising that Michael John Brennan, in [Brennan (1979)] "The Pricing of Contingent Claims in Discrete-Time Models," *Journal of Finance* 34, No. 1 (March 1979), pp. 53–68, is able to show that constant relative risk aversion for the representative agent is not only sufficient but also *necessary* to produce the Black-Scholes formula without continuous trading opportunities in a market where the underlying asset returns are subjectively lognormally distributed.

Robert E. Lucas Jr., in [Lucas (1978)] "Asset Prices in an Exchange Economy," *Econometrica* 46, No. 6 (November 1978), pp. 1429–1445, develops a special case of the standard finance model with many dates and states where the investment opportunity set is assumed to follow a Markov process (in terms of aggregate consumption levels). This is more general than a random walk since it leaves open the possibility that the rate of growth of aggregate consumption in any period could depend on the aggregate level of consumption at the beginning of the period, but is clearly less general than, say, Rubinstein (1976/May) and Rubinstein (1976/Autumn), which largely place no restrictions on this process whatsoever. Although Lucas's paper is widely cited, in view of earlier work it is hard to see what its marginal contribution is. Lucas seems to think that what is new is his observation that "the presence of a diminishing rate of substitution of future for current consumption is inconsistent with . . . the conditions under which the Martingale property is likely to approximately describe a price series." But this seems to me to be all too evident from several earlier papers—for example, LeRoy (1973) and Rubinstein (1975).

1976   Sanford J. Grossman, "On the Efficiency of Competitive Stock Markets Where Traders Have Diverse Information," *Journal of Finance* 31, No. 2 (May 1976), pp. 573–585.

1978   Stephen Figlewski, "Market 'Efficiency' in a Market with Heterogeneous Information," *Journal of Political Economy* 86, No. 4 (August 1978), pp. 581–587.

EFFICIENT MARKETS, RATIONAL EXPECTATIONS,
AGGREGATION OF INFORMATION, EXPONENTIAL UTILITY,
CONSENSUS BELIEFS, DARWINIAN SURVIVAL

Building on Lucas (1972) and Green (1973), Grossman (1976) formally models the Hayek (1945) idea that equilibrium prices in competitive markets are aggregators of information. It follows from this that a rational investor will try to learn what other investors know from the equilibrium price itself. Grossman provides a closed-form example that captures this circularity assuming exponential utility and normal distributions, known from Wilson (1968) to possess desirable aggregation properties. In his model, information is truly dispersed: Each investor gets his own private signal and each investor believes that his information is no better than any other investor's. Grossman's self-fulfilling expectations equilibrium has the property that all the disparate information is captured in current prices that at the same time provide information to investors that leads them to produce in equilibrium those same prices.

In a simpler and somewhat earlier paper, Richard E. Kihlstrom and Leonard J. Mirman, in [Kihlstrom-Mirman (1975)] "Information and Market Equilibrium," *Bell Journal of Economics* 6, No. 1 (Spring 1975), pp. 357–376, create a model where the information possessed by a single informed agent becomes fully revealed by the current price because there is a one-to-one correspondence between the equilibrium price and the relevant information. This equilibrium arises because the uninformed investors start with the knowledge of the equilibrium pricing function and can invert it. Alternatively, the uninformed investors start with almost no knowledge of this correspondence, but as the market continues to reconvene over time, the uninformed investors, using Bayesian expectations based on accumulating past observed prices, gradually figure it out.

For Grossman, rational pricing occurs because of competitive entry into the information-gathering business. However, since Grossman assumes exponential utility for all investors, he forsakes the opportunity to study wealth distribution effects on the rationality of equilibrium prices and to test for the efficacy of one of the key forces claimed to create rational pricing. As Paul

H. Cootner, in [Cootner (2000)] *The Random Character of Stock Market Prices* (original published in 1964, reprinted London: Risk Publications, 2000), p. 94, writes:

> *Given the uncertainty of the real world, the many actual and virtual investors will have many, perhaps equally many, price forecasts. . . . If any group of investors was consistently better than average in forecasting stock prices, they would accumulate wealth and give their forecasts greater and greater weight. In the process, they would bring the present price closer to the true value.*

This argument for rational pricing is, of course, quite similar to the Friedman (1953/A) survival argument for profit maximization.

Rubinstein (1974) and Kraus-Litzenberger (1975) show that in a complete market single-period economy under perfect and competitive security markets, if all investors i have logarithmic utility functions $U_i(W_1^i) = \log W_1^i$ of future wealth W_1^i but have different subjective probability beliefs p_s^i (over states s) and current wealth W_0^i, equilibrium state-prices will be set as if there is a single investor with subjective probabilities p_s over states constructed according to the following rule:

$$p_s = \Sigma_i \left(\frac{W_0^i}{W_0^M} \right) p_s^i \quad \text{with} \quad W_0^M \equiv \Sigma_i W_0^i \quad \text{for all states } s$$

This simple model illustrates how prices are determined by an aggregation of the heterogeneous beliefs of all investors in the economy where the individual beliefs are weighted by the relative current wealth of each investor. Wealthier investors therefore have proportionately more influence on market prices.

These static results are modeled dynamically in Figlewski (1978). He asks whether, over time, Cootner's prediction of rational pricing will occur. To keep matters simple, Figlewski assumes a sequence of markets in which at the end of each period nature determines the correct price of a single security, while at the beginning of each period the market participants buy and sell among themselves based on a price determined by their own guesses about the price at the end of the period. This is very similar to pari-mutuel horse race betting where over a single day the market reconvenes at the beginning of perhaps 10 races, with 10 corresponding results from each race (hopefully draws from nature) determining the actual payoffs. In both cases, the complications of the Keynesian (1936) "beauty contest" are avoided. Before trading, at the beginning of each period each trader receives his own information, which is aggregated across traders to determine the market price. Some traders receive better information than others. A linear combination of the prices each predicts with this information, with weights determined by their relative wealth and risk aversion, equals the market equilibrium price. In each period, traders who have sold just before prices rise will transfer wealth to those who have bought, and vice versa. Over time, some traders will become richer and others poorer by a continuation of this process. Figlewski compares these equilibrium prices to the rational price, which is defined as the price that would have been predicted by a trader who knows all the information possessed by the actual traders.

The key result of this model is that poorly informed traders tend not to be driven out of the market. At first, their information may be over-weighted in determining the market price, but as they become poorer, their lower wealth actually leads to an underweighting of their information so they no longer lose money to the better-informed traders. While there is a general tendency not to stray far from the rationally set price, except by accident, the price actually set by the market is never exactly equal to the rational price. So Cootner is half right!

1976   Stephen A. Ross, "The Arbitrage Theory of Capital Asset Pricing," *Journal of Economic Theory* 13, No. 3 (December 1976), pp. 341–360.

ARBITRAGE PRICING THEORY (APT), DIVERSIFICATION,
LAW OF LARGE NUMBERS, MULTIFACTOR MODELS,
APT VS. CAPM, PORTFOLIO SEPARATION,
PRICED VS. NONPRICED FACTORS, MARKET PORTFOLIO

Ross (1976/December) is the classic paper deriving the approximate arbitrage pricing model, known as the arbitrage pricing theory (APT). The rough intuition behind the APT was illustrated empirically eight years earlier by Evans-Archer (1968). They showed that as randomly selected stocks are added to a portfolio, the standard deviation of the return of the portfolio very quickly converges to the standard deviation of the return of the market. Indeed, with even 10 randomly selected stocks, their six-month standard deviation is expected to be about 1 percent per annum higher than the standard deviation of the portfolio universe of the 470 securities from which they were selected.

The Ross APT begins with a multifactor model of security returns r_j, with expected returns μ_j, with enough factors F_k so that the residual component ε_j is independent across all the securities in the selected universe:

$$r_j = \mu_j + \Sigma_k \beta_{jk} F_k + \varepsilon_j \text{ for securities } j, l = 1, 2, \ldots,$$
$$m \text{ and factors } h, k = 1, 2, \ldots, K$$

By construction, $E(\varepsilon_j) = E(F_k) = \rho(\varepsilon_j, F_k) = 0$, $\rho(F_h, F_k) = 0$ for $h \neq k$, and $\text{Var}(F_k) = 1$, and by assumption $\rho(\varepsilon_j, \varepsilon_l) = 0$ for $j \neq l$, and $\text{Var}(\varepsilon_j)$ has a finite upper bound. Then, by forming portfolios of the other securities to mimic the factors, the return of a particular security can be replicated up to the residual terms in the factor model—hence the name the "arbitrage pricing theory." Ross then argues that it is reasonable in a "large" market (with many securities, none of which is large relative to the entire market) for the law of large numbers to cause the residual risk not to be priced. This results in a multifactor model of expected returns, which is an alternative to the CAPM—for example, Sharpe (1964):

$$\mu_j = r + (\mu_1 - r)\beta_{j1} + (\mu_2 - r)\beta_{j2} + \cdots + (\mu_k - r)\beta_{jk} + \cdots + (\mu_K - r)\beta_{jK}$$

where r is the riskless return and $\mu_1, \mu_2, \ldots, \mu_k, \ldots, \mu_K$ are the expected returns of the factor-mimicking portfolios.

While the assumptions of the model are more general than the CAPM (not requiring assumptions about investor preferences and very weak assumptions on probability distributions), at the same time the conclusions are much less specific since the number of factors and the factors themselves are not identified. Moreover, which of these factors will actually end up being priced in equilibrium (that is, many factors could have $\mu_k = r$ and therefore not affect expected returns) is not identified.

Although the two models seem to be sewn from different cloth, they are related in a very simple way. To a useful approximation (indeed the very approximation made by the APT itself), the CAPM can be viewed as nested within the APT. The APT points to a number of factors that might affect security expected returns. The Sharpe (1964), Lintner (1965/February), Mossin (1966), Treynor (1999) CAPM says that the market portfolio will be one of these factors, and it will be the only one that is priced. This is a direct result of the portfolio separation property of the CAPM: All investors, irrespective of their differences, divide their wealth between the same two mutual funds, one riskless and the other the market portfolio. That is, even though securities may be correlated with each other for other reasons than through their joint dependence on the market portfolio, this correlation will not matter to these investors since they only hold the market portfolio. For example, if they were to hold, in addition, a second risky security portfolio that protected them against intertemporal changes in the opportunity set, as in Merton (1973/September), then investors would also be concerned with the correlation of security returns with that portfolio. That concern would enter their utility functions and give rise to Merton's three-fund separation. Correspondingly, that would be another of the APT factors that would almost surely be priced, while all others would continue not to be. So, it is really the separation properties of more completely specified asset pricing models that separate them from the APT.

The intuitive introduction to the APT in Ross (1977) was, perhaps unintentionally, published after this much more difficult and rigorous analysis, and should probably be read first before Ross (1976/December).

1977   Richard Roll (October 31, 1939–), "A Critique of the Asset Pricing Theory's Tests, Part I: On Past and Potential Testability of the Theory," *Journal of Financial Economics* 4, No. 2 (March 1977), pp. 129–176.

CAPITAL ASSET PRICING MODEL (CAPM), MEAN-VARIANCE EFFICIENCY, MARKET PORTFOLIO

As Lintner (1965/February), Mossin (1966), and Treynor (1999) show under the conditions of the CAPM, the market portfolio is mean-variance efficient. That is, given its level of expected return, the market portfolio has a lower variance of return than any other available portfolio. Indeed, combinations of the riskless security and the market portfolio (which allow spanning of all levels of expected return) are the only portfolios that are mean-variance efficient. Roll (1977) turns this around arguing that if the market portfolio is mean-variance efficient, then the CAPM expected return pricing relation holds. Therefore, the empirical content of the CAPM comes down to the proposition that the market portfolio is mean-variance efficient; it must be accepted or rejected solely based on that. The same point is also made by Stephen A. Ross, in [Ross (1977/March)] "The Capital Asset Pricing Model (CAPM), Short-Sale Restrictions and Related Issues," *Journal of Finance* 32, No. 1 (March 1977), pp. 177–183.

Roll further argues that any mean-variance efficient portfolio must satisfy the CAPM expected return pricing relation, no matter what the surrounding economic conditions (even if the CAPM were false). That is, if P is a mean-variance efficient portfolio and security j is held in that portfolio, then $\mu_j = r + (\mu_P - r)\beta_{jP}$ where $\beta_{jP} \equiv Cov(r_j, r_P)/Var(r_P)$. This is easy to see from inspection of the first-order conditions of the mean-variance portfolio optimization problem.

In practice, investors can only use, and empiricists can only test, the CAPM using a proxy for the true market portfolio. For many years before this paper, it was widely believed that if the CAPM fails to be verified by an empirical test, it could be that the CAPM is true, but the proxy used for the market portfolio is poor. After this paper, it was now also apparent that even if the CAPM is verified by an empirical test, that merely means that the proxy used for the market portfolio is mean-variance efficient, not that the CAPM is true. For example, suppose the true model were one in which in addition to covariance with the market portfolio return, coskewness with the market as in Rubinstein (1973/January) or covariance with a variable proxying for stochastic changes in investment opportunities as in Merton (1973/September) were the true model. Of course, the true market portfolio would have to satisfy the true model. Unfortunately, one could still observe, using a particular proxy portfolio for the market (which is not the same as the true market portfolio) like the S&P 500 index, that the proxy portfolio is mean-variance efficient and therefore satisfies the CAPM pricing relation (even though the CAPM is a false model). So we have a case of being damned if we do, and damned if we don't. Assume the proxy for the market portfolio is not the true market portfolio: (1) if the CAPM is true, we may reject it because the proxy is poor (known before Roll's paper); or (2) if the CAPM is false, we may accept it because even though the proxy is poor, it happens to be mean-variance efficient (not understood until Roll's paper).

Roll believes it is, in practice, impossible to measure the return of the market portfolio, so in practice the CAPM cannot be proved or disproved. Jay Shanken, in [Shanken (1987)] "Multivariate Proxies and Asset Pricing Relations: Living with the Roll Critique," *Journal of Financial Economics* 18, No. 1 (March 1987), pp. 91–110, adjusting as well as possible to Roll's challenge develops tools for testing the joint hypothesis that (1) the CAPM is valid and (2) the correlation between the true but unknown market portfolio return and that of a known proxy is at least some prespecified amount.

1977 Burton G. Malkiel, "The Valuation of Closed-End Investment-Company Shares," *Journal of Finance* 32, No. 3 (June 1977), pp. 847–859.

CLOSED-END FUND DISCOUNTS,
CLOSED-END VS. OPEN-END FUNDS, EFFICIENT MARKETS

If a managed portfolio of securities is traded in addition to its constituent securities that trade separately in the market, one would naively think that in a rational market the market value of the portfolio should trade for the sum of the market values of its securities. If this were not true, then obvious arbitrage opportunities would be available. If the managed portfolio traded for more (or less) than the separate securities, investors would replicate the portfolio by buying (or shorting) the individual securities and shorting (or buying) the portfolio. However, even if short sales were unconstrained, as long as only a few investors tried to implement the strategy, it might fail since the managed portfolio might simply remain over- or underpriced relative to the individual securities and the arbitrage profit might never be realized. Another arbitrage strategy is to buy the shares of a managed portfolio selling at a discount, take control of the portfolio, and liquidate it at the higher market prices of its constituent securities. Unfortunately, in practice, the very act of trying to buy enough shares to take control of the managed portfolio tends to push the price of the shares up to the point when they even begin to sell at a premium, as the die-hard core holders of the fund resist selling. This positively sloped supply curve typically will throw the buyout strategy into a loss.

Open-end (mutual) funds make a market in their own shares every day at the close of trading, standing willing to buy and sell those shares at their net asset value (that is, the value of the portfolio constructed from buying the constituent securities at their contemporaneous closing market prices). Those funds, in effect, force out any arbitrage opportunities of the type discussed in the previous paragraph. However, although closed-end funds trade like shares on exchanges, these funds do not make a market in their own shares. So for these funds, discounts or premiums to net asset value are possible.

Closed-end funds are perhaps the most evident examples of traded portfolios that often sell at significant discounts to net asset value, often as large as 10 to 20 percent. The closed-end fund anomaly poses one of the most consistent and serious objections to the rational market hypothesis. A single stock can be interpreted as a closed-end fund of physical projects, but more complex than an actual closed-end fund because of potential synergies. If the market cannot even price the simpler closed-end funds right, how can it correctly price individual stocks?

Many a financial economist has tried his hand at showing that closed-end fund discounts can be consistent with rational markets. Malkiel (1977), one of the earliest of such quixotic knights, considers a number of explanations: (1) built-in capital gains appreciation, (2) ownership of restricted stock, (3) holdings of foreign stock, (4) inferior performance of closed-end fund managers, (5) high portfolio turnover and consequent trading costs, and (6) high management fees. He looks at 24 closed-end funds from 1967 to 1974. Unfortunately, these rational explanations appear to explain only a small part of the typical discounts. Indeed, his observations that the discount on closed-end fund narrows when the market falls and widens when it rises would suggest that compared to individual stocks, closed-end funds are better hedges against market risk and so should, if anything, sell at a premium.

A second study by Rex Thompson, in [Thompson (1978)] "The Information Content of Discounts and Premiums on Closed-End Fund Shares," *Journal of Financial Economics* 6, No. 2 (1978), pp. 155-186, reports that closed-end funds selling at discounts tend to outperform the market, seemingly at variance with the hypothesis of rational pricing.

1977 Stephen A. Ross, "Return, Risk, and Arbitrage," in *Risk and Return in Finance*, edited by Irving Friend and James Bicksler (Cambridge, MA: Ballinger, 1977), pp. 189–218.

FUNDAMENTAL THEOREM, SINGLE-PRICE LAW OF MARKETS,
ARBITRAGE, STATE-PRICES, COMPLETE MARKETS,
CAPITAL ASSET PRICING MODEL (CAPM),
BLACK-SCHOLES FORMULA,
PERFECT MARKETS, VALUE ADDITIVITY

Ross (1977) provides an intuitive introduction to the Ross (1976/December) arbitrage pricing theory (APT). The paper also includes a brief statement and proof of one of the key results in financial economics. Arrow (1953) derived sufficient conditions for state-prices to exist in equilibrium. Ross and to a significant extent Rubinstein (1976/Autumn) show that concavity of preferences, although important to Arrow's other results, is not needed simply for existence. Ross defines "no arbitrage" to be a situation in which one cannot form a portfolio of existing securities that has a nonnegative payoff in all states, a positive payoff in at least one state, but has a zero or negative cost. Ross gives what is the first completely clear formulation of "the fundamental theorem of financial economics":

There is no arbitrage if and only if state-prices exist.[35]

(See in particular pp. 201–203, 214–215.)[36] Ross' proof is in the context of an equilibrium of nonsatiated investors, but otherwise he requires no restrictions on preferences. The first published version of this proof actually appeared in [Cox-Ross (1976)] John C. Cox and Stephen A. Ross, "A Survey of Some New Results in Financial Option Pricing Theory," *Journal of Finance* 31, No. 2 (May 1976), pp. 383–402 (in particular see p. 385). Ross provides a formal proof of his result in [Ross (1978/July)] "A Simple Approach to the Valuation of Risky Streams," *Journal of Business* 51, No. 3 (July 1978), pp. 453–475, the article that won the 1978–1979 Leo Melamed Prize, awarded biennially by the University of Chicago for the most outstanding work published by a business school teacher during the award period. A very nice summary of Ross' results is contained in [Varian

(1987)] Hal R. Varian, "The Arbitrage Principle in Financial Economics," *Journal of Economic Perspectives* 1, No. 2 (Fall 1987), pp. 55–72.

A related condition known as the single-price law says that two portfolios cannot be constructed with the same payoffs but different costs. The absence of arbitrage implies the single-price law, but the single-price law does not imply the absence of arbitrage. The presumption typically made in finance models that there is no arbitrage is a no-lose proposition: If it is right, it will help us to explain security prices; if it is wrong, then our analysis will help us identify arbitrage opportunities that we can take advantage of and earn unlimited profits. This also makes it easy to see why, in practice, arbitrage opportunities should be limited since in perfect markets the trading activities of just one "rational" investor would eliminate them.

Ross assumes that there are *perfect markets* so that there are no transactions frictions such as buying and selling commissions, the bid-ask spread, short-sale constraints, differential taxes on different securities, or leverage constraints. As an implication, from the set of available securities investors can form arbitrary portfolios such that the *payoff* from the portfolio equals the sum of the payoffs of the constituent securities. In this case, the single-price law implies present value additivity, that is, since both have the same payoffs, the cost or current *price* of a portfolio equals the summed costs of all the securities in the portfolio.

Ross' No Arbitrage Theorem

To make this concrete, suppose there are just three states $s = 1, 2, 3$ and three securities $j = 1, 2, 3$; X_{sj} is the payoff of security j in state s, and P_j is the price of security j. Say we form portfolios by holding n_j units of each security ($n_j > 0$ if the security is held long, and $n_j < 0$ if it is held short). The payoff of the portfolio in each state is then:

State 1 payoff $= n_1 X_{11} + n_2 X_{12} + n_3 X_{13}$
State 2 payoff $= n_1 X_{21} + n_2 X_{22} + n_3 X_{23}$
State 3 payoff $= n_1 X_{31} + n_2 X_{32} + n_3 X_{33}$
Portfolio cost $= n_1 P_1 + n_2 P_2 + n_3 P_3$

So to say that there is no arbitrage means that no matter what portfolio weights (n_1, n_2, and n_3) we choose, if state 1 payoff ≥ 0, state 2 payoff ≥ 0, and state 3 payoff ≥ 0, then portfolio cost ≥ 0 (the last inequality is taken to mean that if at least one of the states has a positive payoff, then the portfolio cost will be positive).

Ross' No Arbitrage Theorem *(Continued)*

The theorem makes two separate claims:

1. If there is no arbitrage, then state-prices exist.
2. If state-prices exist, then there is no arbitrage.

The second claim is easier to prove, so I will prove that first. Since I assume state-prices exist where the $\pi_s > 0$:

$$P_1 = \pi_1 X_{11} + \pi_2 X_{21} + \pi_3 X_{31}$$

$$P_2 = \pi_1 X_{12} + \pi_2 X_{22} + \pi_3 X_{32}$$

$$P_3 = \pi_1 X_{13} + \pi_2 X_{23} + \pi_3 X_{33}$$

Examine a portfolio that has nonnegative payoffs so that:

$$n_1 X_{11} + n_2 X_{12} + n_3 X_{13} \geq 0$$

$$n_1 X_{21} + n_2 X_{22} + n_3 X_{23} \geq 0$$

$$n_1 X_{31} + n_2 X_{32} + n_3 X_{33} \geq 0$$

Multiplying through these equations by the (positive) state-prices π_1, π_2, and π_3 does not alter the inequalities:

$$\pi_1 n_1 X_{11} + \pi_1 n_2 X_{12} + \pi_1 n_3 X_{13} \geq 0$$

$$\pi_2 n_1 X_{21} + \pi_2 n_2 X_{22} + \pi_2 n_3 X_{23} \geq 0$$

$$\pi_3 n_1 X_{31} + \pi_3 n_2 X_{32} + \pi_3 n_3 X_{33} \geq 0$$

Summing up all three inequalities, we have:

$$n_1(\pi_1 X_{11} + \pi_2 X_{21} + \pi_3 X_{31}) + n_2(\pi_1 X_{12} + \pi_2 X_{22} + \pi_3 X_{32})$$
$$+ n_3(\pi_1 X_{13} + \pi_2 X_{23} + \pi_3 X_{33}) \geq 0$$

Substituting in the current prices for the terms in parentheses:

$$n_1 P_1 + n_2 P_2 + n_3 P_3 \geq 0$$

(Continued)

Ross' No Arbitrage Theorem *(Continued)*

The second claim is then proven since such a portfolio must have non-negative cost.

   Now for the first claim: If there is no arbitrage, then state-prices exist. If there is no arbitrage, the single-price law must hold, so from our earlier analysis we know that pseudo state-prices λ_s exist. It remains to show that these prices must be positive.

   If there are complete markets, this is easy to prove. In that case, we can always construct a portfolio that has a payoff off $1 in one state and $0 in all other states. Such a security cannot have a negative price since otherwise there is an arbitrage opportunity; therefore, the pseudo state-price must be positive. Since we can do this for any state, all pseudo state-prices must be positive and hence qualify as state-prices π_s.

   On the other hand, if markets are incomplete, then while no arbitrage continues to imply the existence of positive pseudo prices, the proof is more difficult. Indeed, the discovery of this proof was Ross' major contribution to this literature. I will not provide it here but instead refer the reader to John H. Cochrane, in [Cochrane (2001)] *Asset Pricing* (Princeton, NJ: Princeton University Press, 2001), p. 72. Nonetheless, at this point, I hope the reader will feel intuitively comfortable with this result.[37]

   Neither Rubinstein nor Ross requires a complete market for the existence of state-prices. When the number of different securities is less than the number of states, it is still the case that state-prices will exist that will explain the prices of all securities as long as there is no arbitrage. However, the state-prices will not be unique. That is, there could be several sets of state-prices that can explain the prices of the existing securities. This means that in general if we add another security to the economy and try to guess its *exact* price simply from the no arbitrage principle, we will not be able to do so. However, even with fewer securities than states, the prices of these securities will establish upper and lower arbitrage bounds around the price of any additional security.

   Suppose instead that the number of different securities equals the number of states (a complete market). Then the state-prices will be unique (as illustrated earlier). Now, if any new security is added to the economy, as long as there is no arbitrage, we can exactly price that security in terms of the prices of other securities. This is the situation in modern option pricing theory. The fundamental theorem guarantees that derivatives, like other securities, can be priced as weighted averages of their payoffs: $P = \Sigma_s \pi_s X_s$. The trick of the modern theory is to find a way to complete the market and exactly determine the state-prices (π_s). In that case, the options can be priced in terms of the prices of other related securities: in particular, the underlying asset and a riskless bond.

The fundamental theorem can be easily applied to prove the value additivity property of present value: The present value of the two cash flows equals the sum of their present values. Varian (1987) illustrates the use of the fundamental theorem to prove the arbitrage lower bound for the value of a standard European call.

Use of Fundamental Theorem to Derive Lower Bound Value for European Call

π_s = current today of \$1 received if and only if state s occurs at time t

S_s = the payoff from an asset in state s at time t

S_0 = the present value of the asset

d = payout return of asset over time t

r = the riskless return over time t

C_0 = current value of a standard European call, with payoff max(0, $S_s - K$) in state s

K = strike price of call

If there is no arbitrage, from the fundamental theorem, there must exist state prices $\pi_s > 0$ such that:

$$S_0 = \Sigma_s \pi_s S_s \quad \text{and} \quad r^{-t} = \Sigma_s \pi_s$$

$$C_0 = \Sigma_s \pi_s \max(0, S_s - K)$$

From this it follows that $C_0 \geq \Sigma_s \pi_s (S_s - K) = (\Sigma_s \pi_s S_s) - K(\Sigma_s \pi_s) = S_0 d^{-t} - Kr^{-t}$.
And if $S_0 d^{-t} - Kr^{-t} < 0$, clearly $C_0 \geq 0$. Taken together: $C_0 \geq \max(0, S_0 d^{-t} - Kr^{-t})$.

The fundamental theorem can also be used to derive the valuation equation of the CAPM. Begin with the assumption that there is no arbitrage. This means that the price P_j of any security j is related to its cash flows X_{sj} by state-prices $\pi_s > 0$:

$$P_j = \Sigma_s \pi_s X_{sj}$$

Decompose the state-prices into subjective probabilities p_s, risk aversion adjustments Y_s, and the riskless return r, so that $\pi_s = p_s Y_s / r$. Then, using expectation notation:

$$P_j = \frac{\Sigma_s p_s (X_{sj} Y_s)}{r} = \frac{E(X_j Y)}{r}$$

Since, for any two random variables x and y, $E(xy) = \text{Cov}(x, y) + E(x)E(y)$ and since $E[Y] = 1$:

$$P_j = \frac{\text{Cov}(X_j, Y) + E(X_j)}{r}$$

Assuming no dividends, the return on the security $r_j \equiv X_j / P_j$ so that dividing by Pj:

$$1 = \frac{\text{Cov}(r_j, Y) + E(r_j)}{r}$$

Rearranging this:

$$E(r_j) = r + \text{Cov}(r_j, -Y)$$

Interpreting what we have so far, we can say that if there is no arbitrage, there must exist a random variable Y, the same for all securities (and portfolios[38]), such that the expected return of any security (or portfolio) equals the riskless return plus an adjustment for risk.

This conclusion is attractive since it proceeds from the most fundamental assumption in financial economics: There is no arbitrage (as well as perfect markets). It is nice to know at least that whatever determines Y, once we know how to measure that variable, we can use it to value all securities and portfolios. But it is also annoyingly unspecified since it leaves open what determines Y. To identify Y, the CAPM makes further assumptions including the rationality and risk aversion of investors, the joint normality of security returns, and identical beliefs shared by all investors. From this, as I have shown earlier—see the discussion under Sharpe (1964)—it can be shown that Y is determined in a simple way by the return of the market portfolio. But, as work in asset pricing over the past 30 years has shown, we can make other assumptions, and derive other identifications of Y that can lead to a model that more closely resembles empirical reality.

I can also derive the Black-Scholes (or standard binomial) formula from the perspective of the fundamental theorem. The model makes seven assumptions. Starting with the most general and ending with the most restrictive:

1. At least an underlying stock, (riskless) cash, and an option exist.
2. No arbitrage exists among these securities.[39]
3. Without including the option, the market is complete.
4. Markets are conserved through dynamic completeness.
5. Only two securities are required to dynamically complete the market.
6. States at each date recombine.
7. Future state-prices are the same as today's state-prices.[40]

The first and second assumptions give us three equations: For the current stock price S_0, riskless return r, and current call price C_0, respectively:

$$S_0 = \Sigma_s \pi_s X_s$$

$$r^t = \frac{1}{\Sigma_s \pi_s}$$

$$C_0 = \Sigma_s \pi_s \max[0, X_s - K]$$

X_s is the underlying stock price on the option's expiration date, K is the option's strike price, t its annualized time to expiration, and π_s are the state-prices.

The third assumption assures us that if we know the current prices of all securities excluding the option (including S_0 and r, *but in general many others*), we can derive the state-prices π_s in terms of the prices of these securities (as in the earlier example). We can then use these state-prices to solve for the redundant option price. We will end up at this point with an equation relating the option price C_0 to the stock price S_0, the riskless return r, and the prices of *potentially many other securities in the economy.*

The fourth assumption implies from Arrow (1953) that we can con-serve on the number of markets by introducing portfolio revision over time. This leads to a picture of the evolution of the stock price that could be like the evolution of the state-space in the diagram given in the discus-sion of Black-Scholes (1973).

The contribution of Black-Scholes (1973) can be interpreted as making three additional very clever assumptions. First, they assume that only two securities, namely the stock and cash, are sufficient to dynamically com-plete the market. This implies on any date one can form a portfolio con-taining just these two securities that will be able to recreate the return pattern of the option over the next period. This means that the state-space evolution is restricted to *binomial* moves in the stock price over time.

Binomial State-Space Evolution

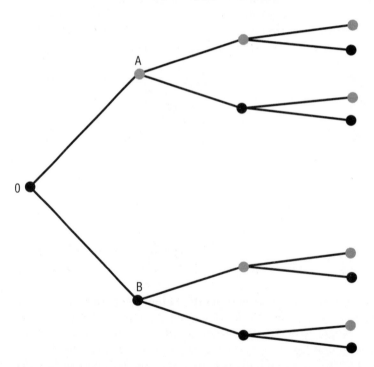

Stopping at this assumption, a key aspect of the Black-Scholes model is now achieved: If the state-space evolution of the stock price is known, the current option value C_0 can now be uniquely determined in terms of S_0 and r without needing to know the prices of any other securities.[41] Indeed, sub-

stantial effort has been expended to value options in such a path-dependent setting; but without further assumptions, no simple formula captures
this value, and the options are usually valued using a numerical working-
backwards approach reminiscent of Pascal-Fermat (1654).

To arrive at their formula, Black and Scholes assume that this state-
space *recombines* so that adjoining nodes coming from different states
join together as in the "Recombining Binomial State-Space Evolution"
diagram.

Recombining Binomial State-Space Evolution

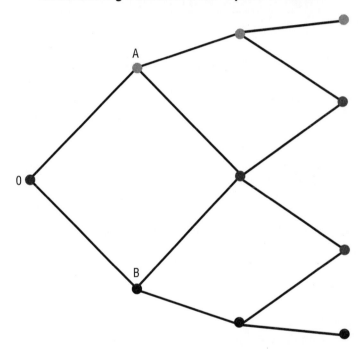

Without assumption 7, this permits the binomial up and down move
sizes to vary over time and to be dependent on the concurrent stock price.
For example, volatility (as captured by the move sizes) could be lower at
high stock prices and higher at low stock prices.[42]

Finally, Black and Scholes assume that the state-prices are constant
over time, so that at any node if π_u and π_d are the state-prices at date 0,
then they will also be the state-prices at all future nodes: In Black-Scholes
terminology, the stock volatility is constant and the riskless return is constant since $r = 1/(\pi_u + \pi_d)$. In sum, starting with the equations given earlier

that follow from assumptions 1 and 2, Black and Scholes have succeeded in identifying the state-prices in a way that leads to their formula. In terms of the standard binomial option pricing model, the state-prices over n binomial up (u) and down (d) moves through expiration become:

$$C_0 = \Sigma_{s=0\ldots n}\, \pi_s \max[0, S_0 u^s d^{n-s} - K]$$

with

$$\pi_s = r^{-n}\left[\frac{n!}{s!\,(n-s)!}\right]q^s(1-q)^{n-s} \quad \text{and} \quad q \equiv \frac{r-d}{u-d}$$

At this point, the economics is finished; with a little mathematics as shown in Cox-Ross-Rubinstein (1979), one can derive the world-famous Black-Scholes formula.

Stewart C. Myers, in [Myers (1968)] "A Time-State-Preference Model of Security Valuation," *Journal of Financial and Quantitative Analysis* 3, No. 1 (March 1968), pp. 1–33, develops many of the implications of the idea that investors can be considered to trade a complete set of state-securities with payoffs across all states and dates. In particular, he derives a general statement for valuing cash flows over time, from the point of view of an individual consumer/investor, expressed as the sum of the expected cash flows, where each cash flow is weighted by the ratio of the marginal utility of consumption at that state and date divided by the marginal utility of current consumption.

Apparently independently, in the context of markets that are not necessarily complete, John B. Long Jr., in [Long (1972)] "Consumption-Investment Decisions and Equilibrium in the Securities Market," in *Studies in the Theory of Capital Markets*, edited by Michael C. Jensen (New York: Praeger, 1972), pp. 146–222 (see in particular pp. 169–170), also derives a similar equation.

Perhaps the earliest appearance of a similar approach to the preceding CAPM proof is in [Beja (1971)] Avraham Beja, "The Structure of the Cost of Capital under Uncertainty," *Review of Economic Studies* 38, No. 3 (July 1971) pp. 359–368, particularly p. 364, eq. 3.4.3. However, although Beja proposes the pricing relation $P = \Sigma_s \pi_s X_s$ and the inequality $\pi_s > 0$, he does not investigate the conditions for the existence of state-prices and he makes the unnecessary assumption of complete markets. Clearly trying to maintain a high standard of generality, he also does not make the correspondence, as in Myers (1968) and Rubinstein (1976/Autumn), between the state-prices (π_s) and marginal utilities.

1977   Edward M. Miller, "Risk, Uncertainty, and Divergence of Opinion," *Journal of Finance* 32, No. 4 (September 1977), pp. 1151–1168.

SHORT SALES, HETEROGENEOUS BELIEFS,
PORTFOLIO SEPARATION, FAVORABLE GAMBLES THEOREM,
AGGREGATION OF INFORMATION

A cademic literature on short sales and stock prices has had a renaissance in the early twenty-first century. This literature argues that several examples of apparently anomalous security price behavior may at their root simply be attributed to the failure to appreciate the full implications of constraints on short sales.

The standard finance paradigm for market equilibrium under uncertainty is the CAPM of Sharpe (1964), Lintner (1965/February), Mossin (1966), and Treynor (1999). That model has one key assumption that will here concern us: Beliefs about the future joint return distributions of all securities are the same for all investors. In this context, as is well known from the portfolio separation property of that model: If all investors have the same beliefs and a riskless security exists, then every investor divides his wealth between cash and a single mutual fund, the market portfolio, which contains all securities in the market. Arrow (1965/B) has proven in a very general risk-aversion setting that every investor will want to invest at least part of his wealth in positive amounts in a favorable gamble. The market portfolio then being a favorable gamble (since its equilibrium expected return exceeds the riskless return), all investors will have a long position in the market. Restrictions on short sales would then not be binding since no investor would go short the market (and therefore any risky security). Investors lend, borrow, and buy risky securities, but none short. However, once one allows for different beliefs, then intuitively investors who are sufficiently pessimistic about the returns of certain securities, other things being equal, may want to short these securities, with the other side of their transaction taken up by comparatively optimistic investors.

Perhaps the most intriguing form of market segmentation derives from short-selling constraints. These constraints are particularly interesting because (1) they are bound up with heterogeneous beliefs (since, as mentioned, in the original CAPM with homogeneous beliefs these constraints are not binding); (2) each investor chooses the extent to which he will be bound by them (unlike the pure segmentation models); and (3) several features of real-world U.S. markets erect barriers to short selling:

1. To short sell, a lender of the shares must be found and motivated to temporarily part with his shares. The proceeds of the short sale are

held as collateral to help protect the stock lender. The interest rate on that collateral that is returned to the short seller is called the "rebate rate." To motivate the lender to lend his shares, the rebate rate is lower than the full interest rate that is earned on the collateral. So the lender earns the difference between that interest rate and the rebate rate. In times of very restricted supply, the rebate rate can even be negative so the short seller not only earns no interest on the short-sale proceeds but pays an additional fee to the lender.

2. To understand the lack of symmetry from loss of interest on short sales, consider a "short sale against the box": being long and short the same stock simultaneously. If the investor does not receive any interest on the proceeds of the short sale, even though he must invest his own funds to buy the long side, this position has a zero payoff. If the short sale were symmetric, the investor should be able to earn the riskless return on the investment (which would have occurred had he earned the interest on the proceeds of the short sale).

3. If after the short sale occurs the broker can no longer find a willing lender to continue the short sale, the short seller may be forced to cover prematurely.

4. Short selling is potentially vulnerable to another investor who succeeds in intentionally monopolizing the floating supply of stock in a "short squeeze."

5. Investors cannot short sell after a downtick or after a zero-downtick.

6. If the stock price jumps up more than 100 percent before a short seller can close out the position, the short seller will experience a greater loss than would the long buyer who suddenly experiences the largest possible stock price decline (of 100 percent due to limited liability). However, shorting by buying put options does not have this drawback.

7. All profits and losses from short sales are treated relatively unfavorably as short-term capital gains irrespective of the short-sale holding period.

8. Many institutional investors, particularly mutual funds, are contractually precluded from short selling.

Short selling by buying put options largely circumvents the first six of these barriers. However, while the loss of the interest on the proceeds of short sales is not clearly visible in a put purchase, it can be inferred using the put-call parity relation from the price of the put relative to the price of an otherwise identical call. Several empirical studies suggest that the implicit rebate rate earned by a put buyer is often significantly less than the market riskless rate—for example, Stephen Figlewski and Gwendolyn P. Webb, in [Figlewski-Webb (1993)] "Options, Short Sales, and Market

Completeness," *Journal of Finance* 48, No. 2 (June 1993), pp. 761–777, and Eli Ofek, Matthew Richardson, and Robert F. Whitelaw, in [Ofek-Richardson-Whitelaw (2002)] "Limited Arbitrage and Short Sale Restrictions: Evidence from the Options Markets," *Journal of Financial Economics* 74 (November 2004), pp. 305–342.

Asymmetric restrictions such as these lead Miller (1977) to postulate that relatively pessimistic investors will often not register their opinions in the market since they will find short selling quite costly. On the other hand, the same reservations do not stop an optimistic investor from going long. As a result, particularly when there is substantial divergence of opinion about a stock and short sales are difficult, Miller argues that current stock prices will tend to reflect only the more optimistic information since the negative opinions of would-be short sellers never make it into the stock price. The Hayek (1945) model of information pooling fails, and the current price of such stocks becomes higher than the price they would have in a market in which all available information is reflected in the price.

A very similar observation was made about 40 years earlier by Williams (1938):

> *In multiple stock markets, each stock will be held only by those who like that particular stock issue better than any other, and those who prefer some other stock will not be owners of that particular stock, even though they may entertain an opinion on that one along with opinions on all others. . . . In other words, in a multiple stock market there is a tendency for most people to think all stocks but their own too high. If most people are right in their opinion of the other fellow's investments, then it would follow that stocks in general have a tendency to sell too high, because almost every stock will enjoy some distinction of its own, and will tend to gather around itself its own special group of enthusiasts who will bid its price up too high. If every stock is somebody's favorite, then every price should be viewed with skepticism. (pp. 28–29)[43]*

To some extent, the Williams-Miller argument can also be traced to Lintner (1969), who presents apparently the first formal analysis of the formation of equilibrium prices under binding short selling constraints (short selling is simply not permitted). Although Miller cites Lintner's paper, strangely he mentions only the portion of the paper that does *not* deal with short-selling constraints. But the clear connection between heterogeneous beliefs and short selling, which was subsequently to be the heart of the short-selling literature, was forged by Lintner.

To derive more specific results, to the assumptions usually made for the CAPM, as in Lintner (1970), Lintner in addition assumes that all investors have exponential utility functions, known from Wilson (1968), which Lintner references, to produce aggregate closed-form results even when agents have differing beliefs. Lintner's first important conclusion is that, for a given security, its equilibrium price is determined only by those investors who hold that security. Those who in the absence of short-selling constraints would have tended to short it and, in the presence of these constraints, now have zero holdings, play no direct role in determining its equilibrium price. That is, only the preferences and beliefs of those investors that end up holding a security have a direct influence on its equilibrium price. The preferences and beliefs of those who do not hold the security only indirectly affect its price via their effect on the prices of other securities that are held in common. For example, suppose there are three securities, 1, 2, and 3 and two investors, A and B. Say in equilibrium investor A holds securities 1 and 2, and investor B holds securities 2 and 3. Then investor B affects the price of security 1 only indirectly though his influence on the price of security 2, which in turn affects the demand for security 1 by investor A. Surprisingly, despite what some seem to believe, Lintner does not draw the Williams-Miller conclusion that securities will tend to be priced higher because they will be held by relatively optimistic investors. Instead, Lintner simply says that the pricing of any security will only depend directly on the beliefs and risk aversions of the investors who hold it, and that in determining its price greater weight is given to the risk aversions and beliefs of those investors who hold more of the security. Indeed, as Lintner points out (pp. 395–396), in his model the fewer investors in a security (in his terminology, "the smaller the market"), the higher the risk premium of that security and the lower therefore its market price, other things being equal. In effect, because investors have available fewer desirable securities, they diversify less and tend to hold portfolios with higher variance. This, in turn, tends to reduce the desirability and therefore prices of risky securities. Lintner also points out that there is a formal correspondence between markets with short-selling constraints and markets without them but where subsets of investors are simply ignorant of subsets of securities and therefore do not trade in them—a correspondence revisited by Merton (1987). So Lintner, since he draws conclusions only about pure segmentation issues, would have concluded the opposite of Williams and Miller: that short-selling constraints, by reducing the size of the market, should tend to reduce prices.

Robert Jarrow, in [Jarrow (1980)] "Heterogeneous Expectations, Restrictions on Short Sales, and Equilibrium Prices," *Journal of Finance* 35, No. 5 (December 1980), pp. 1105-1113, refines the Williams-Miller hypothesis further. A disconcerting implication of the Markowitz (1952/March) and Roy (1952) mean-variance portfolio selection model in the case of unconstrained short sales is that the optimal portfolio often includes very large long positions in some securities hedged and financed by very large short positions in other securities. In an extreme case, suppose securities A and B have almost perfectly positively correlated returns, but the investor believes that the expected return of security A is slightly higher than that of security B. He can exploit this small difference in expected returns by shorting a large amount of security B and using the proceeds to fund correspondingly large purchases of security A—almost a riskless arbitrage. In this case, imposing short-sale constraints not only eliminates the short sales in security B, tending to increase its price, but it also can significantly reduce the size of long positions in security A, tending to *decrease* its price. Jarrow concludes that a priori considering both these effects means that short-sale constraints can drive the prices of some securities up and others down. However, he also proves that in the context of Lintner's heterogeneous expectations model, if the only source of disagreement among investors is their expected returns (in particular, investors have identical beliefs about covariances), then the imposition of short-selling constraints will only increase the prices of risky securities.

Although antecedents to Miller's paper can be found in Williams (1938), Lintner (1969), William Forsyth Sharpe, in [Sharpe (1970)] *Portfolio Theory and Capital* (New York: McGraw-Hill, 1970), pp. 104–113, and perhaps others, Miller is the first to emphasize several implications of this hypothesis and a surprising number of apparently anomalous observations that contradict standard models but can be potentially explained by asymmetric short-selling restrictions:

1. One should not be surprised to find that warrants, particularly near-expiration warrants, tend to be overpriced, as claimed by Thorp-Kassouf (1967), since it is precisely these securities that will be most attractive to optimistic investors as a result of their high implicit leverage.
2. Syllogistically, since divergence of opinion tends to be correlated with increased risk and since securities with the greatest divergence of opinion, by Miller's theory, tend to be the most overpriced, then ironically increased risk and overpricing (hence lower expected returns) for securities with divergent opinions tend to go together. For example, overpricing of stocks at initial public offerings (IPOs), another apparent anomaly, may then be explained by the fact that it is at the moment of the IPO when divergent opinion about the stock is often at its greatest.
3. High turnover and relatively divergent opinions tend to go together; therefore, high turnover is the market trace evidence of divergence.

Again, one should not be surprised to find that stocks with high turnover tend to have lower returns, as claimed by Phillip L. Cooley and Rodney L. Roenfelt in [Cooley-Roenfelt (1975)] "A Comparative Multivariate Analysis of Factors Affecting Stock Returns," *Financial Review* (1975), pp. 31–41.

4. Barr Rosenberg and Walt McKibben, in [Rosenberg-McKibben (1973)] "The Prediction of Systematic and Specific Risk in Common Stocks," *Journal of Financial and Quantitative Analysis* 8, No. 2 (March 1973), pp. 317–333, provide evidence that high turnover and high beta tend to be observed together. Therefore, one should not be surprised to find that high-beta stocks have lower returns than the CAPM would predict, as found by Black-Jensen-Scholes (1972), among many others.

5. Miller speculates that the closed-fund discount anomaly may be at least partially due to short-sale restrictions. It is not that closed-end funds are selling at a discount, but rather that individual securities are selling at a premium. Investors who are optimistic about individual stocks cannot take optimal advantage of their beliefs by purchasing managed portfolios of stocks, but will instead prefer to purchase specific stocks.

The Williams-Miller argument also has an unfortunate side effect: Since prices will not reflect, as Hayek (1945) argued, the beliefs of the pool of all potential investors, realized returns cannot be used without bias to infer their *ex ante* probability distribution, as is often assumed in empirical work.

As Joram Mayshar, in [Mayshar (1983)] "On Divergence of Opinion and Imperfections in Capital Markets," *American Economic Review* 73, No. 1 (March 1983), pp. 114–128, points out, Lintner's model fails to endogenize explicitly the decisions of investors not to hold certain securities. To achieve clean results, Mayshar develops a special case of Lintner's heterogeneous beliefs exponential utility CAPM with short-selling constraints. In particular, he assumes that investors have identical preferences and beliefs except for differing opinions about the mean, which for each security can be arrayed continuously from the least pessimistic to the most optimistic. To prevent the decision to hold security j from depending on the prices of other risky securities and their expected returns, Mayshar cleverly assumes that the realized return of every security has a structure as in the Markowitz (1959) and Sharpe (1963) diagonal or market model, $r_j - r = \alpha_j + (r_M - r)\beta_j + \varepsilon_j$, where both long and short positions are permitted in the market factor and all investors have the same probability beliefs about the market factor. That means, then, that investor diversity is limited strictly to different alphas, α_j. In addition, to get around complexities created by security endowments, he assumes that all investors start with positions that are 100 percent cash, and then trade from there to reach their holdings of risky securities. It then follows that the investors in security *j* will be those with the highest alphas. There will exist some point α_j^* for each security *j* where all investors with alphas below that amount will not hold the security and all investors with alphas above will. Unlike the standard CAPM, the equilibrium price will then be determined in addition to the other variables in that model by the number of investors n_j holding that security and its average alpha: $(\Sigma_k \alpha_k)/n_j$, where the sum is taken from 1 to n_j, only for those investors with long positions.

Stephen Figlewski, in [Figlewski (1981)] "Informational Effects of Restrictions on Short Sales: Some Empirical Evidence," *Financial and Quantitative Analysis* 16, No. 4 (November 1981), pp. 463–476, conducts an early, fairly direct test of the Williams-Miller hypothesis. The hypothesis implies that if one can identify stocks and times when dispersion of beliefs is unusually high, one should find those stocks at those times to be overpriced. Figlewski uses the percentage of outstanding stock held short as an indicator of belief dispersion. Considering the significant cost of short selling, those who do may have very negative information compared to those who hold the stock. The opposite position has often been argued: that stocks with high short interest should be underpriced since at some point the short sellers will need to cover by buying stock and this will force the price up in the future. Covering the period 1973–1979, Figlewski's empirical evidence, however, supports both the Williams-Miller hypothesis and his use of the short-interest percentage as an indicator of belief dispersion, but the identified stocks are not found to be sufficiently overpriced to compensate for the loss of interest on the proceeds of the short sale likely to be experienced by most investors. His results also confirm what may be the earliest published test of the predictability of short interest by Joseph J. Seneca, in [Seneca (1967)] "Short Interest: Bearish or Bullish?," *Journal of Finance* 21, No. 1 (March 1967), pp. 67–70, who covers the earlier 1946–1965 period using midmonthly announcements of open interest.

Joseph Chen, Harrison Hong, and Jeremy C. Stein, in [Chen-Hong-Stein (2002)] "Breadth of Ownership and Stock Returns," *Journal of Financial Economics* 66, Nos. 2–3 (November/December 2002), pp. 171–205, test the Williams-Miller hypothesis by using breadth of stock ownership, defined as the number of investors with long positions in the stock, as a measure of pent-up short-selling demand (that is, the fewer investors, the more pent-up demand since the harder it will be to locate share lenders). If this proxy works and the hypothesis is true, then reductions in breadth of ownership should forecast reduced future stock returns. Chen, Hong, and Stein confirm this prediction for their sample of mutual funds for which they have breadth information. They presume that all investments of these funds are long since very few mutual funds engage in short sales. For this sample, their prediction is confirmed. Moreover, they also show that breadth and momentum are positively correlated. Therefore, it is possible that part of the anomalous observation that momentum can predict returns (see N. Jegadeesh and Sheridan Titman, in [Jegadeesh-Titman (1993)] "Returns to Buying Winners and Selling Losers: Implications for Stock Market Efficiency," *Journal of Finance* 48, No. 1 (March 1993), pp. 65–91) may be simply that momentum is a by-product of changes in breadth, which in turn influences stock returns due to the Williams-Miller hypothesis.

The Williams-Miller hypothesis can also potentially explain other more recent anomalous observations. Karl B. Diether, Christopher J. Malloy, and Anna Scherbina, in [Diether-Malloy-Scherbina (2002)] "Differences of Opinion and the Cross Section of Stock Returns," *Journal of Finance* 57, No. 5 (October 2002), pp. 2113–2141, attempt to explain why it appears that, compared to otherwise similar stocks, stocks with higher dispersion in analysts' earnings forecasts tend to have lower future stock market returns. Arguing that this dispersion proxies for differences in opinion about these returns, the Williams-Miller hypothesis can be used to explain the future lower stock market returns (since these securities tend to be the most overpriced). Supporting this explanation is the additional observation that the dispersion effect is greater for small stocks—stocks that are particularly difficult to short and have no exchange-traded options, where shorting could otherwise be easily accomplished by selling calls or buying puts. The dispersion effect also seems to be stronger for growth stocks where a given level of earnings-estimate dispersion translates into a larger disagreement over current value.

1978 Nils H. Hakansson, "Welfare Aspects of Options and Supershares," *Journal of Finance* 33, No. 3 (June 1978), pp. 759–776.

OPTIONS, COMPLETE MARKETS, PORTFOLIO SEPARATION,
MARKET PORTFOLIO, HETEROGENEOUS BELIEFS,
MARKET-EQUIVALENCE THEOREM

To have the benefits of a complete market as in Arrow (1953), it would seem we need as many different securities as there are states of the world. However, in certain interesting cases, the number of securities can be dramatically economized. The CAPM separation theorem says that only two securities are needed: a riskless security and a share in a marketwide index fund. Merton (1973/September) suggests that a third fund may be required to allow investors to hedge stochastic changes in investment opportunities. Rubinstein (1976/May) shows that a natural candidate for such a fund is a default-free annuity maturing at the end of an investor's life (similar to Social Security in the United States). Thus, an intertemporal version of two-fund separation can be achieved even with stochastic investment opportunities, provided the riskless security is interpreted as a default-free annuity.

Hakansson (1978) finds another way to reduce the number of securities and yet satisfy the needs of investors. He permits arbitrary and heterogeneous risk-averse investor utility functions of wealth. He also assumes arbitrary probability beliefs attached to states. His key restriction is to suppose that although different investors have different beliefs, their only source of disagreement is about outcomes of the market portfolio. Since investors' subjective probabilities about individual security returns, conditional on the outcome of the market portfolio, are the same, then state-securities on the market portfolio are the only securities needed by the market. In other words (by the market-equivalence theorem), a complete market would lead to the same allocations and prices.

Breeden-Litzenberger (1978) takes this a step further to intertemporal time-additive utility of consumption. They show that, if conditional on the aggregate level of consumption, all consumer/investors agree on the probabilities of all states, then the market can be effectively completed only by trading state-securities on aggregate consumption. They interpret this as a diversification result. Consider a subset of states for which aggregate consumption is the same, but securities have different returns conditional on aggregate consumption. Consumer/investors will not choose to vary their consumption across these states since that would create unnecessary risk for which they will not be compensated (by, say, higher expected returns) since that conditional risk is not priced in equilibrium. Without the assumption of conditional agreement, the agents would take opposing side bets on the states and more securities would be required. This leads to a simplification in the valuation function for cash flows in terms of macro states. In the general case, over dates $t = 0, 1, \ldots, T$ and dated events $s(t)$,

$$PV_0(X_0, \{X_1\}, \{X_2\}, \ldots, \{X_T\}) = \Sigma_t \Sigma_{s(t)} \, \pi_{t,s(t)} X_{t,s(t)}$$

where $\pi_{t,s(t)}$ is the current price of a state-security that pays \$1 if and only if dated event $s(t)$ occurs at date t.

Consider macro dated events $S(t)$ such that for all dated events $s(t) \in S(t)$, the level of aggregate consumption $C_{t,s(t)}$ is the same. Under the conditions of Breeden and Litzenberger, the preceding present value formula simplifies to:

$$PV_0[X_0, (X_1), (X_2), \ldots, (X_T)] = \Sigma_t \Sigma_{S(t)} \, \pi_{t,S(t)} \, E[X_t | S(t)]$$

where $\pi_{t,S(t)}$ is current price of \$1 received if and only if macro state $S(t)$ occurs and $E[\bullet]$ is the universally held subjective expected value of X_t conditional on $S(t)$.

In practice, this suggests that if the major source of disagreement among investors relates to aggregate market returns, most of the market's risk distribution function can simply be met by state-securities or options on the market portfolio. Stephen A. Ross, in [Ross (1976/February)] "Options and Efficiency," *Quarterly Journal of Economics* 90, No. 1 (February 1976), pp. 75–89, had already shown that in place of state-securities, a full set of standard calls can also complete the market.

Hakansson's paper preceded the creation of exchange-traded index options in the United States by five years. Today, despite the fact that the individual equity option market had a 10-year head start and despite the fact that options are now traded on thousands of equities, the daily trading volume of S&P 500 and S&P 100 index options alone typically exceeds the volume of all traded equity options.

1978   Haim Levy, "Equilibrium in an Imperfect Market: A Constraint on the Number of Securities in the Portfolio," *American Economic Review* 68, No. 4 (September 1978), pp. 643–658.

1987   Robert C. Merton, "A Simple Model of Capital Market Equilibrium with Incomplete Information," *Journal of Finance* 42, No. 3 (July 1987), pp. 483–510, his Presidential Address to the American Finance Association.

MARKET SEGMENTATION, NONMARKETABLE ASSETS,
CAPITAL ASSET PRICING MODEL (CAPM), NEGLECTED STOCKS

Realistic modeling of barriers to exchange such as trading costs, short selling, and so on, present challenging tractability problems. One way to circumvent these is to exogenously impose some form of market segmentation where investors are simply precluded from holding, exchanging, or short selling some securities. One of the earliest and perhaps the simplest of these is described by David Mayers, in [Mayers (1972)] "Nonmarketable Assets and Capital Market Equilibrium under Uncertainty," in *Studies in the Theory of Capital Markets*, edited by Michael C. Jensen (New York: Praeger, 1972), pp. 223–249. Mayers considers a generalization of the standard Sharpe-Lintner-Mossin-Treynor CAPM that allows for nonmarketable assets that are held in the portfolio of each investor, for example the present value of future labor income. In another context, Kenneth Joseph Arrow and R.C. Lind in [Arrow-Lind (1970)] "Uncertainty and the Evaluation of Public Investment Decisions," *American Economic Review* 60, No. 3 (June 1970), pp. 364–378, consider the effect of the number of investors in a firm on the firm's socially optimal discount rate for its physical investments. They conclude that in a segmented market this discount rate varies inversely with the spread of ownership, which implies that discount rates should typically be lower for publicly financed (that is, federal government) investments than for privately financed investments since the former has more (implicit) investors.

Another very simple example developed by Mark Rubinstein, in [Rubinstein (1973/December)] "Corporate Financial Policy in Segmented Securities Markets," *Journal of Financial and Quantitative Analysis* 8, No. 4 (December 1973), pp. 749–761, serves to bring out the key point of this literature.

Example of Segmented Securities Markets

One way of writing a basic conclusion of the Sharpe-Lintner-Mossin-Treynor CAPM is:

$$E(W_1^M) - r W_0^M = \left(\frac{\theta}{I_M} \right) \mathrm{Var}(W_1^M)$$

where r = the riskless return

W_t^M = the dollar value of overall market wealth at dates $t = 0, 1$

I_M = the number of investors in the economy, assumed to be identical

θ = a measure of the risk aversion of the representative investor

One way to think of this result is as an equation determining the current wealth W_0^M as a function of the other variables, all of which are given.

(Continued)

Example of Segmented Securities Markets *(Continued)*

Suppose the economy M were broken into two similar and disjoint parts, J and K, such that

$$W_1^M = W_1^J + W_2^K \qquad I_J = I_K = \frac{1}{2} I_M$$

$$E(W_1^J) = E(W_2^K) \qquad \text{Var}(W_1^J) = \text{Var}(W_1^K)$$

For the two similar smaller economies, we would then have:

$$E(W_1^J) - rW_0^J = \frac{\theta}{I_J}\,\text{Var}(W_1^J) \quad \text{and} \quad E(W_1^K) - rW_0^K = \frac{\theta}{I_K}\,\text{Var}(W_1^K)$$

The market has now been *completely segmented* since the investors in economy J can only trade securities in economy J but not the other, and likewise investors in economy K can only trade securities in economy K but not the other. A standard example comes from international finance where J and K are viewed as two countries with no overlapping securities or investors.

The question I wish to answer is whether segmenting the market tends to increase or decrease overall current wealth; that is, is $W_0^M > W_0^J + W_0^K$ or is $W_0^M < W_0^J + W_0^K$?

Rewriting the equation for larger economy M:

$$E(W_1^J + W_1^K) - rW_0^M = \frac{\theta}{I_J + I_K}\,\text{Var}(W_1^M + W_1^K)$$

Now subtracting this from the separate equations for economies J and K we can conclude:

$$W_0^M > W_0^J + W_0^K \text{ if and only if } \rho(W_1^J, W_1^K) < 1$$

where $\rho(W_1^J, W_1^K)$ is the correlation of W_1^J and W_1^K. (Assumed here is that θ will remain unchanged after segmenting the original market; although this is not always correct, any change is likely to be second order.)[44]

Intuitively, as long as the two smaller economies J and K have future market wealth that is not perfectly positively correlated, the investors in each will be better off if the economies merge into M since all investors can reduce portfolio risk through expanded opportunities for diversification. Current wealth therefore becomes more valuable in the merged economy. In international finance, this is the prima facie case for international diversification, where expanding the size of the market tends to increase security prices.

Blume-Friend (1975/May) document that investors typically hold stock portfolios with very few securities. The Sharpe-Lintner-Mossin-Treynor CAPM implies that *every firm* must have the same number of shareholders; in particular, every investor must be a shareholder. This finding motivates Levy (1978). Levy modifies the original CAPM by assuming that each investor i has an exogenously specified number of risky securities m_i that he can hold in his portfolio (in addition to the riskless security). So while all securities are held by some investors, not all investors hold the same risky securities. In the cross-sectional regression:

$$r_j - r = \gamma_0 + \gamma_1 \beta_j + \gamma_2 \omega_j^2 + \varepsilon_j$$

where r_j = the realized return of security j
r = the corresponding riskless return
β_j = the measured beta of security j
ω_j^2 = the variance of the residual term (ε_j) of a market model regression
ε_j = the remaining unexplained variation in r_j

The original CAPM predicts that $\gamma_0 = 0$, $\gamma_1 = r_M - r$, and $\gamma_2 = 0$ where r_M is the return on the market portfolio. In fact, almost every investigator reports that $\gamma_0 > 0$, $\gamma_1 < r_M - r$, and $\gamma_2 > 0$. Levy shows that in principle his model is capable of simultaneously explaining all three empirical deviations from the CAPM. In particular, with most investors holding perhaps only a few securities in their portfolios, it is not surprising that ω_j^2 becomes more important to them than β_j as a measure of security risk. In Levy's model, β_j reflects the correlation of the return of security j with the return of a portfolio containing all the securities in the market. A Levy investor who may hold only very few securities may not be very concerned about the market as a whole.

More general models of segmentation with international segmentation in mind include [Errunza-Losq (1985)] "International Asset Pricing under Mild Segmentation: Theory and Test," *Journal of Finance* 40, No. 1 (March 1985), pp. 105–124, by Vihang Errunza and Etienne Losq. In this paper, a group of unrestricted investors can trade all securities, but a second group, the restricted investors, can trade only a subset of these securities. The securities that can be traded by all investors are called eligible and those available only to the unrestricted investors are called ineligible. Not surprisingly, the eligible securities are priced as if the market is not segmented, while the ineligible securities have lower prices (with what the authors call "super" risk premiums) than they would have in a fully unsegmented market. The intuition here is the same as in the simpler setting of Rubinstein (1973/December).

Perhaps the most elaborately developed segmentation model is that of Merton (1987). Merton uses a model very similar to that of Levy in which different investors are exogenously assumed to be restricted to just a few securities, with each investor potentially constrained to allocate his wealth among a different and possibly small subset of all available securities. On top of Levy's assumptions, using a version of the Markowitz-Sharpe market model, he assumes that all investors can invest as well in an "index fund," which captures the common exposures of all existing securities to a marketwide risk factor. Different investors know about different subsets of securities, but all investors who know about a security agree about the key parameters describing its return distribution. As a result, Merton's model fits into a category of segmentation models with homogeneous beliefs.

In addition to the findings of Blume-Friend (1975/May), Merton motivates his model from results of subsequent papers by Avner Arbel, Steven Carvell, and Paul J. Strebel, summarized by Avner Arbel in [Arbel (1985)] "Generic Stocks: An Old Product in a New Package," *Journal of Portfolio Management* 11, No. 4 (Summer 1985), pp. 4–13, that show that "neglected" but not necessarily small firms (that is, firms with relative little institutional following) tend to have higher realized returns than would be predicted even considering the "small firm effect." Indeed, they present evidence that once one has controlled for neglect, size has no separate effect on returns. They hypothesize that neglected or generic firms tend to have higher returns because investors need compensation for the greater difficulty of obtaining information about these firms, in comparison to the "brand name" and typically larger well-known firms. Supporting this is evidence of greater dispersion of earnings forecasts among analysts for neglected firms compared to widely followed firms. They argue that the January effect, found by Marc Reinganum, in [Reinganum (1983)] "The Anomalous Stock Market Behavior of Small Firms in January: Empirical Tests for Year-End Tax Effects," *Journal of Financial Economics* 12, No. 1 (June 1983), pp. 89–104, if caused by end-of-year tax selling to realize losses, is much more likely to characterize neglected firms since much of the stock of well-known firms tends to be owned by tax-exempt institutions. Moreover, release of new information by all firms tends to be concentrated in January, but this release is more critical for neglected firms in dispelling uncertainty. Supporting this, they present evidence that not only does the dispersion of earnings forecasts tend to reach a seasonal low for all firms in January, but this reduction is particularly pronounced for neglected firms.

Among his many results, Merton confirms the simpler segmentation models that prices vary with the size of the market. In particular, other things being equal, firms with larger exposure to the common factor (similar to β_j), larger residual variance (similar to ω_j^2), larger market value, and fewer investors will tend to have lower prices and higher expected returns. Perhaps his most interesting result is to point out that it is not size measured by the proportion of the market value of the firm to total market wealth that counts, but rather the market value of the firm relative to the aggregate wealth of the investors who consider investing in that firm (p. 495). The simple intuition underlying these results is that if the typical investor must confine himself to just a few securities instead of the market portfolio, the investor will benefit less from diversification and place a lower current value on the risky securities he owns. Similarly, if fewer investors must hold the stock of the same firm, then its risk is less easily reduced through diversification and therefore investors are only willing to pay less for the stock of that firm.

1978   Douglas T. Breeden (September 29, 1950–) and **Robert H. Litzenberger**, "Prices of State-Contingent Claims Implicit in Option Prices," *Journal of Business* 51, No. 4 (October 1978), pp. 621–651.

OPTION PRICING, STATE-PRICES, BUTTERFLY SPREADS,
LOGNORMAL DISTRIBUTION, BLACK-SCHOLES FORMULA,
CRRA INTERTEMPORAL CAPM

The mean-variance approach to portfolio selection and equilibrium has had widespread application in practice, while the state-price approach, although quite useful as a theoretical device, has been much harder to apply. Practical application becomes grounded on the shoals of measuring the state-prices. As late as 1972, Michael C. Jensen, in [Jensen (1972/Autumn)] "Capital Markets: Theory and Evidence," *Bell Journal of Economics and Management Science* 3, No. 2 (Autumn 1972), pp. 357–398, had written:

> *While the state-preference [state-price] approach is perhaps more general than the mean-variance approach and provides an elegant framework for investigating theoretical issues, it is unfortunately difficult to give it empirical content.*

All this was to change with the development of the Black-Scholes (1973) option pricing model. Latané-Rendleman (1976), in the very restrictive context of risk-neutral lognormality, showed how the missing parameter of the state-price distribution, volatility, can be recovered from the prices of exchange-traded options. Breeden-Litzenberger (1978) show how this can be done without presupposing that the risk-neutral distribution is anything in particular, let alone lognormal. They recover the state-prices from the current prices of standard European options on the same underlying asset with the same time to expiration, when there exists a continuum of options spanning all strike prices.

Intuition Behind the Breeden-Litzenberger Formula for State-Prices

First, discretize the state space. Consider expiration-date security prices between a low price of K_i and a high price of K_{i+1}. The discrete state-price for this interval is approximated by examining the price of a butterfly spread: Buy one call with strike K_i and price $C(K_i)$, buy one call with strike K_{i+1} and price $C(K_{i+1})$, and sell two calls with strike $K \equiv (K_i + K_{i+1})/2$ and price $C(K)$. The price of the butterfly is then $C(K_i) - 2C(K) + C(K_{i+1})$. Define $\Delta K \equiv K - K_i = K_{i+1} - K$. The ratio $[C(K_i) - 2C(K) + C(K_{i+1})]/(\Delta K)^2$ can be interpreted as a finite difference approximation to $\partial^2 C/\partial K^2$, which in turn equals the recovered state-price density.

In this wide-ranging paper, Breeden and Litzenberger also derive similar results to Rubinstein (1976/Autumn) for valuing a stream of uncertain cash flows under time-additive CRRA utility of consumption. Rosenberg-Ohlson (1976) had already shown that the Merton (1973/September) continuous-time, continuous-state security pricing model under intertemporally *nonstochastic* investment opportunities implies that the returns of all risky securities are identical. Breeden and Litzenberger show, moreover, that Merton's model also implies that consumer/investors must have CRRA to sustain the constant opportunity set. This means that, despite appearances to the contrary, Merton's model is a special case of the Rubinstein (1976/Autumn) discrete-time CRRA equilibrium model, where the returns of the (single) risky security follow geometric Brownian motion, the riskless return is constant, and trading takes place continuously.

1978   Michael C. Jensen, "Some Anomalous Evidence Regarding Market Efficiency," *Journal of Financial Economics* 6, No. 2 (1978), pp. 95–101.

EFFICIENT MARKETS

Jensen (1978) introduces the most famous issue of the *Journal of Financial Economics*, marking a turning point in acceptable academic work in finance. Heretofore, research questioning the rationality of market prices was difficult to publish because, like good Bayesians, most financial economists had such a strong prior belief in rational markets that they suspected apparent nonconfirming evidence contained empirical errors. As Jensen states in a famous paragraph:

> *I believe there is no other proposition in economics which has more solid empirical evidence supporting it than the Efficient Market Hypothesis. That hypothesis has been tested and, with very few exceptions, found consistent with the data in a wide variety of markets: the New York and American Stock Exchanges, the Australian, English and German stock markets, various commodity futures markets, the Over-the-Counter markets, the corporate and government bond markets, the option market, and the market for seats on the New York Stock Exchange. Yet, in a manner remarkably similar to that described by Thomas Kuhn in his book,* The Structure of Scientific Revolutions, *we seem to be entering a stage where widely scattered and as yet incohesive evidence is arising which seems to be inconsistent with the theory. As better data become available (e.g. daily stock price data) and as our econometric sophistication increases, we are beginning to find inconsistencies that our cruder data and techniques missed in the past. It is evidence which we will not be able to ignore. (p. 95)*[45]

The issue includes papers on the delayed reaction of stock prices to earnings announcements, potentially profitable trading rules based on closed-end fund discounts, violations of the general arbitrage conditions for standard option prices (Merton 1973/Spring), profitable trading strategies using information contained in option implied volatilities (Latané-Rendleman 1976), an example of two virtually identical investments selling at different prices, and positive abnormal returns using stock split information (Fama-Fisher-Jensen-Roll 1969). The floodgates holding back research results questioning rational markets had been breached.

1979　John C. Cox, Stephen A. Ross, and Mark Rubinstein, "Option Pricing: A Simplified Approach," *Journal of Financial Economics* 7, No. 3 (September 1979), pp. 229–263.

1979　Richard J. Rendleman Jr. and Brit J. Bartter, "Two-State Option Pricing," *Journal of Finance* 34, No. 5 (December 1979), pp. 1093–1110.

OPTION PRICING, BINOMIAL OPTION PRICING MODEL,
BLACK-SCHOLES FORMULA, RECOMBINING BINOMIAL TREES,
WORKING BACKWARDS, OPTION EARLY EXERCISE

Here is the widely known article developing the binomial option pricing model. Cox-Ross-Rubinstein (1979) (CRR) assume a sequence of markets over time with just two long-lived securities available at each dated event, one riskless (cash) and the other risky (underlying asset). The risky security is assumed to experience a binomial return between each trading date, say up or down; moreover, the up and down returns are assumed to be the same at every dated event. Graphically, this traces out a recombining binomial tree of prices; see discussion under Ross (1977). Each time the market reconvenes (a node in the tree), an investor can revise his portfolio; then one of the two dated events occurs; then the market reconvenes again; then the investor reinvests his accumulated profits and losses in a revised portfolio; and so on. Because at each date there are just as many securities (two) as possible dated events (two), the market is dynamically complete. If one considers yet an additional security (an option) with payoff completely determined by the realized price of the original risky security at the expiration date and if there is no arbitrage, then the added security is redundant, in the sense that its payoff can be replicated by revising a (self-financing) portfolio of the original two securities over time. This strategy leads to a replicating portfolio that perfectly mimics the payoff of the added security. Therefore, it is possible to determine the current value of an arbitrary security in terms of the current price of the original risky security and the riskless return. CRR then parameterize the binomial process of the original risky security so that as the time interval between successive binomial price changes (and successive opportunities to revise the replicating portfolio) approaches zero, the price process of the original risky security approaches geometric Brownian motion. They suppose the added security is a standard call. Then the current binomial value of the call approaches its Black-Scholes value in the limit.

The binomial approach to derivatives has three advantages over Black-Scholes (1973): (1) its much simpler mathematical structure clarifies the underlying economics; (2) since its proof only requires an elementary mathematical background, it has popularized Black-Scholes option pricing techniques among professionals and no doubt encouraged the rapid expansion of derivatives trading around the world; and (3) the backwards recursive solution algorithm can easily be modified to handle a substantial expansion of the types of securities that can be valued. It is obvious, for example, that the approach can be used to value any security whose entire payoff occurs at a single date in the future and is an arbitrary function of the price of the underlying risky security at that date. CRR show that American options (options that can be exercised prior to their expiration) can easily be valued using a slight modification of the recursive solution algorithm. American options are examples of a more general class of derivatives whose payoff depends not just on their underlying asset price at expiration, but also on the path taken by the underlying asset in getting there. Others have subsequently shown how the binomial approach can be extended to value a large variety of exotic or nonstandard derivatives, including path-dependent derivatives based on barriers or look-back features, derivatives with payoffs depending on the price of more than one risky security, derivatives whose payoff depends on value of other derivatives, derivatives with forward start features, derivatives with extendible expiration dates, derivatives with payoffs at different dates, and so on.

From the more general perspective of asset pricing, the binomial approach to derivatives significantly enlarges the complexity of long-lived securities that can be handled in equilibrium models. The paper suggests that the continuous-time, continuous-state models initiated by Merton (1969, 1971, 1973/September) can be alternatively modeled as discrete-time processes suitably parameterized so that as the time interval between successive returns goes to zero, the return process of all the securities approaches multivariate geometric Brownian motion. Initially, there was some question about how this analogy could be carried over to more complex economies with more than one risky long-lived security. In the context of Merton's continuous-time, continuous-state economy, to complete the market by portfolio revision it quickly became apparent that there needed to be just as many long-lived risky securities as state-variables for the arbitrage reasoning to work. To see the difficulty, suppose there were just three securities: one riskless and two risky (A and B), each with binomial returns. Over a single period, it would now seem that there would be four joint outcomes (up for both A and B; up for A, down for B; down for A, up for B; down for both A and B). Unfortunately, that leads to four states and these cannot be spanned by only three securities; so the value of a fourth security (say, a call) cannot be determined simply by arbitrage reasoning. However, Hua He, in [He (1990)] "Convergence from Discrete- to Continuous-Time Contingent Claims Prices," *Review of Financial Studies* 3, No.

4 (1990), pp. 523–546, shows how this generalization would work. He proves that if the distribution of A and B were reduced to only three joint outcomes and properly parameterized, this would preserve the arbitrage reasoning while at the same time converging to joint geometric Brownian motion in the continuous-time, continuous-state limit. This is an important result because it shows how binomial models need to be generalized to mimic a continuous-time model with many state variables, rendering the distinction between discrete-time and continuous-time, continuous-state models moot.

A glimmer of the model appeared in Cox-Ross (1976), which contains a continuous-time binomial jump model (see particularly p. 389). The discrete-time binomial approach to option pricing was originally suggested by William Forsyth Sharpe in [Sharpe (1978)] *Investments* (Englewood Cliffs, NJ: Prentice-Hall 1978). Rendleman-Bartter (1979) independently developed many of its implications.

1979   Douglas T. Breeden, "An Intertemporal Asset Pricing Model with Stochastic Consumption and Investment Opportunities," *Journal of Financial Economics* 7, No. 3 (September 1979), pp. 265–296.

INTERTEMPORAL CONSUMPTION AND INVESTMENT,
CONSUMPTION-BASED CAPM, CONTINUOUS-TIME,
CONTINUOUS-STATE CAPM, CONSUMPTION BETA,
MARKET PORTFOLIO, LOGNORMAL DISTRIBUTION,
STOCHASTIC OPPORTUNITY SET

The Merton (1973/September) derivation of an intertemporal asset pricing model with stochastically changing investment opportunities over time resulted in a multibeta version of the CAPM, with an additional beta term for each additional state variable. Breeden (1979) shows that in Merton's continuous-time, continuous-state framework, if a beta is defined relative to the growth rate of aggregate consumption, rather than the return of the market portfolio, then the model is considerably simplified since the multiple beta terms collapse to a single beta capturing the sensitivity of the return of a security to the growth of aggregate consumption. Breeden also shows that each consumer/investor chooses a portfolio that provides the highest possible correlation of his consumption with aggregate consumption.

The single-beta result was first shown by Rubinstein (1976/Autumn) in a discrete-time multiperiod generalization of the CAPM with joint normality of cash flows and consumption at the same date. It was also shown to hold under joint lognormality in discrete time in Breeden-Litzenberger (1978). Here it is shown to hold in continuous time for all securities provided their returns follow a continuous-state process. This means that in empirical application of this consumption-based CAPM (CCAPM), it is not necessary to identify or measure the potential multitude of factors that could arise in a Merton-type generalization of the single-factor CAPM expressed in terms of the return of the market portfolio. However, it then becomes necessary to measure aggregate consumption, in practice a very difficult task. Moreover, if there are reasons—other than a stochastically changing investment opportunity set—why the indirect utility of wealth function is state-dependent, there will be no getting around having to measure extra beta terms.

The Modern Period
Post-1980

1980   Hayne Ellis Leland, "Who Should Buy Portfolio Insurance?" *Journal of Finance* 35, No. 2 (May 1980), pp. 581–594.

2000   John C. Cox and Hayne Ellis Leland, "On Dynamic Investment Strategies," *Journal of Economic Dynamics and Control* 24, Nos. 11–12 (October 2000), pp. 1859–1880.

MARKET PORTFOLIO, DYNAMIC STRATEGIES, PATH DEPENDENCE

L eland (1980) shows how to recover qualitative features of the utility function of an investor from the distribution of his future wealth that he optimally chooses over states, given the way securities are priced in equilibrium. In particular, he answers the question why some investors prefer wealth payoffs over states that are convex functions of the return of the market portfolio, while others prefer concave payoffs. Which will be chosen depends on how the rate an investor's risk aversion changes as his wealth changes relative to the rate of change for the market as a whole.

In most other work, optimal self-financing dynamic strategies are derived from prespecified risk preferences. In Cox-Leland (2000), the inverse problem is solved: Given a proposed dynamic strategy, how can we tell if it will be self-financing, has path-independent outcomes, and is consistent with expected utility maximization of future wealth? The paper concentrates on a situation involving a choice between a single risky security (the market portfolio) following geometric Brownian motion, and cash with an exogenously specified constant riskless return. A key result is that *path-independent* dynamic strategies are a necessary condition for expected utility maximization.

1980   Sanford J. Grossman and Joseph E. Stiglitz, "On the Impossibility of Informationally Efficient Markets," *American Economic Review* 70, No. 3 (June 1980), pp. 393–408.

1981 Douglas W. Diamond and **R.E. Verrecchia**, "Information Aggregation in a Noisy Rational Expectations Economy," *Journal of Financial Economics* 9, No. 3 (September 1981), pp. 221–235.

2001 Mark Rubinstein, "Rational Markets: Yes or No? The Affirmative Case," *Financial Analysts Journal* 57, No. 3 (May-June 2001), pp. 15–29.

MARKET EFFICIENCY, RATIONAL EXPECTATIONS,
AGGREGATION OF INFORMATION,
PARTIALLY VS. FULLY REVEALING
RATIONAL EXPECTATIONS EQUILIBRIA,
INFORMED VS. UNINFORMED TRADERS,
OVERCONFIDENCE, HYPEREFFICIENT MARKETS

Grossman-Stiglitz (1980) tries to reconcile the paradox of circularity at once evident from a literal interpretation of Grossman (1976): If all information is fully revealed in prices, investors have no incentive to gather the information in the first place, so no information would be contained in prices, but then investors would have an incentive to gather it and so forth. Hence, considering the incentives to gather information, an equilibrium does not exist—therefore, the title of the paper. To correct this difficulty, the following model is proposed: Two securities exist, one riskless and the other risky. The return of the risky security consists of the sum of two terms, the first (θ) observable by paying cost (c), and the second (ε) unobservable with mean zero and zero correlation with the observable term. There are two types of agents: fraction λ informed traders who have paid c and observe the first term, and fraction $1 - \lambda$ uninformed traders who observe neither term. Otherwise, the traders are identical (same endowments, preferences, and prior beliefs before observing the first term). Although the uninformed traders cannot observe θ, they nonetheless can observe the current price P. As in Grossman (1976), these traders are assumed to have rational expectations in the sense that they draw out as much information as they can about θ from P in forming their own expectations. If x denotes the supply of the risky security, then the equilibrium price can be interpreted as the function $P_\lambda(\theta, x)$. All traders are assumed to know they are identical except that there are percentage λ informed traders. All traders therefore know the equilibrium pricing function $P_\lambda(\theta, x)$. Therefore, if all traders know aggregate supply x, they can determine θ simply by observing the price P. Hence we would have a fully revealing rational expectations equilibrium. But this creates precisely the aforementioned paradox of circularity.

To break the circle, Grossman and Stiglitz assume that the uninformed traders also cannot observe x. Thus they are prevented from inferring θ from P since they cannot sort out the separate effects of θ and x. Thus, the equilibrium is only partially revealing. The full equilibrium proposed allows traders to choose whether to become informed. As more traders become informed, the benefits of being informed decline until it does not pay additional traders to pay c to become informed as well. To obtain closed-form results, all traders are assumed to have exponential utility functions, and θ and ε are assumed to be jointly normally distributed random variables.

Among the conclusions is the idea that markets will be thinner, and indeed may not exist, when either very few or very many traders are informed (that is, λ is near 0 or 1). Another idea is that while differences in beliefs would initially seem to foster markets, to the extent the information of informed investors is revealed by prices, the creation of markets eliminates the very cause that gives rise to them, and may, in the end, cause those markets to disappear. The net result is that markets cannot be fully efficient in the sense of reflecting all available information, but markets can be efficient in the deeper sense of reflecting sufficient information so as to leave zero profit, at the margin, from gathering additional information.

As we have seen, Grossman (1976) developed a fully revealing rational expectations equilibrium where the diverse information of many agents is aggregated into prices. Grossman-Stiglitz (1980), on the other hand, developed a partially revealing rational expectations equilibrium where noise is created by each trader's uncertainty about aggregate endowment, but did not at the same time model the aggregation of diverse information. Diamond-Verrecchia (1981) do both: They model how the aggregation of the diverse information of many agents and the noise created by uncertainty about aggregate endowment leads to a partially revealing (that is, "noisy") rational expectations equilibrium. In their model, each agent (with identical prior beliefs) observes an independent signal about what will be the realized return of the risky security as well as an independent signal about aggregate endowment (namely, his own endowment). Their model is identical to Grossman (1976) when agents face no uncertainty about aggregate endowment.

Contending that agents suffer from a type of overconfidence, Rubinstein (2001) carries Grossman and Stiglitz one step further. He argues that overconfidence prompts agents to *overspend on gathering information* beyond the cost-effective point, so that prices actually end up, in a sense, reflecting too much information and are therefore "hyper-rational." This means that any new investor will find the cards stacked against him in the sense that he will not be able to earn a fair return on further investment in information. Empirical evidence that this is so is found in the poor performance of professionally and actively managed equity mutual funds that may fail to earn back their expenses.

1980   Robert C. Merton, "On Estimating the Expected Return of the Market: An Exploratory Investigation," *Journal of Financial Economics* 8, No. 4 (December 1980), pp. 323–361.

EXPECTED RETURNS, RANDOM WALK,
MARKET PORTFOLIO, EQUITY RISK PREMIUM,
SAMPLE VS. POPULATION STATISTICS,
JUMP OR POISSON PROCESS

Merton (1980) is perhaps the first paper to show careful thought about how to measure the equity risk premium. Merton points out that estimating the anticipated future mean from an observed historical time series of equity returns is much more difficult than estimating its variance. Unfortunately, one of the most basic of financial decisions—how much of your money to allocate among equities and other securities—is heavily dependent on your opinion about the size of the equity risk premium.

To illustrate the problem, assume the logarithm of returns is independent and identically distributed (i.i.d.). Suppose we examine a sample of n observations drawn over observation period t years where $h \equiv t/n$ is the sampling interval. It is easy to prove that the annualized *sample mean* (μ) is an unbiased predictor of the *population mean* (μ) and that the *variance of the sample mean* equals σ^2/t where σ is the annualized *population standard deviation*. Note that given t, the variance of the sample mean does *not* depend on the frequency of the observations (n or h). On the other hand, the annualized *sample variance* $\underline{\sigma}^2$ (where the sum of the squared differences between sampled return and its sample mean has been divided by $n-1$) is also an unbiased predictor of σ^2, and the *variance of the sample variance* is $2\sigma^4/(n-1)$. Unlike the sample variance, not only is the sample mean not improved by sampling more frequently but, in practice for portfolios of stocks, the variance of the sample mean also remains disturbingly large even after many years of observations. Moreover, if the i.i.d. assumption is dropped, then estimation problems for the mean can become even more difficult. The problem of estimating expected mean returns for individual stocks and even diversified portfolios of stocks is surely one of the most challenging, vexing, and important problems in financial economics.

Proof of Unbiasedness of the Sample Mean in the Random Walk Model

To illustrate how these results are derived, we begin with the random walk model:

$$\log r_k = \mu h + \sigma \sqrt{h}\, \varepsilon_k$$

for serially independent observations $k = 1, 2, \ldots, n$ where $E(\varepsilon_k) = 0$ and $\mathrm{Var}(\varepsilon_k) = 1$.

The sample mean is defined as $\underline{\mu}h \equiv \Sigma_k (\log r_k)/n$. Substituting for $\log r_k$ and taking expectations of both sides:

$$E(\underline{\mu}h) = E\left(\frac{\Sigma_k \mu h + \sigma \sqrt{h}\, \varepsilon_k}{n}\right) = \mu h + \sigma \sqrt{h}\, \frac{E(\varepsilon_k)}{n} = \mu h$$

so that $E(\underline{\mu}) = \mu$, and hence $\underline{\mu}$ is unbiased. (*Note:* Serial independence is not needed for this particular result.)

In [Merton (1976/May)] "The Impact of Option Pricing of Specification in the Underlying Stock Price Returns," *Journal of Finance* 31, No. 2 (May 1976), pp. 333–350, Merton adds an important caveat to this. He notes that if the security return, instead of following geometric Brownian motion in the continuous-time limit, as earlier, follows a mixed Brownian motion Poisson jump process, which he had used to value options in [Merton (1976/January–March)] "Option Pricing When Underlying Stock Returns Are Discontinuous," *Journal of Financial Economics* 3, No. 1 (January–March 1976), pp. 125–144, reprinted in Robert C. Merton, *Continuous-Time Finance*, Chapter 9 (Malden, MA: Blackwell, 1990), pp. 309–329, then the variance of the sample variance approaches a positive lower bound as h (holding t fixed) goes to zero. If the jump portion of the process is significant enough, estimating the sample variance can be near the same order of difficulty as estimating the sample mean. The addition of jumps adds the further complication that one could easily interpret the realized returns as having been drawn from a nonstationary, purely continuous distribution, when in fact they are drawn from a stationary distribution with a jump component. These caveats should be intuitively easy to understand.

These observations motivate Merton's search for a better way to forecast the equity risk premium (which he takes to be the difference between the monthly expected return inclusive of dividends of the New York Stock Exchange (NYSE) stock index minus the corresponding monthly holding period return on a U.S. Treasury bill with the shortest maturity exceeding 29 days). He assumes the equity market portfolio return follows geometric Brownian motion over a given observation period. Although he allows his measure of volatility to change from month to month, he assumes for the purpose of his "exploratory study" that it is sufficiently constant within the month to be exactly measured by the sample volatility from daily returns within the month. He examines three alternative constraints that can be placed on estimates of the risk premium. The first is that the risk premium be positive and proportional to the equity return variance: $(\mu - r)/\sigma^2 = a_1$, where $a_1 > 0$; this is the conclusion reached from representative investor constant relative risk aversion (CRRA) market equilibrium models. Merton (1973/September) and Rubinstein (1973/October) have shown that a_1 can be interpreted as the sum over a measure of all investors' individual risk aversions. His second model, which has no simple theoretical motivation, is that the risk premium be positive and proportional to the equity return standard deviation: $(\mu - r)/\sigma = a_2$, where $a_2 > 0$. The third is merely that the risk premium be positive and constant: $\mu - r = a_3$, where $a_3 > 0$; Merton calls this last the "state-of-the-art model." These different models will produce different predictions if, as Merton believes, the variance changes from month to month. Indeed, the prior work of Rosenberg (1972) strongly indicates this is true.

Methodologically, Merton incorporates the prior restriction that risk premiums be positive (true for all three alternatives) by assuming a prior distribution for a_j (j = 1, 2, 3) that is uniform over the positive real line. He then uses Bayes' theorem[1] to estimate the posterior distribution of the a_j based on historically observed returns. He examines various subperiods spanning a minimum of 1 year to a maximum of 52 years from 1926 to 1978, over each of which he assumes the a_j are constant, but varying across subperiods. He shows, as one might expect, that the non-negativity restriction is particularly significant when the historical period used to determine the posterior distribution contains large negative return observations.

He reaches three main conclusions. All three measures of a_j are significantly affected by imposing the constraint that these estimates be positive, even when the unconstrained estimate would have been positive. He therefore advises that careful estimates of the risk premium should build in a nonnegativity restriction. Second, the three constrained measures of a_j can easily imply quite different predictions of the equity risk premium. And third, regression estimates should divide realized returns by the variance corresponding to the month in which the returns are measured to correct for nonconstant variance (that is, heteroscedasticity).

1981   Robert C. Merton, "On Market Timing and Investment Performance I: An Equilibrium Theory of Value for Market Forecasts," *Journal of Business* 54, No. 3 (July 1981), pp. 363–406.

INVESTMENT PERFORMANCE,
MARKET TIMING, LUCK VS. SKILL

Merton (1981) finds a way to test for market timing skill without making assumptions about how the market adjusts returns for risk, as in the Jensen (1968) alpha tests using the capital asset pricing model (CAPM). Merton's results are independent of assumptions concerning the probability distribution of investment returns and the preferences and wealth of investors. However, they are restricted to the situation where a market timer forecasts whether stocks will outperform bonds and invests accordingly, but does not try to forecast by how much.

First, consider perfect market timing forecasting. Suppose you can invest in a mutual fund that can infallibly predict whether the stock market will do better than the riskless bonds over one year. Say 1 dollar is your current investment and r_M is the value it reaches at the horizon if it is invested in the market and r is the value it reaches if invested in riskless bonds. The fund cannot borrow or sell short. If it thinks $r_M > r$, the fund invests everything in the market; if it thinks $r_M \leq r$, it invests everything in bonds. Merton shows that the current value of being able to invest with this fund is 1 plus P, the present value of a purchased put on the market with strike price equal to r, expiring in one year.

To see this, the payoff of the fund is $\max(r, r_M) = r_M + \max(0, r - r_M)$, and the present value of this payoff is then $1 + P$, the present value of a put with strike r. Under the Black-Scholes (1973) option pricing model, it is easy to see that $P = [2N(\frac{1}{2}\sigma) - 1]$, where $N(\bullet)$ is the standard normal distribution function and σ is the annualized volatility of the logarithm of the stock portfolio return.

More realistically, assume that the forecast is imperfect such that:

p_1 = conditional probability the forecast is *correct* given that the realization is $r_M \leq r$.

$1 - p_1$ = conditional probability the forecast is *incorrect* given that the realization is $r_M \leq r$.

p_2 = conditional probability the forecast is *correct* given that the realization is $r_M > r$.

$1 - p_2$ = conditional probability the forecast is *incorrect* given that the realization is $r_M > r$.

Clearly, if $p_1 = p_2 = 1$ (in which case, $p_1 + p_2 = 2$), then the fund has perfect forecasting skill; Merton also shows that if $p_1 + p_2 = 1$, the fund has no forecasting skill. Assume that $p_1 + p_2 \geq 1$ (that is, the fund does not have negative forecasting skill). Again, suppose the fund invests completely in bonds if it forecasts that $r_M \leq r$ and completely in the market if it forecasts that $r > r_M$, and suppose you are indifferent to any risk that is uncorrelated with r_M. Merton shows that then the present value of the 1 dollar investment with the imperfectly forecasting fund is $1 + P(p_1 + p_2 - 1)$. $P(p_1 + p_2 - 1)$ is the present value of the forecast (or the highest fee the fund could charge for its services). With perfect forecasting skill, $P(p_1 + p_2 - 1) = P$; and with imperfect forecasting skill, $P(p_1 + p_2 - 1) < P$.

Proof of Merton's Result on Market Timing

To see this, compare the returns from the fund's imperfect forecast to the returns of the following portfolio:

Fraction p_2 invested in the market.

Fraction $\lambda \equiv P(p_1 + p_2 - 1)$ invested in puts on the market with strike price r.

Fraction $(1 - p_2 - \lambda)$ invested in bonds.

The return of this portfolio is then:

$$p_2 r_M + \frac{\lambda \max(0, r - r_M)}{P} + (1 - p_2 - \lambda)r$$

Proof of Merton's Result on Market Timing *(Continued)*

This portfolio return has four types of outcomes:

1. $r_M \leq r$ and the forecast is correct: $r - \lambda r - (1 - p_1)(r - r_M)$.
2. $r_M \leq r$ and the forecast is incorrect: $r_M - \lambda r + p_1(r - r_M)$.
3. $r_M > r$ and the forecast is correct: $r_M - \lambda r - (1 - p_2)(r_M - r)$.
4. $r_M > r$ and the forecast is incorrect: $r - \lambda r + p_2(r_M - r)$.

Each of the outcomes has been expressed as the sum of three terms: first, r or r_M, the return that would have been earned utilizing the forecast; second, a constant amount, $-\lambda r$; and third, a random amount depending on the size of $r_M - r$. Now if the forecast is perfect, then $p_1 = p_2 = 1$, and we have only outcomes 1 and 3. In outcome 1, while the fund would have had return r, the portfolio has return $r - \lambda r$; in outcome 2, while the fund would have had return r_M, the portfolio has return $r_M - \lambda r$. Therefore, the forecast always has an excess return of λr, and the present value of this equals $\lambda r / r = \lambda = P$, a conclusion we have already reached more directly.

With an imperfect forecast, $p_1 < 1$, $p_2 < 1$, or both, so that the return from utilizing the forecast would yield λr plus a positive or negative random amount more than the portfolio. However, if we can show that the random component has zero expected value and its risk is uncorrelated with the market, then we can ignore it and conclude that the present value of the forecast is $\lambda r / r = \lambda = P(p_1 + p_2 - 1)$.

Observe that the expected return of the random component conditional on $r_M \leq r$ is:

$$p_2[-(1 - p_1)(r - r_M)] + (1 - p_1)[p_1(r - r_M)] = 0$$

and the expected return of the random component conditional on $r_M > r$ is:

$$p_2[-(1 - p_2)(r_M - r)] + (1 - p_2)[p_2(r_M - r)] = 0$$

Not only does this imply that the *unconditional* expected return of the random component is zero, but it also implies that the return of the random component is uncorrelated with the market. Thus, we can ignore the influence of the random component in valuing the forecast. That leaves $P(p_1 + p_2 - 1)$ as the present value of the forecast.

Merton's main conclusion is that $p_1 + p_2 > 1$ is a necessary and sufficient condition for successful market timing. Note that the fact that the unconditional probability $p > \frac{1}{2}$ of having a successful forecast does not indicate forecasting skill. For example, consider a manager who always forecasts that $r_M > r$. If 75 percent of the time $r_M > r$, then, like a stopped clock, such an investor will have $p = \frac{3}{4}$, even though the investor surely has no forecasting skill. Moreover, by Merton's criteria, for such an investor, since $p_1 = 0$ and $p_2 = 1$, then $p_1 + p_2 = 1$. Or suppose, more generally, that the investor forecasts the market based on flipping a potentially biased coin. Say it lands tails with probability q, and if it lands tails (or heads), the investor predicts $r_M \leq r$ (or $r_M > r$). Then $p_1 = q$ and $p_2 = 1 - q$, so that $p_1 + p_2 = 1$, again indicating no forecasting skill. Suppose $p(1)$ is the unconditional probability of a successful forecast by manager 1 and $p(2)$ is the unconditional probability of 1 by manager 2. It also follows from this that just because $p(1) > p(2)$, that does not by itself imply that the market forecasts of manager 1 are more valuable than the forecasts of manager 2. In short, Merton concludes: "It is not so much how *often* the market timer is correct, but *when* he is correct that determines the value of his forecasts" (p. 388).

In a sequel paper, Roy D. Henriksson and Robert C. Merton, in [Henriksson-Merton (1981)] "On Market Timing and Investment Performance II: Statistical Procedures for Evaluating Forecasting Skills," *Journal of Business* 54, No. 4 (October 1981), pp. 513–533, go on to implement Merton's performance measure empirically. First, they assume that the manager's forecasts are observable. In that case, implementation is simply a matter of counting the number of times the manager timed the market successfully in down markets (say n_1 times out of a total of N_1), and the number of times he was successful in up markets (say n_2 times out of a total of N_2). n_1/N_1 is then an estimate of p_1, and n_2/N_2 is an estimate of p_2. However, in many real-life situations, the manager's forecasts cannot be observed, and performance must be inferred using only the time series of fund returns. In that case, Henriksson and Merton are forced to use a parametric test. Their test adds an extra term to the market model regression (Markowitz 1959 and Sharpe 1963), which instead of being the market return squared, as in Treynor-Mazuy (1966), is the payoff of a put on the market with strike price r. They also show that their technique is exempt from the argument made by Michael C. Jensen, in [Jensen (1972)] "Optimal Utilization of Market Forecasts and the Evaluation of Investment Performance," in *Mathematical Methods of Investment and Finance*, edited by Giorgio P. Szego and Karl Shell (Amsterdam: North Holland, 1972), that using returns alone, performance from market timing and security selection skills cannot be separated.

1984 **Richard Roll,** "Orange Juice and the Weather," *American Economic Review* 74, No. 5 (December 1984), pp. 861–880.

1986 **Kenneth R. French** (March 10, 1954–) and **Richard Roll,** "Stock Return Variances: The Arrival of Information and the Reaction of Traders," *Journal of Financial Economics* 17, No. 1 (September 1986), pp. 5–26.

1988 **Richard Roll,** "R^2," *Journal of Finance* 43, No. 3 (July 1988), pp. 541–566, Presidential Address to the American Finance Association.

1989 **William G. Schwert,** "Why Does Stock Market Volatility Change over Time?" *Journal of Finance* 45, No. 5 (December 1989), pp. 1115–1153.

2001 **John J. Binder** and **Matthias J. Merges,** "Stock Market Volatility and Economic Factors," *Review of Quantitative Finance and Accounting* 17, No. 1 (July 2001), pp. 5–26.

EFFICIENT MARKETS,
WEEKEND VS. TRADING DAY VARIANCE,
EXCESS VOLATILITY

A key issue in the controversy over rational markets is whether the volatility of stock returns can be explained by rational economic factors. In one of the earliest articles, Robert R. Officier, in [Officier (1973)] "The Variability of the Market Factor of the New York Stock Exchange," *Journal of Business* 46, No. 3 (July 1973), pp. 434–453, uses monthly returns over nonoverlapping 12-month periods from 1919 to 1968, and finds that regressing the realized volatility of stock returns against the contemporaneous volatility of industrial production has an R^2 of .261.

Roll (1984) argues that variation in the prices of orange juice futures should largely be determined by the weather, yet he finds that, although the weather affects these prices, its effect is much less than expected. Roll (1988) expands this type of analysis in his Presidential Address to the American Finance Association, published as "R^2"—a clever pun on his initials. Here he examines how much the price movements of stocks can be explained by aggregate economic variables, the returns on other stocks in the same industry, and publicly announced firm-specific news. He finds an R^2 of only .35 for monthly returns and .2 for daily returns, suggesting that much of the price movement may be irrational.

Fama (1965) was one of the first to note the low volatility of stock returns over the weekend. Refining this observation, French-Roll (1986) show that stock volatility is much higher per hour (13 to 100 times) when exchanges are open than when they are closed. For example, three-day weekend variance is only slightly higher than single trading day variance. This would seem to contradict rational markets since it is hard to see why significantly more fundamental information becomes available when markets are open than when they are closed. In fact, Niederhoffer (1971) has provided evidence that world events are more likely to occur over the weekend (Saturday and Sunday) than on any trading day (see his table 3, p. 200). However, information about fundamentals (cash flows) is not the only determinant of changing prices. Information about the demands of investors also affects prices. In a partially revealing rational expectations equilibrium (not contemplated in this paper), this information may be conveyed by the past and evolving history of prices and trading volume. This history may gradually reveal to each agent more about the private information, preferences, and endowments of other agents. In response, as each agent begins to modify his demands, prices may change much more than can be justified by any new fundamental information that becomes available. Obviously, only when markets are open can information be conveyed in this way. David P. Brown and Robert H. Jennings, in [Brown-Jennings (1989)] "On Technical Analysis," *Review of Financial Studies* 2, No. 4 (1989), pp. 527–551, make some progress toward formalizing a rational expectations equilibrium in which investors learn from both current and past prices.

Schwert (1989) uses daily returns over monthly periods on the Dow Jones Composite Portfolio from 1885 to 1927 and the S&P Composite Index from 1928 to 1987, and finds that regressing this market volatility against volatility of the growth rate in industrial production, the volatility of producer price inflation, financial leverage, and past volatility produces an R^2 of .57. However, most of this comes from past volatility, which is not necessarily a by-product of market rationality. Excluding this variable reduces his R^2 to only .208. In addition, he fails completely to explain the sustained significant increase in volatility during the Great Depression.

Binder-Merges (2001), using daily S&P Composite Index data from 1929 to 1989, regresses realized monthly volatility against the concurrent volatility of the general price level, the level of the riskless interest rate, the spread between Baa and Aaa corporate bonds (a proxy for the equity risk premium), and the ratio of expected corporate profits to expected corporate revenues (to capture the simultaneous effects of financial and operating leverage). A simple model shows that these are all rational factors that should determine market volatility. In particular, the last of the four variables can potentially explain the countercyclical behavior of market volatility (high in recessions, low in prosperity). They find that these variables are all statistically significant and have an R^2 of .512, and that their fourth variable keeps the regression on target even during the Great Depression (however, their regression fails to explain the October 1987 crash).

1985 Rajnish Mehra and **Edward C. Prescott** (December 26, 1940–), "The Equity Premium: A Puzzle," *Journal of Monetary Economics* 15, No. 1 (March 1985), pp. 145–161.

1990 George M. Constantinides, "Habit Formation: A Resolution of the Equity Premium Puzzle," *Journal of Political Economy* 98, No. 3 (June 1990), pp. 519–543.

EQUITY RISK PREMIUM PUZZLE, CRRA INTERTEMPORAL CAPM,
TIME-ADDITIVE VOLATILITY, HABIT FORMATION,
VOLATILITY, EXCESS VOLATILITY, RISK AVERSION

Mehra-Prescott (1985) draw attention to an unfortunate prediction of the standard finance model based on constant relative risk-averse utility functions: For the empirically observed risk premium of the market portfolio to be as high as it is relative to empirically observed volatility of aggregate consumption, the risk aversion required of the representative investor would need to be unreasonably high. The paper also argues that a variety of generalizations of this basic model will not correct this problem, which the authors therefore term "a puzzle." Rubinstein (1976/Autumn) anticipated this result by showing in almost the same economy that the return of the market portfolio and the growth of aggregate consumption are perfectly positively correlated, differing only by a positive multiplicative constant, and therefore have the same logarithmic volatility.

Together with Robert J. Shiller, in [Shiller (1981)] "Do Stock Prices Move Too Much to Be Justified by Subsequent Changes in Dividends?," *American Economic Review* 71, No. 3 (June 1981), pp. 421–436, this paper marks a watershed in the financial theory of investments. From this point, the empirical predictions of the standard finance model (its implications, for example, for the size of risk premiums, the variability of the return of the market portfolio, and the level of interest rates) were taken more seriously. The bar had been raised. Those working in the field began to look for ways to adjust the standard model so that *all* its predictions were good approximations of reality. The search for a solution to the puzzle has spurred many attempts to extend the standard finance model in a number of different directions; and there have been many premature announcements of victory. As attempts to solve the puzzle are seemingly frustrated as new related puzzles appear, as more elaborate versions of the model with less degrees of freedom are proposed, and as more anomalous empirical evidence is unearthed, some react by searching for a new paradigm. The new paradigm, if it succeeds, will almost surely make a break from the insistence of the standard model on agent rationality. But 15 years later, even as the twentieth century drew to a close, whether the standard model could be saved or a new paradigm would be necessary was still very much in doubt.

Constantinides (1990) attempts to solve Mehra and Prescott's risk premium puzzle. He drops their assumption of noncomplementarity of preferences for consumption over time (that is, additive utility). To inject habit formation, Constantinides postulates an additive utility function of consumption over time where the utility of consumption at each date takes the form $(C_t - X_t)^\gamma$ and X_t equals an exponentially weighted average of past consumption $C_0, C_1, C_2, \ldots, C_{t-1}$. X_t can be regarded as the subsistence level of consumption at date t, below which the consumer/investor will take no chance of falling. This subsistence level builds in habit formation because it is an increasing function of past levels of consumption. This leads to a smoothing of consumption since the normal increase in the utility of consumption from greater utility is at least partially offset by a reduction in the utility of future consumption from raising the bar of the subsistence level. In turn, this leads to reduced variability of the growth rate of aggregate consumption relative to the variability of the return of the market portfolio, suggesting a potential rational explanation of the equity risk premium puzzle. Suresh M. Sundaresan, in [Sundaresan (1989)] "Intertemporally Dependent Preferences and Volatility of Consumption and Wealth," *Review of Financial Studies* 2, No. 1 (1989), pp. 73–89, derives very similar results.

In 2004, Prescott won the Nobel Prize in Economic Science for the study of how economic policy drives global business cycles.

1987   Douglas W. Diamond and **Robert E. Verrecchia,** "Constraints on Short-Selling and Asset Price Adjustment to Private Information," *Journal of Financial Economics* 18, No. 2 (June 1987), pp. 277–311.

2003   Harrison Hong and **Jeremy C. Stein,** "Differences of Opinion, Short-Sales Constraints, and Market Crashes," *Review of Financial Studies* 16, No. 2 (Summer 2003), pp. 487–525.

SHORT SALES, HETEROGENEOUS BELIEFS,
STOCK MARKET CRASHES, AGGREGATION OF INFORMATION,

RATIONAL EXPECTATIONS, SKEWNESS,
PUT-CALL PARITY RELATION, BUBBLES

An important objection to the Williams-Miller theory, as mentioned in a footnote by Figlewski (1981), p. 465, is that it contradicts rational expectations. This idea is thoroughly developed by Diamond-Verrecchia (1987) in possibly the most interesting paper written on the Williams (1938) and Miller (1977) hypothesis since 1977. If investors know that divergence of opinion with asymmetric short-selling restrictions tends to leave only the most optimistic investors trading in the market, then those investors should temper their optimism, implicitly trying to incorporate in current prices the information held by the more pessimistic investors who fail to trade because of short-sale restrictions. For example, it is hard to believe that investors will persistently overprice IPOs and never learn from their experience. So in the Diamond-Verrecchia model, stocks are not on average overpriced. The authors distinguish carefully between two types of short-selling constraints: (1) "short-prohibition" constraints, such as an institutional ban against short selling, which do not discriminate between optimistic or pessimistic investors, and (2) "short-restriction" constraints, such as a below-market rebate rate, which do discriminate. Only the latter type of short-selling constraint can create the asymmetric pricing response that is their chief innovative conclusion, to which I shall now turn.

Suppose, for some reason, perhaps not fully rational, some traders are optimistic and others pessimistic about individual stock returns. As in Williams-Miller, because of short-restriction constraints, the views of the pessimists are not clearly reflected in prices. However, because of rational expectations, all investors take into account the extent the bad news known by the pessimists is not reflected in prices, and correspondingly bid down prices to reflect an expectation of the unknown pessimistic information. So unlike the hypothesis of Williams-Miller, prices on average are not too high (or too low). However, and this is key, only the expected and not the actually known negative information is reflected in prices. During periods when the optimists subsequently receive bad news and prices fall, the rational traders would now expect some of those who were formerly pessimistic to enter as buyers and cushion the fall. However, occasionally there are periods when the negative information that was originally not reflected in prices is surprisingly bad. At these times, prices will fall much more than anticipated before the pessimists are ready to step in and buy—hence a stock market crash. Note that this effect is asymmetric since on the upside there is no hidden positive information not embedded in prices. So the Diamond-Verrecchia model contains the novel prediction that observed stock returns should be skewed to the left; that is, around the mean, large downward changes should be more frequent than correspondingly large upward changes.

The Diamond-Verrecchia model also provides a good example of a more general issue that surely must characterize realistic financial markets: With dispersed fundamental information but some constraint on trade, market prices, contrary to Hayek (1945), will not reflect pooled investor wisdom; rather, over time trading itself will gradually reveal this dispersed fundamental information and only then will it find itself completely embedded in prices. In the meantime, prices can change rationally even in the absence of news concerning fundamentals. This view offers a rational way to explain the evidence of French-Roll (1986) that stock volatility is much higher when exchanges are open than when they are closed. David Romer, in [Romer (1993)] "Rational Asset-Price Movements without News," *American Economic Review* 83, No. 5 (December 1993), pp. 1112–1230, presents alternative ways that do not rely on constrained short sales by which rationally set prices can move in the absence of fundamental news. These ideas suggest that much of the excessive volatility that behavioralists hold out as evidence of marketwide irrationality is actually required in a rational market where investors use price trends, volume, and other technical information such as short interest to learn about dispersed fundamental information that is not yet embedded in current prices.

Of course, while rational expectations are often held out as an assumption that good finance models must not contradict, many intelligent observers believe that as a practical matter, rational expectations often fail to explain real-world behavior and should not be taken too seriously. If, as Figlewski (1981) supports, the percentage short interest is a good proxy for belief dispersion, then a clear test of the Williams-Miller theory versus the Diamond-Verrecchia rational expectations modification would be to examine whether announcements of significant increases in short interest forecast lower future returns (Williams-Miller) or whether prices immediately adjust downward synchronous with the announcement (Diamond-Verrecchia). In Diamond-Verrecchia, since investors cannot distinguish ordinary sells from short sales just by observing the order flow, news of increased short interest, since it effectively reveals the pessimistic information, when it becomes available should immediately lead to a downward revision in stock prices. In addition, days of relatively little trading volume may be another indicator of greater dispersion of beliefs than usual and therefore may play an informational role similar to that of announced increased short interest in depressing prices.

A.J. Senchack Jr. and Laura T. Starks, in [Senchack-Starks (1993)] "Short-Sale Restrictions and Market Reaction to Short-Interest Announcements," *Journal of Financial and Quantitative Analysis* 28, No. 2 (June

1993), pp. 177–194, test just such an implication of the Diamond-Verrecchia model: Since would-be short sellers are assumed to have pessimistic information generally not accurately reflected in prices (that is, only an unbiased guess about this information is embedded in prices), news of increases in short sales should reduce the previous relative optimism of the holders of these securities, and the prices of the securities should fall. Moreover, the significant cost that short sellers can face suggests that to go short one must typically have very negative information. As I have argued, this is not a prediction of the Williams-Miller hypothesis since in that context investors do not learn from the trading of other investors. The obvious test is to examine whether changes in recently announced short interest are negatively correlated with contemporaneous returns. Senchack and Starks not only confirm this implication empirically, they also show that the correlation is much less pronounced for stocks with exchange-traded options, which permit indirect short selling, again confirming another implication of the Diamond-Verrecchia model.

A very similar model to Diamond-Verrecchia is contained in the more recent article, Hong-Stein (2003). Hong and Stein argue that this model is capable of explaining three virtually defining features of crashes:

1. The post–World War II empirical fact that of the 10 largest moves in stock prices, nine have been down (the one increase was two days after the October 19, 1987, crash).
2. That most of these moves have not seemed to be accompanied by sufficiently significant public news to justify the price movement (this has been particularly remarked about the largest of these crashes, in 1987).
3. That correlation across stocks, both domestically and internationally, seems to increase sharply and suddenly during a crash.

It is easy to see why the first two features are consistent with their short-selling model, as they are with Diamond-Verrecchia. In turn, the third is explained if declines in some stocks reveal the presence of unexpectedly negative systematic (or marketwide) information heretofore hidden by short-sale constraints. Related to the first feature are the empirical observations, both from time series and from option-implied probability distributions, that stock index returns are negatively skewed, and that this negative skewness attenuates at longer time horizons. Both these observations would also be predicted from the Hong-Stein model.

Their model also predicts that abnormally high trading volume should accompany large negative stock market moves more than large positive stock market moves. This association between negative return skewness and trading volume is tested and confirmed in [Chen-Hong-Stein (2001)]

Joseph Chen, Harrison Hong, and Jeremy C. Stein, "Forecasting Crashes: Trading Volume, Past Returns, and Conditional Skewness in Stock Prices," *Journal of Financial Economics* 61, No. 3 (September 2001), pp. 345–381. This result is also supported in the domain of option-implied stock distributions by Patrick Dennis and Stewart Mayhew, in [Dennis-Mayhew (2002)] "Risk-Neutral Skewness: Evidence from Stock Options," *Journal of Financial and Quantitative Analysis* 37, No. 3 (September 2002), pp. 471–493, who conclude that periods of larger than usual implied negative skewness in stock returns also tend to be periods with abnormally high market volatility. As Hong and Stein point out, other types of crash explanations fail to explain either the asymmetry, that is, why large post–World War II jumps in the United States seem to occur primarily on the downside (behavioral theories), or why crashes tend to occur without apparent significant public news (volatility feedback theories). Only the short-selling explanation coupled with investor heterogeneity seems to deal with all three of the defining features of crashes that they identify. However, to illustrate that the world is never so simple as one would like, the observation remains unexplained that skewness of returns, both time-series and option-implied, is negative for stock index returns while being positive or at least much less negative for individual component stocks. At the conclusion of their paper, Hong and Stein write:

> This article can be seen as part of a recent resurgence of theoretical and empirical interest in the general topic of how short-sale constraints shape stock prices. . . . This work is also beginning to suggest that short-sale constraints may play a bigger role than one might have guessed based on just the direct transactions costs associated with shorting. . . . There remains much to be done, both in terms of developing a fuller understanding of why so many investors behave as if they were facing prohibitive shorting costs, and of exploring the consequences of such behavior for stock prices. (p. 516)[2]

Perhaps the greatest puzzle surrounding the relationship between short selling and stock prices, as Hong and Stein suggest, is one of demand: Why is so little stock is shorted? During 1976–1993, for example, more than 80 percent of all NYSE stocks had short interest of less than 0.5 percent of their outstanding shares. Figlewski (1981) reports that even the top decile from a universe of over 400 S&P 500 companies from 1973 to 1979 had an average short-interest percentage of less than 1 percent. However, it appears from Ofek-Richardson (2003) that short interest has dramatically increased in recent years. For their sample of about 4,200 U.S. stocks in February

2000, the average percentage of short interest to shares outstanding was about 2 percent. (Ofek and Richardson emphasize that Internet stocks had a significantly higher short-interest percentage closer to 3 percent. The highest 5 percent of Internet stocks had a short-interest percentage of about 10.5 percent, with only about a 0.5 percent annualized rebate rate when the rebate rate to the short seller for a normal stock was over 5.0 percent.) How can this bias be explained? Even with symmetric short-selling conditions, there are many reasons to expect significantly less short than long interest:

- Since a long position must preexist equal to the number of outstanding shares and a short sale must give rise to an additional exactly offsetting long position, the number of shorted shares must necessarily be less than shares held long.
- In a market with identical investors, since they would all hold the same marketwide index fund, there would be no desire to short. Even in the standard finance equilibrium model, the CAPM, no investor sells any stock short.
- Starting from that default, an investor with somewhat relatively pessimistic beliefs can assert these by taking less of a long position without needing to go so far as to short.
- For many securities, short selling can be accomplished by trading in their derivatives (selling futures, selling calls, or buying puts). Using back-of-the-scratch-pad estimates in October 2003, while the short-interest percentage (that is, percentage of shorts to outstanding shares) is typically about 2 percent for stocks with listed options, the aggregate amount of open interest including exchange-traded delta-adjusted calls and puts on stock indexes and individual stocks, as well as stock index futures, adds about another 4 percent to the typical direct short interest, bringing it to about 6 percent (if the implicit short positions of open derivative positions are included).

Detailed published estimates of the extent of the loss of the interest on the proceeds of short sales is now finally available in a recent article by Charles M. Jones and Owen A. Lamont, in [Jones-Lamont (2002)] "Short-Sale Constraints and Stock Returns," *Journal of Financial Economics* 66, Nos. 2–3 (November/December 2002), pp. 207–239. The estimates cover 1926–1933, when there was briefly a centralized market on the NYSE for borrowing stocks. These authors then use these estimates to test the Miller prediction (and I think implicitly Williams as well) that stocks with high barriers to short sales should be overpriced and experience lower subsequent returns. They find that the overpricing of stocks that are expensive to short is sufficiently large to produce profits to short sellers even after subtracting these costs.

Supplementing Jones and Lamont, Gene D'Avolio, in [D'Avolio (2002)] "The Market for Borrowing Stock," *Journal of Financial Economics* 66, Nos. 2–3 (November/December 2002), pp. 271–306, also documents the costs of short selling using 18 months during 2000–2001 of transactions obtained from a large stock-lending intermediary. He again confirms the Williams-Miller hypothesis for a number of proxies for large differences of opinion—high share turnover, large dispersion of analysts' forecasts, high visibility among unsophisticated investors, high P/E ratios, and low cash flows relative to stock price (these latter two create increased uncertainty and room for differences of opinion). D'Avolio also reports that forced premature covering of short positions affects about 2 percent of lent stocks each month across his sample. But the costs of shorting, inclusive of lost interest and potential forced covering, just don't seem significant enough to explain the low incidence of short sales (even if the implicit short sales via derivatives are included), particularly for large S&P 500 companies for which these costs are quite low.

A related supply puzzle is why more investors don't take advantage of opportunities to lend their stock. In [Almazon-Brown-Carlson-Chapman (2004)] "Why Constrain Your Mutual Fund Manager?", *Journal of Financial Economics* 73, No. 2 (August 2004), pp. 289–321, Andres Almazon, Keith C. Brown, Murray Carlson, and David A. Chapman report that 70 percent of institutional managers are precluded from short selling by contract, and of those that remain only 10 percent actually short sell. Despite this, on occasion the payment for security lending becomes so high that it would seem that no one holding the stock long should not be lending it. For example, the recent spin-off of Palm by 3Com implied significant returns to stock lending. At the beginning of March 2000, 3Com spun off 5 percent of a wholly owned subsidiary, Palm, Inc., stating (and there was virtually no doubt this would happen) that it would distribute the remaining 95 percent of Palm shares on July 27. At that time, for each 3Com share, a shareholder would receive 1.483 shares of Palm. This suggests that 3Com's shares should be worth at least 1.483 times the price of Palm's shares. To take a typical day, on April 18, the following prices were being quoted by Charles Schwab:

$$3\text{Com } \$39^3/_8 \qquad \text{Palm } \$30^1/_2$$

Under these circumstances, an arbitrage opportunity would seem to exist: For each share of 3Com that you buy, short 1.483 shares of Palm:

Cash flow on April 18: $-\$39.375 + 1.483(\$30.50) = \$5.85$ (received)

Cash flow on July 27: 0 (since cover short with distribution of Palm)

However, Palm was very expensive to short. Indeed, instead of receiving interest on the proceeds of the short sale, the short seller received no interest and actually had to pay a fee on top. As it turned out, the fee demanded by lenders of Palm (about $5.85) was exactly enough to make the arbitrage opportunity disappear.

As an alternative, one could have tried to short indirectly using exchange-traded Palm options. From the put-call parity relation (Stoll 1969),

$$-S_0 = P_0 - C_0 + Kr^{-t}$$

That is, a short position in a stock with current price S_0 and with no payouts (Palm did not pay dividends) can be replicated by buying a European put with current price P_0 and selling a European call with current price C_0 on the stock, both with the same strike price K and time to expiration t (r being the return on a riskless zero-coupon bond maturing after time t). On April 18, estimating $r = 1.06$ and using this equation to imply the stock value from option prices:

Option	t	K	C_0	P_0	Implied S_0
Aug 25	.33425	25	7.125	5.375	26.27
Aug 30	.33425	30	4.675	8.35	25.85
Aug 35	.33425	35	3.125	3.125	25.70

Therefore, the average implied stock value is ($26.27 + $25.85 + $25.70)/3 = $25.94. Short selling stock at this price indirectly through the options market unfortunately leads to a current cash flow from this arbitrage of:

$$-.39.38 + 1.483(\$25.94) = -\$0.91 \text{ (loss)}$$

So that wouldn't work, either. The options market had clearly caught on to the arbitrage and had aligned the prices of each put-call pair such that each implied about the same stock price for Palm, sufficiently low to eliminate the arbitrage. But the key puzzle remains: There must always be more shares held long than shorted. So there must be some who held Palm who did not lend it out. So one wonders why anyone who held Palm long did not try to lend his stock out and pick up a free $5.85 per share!

Further reflection shows that in the presence of security lending costs, the equilibrium price of a security (measured before considering these costs) could be indeterminate. To repeat the example given by Darrell Duffie, Nicolae Gârleanu, and Lasse Heje Pedersen, in [Duffie-Gârleanu-Pederson (2002)] "Securities Lending, Shorting and Pricing," *Journal of Fi-*

nancial Economics 66, Nos. 2–3 (November/December 2002), pp. 307–339, suppose optimists believe the value of a stock is $100 while pessimists believe its value is $90. If short selling were not possible, the optimists would determine the market price, which would then be $100. But suppose instead there were a market for lending the stock to the pessimists for short selling, and suppose the optimistic lenders had all the market power. In that case, since the pessimists would pay at most $10 ($100 – $90) to borrow the stock, the lending fee would be $10. But then optimists would be willing to pay $110 for the stock since they would now get $100 stock value plus the $10 lending fee. So the stock price would rise to $110. Now the pessimistic short sellers would be willing to borrow the stock for at most a $20 fee ($110 – $90), so the price could then rise to $120, and so on. This upward spiral would cease if eventually all the outstanding stock not yet lent out somehow ended up in the hands of investors who for some reason refused to lend their stock. Ironically, as the authors point out, the price of the stock with possible short selling can actually end up higher than if short selling were prohibited, and even higher than the value placed on it by the most optimistic investor in the market!

Rational market theorists might hope that in this lies the key to explaining the Internet bubble. In fact, as documented by Eli Ofek and Matthew Richardson, in [Ofek-Richardson (2003)] "DotCom Mania: The Rise and Fall of Internet Stock Prices," *Journal of Finance* 58, No. 3 (June 2003), pp. 1113–1137, the rebate rates for shorting Internet bubble stocks averaged 1 percent to 1.5 percent per annum less than for non-Internet stocks. Moreover, other signs of constrained short selling for Internet stocks included higher short interest and frequent put-call parity violations. Also, supporting the hypothesis of high belief dispersion is evidence the authors present that retail investors, in contrast to institutions, played a greater role than usual as buyers of Internet stocks. Unfortunately for rational market advocates, although providing some support for the Williams-Miller hypothesis, the magnitudes of these effects do not come close to explaining the rise phase of the bubble. Where were all the short sellers who, even with somewhat higher costs, should have stepped in with so much that was apparently to gain?

However, the authors also emphasize that something quite similar to temporarily very strong shorting restrictions may explain the collapse. An extraordinarily large amount of insider IPO-related stock that was locked up during the rising phase of the bubble (early 1998 to February 2000) became unlocked just as the bubble was collapsing (March 2000 to December 2000). This meant that for the first time relatively well-informed shareholders whose relative pessimism may have been hidden during the rise now entered the market, and their selling may have at least precipitated the collapse, which then subsequently became fed by the previously optimistic investors who now began to factor the implied beliefs of the new traders into their calculations.

1994 Mark Rubinstein, "Implied Binomial Trees," *Journal of Finance* 49, No. 3 (July 1994), pp. 771–818, Presidential Address to the American Finance Association.

DERIVATIVES, OPTIONS, OPTION PRICING,
BINOMIAL OPTION PRICING MODEL, IMPLIED BINOMIAL TREES,
RECOMBINING BINOMIAL TREES, WORKING BACKWARDS,
STATE-PRICES, STOCHASTIC VOLATILITY

The binomial option pricing model of Cox-Ross-Rubinstein (1979) and Rendleman-Bartter (1979) assumes that the up and down returns of the underlying risky security are the same at every node in the binomial tree describing the evolution of the price of the security. This leads to a recombining tree and a binomial distribution of prices at the end of the tree that is shown to converge to a lognormal distribution as the time between successive nodes goes to zero. Unfortunately, many securities do not have prices that are adequately approximated by risk-neutral lognormality. Indeed, exchange-traded European options on popular stock market indexes have prices that cannot be rationalized by the Black-Scholes formula. To deal with this problem, Rubinstein (1994) allows the binomial returns to be different at all nodes in the tree, but he still retains the feature of the standard binomial model that, at the end of the tree, at a given node, the risk-neutral probability of all paths leading to that node is the same. He shows that, with this generalization, it is possible to value options with arbitrary expiration-daterisk-neutral distributions of their underlying asset price and yet be consistent with a recombining tree in which the backwards recursive procedure conveniently unravels the current value of the option.

A second part of the paper develops an algorithm for recovering the expiration-date risk-neutral distribution from the pre-expiration-date market prices of several standard European options trading on the same underlying asset with the same maturity (they differ only in strike prices). Breeden-Litzenberger (1978) had already shown how this could be done from an infinite number of options with a continuum of strike prices from zero to infinity. By using a quadratic programming approximation technique, Rubinstein adapts this inference to practical situations where only a finite number of options are available.

Taken together, the paper shows how to recover from options not just the state-price distribution corresponding to a given future date, but also the entire stochastic process of state-prices over time that gives rise to that terminal distribution. Compared to Black-Scholes (1973), Cox-Ross-Rubinstein (1979), and Rendleman-Bartter (1979), who assume a constant local volatility, this generalization permits the volatility of the underlying asset to be a function of the concurrent underlying asset price and time. Even with this generalization, the recovered stochastic process is still limited to the class of recombining time-dependent Markov processes.

1995   James A. Ohlson, "Earnings, Book Values, and Dividends in Equity Valuation," *Contemporary Accounting Research* 11, No. 2 (Spring 1995), pp. 661–687.

> DIVIDENDS, EARNINGS, DIVIDEND DISCOUNT MODEL,
> CLEAN-SURPLUS RELATION,
> ABNORMAL EARNINGS DISCOUNT MODEL,
> INVESTMENT OPPORTUNITIES APPROACH,
> ECONOMIC VALUE ADDED (EVA)

Security analysts and academic accountants have long sought a convenient way to use the information commonly found in accounting statements to determine the value of stocks. With this objective, it is difficult to be grateful for the advice from Williams (1938) that one should simply discount the value of future dividends over the remaining life of a firm. As Ohlson (1995) puts it:

> [T]he paper highlights the key role of accounting data when one tries to come to grips with an apparent paradox in neoclassical security valuation: the present value of expected dividends determines a firm's value, yet the prediction of the dividend sequence is basically irrelevant if the underlying dividend policy is irrelevant. (Who wants to predict next year's expected dividends when all dividend policies yield the same market value?)[3]

One way to accomplish this is to make future dividends a function of current dividends, as in the Williams (1938) perpetual dividend growth model, but this is not satisfactory since the sequence of future dividends can be changed without altering the current stock value. One is tempted to discount future earnings, but this suffers from double counting. Ohlson tries to find a way around this. For simplicity, he assumes risk neutrality and starts with the dividend discount model: $P_0 = \Sigma_t E[D_t]/r^t$, where the sum is taken from 1 to ∞, and the dividends D_t can be thought of as dividends net of capital contributions. He uses what accountants call the "clean-surplus relation" to substitute other accounting variables for dividends: $Y_t = Y_{t-1} + X_t - D_t$, which says that book value at date t equals book value at date $t-1$ plus date t earnings minus date t dividends. Substituting for D_t in the present value formula:

$$P_0 = Y_0 + \Sigma_t E\left(\frac{X_t - r^* Y_{t-1}}{r^t} \right)$$

where the summation is taken from 1 to ∞ and $r^* \equiv r - 1$. The expression in parentheses may be interpreted as "abnormal earnings" since it is earnings over and above a fair return on book value. The formulation, to this point, can be found in [Preinreich (1938)] Gabriel A.D. Preinreich, "Annual Survey of Economic Theory: The Theory of Depreciation," *Econometrica* 6, No. 3 (July 1938), pp. 219–241 (see particularly p. 240), and appeared even earlier and perhaps originally in *Appeals and Review Memorandum* 34, United States Treasury Department (1920).

Note that this formulation is quite close to the stream of earnings approach of Miller-Modigliani (1961):

$$P_0 = \Sigma_t \left(\frac{X_t - \Sigma_\tau r^* I_\tau}{r^t} \right)$$

where the first summation is taken from 1 to ∞, the second summation is taken from 1 to t, and I_t is investment at date t, except that it is written in terms of the time series of book values rather than of investment. Ohlson's formulation is also similar to the investment opportunities approach of Miller-Modigliani (1961):

$$P_0 = \frac{X_0}{r^*} + \frac{\Sigma_t I_t (\rho_t - r^*) / r^*}{r^t}$$

where the summation is taken from 1 to ∞, X_0 is earnings at date 0, and ρ_t is the annualized rate of return on the investment undertaken at date t. It is easy to see that $X_0/r^* = Y_0 + Y_0(\rho_0 - r^*)/r^*$ where ρ_0 is the rate of return earned on date 0 book value.

Ohlson then assumes either that (1) abnormal earnings themselves are independent of dividends, or more fundamentally that (2) I_t and ρ_t (investment policy) are independent of dividends, or that (3) changes that dividends cause in investment are value-neutral. For example, the return on investment financed by paying less dividends can earn only return r^*. In any of these cases, of course, P_0 will then be independent of dividend policy. That this should be true under (1) is obvious, and that this should be true under (2) follows from the analysis of Miller-Modigliani (1961), and (3) follows from Brennan (1971) and Rubinstein (1976/September). Any of these assumptions would follow from the more fundamental notion that a stock-price-maximizing firm should not let dividend policy dictate its investment policy.

To finish the task of making the current stock price depend only on concurrent accounting information, Ohlson then assumes that (1) abnormal earnings are a linear function of the most recent past abnormal earnings, information other than abnormal earnings, and noise; and (2) that this other information is itself a linear function of its previous level and noise. This specification is quite arbitrary and its efficacy clearly depends on empirical verification. This approach of linking future information determining present value to current information can be viewed as a more sophisticated version of the Williams (1938) perpetual dividend growth model, which assumes that future dividends are a simple function of current dividends.

In the light of earlier work, I conclude then that Ohlson's paper makes very little contribution to theory. Nonetheless, his paper has made an important contribution to subsequent empirical research by reorienting the way accounting data is used to explain stock prices. Previously, this line of research either used accounting data with no constraint imposed by the dividend discount model to explain prices, or if this constraint were imposed and earnings were forecast, dividends were assumed to be some simple (perhaps linear) function of earnings. Ohlson's approach, within the constraint of the dividend discount model, does not bother with forecasting dividends even indirectly, but instead forecasts abnormal earnings or its determinants. Victor I. Bernard, in [Bernard (1995)] "The Feltham-Ohlson Framework: Implications for Empiricists," *Contemporary Accounting Research* 11, No. 2 (Spring 1995), pp. 733–747, shows empirically that the cross-sectional variation in stock prices is far better explained by forecasts of abnormal earnings than direct forecasts of dividends.

Gerald A. Feltham and James A. Ohlson, in [Feltham-Ohlson (1995)] "Valuation and Clean Surplus Accounting for Operating and Financial Assets," *Contemporary Accounting Research* 11, No. 2 (Spring 1995), pp. 689–731, illustrate the theoretical advantages of the framework established by Ohlson. They apply clean-surplus accounting separately to financial assets and operating assets, assuming that market and book value for the former are equal. Not surprisingly, this leads to a present value relation in terms of book value and abnormal operating income that is similar to Ohlson's present value relation in terms of book value and abnormal earnings. One of the most interesting features of accounting earnings is its tendency (by design) to be biased, so that book value tends to be less than market value for most stocks. Feltham and Ohlson define conservative accounting mathematically as the property that the difference between market price and book value at date t is expected at fixed date $t_0 < t$ to be positive as $t \to \infty$. To tie future earnings to current earnings and book value, they adopt a linear time-series model with noise determining future operating earnings and operating assets and show how the time-series coefficients depend on whether accounting is unbiased or conservative.

Closely related to abnormal earnings is the concept of "residual income": net operating income after taxes minus the product of the overall cost of capital (debt plus equity) times the amount of capital (that is, assets net of depreciation and amortization invested in operations). Abnormal earnings and residual income are equivalent in the absence of debt financing. Stern Stewart & Company has successfully popularized an annual residual income measure trademarked EVA (economic value added), which considers a number of accounting modifications to net operating income such as amortizing research and development (R&D) and marketing expenditures, recording operating leases as an asset and offsetting liability, and converting last in, first out (LIFO) to first in, first out (FIFO) inventory accounting, and uses the CAPM to measure the overall cost of capital. Stern Stewart argues that these adjustments turn residual income into a number that measures the annual performance of management. Joel M. Stern, in [Stern (1999)] "Stern Stewart Roundtable on EVA in Europe," *Journal of Applied Corporate Finance* 11, No. 4 (Winter 1999), pp. 98–121, says:

> *So, even as finance professors were teaching their students that discounted cash flow and NPV were the primary determinants of value, EPS concerns continued to rule the day inside corporations. Why did companies reject NPV? The problem with NPV is that it is a multi-period, "stock" measure of value that does not lend itself to a single-period performance evaluation. EVA solved this problem by in effect decomposing NPV into annual—or even monthly—"installments" of value added. Over a sufficiently long period of time EVA and NPV give identical answers in evaluating performance. But because EVA is a "flow" rather than a "stock" measure, it can be used as the basis for a period-by-period performance evaluation and incentive system. (p. 102)[4]*

1995   Jonathan B. Berk (April 22, 1962–), "A Critique of Size-Related Anomalies," *Review of Financial Studies* 8, No. 2 (Summer 1995), pp. 275–286.

SIZE EFFECT, PRICED VS. NONPRICED FACTORS

The size anomaly had been regarded by many researchers as one of the most prominent contradictions of the current asset pricing paradigm in finance; see, for example, Eugene F. Fama and Kenneth R. French, in [Fama-French (1992)] "The Cross-Section of Expected Stock Returns," *Journal of Finance* 47, No. 2 (June 1992), pp. 427–465. The size anomaly is the finding that firm size (measured by market value) is inversely related to stock market returns. This size effect also extends to other size-related variables including the price-earnings ratio, the dividend yield, the debt-equity ratio, and the ratio of book value of equity to market value of equity. Many researchers simply concluded that somehow size must be a proxy for risk. Unfortunately, it has been difficult to come up with a theoretical justification for such a relationship between size and risk.

Berk (1995) provides a very clever explanation for why the size effect is really not an anomaly. Moreover, his explanation for the size anomaly does not rely on any particular relationship between firm size and risk. To understand it, consider two firms with the same expected future cash flows. If one of those firms is more risky than the other, then its current market value will be lower. This immediately implies that a firm with a lower market value will have a higher expected future return, consistent with the alleged size anomaly. As Berk shows, this result also implies that a firm's market value will add explanatory power to any asset pricing model that does not fully explain expected return. The beauty of this result is its simplicity and intuitive appeal.

Berk supports his theory with empirical tests in [Berk (1999)] "A View of the Current Status of the Size Anomaly," in *Security Market Imperfections and World Wide Equity Markets*, edited by Donald Keim and William Ziemba (Cambridge: Cambridge University Press, 1999). In one set of tests, Berk examines whether measures of size other than market value are related to a firm's average return. Under the conventional explanation of the size effect, there should be a relationship; under Berk's, there should not. The four measures of size that are used are book value of equity, sales, number of employees, and acquisition cost of property, plant, and equipment. Using tests similar to those employed to document the size effect, Berk finds no relationship between any of these measures and average returns, consistent with his theory.

1996 Jiang Wang, "The Term Structure of Interest Rates in a Pure Exchange Economy with Heterogeneous Investors," *Journal of Financial Economics* 41, No. 1 (May 1996), pp. 75–110.

AVERAGE OR REPRESENTATIVE MAN, AGGREGATION, CAUTIOUSNESS, CONSTANT RELATIVE RISK AVERSION (CRRA)

Until 1996, closed-form aggregation results in a competitive pure-exchange economy appeared to limit the heterogeneity of investors to utility functions of identical "cautiousness," as in Rubinstein (1974). For example, Bernard Dumas, in [Dumas (1989)] "Two-Person Dynamic Equilibrium in the Capital Market," *Review of Financial Studies* 2, No. 2 (Summer 1989), pp. 157–188, considers an economy of two investors, one with logarithmic utility and the other with power utility. In this case, the allocation of wealth across investors now affects equilibrium prices. Although Dumas succeeds in deriving some comparative statics results, he is not able to derive closed-form solutions.

Thought to be impossible, Wang (1996) nonetheless derives closed-form equilibrium results in an economy under uncertainty where investors individually have CRRA utility functions but of different powers. For example, he considers an economy with just two consumer/investors, one with logarithmic utility and one with square-root utility. And he shows that for certain other specific combinations of powers, closed-form results are possible. He then asks how the results are qualitatively different from an economy with a CRRA representative agent.

1997 Mark M. Carhart, "On Persistence in Mutual Fund Performance," *Journal of Finance* 52, No. 1 (March 1997), pp. 57–82.

1997 Kent Daniel, Mark Grinblatt, Sheridan Titman, and **Russ Wermers,** "Measuring Mutual Fund Performance with Characteristic-Based Benchmarks," *Journal of Finance* 52, No. 3 (July 1997), pp. 1035–1058.

2000 Russ Wermers, "Mutual Fund Performance: An Empirical Decomposition into Stock-Picking, Talent, Style, Transactions Costs, and Expenses," *Journal of Finance* 55, No. 4 (August 2000), pp. 1655–1695.

MUTUAL FUND PERFORMANCE, PERSISTENCE,
THREE- VS. FOUR-FACTOR MODEL, ALPHA,
MOMENTUM, LUCK VS. SKILL

Using a four-factor Fama-French (1992)-style model (where a one-year momentum factor has been added to the three Fama-French factors—the excess return of a value-weighted market index and the return on value-weighted, zero-investment, factor-mimicking portfolios for size and book-to-market equity), Carhart (1997) calculates a Jensen (1968)-style alpha for a sample of 1,892 diversified equity mutual funds over the period 1962–1993, free of survivorship bias since the sample contains all known funds over the period. The four-factor model does a much better job than the single-factor CAPM or the three-factor Fama-French model in matching the returns of managed portfolios. He finds that, after correcting for the four factors and persistent differences in trading costs and management fees, there is very little evidence of persistent skill in stock selection, and any remaining small persistence disappears after one year. He also argues that although funds do show higher returns from following momentum-based strategies, most of these returns seem to be by chance since the funds automatically find themselves with larger positions in the previous year's winning stocks. He also claims that mutual funds do not earn back their expenses in the form of higher returns; in fact, for every 1.5 basis points of additional management expense, the fund recoups only 1 basis point of return, and increases in turnover also reduce net returns.

When a professional portfolio manager proposes an investment strategy based on fundamental analysis of equities, the presumption is that he or she expects the strategy to outperform simpler, purely mechanical, strategies based on stock characteristics like book-to-market, size, and momentum. As companies like Vanguard have demonstrated, simple mechanical portfolio strategies can be implemented at substantially lower cost than the more subjective strategies used by most mutual funds. Therefore, if the active mutual funds fail to beat the mechanical strategies, they may be wasting resources.[5]

With this justification, Daniel-Grinblatt-Titman-Wermers (1997) tries to improve preexisting methods for mechanically replicating the performance of individual mutual funds. Previous work such as Jensen (1968) and Martin J. Gruber, in [Gruber (1996)] "Another Puzzle: The Growth in Actively Managed Mutual Funds," *Journal of Finance* 51, No. 3 (July 1996), pp. 783–810, Presidential Address to the American Finance Association, determined the effect of market, size, and growth factors by regressing the fund's portfolio return against these factors. Instead, using data on fund holdings, Daniel, Grinblatt, Titman, and Wermers first match stock returns to three factors—market value of equity, book-to-market ratio, and the prior years' returns—and then aggregate up to portfolios by weighting the stock exposures by the value weights in the fund. This approach has several advantages: (1) it provides a better match between fund returns and mechanical strategies, leaving less unexplained fund returns, and (2) it allows decomposition of total fund returns into fund returns from "average style," "characteristic selectivity," and "characteristic timing," which together sum to the total fund return. Specifically, using all New York Stock Exchange, American Stock Exchange, and Nasdaq stocks, at the beginning of each quarter these are grouped into three quintiles based on size, book-to-market ratio, and momentum. This 5 by 5 by 5 sorting produces 125 value-weighted portfolios. Each quarter, each stock is then matched to the single passive portfolios with same values for all three factors. The "characteristic selectivity" return is then the difference between the realized return over the quarter for the stock and its matching portfolio. A fund's return over a longer period is then simply the compound return, so measured, over constituent quarters.

Their results on "characteristic selectivity" are similar to Carhart's alpha, but they attribute to it somewhat higher fund returns and have greater statistical significance. They confirm Carhart's conclusion that a fund's persistence is almost completely explained by its average exposure to the three factors, and report that there is no evidence of returns from timing characteristics. They also show that most of the superior stock selectivity is concentrated in the first five years of their 20-year (1975–1994) sample period.

The historical performance of equity mutual funds is perhaps the most significant empirical evidence bearing on the hypothesis that prices in developed financial markets are determined rationally. Unlike most other empirical evidence bearing on this issue, mutual fund performance is based on actual, not paper, profits. It bypasses the issue of whether various anomalous strategies can actually be implemented; whatever strategies the mutual funds followed were, of course, implemented. Provided care is taken to correct for survivorship bias, there is little danger of data mining or other empirical problems. We can argue as long as we like about whether a legitimate successful strategy should have been discovered in a rational market, given the costs of research and the technology then existing, and we will not know. But we can look at the results of 60 years of investing by thousands of smart and highly compensated individuals who spent most of their waking hours studying markets. If these individuals could not beat the market, then at least we can say it is very difficult to do so. Several performance issues have been examined:

1. Can the average mutual fund outperform standard widely diversified market indexes such as the S&P 500?

2. Even if the answer to question 1 is no, is there statistically significant evidence that any small group of mutual funds has outperformed the market averages by skill?
3. Is there any evidence of mutual fund performance persistence?
4. To the extent mutual funds experience different net performance than an index fund (such as the Vanguard S&P 500 Index Fund), how much of this performance can be attributed to: (1) stock selection, (2) market timing, (3) differences in investment style, (4) differences in trading costs and turnover, (5) differences in management fees, (6) differences in the percentage of assets held in cash?

From the point of view of an investor deciding between investing in a passively or actively managed fund, the answers to all the questions are important. For example, suppose the average active fund underperforms the market average (question 1). Even if some mutual funds outperform the market by skill (question 2), if the funds do not exhibit performance persistence (question 3), it may be impossible to identify the superior-performing funds in advance. Therefore, passive investment would be preferred. Or, even if an active mutual fund underperforms the market, it may do so with less risk (question 4) and still be the preferred investment. Evidence that suggests investors are divided on this issue is the fact in the year 2000 the two largest equity mutual funds were an actively managed fund, Fidelity Magellan, and a passively managed fund, Vanguard S&P 500 Index Fund.

Using a new database, Wermers (2000) is able to provide an answer to questions 1 and 4. He examines the entire universe of U.S. equity mutual funds from 1975 to 1994, a total of 1,788 distinct funds. His database contains both funds that survived the entire 20 years and those that disappeared due to liquidation or merger, and hence is free of the survivorship bias that has bedeviled many earlier studies. He limits his analysis only to funds holding diversified portfolios of U.S. equities (self-styled as "aggressive growth," "growth," "growth and income," or "balanced"), excluding international funds, bond funds, commodity funds, real estate funds, and other sector funds.

Wermers measures performance as if the entire mutual fund industry held a single portfolio, that is, a value-weighted average of the returns of the constituent funds. He measures these value-weighted returns quarterly and then compounds these quarterly returns to measure performance over longer intervals. He adjusts for three style factors: size, book-to-market ratio, and prior-year stock return (to capture momentum) using the stock-by-stock matching method taken from Daniel, Grinblatt, Titman, and Wermers (1997).

He attributes the average performance per year of these mutual funds to:

Center for Research in Securities Prices (CRSP) value-weighted return	15.60%
Holding benchmark style portfolios that outperform the market	+ 0.60
Holding stocks that outperform benchmark style portfolios	+ 0.71
Nonstock holdings	–0.70
Management expenses	–0.79
Trading costs	–0.80
Average net return	14.60%

The S&P 500 return over the same period was 15.4 percent—very close to the CRSP value-weighted return. Over almost the same period, the Vanguard S&P 500 Index Fund had management expenses of 0.28 percent and trading costs of 0.07 percent. So if we assume near-perfect tracking—a reasonable inference from Vanguard's reported annual results—Vanguard's average net return would have been 15.05 percent, giving it about a half a percent advantage over active management.

Wermers also finds that due to nonstock holdings, mutual funds tend to underperform market averages much more in high-return years than low-return years. He also finds that high-turnover funds tend to do better than low-turnover funds, which supports the value of active management.

Wermers' measured performance of active mutual funds is probably overstated for six reasons:

1. Some nonstock holdings may be a necessary by-product of efficient active investment.
2. It is likely that over the subsequent five-year period, 1995–1999, active funds performed even more poorly than usual relative to passive funds.
3. Breaking down the results into four sequential five-year periods, it appears that much of the superior performance of active funds occurred in the first five years, 1975–1979, when there were far fewer and much smaller funds; this, taken together with reason 2, means that during the more recent 20-year period 1979–1999, it is likely that passive funds significantly outperformed active funds.
4. The benchmark style portfolio may not fully correct for the risk of omitted factors such as liquidity.

5. For taxable investors, passive funds with their lower average turnover and perforce their tendency to realize less capital gains may have a significant tax advantage increment to their performance.

6. Load fees are not considered.

1999 **Jonathan B. Berk, Richard C. Green,** and **Vasant Naik,** "Optimal Investment, Growth Options, and Security Returns," *Journal of Finance* 54, No 5 (October 1999), pp. 1553–1607.

REAL OPTIONS, CAPITAL BUDGETING,
TIME-VARYING EXPECTED RETURNS

The idea that firm growth opportunities can be interpreted as options may first have been mentioned in passing in Fisher (1930) and then first formally considered in [Myers-Turnbull (1977)] Stewart C. Myers and Stuart M. Turnbull, "Capital Budgeting and the Capital Asset Pricing Model: Good News and Bad News," *Journal of Finance* 32, No. 2 (May 1977), pp. 321–333 (see particularly p. 332). Berk-Green-Naik (1999) develop a dynamic model of the firm in which the firm's option to invest in growth opportunities is explicitly modeled. Heretofore, the endogenous asset composition of a firm's balance sheet had been ignored in asset pricing theory, and yet one might have expected this to be a rich mine of theory for time-varying expected returns. This is all the more significant because the solution to several recent empirical puzzles has either been credited to investor behavioral biases or to time-varying expected returns. At the same time, the case for time-varying expected returns has been weakened by failure to provide sound theoretical reasons to justify the particular forms of variation required to explain the empirical puzzles.

This paper is one of the first to model time-varying expected returns from the ground up, so to speak, by distinguishing between assets in place and the value of options representing growth opportunities; see also Rubinstein (1983). This is possibly the most important cross-sectional and time-series feature of corporate assets for the purpose of explaining time-varying expected returns. The paper shows that the optimal exercise of the growth opportunities causes the firm's asset base and systematic risk to change in predictable ways. The paper then uses simulation to show that these dynamics can simultaneously explain a number of observed empirical findings, such as (1) the performance of contrarian investment strategies over short horizons, (2) the performance of momentum strategies over long horizons, (3) the inverse relation between interest rates and the market risk premium, and (4) the time-series and cross-sectional relationships among book value, market value, and asset returns. This paper should give behavioralists pause before abandoning the more traditional rationalist approach to finance; it provides an excellent illustration that the rationalist approach may only appear to fail because it is applied too naively.

2001 Alan Kraus and **Jacob Sagi**, "Aggregation of State Dependent Preferences When Markets Are Incomplete," unpublished working paper, Haas School of Business, University of California, Berkeley (2001).

PREFERENCE UNCERTAINTY, LEARNING, COMPLETE MARKETS, AGGREGATION

Kraus-Sagi (2001) investigates a promising and highly interesting generalization of standard multiperiod equilibrium models commonly used in finance. The authors generalize existing models by allowing consumers to be uncertain of their future preferences, a sort of failure to completely know themselves. Nonetheless, they are assumed to have probability assessments of possible future preferences that get increasingly refined as the future approaches. This lack of self-knowledge is captured by assuming that preferences depend on consumption (as usual) but also on an unspecified state-variable. In order to characterize the equilibrium, they cleverly assume that aspects of future states that affect prices can be hedged in a complete market, but they allow for aspects of future states that do not affect prices but still affect consumer utility to be uninsurable (and therefore to that extent the market is incomplete).

Quite generally, the additional state-variable could reflect (1) other exogenous aspects of the states that affect utility such as consumer health or the weather, (2) the future prices of commodities on which dollar consumption is to be spent, (3) the value of incompletely marketable assets such as human capital, (4) the results of as yet unperformed calculations, or, more simply, (5) an incomplete self-knowledge. However, it does not seem that this state-variable in the authors' model could depend on either the way in which the stochastic process of future investment opportunities evolves or the choices of other economic agents, as in keeping up with the Joneses.

Despite the very high level of generality of the model, a number of strong and somewhat surprising conclusions are reached. First, although market incompleteness (of their special type) does not affect the market price of risk (that is, the aggregate Sharpe ratio), it does affect the riskless return, and via that, the present value of future aggregate consumption (aggregate wealth), and by that route the equity risk premium. Second, even though the aggregate rate of time preference is stochastic, this uncertainty has no effect on the risk premium. Third, the volatility of aggregate relative risk aversion has a much greater influence on the equity risk premium than the level of aggregate relative risk aversion. Fourth, at least in an interesting special case, the greater the uncertainty surrounding the unspecified state-variable, the lower the equity risk premium. This result is unfortunate in the sense that one might have hoped that the generalizations in the paper would have helped explain the large size of the risk premium; but in fact, the paper makes the equity risk premium puzzle even more puzzling!

2003 **Dilip Abreu** and **Markus K. Brunnermeier**, "Bubbles and Crashes," *Econometrica* 71, No. 1 (January 2003), pp. 173–204.

2005 **Markus K. Brunnermeier** and **Jonathan Parker**, "Optimal Expectations," *American Economic Review* 95, No. 4 (September 2005), pp. 1092–1118.

BUBBLES, STOCK MARKET CRASHES,
INFORMED VS. UNINFORMED TRADERS,
SEPARATION OF PROBABILITIES AND PREFERENCES, FELICITY

The model in Abreu-Brunnermeier (2003) works like this: A "prebubble" starts at time t_0; at this point the market price begins to exceed the fully informed price. This can happen because many investors in the market are noise traders, perhaps trading foolishly on momentum; it really doesn't matter. At the same time there is a group, say, of informed traders. Because it takes time for information to diffuse in the market or time to analyze the information, these traders only gradually become informed that a bubble is in progress. In particular, imagine that there are 21 informed traders and assume that on each of the next 21 days exactly one new trader becomes informed that a finite-lived bubble is in progress. Each of these traders knows that there are exactly 21 traders who will eventually become informed. Suppose each trader has exactly one unit of capital and suppose it takes a total of 15 traders to break the bubble and each trader knows this. Also suppose that when a trader becomes informed, he does not know how many other traders are already informed (this is key).

The real bubble occurs when the informed traders in aggregate have enough capital to break the bubble—that is, 15 days after the prebubble started. Abreu and Brunnermeier claim that in general the bubble will not be broken at $t_0 + 15$ but more generally after that. This is the key claim of the paper, and I am not sure I understand it. Before getting to that, let me say that at this point I like the setup; it seems to mirror key features of real-world bubbles, and after $t_0 + 15$ we are in what I would regard as essentially a rational model where, before this paper, we would have expected the bubble to burst immediately. The generally accepted wisdom is as soon as there is enough arbitrage capital held by a sufficient number of traders to eliminate the arbitrage, it should be eliminated. But the authors say no, this will not generally happen.

Let us say that 14 traders have been informed a bubble is in progress. This will happen by day 14 from the beginning of the prebubble. Even if they all sold in aggregate they could not break the bubble. Now on day 15 the 15th trader is informed. He is the one who will end up breaking the bubble, but he doesn't know that. But knowing that there are 21 traders who will be eventually informed, he thinks that probably only 10 traders have already been informed, so his guess is that the bubble cannot yet be broken. But, of course, he is worried that since the bubble is in progress already it may break if he waits. So he has to trade off the expected loss versus the expected gain in waiting. One can well imagine that if the bubble price is going up fast enough at an accelerating rate, he may decide it is better to wait (in particular, his best guess is that it will be another 4 or 5 days before 15 traders are informed there is a bubble).

Brunnermeier-Parker (2005) take on what has long been a very interesting psychological (or behavioral, if you prefer) issue: a particular way many people let their probabilities be influenced by their preferences. When evaluating what they should do, they increase the probabilities of outcomes they prefer and decrease the probabilities of outcomes they don't like, and then act on the rational decision that emerges. An example is the belief in the afterlife that underlies most Western religions. First, people make the mistake of overestimating the probability there is some type of conscious existence after death; then they sign up for the tenets of some religion in order to maximize the utility of that existence when they get there. The net result is that during their life, they feel much better about everything they do believing that they will be ending up in some version of heaven. Even the most unbearable impoverished existence becomes bearable. But they have a trade-off. If that was all there was to it, they might have to live in a monastery and forgo earthly pleasures. The actual realized utility of that choice is sufficiently negative that they compromise by tasting but limiting their indulgence in the vices, to get the best of both worlds, so to speak.

Brunnermeier and Parker try to create a mathematical model of this type of departure from standard rationality and then examine its consequences for several issues primarily in finance. In a simple example of their more general model, in place of the standard expected utility of ending wealth $E[U(W)]$, they instead assume investors maximize "expected felicity," which is $E\{E^*[U(W)] + U(W)\}$. Here the first expectation is taken over the objective or true probabilities, and the embedded expectation is taken over the "optimal probabilities," which are actually those probabilities that maximize expected felicity, so they are endogenous to the problem. Not too surprisingly, the authors show that this investor tends to take more risk than the purely rational investor since he acts as if he believes expected returns are higher for the risky asset (he may even be seen gambling, heaven forbid!). In a multiple security context, we would expect the investor to be willing to hold portfolios that are much less diversified than a purely rational investor. In another example of a two-person exchange equilibrium, the authors assume that the two investors differ only in endowments. Because they maximize expected felicity, each wants to believe that his endowment is more valuable than the other's (in terms of state-securities, each would believe that the states where his endowment is concentrated are more likely to occur than those where it is not). What is particularly nice is that these heterogeneous beliefs that emerge in equilibrium are derived endogenously. Each investor wants to believe whatever will make him happiest. Gambling occurs here because of a disagreement about probabilities.

The authors suggest that this type of behavior could explain home bias. In a model of intertemporal savings and consumption, not surprisingly consumers would tend to consume more and save less than fully rational agents (agents are both overconfident in the sense that they underestimate risk, and unrealistically optimistic in the sense that they overestimate expected return). Every period consumers are inclined to be surprised that the consumption they end up choosing tends to be lower than they had previously expected. Forms of insurance are not as popular as they should be. It is even possible that introducing options to insure income, where before they did not exist, can actually reduce expected felicity. Agents in their models may also prefer to delay the resolution of uncertainty if they can. To be sure, there is no learning in these models, but the authors contend that continual overconfidence and optimism match many empirical observations.

Notes

PREFACE

1. Too recently discovered to be included in this history is a 1940 paper of the Italian mathematician Bruno de Finetti, predating Markowitz and Roy by 12 years, which formulates mean-variance portfolio theory, including a justification for measuring risk by portfolio variance, the equation relating the covariances of security returns to the portfolio variance of return, mean-variance efficient sets, and a critical line algorithm to numerically solve the portfolio selection problem. Although de Finetti's paper formulates the general quadratic programming problem including short-sale constraints for the general case, only an algorithm for solving it in the special case of uncorrelated returns is fully worked out. Written in Italian, the paper has remained unknown among financial economists until it was just recently brought to my attention and translated into English.

The Ancient Period: Pre-1950

1. A recently updated translation of the Archimedes palimpsest that contains his *Method* ends with a single page apparently beginning another work, which seems to concern combinatorics.
2. Pascal and Fermat go on to examine an important generalization that arises only when there are more than two players. Suppose player A needs 1 point to win and players B and C each need 2 points to win. Then the game requires a maximum of three more awarded points to determine the outcome. One such sequence is (abb). In this sequence, although both A and B would end up with the same number of points, the first player wins since he is the first player to accumulate the required number of points. This simple example illustrates the importance of what would much later be called "path dependence," a characteristic, for example, of an American option where different permutations of the same combination of serially realized returns of an underlying asset can lead to a different payoff to the buyer of the option.
3. As an aside that I cannot resist, it took more than 300 years before it was shown that Huygens might have a problem with this setup. Ivo Schneider, in "Christiaan Huygens' Non-probabilistic Approach to the Calculus of Games of Chance," *De Zeventiende Eeuw* 12, No. 1 (1996), pp. 171–185, first shows that this table describes the payoffs required by Huygens' assumptions. Each

player is seen to have an equal chance of receiving each of the three payoffs, *A*, *B*, or *C*, and the stakes are always all paid out to the players. But suppose we also naturally assume that when a player wins the stakes, after the side payments, he also wins in the sense that he has a greater payoff than the other two players. Then, there must be an inconsistency. To see this, if P1 wins in this sense, then clearly $A > B, C$. But then when P2 wins the stakes, after side payments he ends up with only $C < A$. Did Huygens, one of the most careful and mathematically sophisticated minds of his time, make an error? In spirit, perhaps, but technically no, since he does not explicitly state that $A > B, C$.

4. Savage (1954), pp. 94-95, apparently incorrectly, attributes the finding concerning bounded utility to Cramer's letter. A detailed analysis of the cause of Savage's error can be found in [Bassett (1987)] Gilbert W. Bassett Jr., "The St. Petersburg Paradox and Bounded Utility," *History of Political Economy* 19, No. 4 (1987), pp. 517–523. I learned of this from the economic historian, Joseph Persky, who asked the author to send me a copy of his paper.

5. Proceedings of the Berkeley Symposium on Mathematical Statistics and Probability by Kenneth Joseph Arrow/Jerzy Neyman. Copyright 1951 by the University of California Press. Reproduced with permission of University of California Press in the format Trade Book via Copyright Clearance Center.

6. Abraham de Moivre's [de Moivre (1738)] *The Doctrine of Chances* was first published in 1718. The second edition published in 1738 contains de Moivre's most important result, which he published separately in 1733 in seven pages as *Approximatio ad Summam Terminorum Binomii* $(a + b)^n$ *in Seriem Expansi,* the normal approximation to the binomial. An expanded third edition was published posthumously in 1756, reprinted (New York: Chelsea Publishing Company, 1967); a portion was originally published in Latin in 52 pages as "De Mensura Sortis" ("On the Measurement of Lots"), *Philosophical Transactions of the Royal Society* 27 (1710–1712), pp. 213–264.

De Moivre's contribution to mathematics has been substantial, including results in finite differences, the theory of infinite series, and a theorem from trigonometry that bears his name. His work on life annuities has assured him an honored place in the development of actuarial science and the theory of investments more generally. But clearly his most significant contribution is the earliest version of the central limit theorem, the normal approximation to the binomial. Here we see an example of Stephen Stigler's law that laws and formulas are never named after their original discover: The normal distribution is sometimes referred to as "Gaussian," after the great mathematician Carl Friedrich Gauss, who was born 23 years after de Moivre's death. The *Approximatio* was only discovered recently by Karl Pearson, which he describes in [Pearson (1924)] "Historical Note on the Origin of the Normal Curve of Errors," *Biometrika* 16, Nos. 3/4 (December 1924), pp. 402–404. The *Approximatio* contains the first known occurrence of the normal distribution, which was then widely distributed in English in 1738 as part of the second edition of de Moivre's *Doctrine of Chances*. The *Approximatio* also contains the first known statement of what is also incorrectly called Stirling's formula for approximating factorials: $n! \approx 2.5074(\sqrt{n})e^{-n}n^n$. Stirling's amendment to this was to replace 2.5074 with the exact expression $\sqrt{2\pi}$.

7. Jules Regnault in [Regnault (1863)] *Calcul des chances et philosophie de la Bourse* (Mallet-Bachelier et Castel, Paris, 1863) anticipated this result several decades earlier, deducing it from, of all things, the empirical observation of stock price movements.

8. Source: Paul Anthony Samuelson, PBS television program "NOVA 2074: The Trillion Dollar Bet," broadcast February 8, 2000. www.pbs.org/wgbh/nova/stockmarket. For program purchase: http://shop.wgbh.org/webapp/wcs/stores/servlet/ProductDisplay?productId=11030&storeId=11051&catalogId=10051&langId=-1.

9. Source: Irving Fisher, *The Theory of Interest: As Determined by Impatience to Spend Income and Opportunity to Invest It* (New York: Macmillan, 1930); reprinted (New York: Augustus M. Kelley, 1955), p. 315.

10. Ibid., p. 313.

11. Ibid., p. 341.

12. Source: Joan Violet Robinson, "What Is Perfect Competition?" *Quarterly Journal of Economics* 49, No. 1 (November 1934), pp. 104–120 (p. 119).

13. Source: Fisher, *Theory of Interest*, pp. 194–199.

14. Ibid., p. 316.

15. Reprinted by permission of Blackwell Publishing.

16. Excerpt from *The Intelligent Investor: The Classic Text on Value Investing* by Benjamin Graham. The Original 1949 Edition, featuring a new Foreword from John C. Bogle. Copyright 1949 by Benjamin Graham; Foreword copyright © 2004 by John C. Bogle. Reprinted by permission of HarperCollins Publishers, Inc.

17. Ibid.

18. Source: Warren E. Buffett, "The Superinvestors of Graham-and-Doddsville," *Hermes*, Columbia School of Business (Fall 1984), pp. 4–15. Copyright 1984. Reprinted with permission.

19. Buffett, though generally refreshingly conversant with modern financial theory, seems to have misunderstood this theory at this point. The modern theory, because of the implications of diversification, implies that prices are set at the margin by *all* investors (or, in special cases, by the *average* investor), not as Buffett puts it by the single least rational investor.

20. Source: Buffett, "The Superinvestors of Graham-and-Doddsville," pp. 4–15.

21. Since this is a history, it is perhaps appropriate to mention that the word *bankruptcy* takes its origin from the Italian *banco*, a bench set up by moneylenders in Venice during the Renaissance. When a moneylender was discovered cheating, he would be forcefully closed down and publicly disgraced by having his bench broken—hence the suffix *ruptus*.

22. Source: John Maynard Keynes, *The General Theory of Employment, Interest and Money* (Palgrave Macmillan, 1936), pp. 153–155. Reproduced with permission of Palgrave Macmillan.

23. Source: John Maynard Keynes, "The General Theory of Employment," *Quarterly Journal of Economics* 51, No. 2 (February 1937), pp. 209–223.

24. Strangely, although Gordon and Shapiro are clearly aware of Williams' book, they do not credit him with this formula in their article. To the contrary, they write:

> *In his* Theory of Investment Value, *a classic on the subject, J.B. Williams tackled this problem of growth. However, the models he developed were arbitrary and complicated so that the problem of growth remained among the phenomena dealt with qualitatively. It is our belief that the following proposal for a definition of the rate of profit that takes cognizance of prospective growth has merit.* Source: Myron J. Gordon and Eli Shapiro, "Capital Equipment Analysis: The Required Rate of Profit," *Management Science* 3, No. 1 (October 1956), pp. 102–110 (p. 105).

    They then go on to derive the same simple growth formula as Williams—equation (7), p. 105.

25. Reprinted by permission of Fraser Publishing, www.fraserpublishing.com. All rights reserved.

26. Ibid.

27. Source: Friedrich August von Hayek, "The Use of Knowledge in Society," *American Economic Review* 35, No. 4 (September 1945), pp. 519–530 (pp. 526–527).

28. Adam Smith (June 5, 1723–July 17, 1790), *An Inquiry into the Nature and Causes of the Wealth of Nations*, Great Books of the Western World: Smith (Franklin Center, PA: Franklin Library, 1978).

29. Source: von Hayek, "The Use of Knowledge in Society," p. 527.

30. More precisely, Markowitz assumed two of the three departures from standard utility theory made by prospect theory: (1) utility normalized relative to current wealth and (2) a steeply convex segment to the left of the origin. In addition, Kahneman and Tversky also (3) weaken the assumption that the probability weights on utility sum to one.

31. M. G. Kendall, "The Analysis of Economic Time-Series—Part I: Prices," *Journal of the Royal Statistical Society: Series A (General)* 116, No. 1 (1953), pp. 11–34.

32. Source: Holbrook Working, "The Investigation of Economic Expectations," *American Economic Review* 39, No. 3 (May 1949), pp. 150–166.

The Classical Period: 1950–1980

1. Most sources, including *Bartlett's Familiar Quotations*, 17th edition, 2002, attribute this advice to Mark Twain (November 30, 1835–April 21, 1910) since

he provides it without attribution in his book, *The Tragedy of Pudd'nhead Wilson* (1894), at the start of Chapter 15:

> *Behold, the fool saith, "Put not all thine eggs in the one basket"— which is but a matter of saying, "Scatter your money and your attention;" but the wise man saith, "Put all your eggs in one basket and—WATCH THAT BASKET."*

A few years earlier Twain had heard Andrew Carnegie advise this as a result of Carnegie's own experience in industry, and was so taken with it that he included it in his book. Carnegie's advice seems to be a response to Sancho Panza in Miguel de Cervantes (1547–1616), *Don Quixote* (1605), Part I, Book III, Chapter 9:

> *'Tis the part of a wise man to keep himself today for tomorrow, and not venture all his eggs in one basket.*

2. Reprinted by permission of Blackwell Publishing.
3. Ibid.
4. Copyright 1999, CFA Institute. Reproduced from *The Financial Analysts Journal* with permission from the CFA Institute. All rights reserved.
5. Kendall, "Analysis of Economic Time-Series."
6. It is often claimed that this last point appears in Friedman's article, but I must confess that I can't find it.
7. Reprinted by permission of Blackwell Publishing.
8. Source: Franco Modigliani and Merton Howard Miller, "The Cost of Capital, Corporation Finance and the Theory of Investment," *American Economic Review* 48, No. 3 (June 1958), pp. 261–297 (p. 271).
9. Source: Walter A. Morton, "The Structure of the Capital Market and the Price of Money," *American Economic Review* 44, No. 2 (May 1954), pp. 440–454 (p. 442).
10. Source: Franco Modigliani and Merton Howard Miller, "The Cost of Capital, Corporation Finance and the Theory of Investment," *American Economic Review* 48, No. 3 (June 1958), pp. 261–297 (p. 271).
11. Reprinted by permission of Fraser Publishing, www.fraserpublishing.com. All rights reserved.
12. Source: Holbrook Working, "A Theory of Anticipatory Prices," *American Economic Review* 48, No. 2 (May 1958), pp. 188–199 (p. 196).
13. Reprinted by permission of Blackwell Publishing.
14. Proceedings of the Berkeley Symposium on Mathematical Statistics and Probability by Leo Breiman. Copyright 1961 by the University of California Press. Reproduced with permission of University of California Press in the format Trade Book via Copyright Clearance Center.
15. Source: Hans-Werner Sinn, "Weber's Law and the Biological Evolution of Risk Preferences: The Selective Dominance of the Logarithmic Utility Function," CESifo Working Paper No. 770 (September 2002), pp. 3–4.

16. Translating this example into our earlier notation, set $W(s) = 1\ 2\ 3\ 4\ 5\ 6$, $p_A(s) = 0\ .5\ 0\ 0\ 0\ .5$ and $p_B(s) = .5\ 0\ .5\ 0\ 0\ 0$ for states $s = 1, 2, \ldots, 6$, respectively.

17. Reprinted by permission of Blackwell Publishing.

18. Amazingly, it has just recently come to light that about 10 years earlier Bruno de Finetti in "Sulla preferibilità," *Giornale degli Economisti e Annali di Economia* 11 (1952), pp. 685–789, developed the notion of absolute risk aversion in a paper written in Italian that I do not believe has ever been translated into English. According to Claudio Albanese, who has been able to read the paper, de Finetti defines absolute risk aversion, observes that it uniquely defines the utility function, and uses it to examine risk premiums in the context of small bets. As an example, he looks at the case of constant absolute risk aversion, which corresponds to exponential utility.

19. Reprinted by permission of Blackwell Publishing.

20. Ibid.

21. Source: Eugene F. Fama, "The Behavior of Stock-Market Prices," *Journal of Business* 38, No. 1 (January 1965), pp. 34–105 (p. 87). Reprinted by permission of the University of Chicago Press.

22. Source: Warren H. Hausman, "A Note on 'The Value Line Contest: A Test of the Predictability of Stock-Price Changes'," *Journal of Business* 42, No. 3 (July 1969), pp. 317–330. Reprinted by permission of the University of Chicago Press.

23. Source: Barr Rosenberg, "The Behavior of Random Variables with Nonstationary Variance and the Distribution of Security Prices," (unpublished but frequently cited working paper), Graduate School of Business, University of California at Berkeley (December 1972), pp. 39–40.

24. Reprinted by permission of Blackwell Publishing.

25. Source: Mark Rubinstein, "Securities Market Efficiency in an Arrow-Debreu Economy," *American Economic Review* 65, No. 5 (December 1975), pp. 812–824.

26. Source: Mark Rubinstein, "The Fundamental Theorem of Parameter-Preference Security Valuation," *Journal of Financial and Quantitative Analysis* 8, No. 1 (January 1973), pp. 61–69.

27. Source: Jack L. Treynor and Fischer Sheffey Black, "How to Use Security Analysis to Improve Portfolio Selection," *Journal of Business* 46, No. 1 (January 1973), pp. 66–86. Reprinted by permission of the University of Chicago Press.

28. Reprinted with permission of Blackwell Publishing.

29. Arrow's actual example was somewhat different. He supposed instead that the economy consists of agents who consume C different commodities. With S states, $S \times C$ is the total number of state-contingent commodities needed to complete the market. These state-contingent commodities pay off one unit of a specific commodity in a given state. To conserve on the number of markets, Arrow introduces S securities that pay off state-contingent dollars, one for each state, which can then be used to purchase a basket of commodities in the corresponding state. Instead of directly buying state-contingent commodities, agents first

buy state-securities with dollar payoffs. The true state is revealed, and only then do markets for the individual commodities open up. This market organization reduces the number of markets to $S + C$. If $S, C > 2$, then $(S + C) < (S \times C)$, and the number of markets is reduced in the second way of organizing the market.

30. For example, in the Problem of Points (Pascal-Fermat 1654), to determine the current fair division of stakes, one must know the future probabilities of participants winning rounds; for this simple game, these are all assumed to be $\frac{1}{2}$. In this case, this probability is objective in the sense that it is given in the terms of the game. However, when Pascal's backwards solution approach is applied in situations such as those discussed in this paper where probabilities are subjective, assuming this type of foreknowledge is problematic.

31. The well-known binomial option pricing model makes this point crystal clear. The annualized volatility (σ) determines the up (u) and down (d) moves of the underlying stock price; one formula for this is $u = d^{-1} = e^{\sigma\sqrt{(t/n)}}$ where t is the option's time to expiration and n is the number of binomial steps. Cox-Ross-Rubinstein (1979) show that the state-prices are $\pi_u = (r - d)/[r(u - d)]$ and $\pi_d = (u - r)/[r(u - d)]$ where $r = 1/(\pi_u + \pi_d)$ is the riskless return over a binomial interval. Therefore, specifying the annualized σ and annualized riskless return determines u, d, and r, which in turn determines the state prices π_u and π_d. Like Black-Scholes, this model makes the highly simplifying assumption that future state-prices for claims to dollars in one period are always the same.

32. The realization that the equilibrium stochastic process (over time) of security returns depends on the preferences of investors and should not be exogenously specified may have appeared first in Osborne (1959) where he justifies his assumption of multiplicative Brownian motion by the Weber-Fechner hypothesis of psychophysics: Equal ratios of physical stimulus correspond to equal intervals of subjective sensation.

33. Source: Mark Rubinstein, "An Aggregation Theorem for Securities Markets," *Journal of Financial Economics* 1, pp. 225–244. Copyright 1974. Reprinted with permission from Elsevier Science.

34. To state this condition more carefully, what is allowed is geometric Brownian motion but with a subjective mean that could be arbitrarily random, even dependent on external state variables, as long as it does not lead to jumps in the asset price. But the log volatility (or diffusion coefficient) of the process must be constant. However, in terms of the risk-neutral probabilities, the geometric Brownian motion must have a nonstochastic mean equal to the riskless return.

35. Source: Stephen A. Ross, "Return, Risk, and Arbitrage," in *Risk and Return in Finance* (edited by Irving Friend and James Bicksler, Ballinger 1977), pp. 189–218.

36. The name "fundamental theorem" seems to have originally appeared in [Dybvig-Ross (1996)] Phillip H. Dybvig and Stephen A. Ross, "Arbitrage," in *The New Palgrave: A Dictionary of Economics*, Volume 1, edited by John Eatwell, Murray Milgate, and Peter Newman (reprinted London: Macmillan Press, 1996), pp. 100–106.

As Arrow (1953) shows, unless the number of different securities equals the number of states, these state-prices will not be unique—a result sometimes referred to as "the second fundamental theorem of financial economics."

The formulation of the fundamental theorem explicitly allows for uncertainty: In the future only one of many now possible "states" will occur. Under certainty, with the focus on cash flows from securities over time, the corresponding theorem would be:

> *A term structure of interest rates exists if and only if there is no arbitrage.*

To say that "a term structure of interest rates exists" is shorthand for:

- The current price of any bond equals the present value of its cash flows calculated by using the same term structure of interest rates for every bond.
- All forward interest rates (implied in the term structure) are positive.

37. Source: Ross, "Return, Risk, and Arbitrage."
38. We can easily show that this same result holds for any portfolio as well. Suppose the proportions of each security j held in a portfolio are represented by x_j; then the return r_p of the portfolio is $r_p = \Sigma_j x_j r_j$. We have for any security j:

$$E(r_j) = r + \text{Cov}(r_j, -Y)$$

Multiply through by x_j and sum over all securities j:

$$E(\Sigma_j x_j r_j) = r + \text{Cov}(\Sigma_j x_j r_j, -Y)$$

which implies that:

$$E(r_p) = r + \text{Cov}(r_p, -Y)$$

39. One of the innovations of Black and Scholes, compared to say Arrow (1953), was to rule out arbitrage only among a small subset of all available securities and investigate just the relations among the prices of securities in this subset. Therefore, it would be perfectly consistent with Black and Scholes if arbitrage profits could be earned from positions involving two different stocks, as long as they could not be earned from positions containing only a given stock, its options, and cash. So Black-Scholes provides a theory pertaining to "island universes" within the cosmos.
40. To be complete, as Cox-Ross-Rubinstein (1979) point out, we need an eighth assumption to rule out the possibility of a binomial jump process, wherein at each node the stock moves up (or down) by a small amount with high risk-neutral probability or moves down (or up) a large fixed amount with low risk-neutral probability, and where these probabilities become increasingly extreme as the time interval between moves goes to zero. Finally, we should add that Black and Scholes ask what happens to the value of an option in this nonjump setting when the time interval between moves goes to zero.

41. The formulation at this point even allows the riskless return to be different at each node, provided that given one is at a node, the riskless return is known, and, à la Drèze (1970), that the pattern of these contingent riskless returns is known in advance.

42. If we stop here and do not make the last assumption, we will have arrived at the option pricing model described by Rubinstein (1994) in his paper "Implied Binomial Trees."

43. Reprinted by permission of Fraser Publishing, www.fraserpublishing.com. All rights reserved.

44. Source: Mark Rubinstein, "Corporate Financial Policy in Segmented Securities Markets," *Journal of Financial and Quantitative Analysis* 8, No. 4 (December 1973), pp. 749–761.

45. Source: Michael C. Jensen, "Some Anomalous Evidence Regarding Market Efficiency," *Journal of Financial Economics* 6, pp. 95–101. Copyright 1978. Reprinted with permission from Elsevier Science.

The Modern Period: Post-1980

1. Thomas Bayes (circa 1701–April 7, 1761), in [Bayes (1763)] "An Essay Towards Solving a Problem in the Doctrine of Chances," *Philosophical Transactions of the Royal Society* 53 (1763), pp. 370–418; reprinted along with a transmittal letter by Richard Price, who located the paper among the documents left after Bayes' death in 1761 in *Studies in the History of Statistics and Probability*, Volume 1, edited by Egon S. Pearson and Maurice G. Kendall (London: Griffin, 1970), pp. 131–153.

2. Reprinted by permission of Blackwell Publishing.

3. Source: James A. Ohlson, "Earnings, Book Values, and Dividends in Equity Valuation," *Contemporary Accounting Research* 11, No. 2 (Spring 1995), pp. 661–687.

4. Reprinted by permission of Blackwell Publishing.

5. Ibid.

Index of Ideas

Index of Sources

Full citations can be found on page numbers in **bold**.